Will you count with me

My teeth marks

On you

D0009422

# BLEACH 52 End of Bond

# STARS AND

Orihime Inoue

井上織姫

銀城空吾

Kugo Ginjo

Ichigo Kurosaki

黒崎一護

★ plot

Ichigo Kurosaki meets Soul Reaper Rukia Kuchiki and ends up helping her eradicate Hollows. After developing his powers as a Soul Reaper, Ichigo enters the battle against Aizen and his dark ambitions! Ichigo finally defeats Aizen in exchange for his powers as a Soul Reaper.

With the battle over, Ichigo regains his routine life. But his tranquil days end when he meets Ginjo, who offers to help Ichigo get his powers back. But suddenly Ginjo's mysterious adversary Tsukishima also emerges! Ichigo continues his Fullbring training while avoiding Tsukishima, but just when he doubts the purpose of his grueling training, Ginjo's blade slashes both his eyes!!

# BLEACH ALL

 月島秀九郎
Shukuro Tsukishima

茶渡泰虎
Chad Yasutora

Moeh Shishigawara

獅子河原萌笑

# STORIES

# BLEACH 52

## End of Bond

## Contents

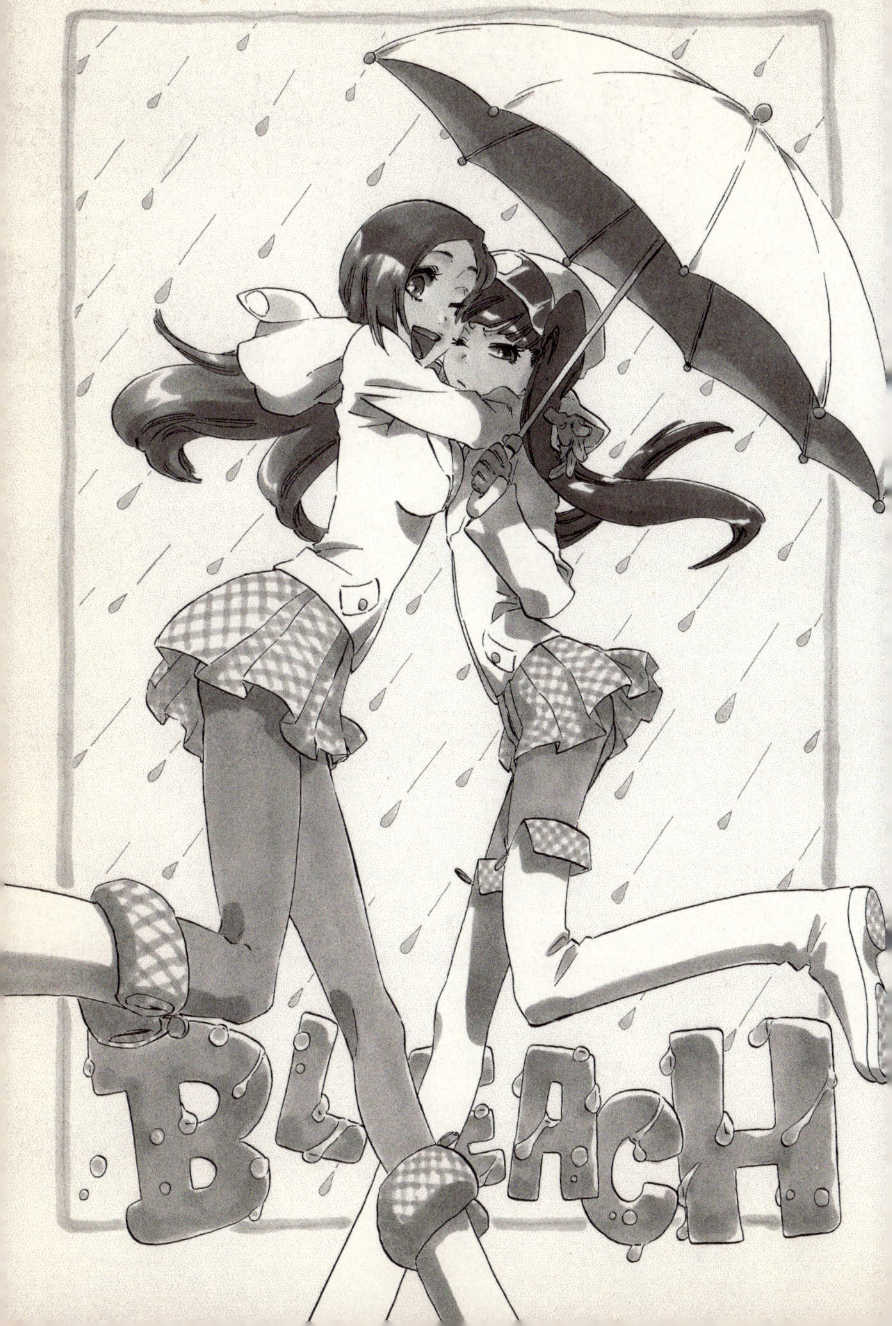
BLEACH

BLEACH ブリーチ

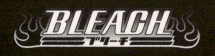

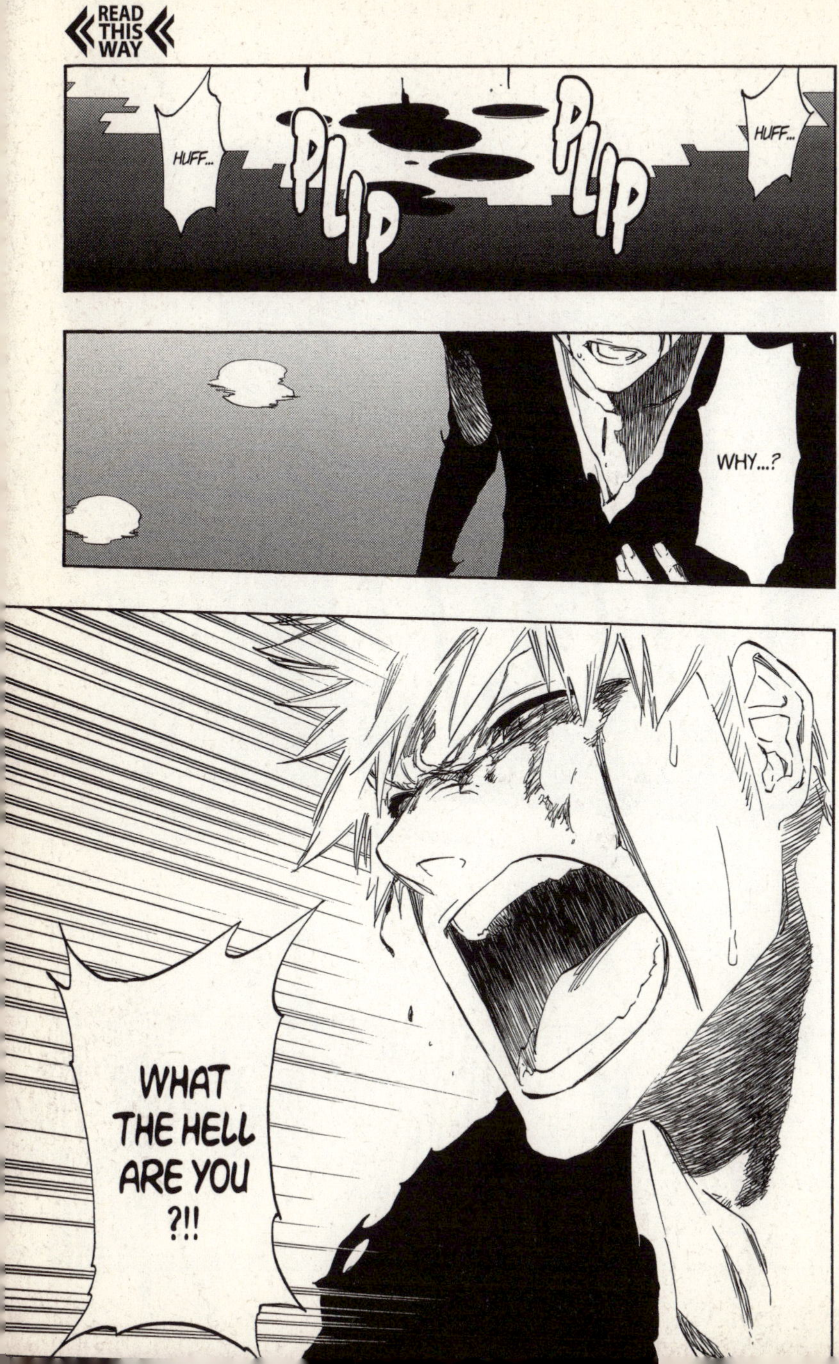
READ THIS WAY
HUFF...
PLIP
PLIP
HUFF...
WHY...?
WHAT THE HELL ARE YOU ?!!

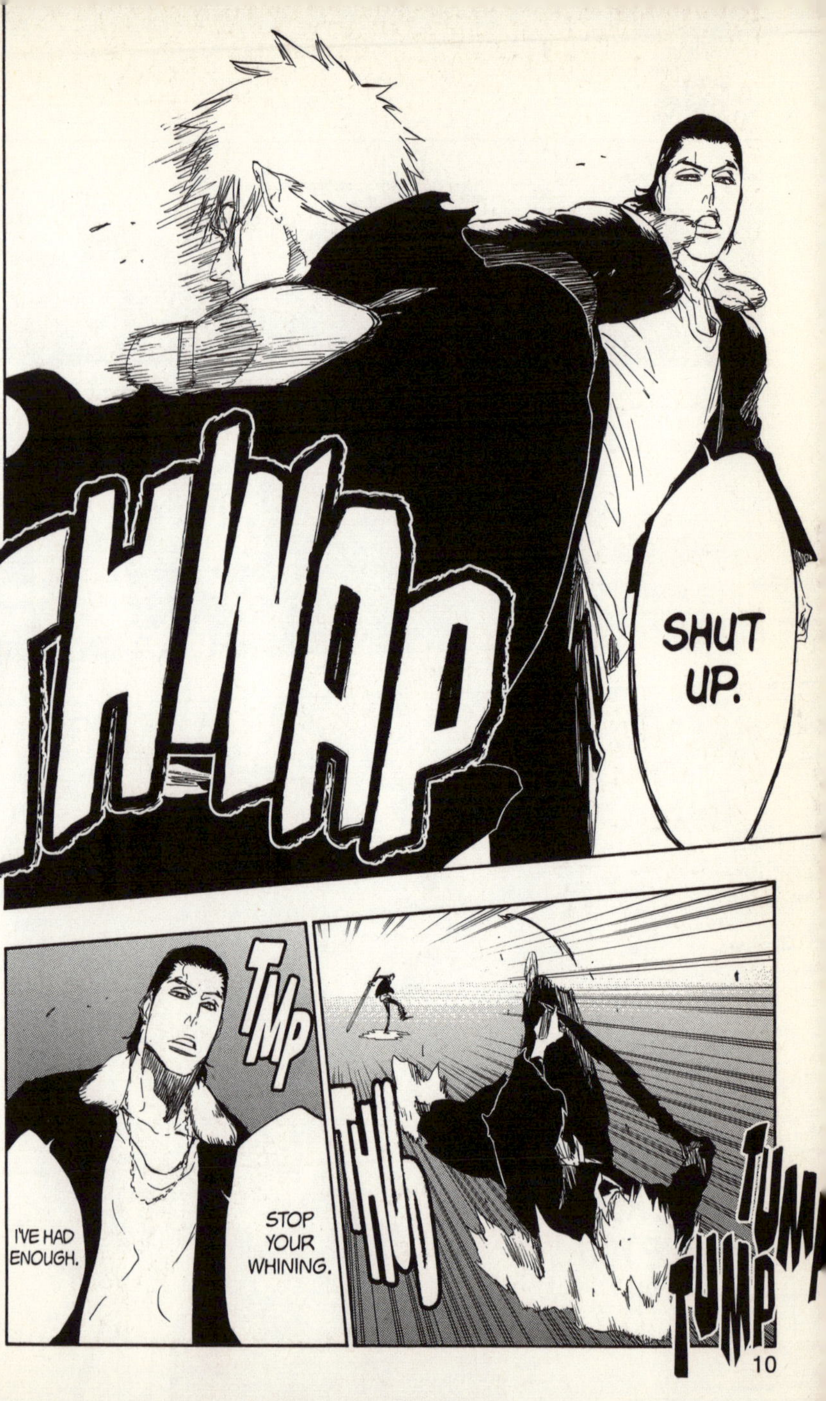
SHUT UP.
THWAP
TUMP TUMP.
THUD
TMP
STOP YOUR WHINING.
I'VE HAD ENOUGH.

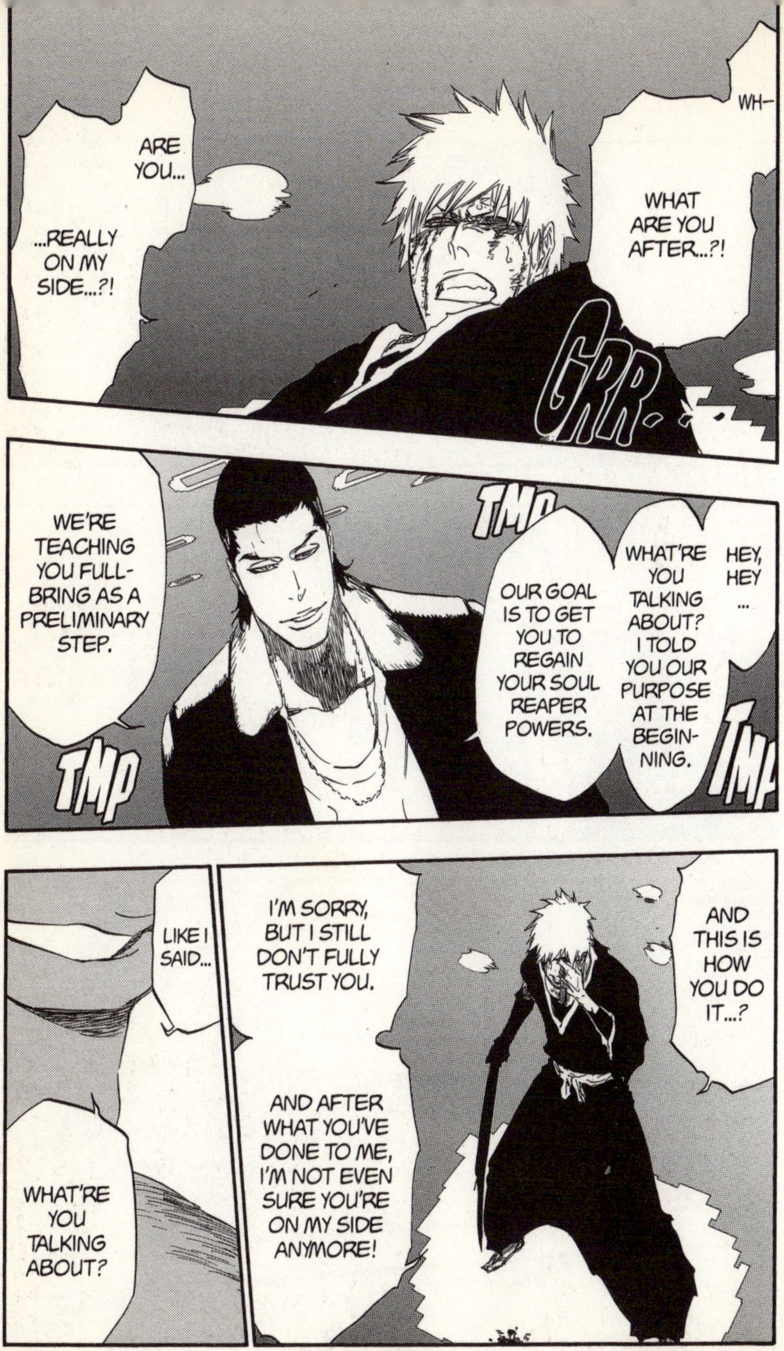
WH–
WHAT ARE YOU AFTER...?!
ARE YOU...
...REALLY ON MY SIDE...?!
GRR
TMP
HEY, HEY ...
WHAT'RE YOU TALKING ABOUT? I TOLD YOU OUR PURPOSE AT THE BEGIN-NING.
OUR GOAL IS TO GET YOU TO REGAIN YOUR SOUL REAPER POWERS.
WE'RE TEACHING YOU FULL-BRING AS A PRELIMINARY STEP.
TMP
TMP
AND THIS IS HOW YOU DO IT...?
I'M SORRY, BUT I STILL DON'T FULLY TRUST YOU.
AND AFTER WHAT YOU'VE DONE TO ME, I'M NOT EVEN SURE YOU'RE ON MY SIDE ANYMORE!
LIKE I SAID...
WHAT'RE YOU TALKING ABOUT?

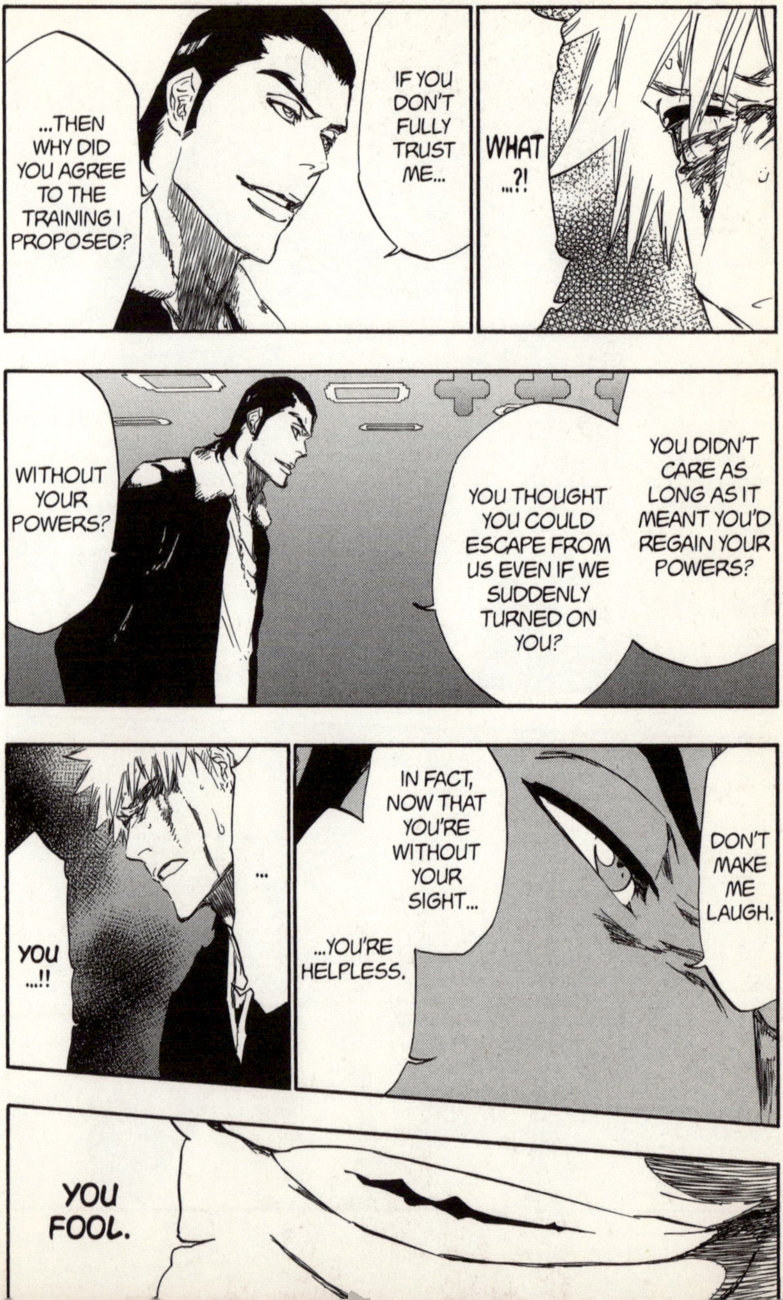
WHAT ...?!
IF YOU DON'T FULLY TRUST ME...
...THEN WHY DID YOU AGREE TO THE TRAINING I PROPOSED?
YOU DIDN'T CARE AS LONG AS IT MEANT YOU'D REGAIN YOUR POWERS?
YOU THOUGHT YOU COULD ESCAPE FROM US EVEN IF WE SUDDENLY TURNED ON YOU?
WITHOUT YOUR POWERS?
DON'T MAKE ME LAUGH.
IN FACT, NOW THAT YOU'RE WITHOUT YOUR SIGHT...
...YOU'RE HELPLESS.
...
YOU ...!!
YOU FOOL.

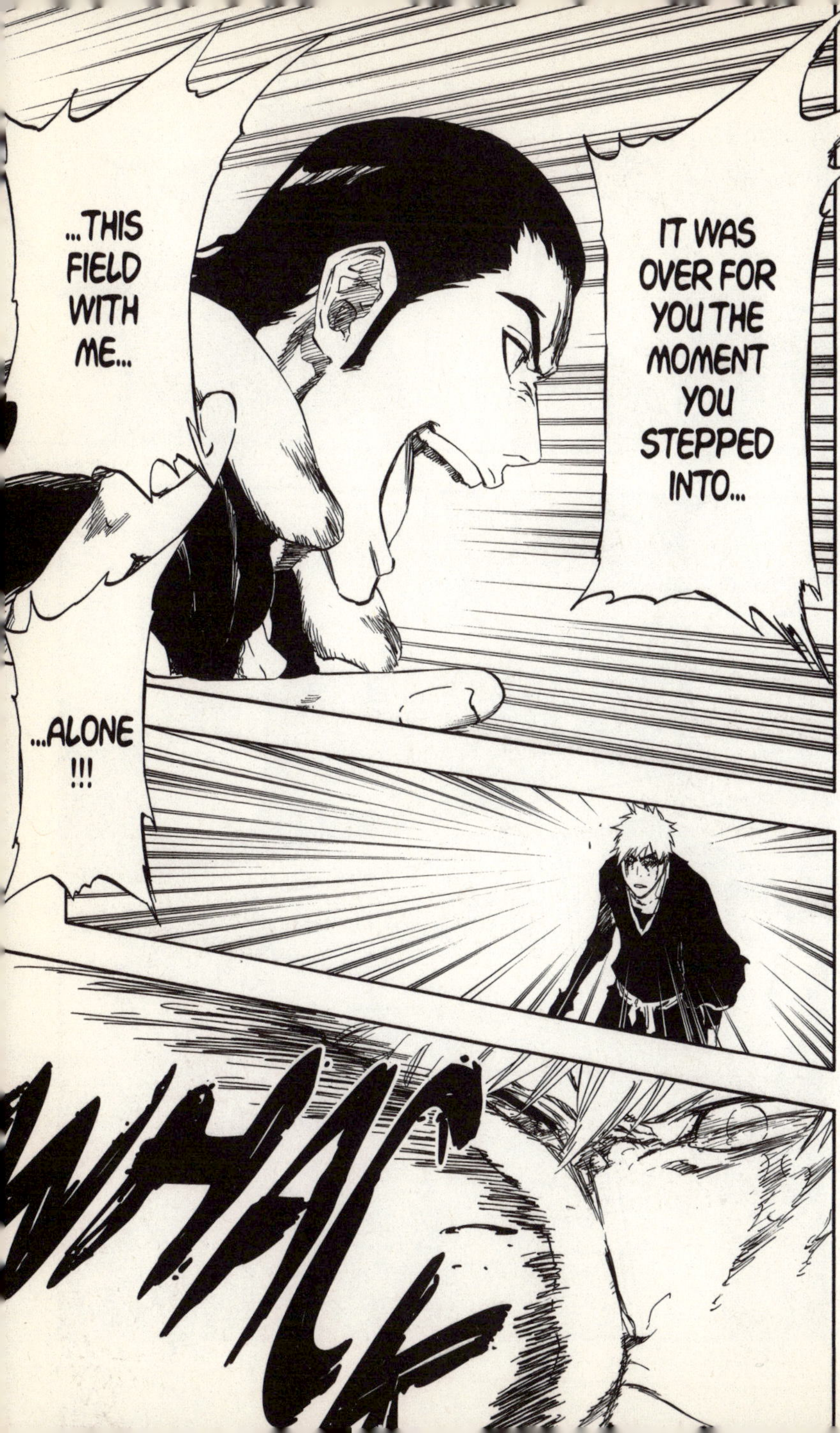
IT WAS OVER FOR YOU THE MOMENT YOU STEPPED INTO...
...THIS FIELD WITH ME...
...ALONE !!!
WHAK

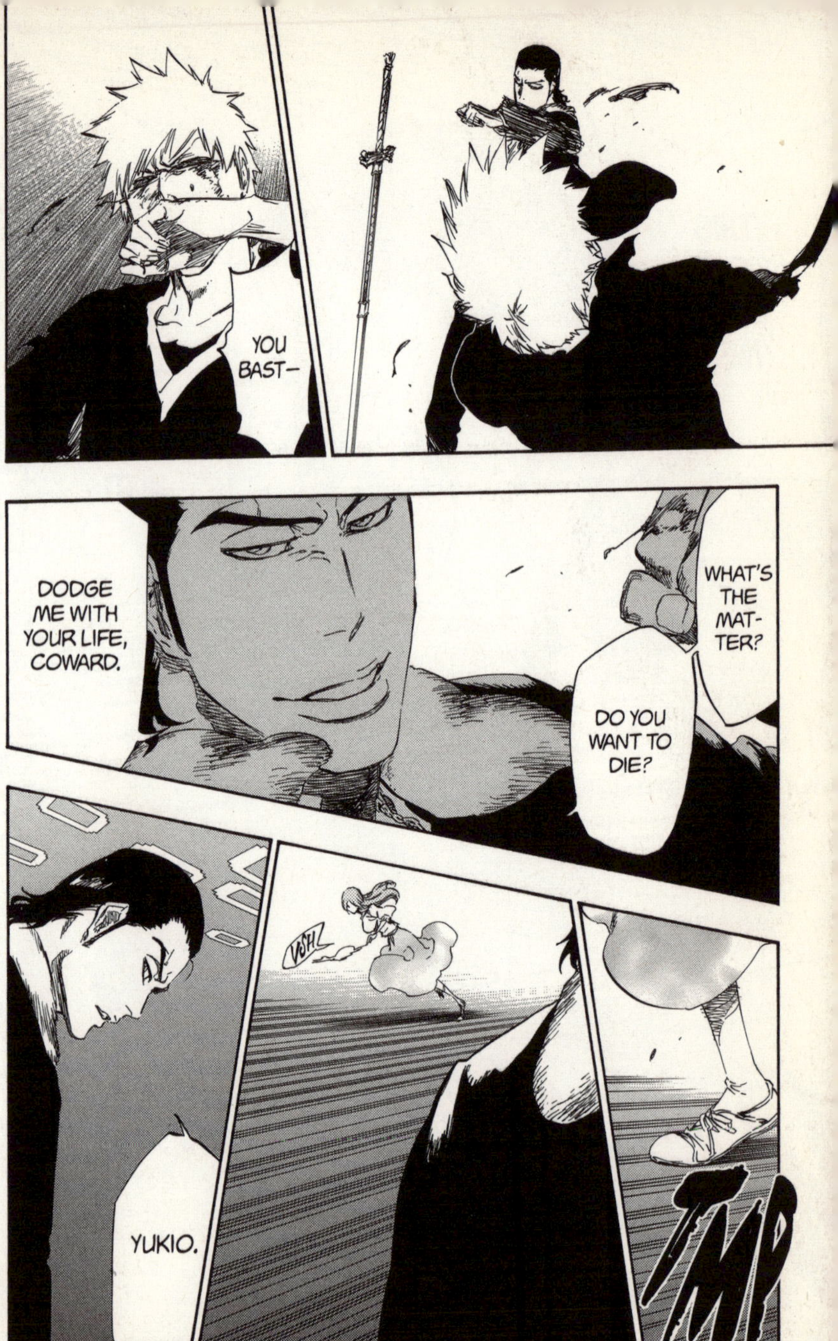
YOU BAST—
WHAT'S THE MAT-TER?
DO YOU WANT TO DIE?
DODGE ME WITH YOUR LIFE, COWARD.
TMP
VSH
YUKIO.

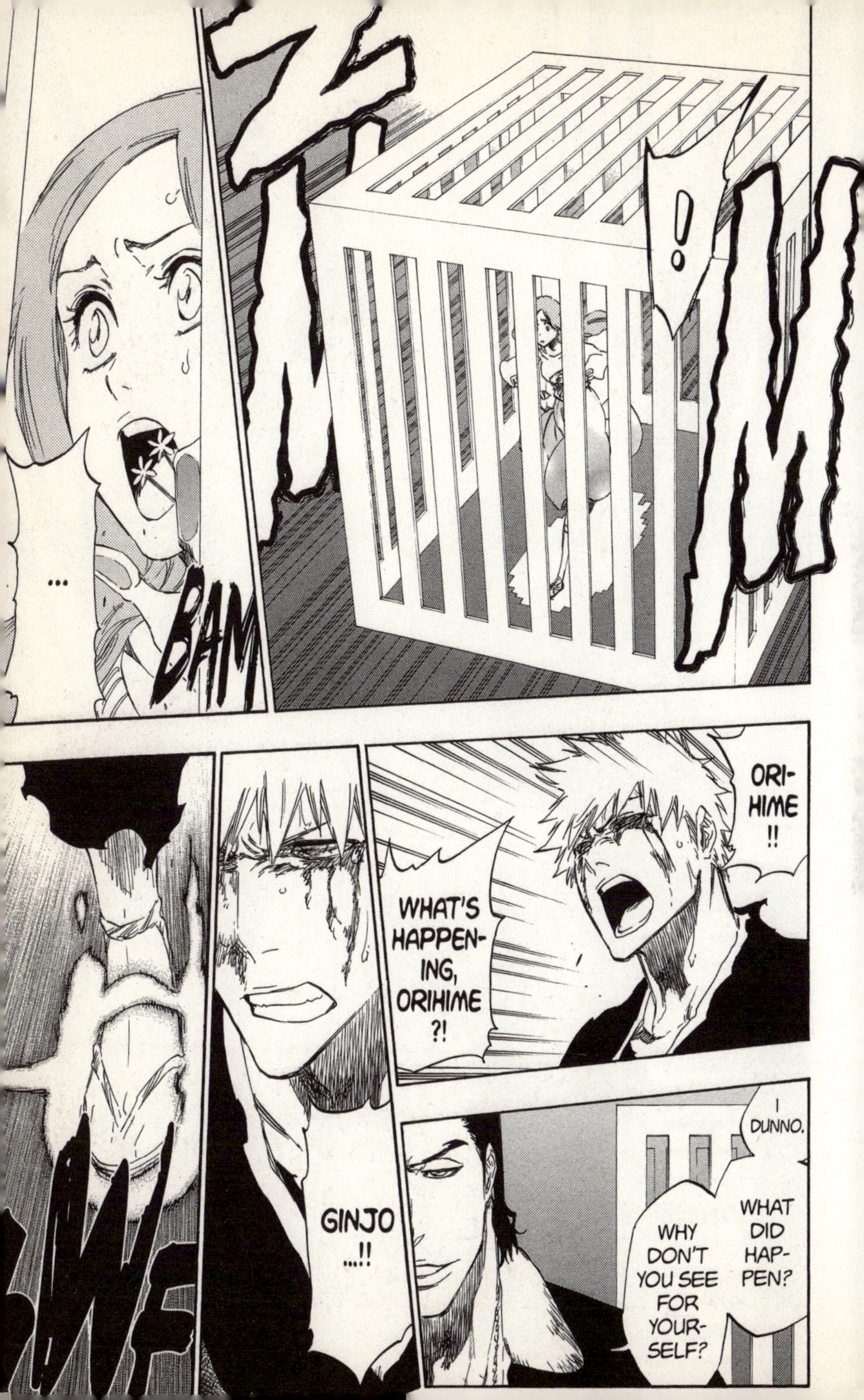
ZUM
!
...
BAM
ORI-HIME !!
WHAT'S HAPPEN-ING, ORIHIME ?!
GINJO ...!!
I DUNNO.
WHAT DID HAP-PEN?
WHY DON'T YOU SEE FOR YOUR-SELF?

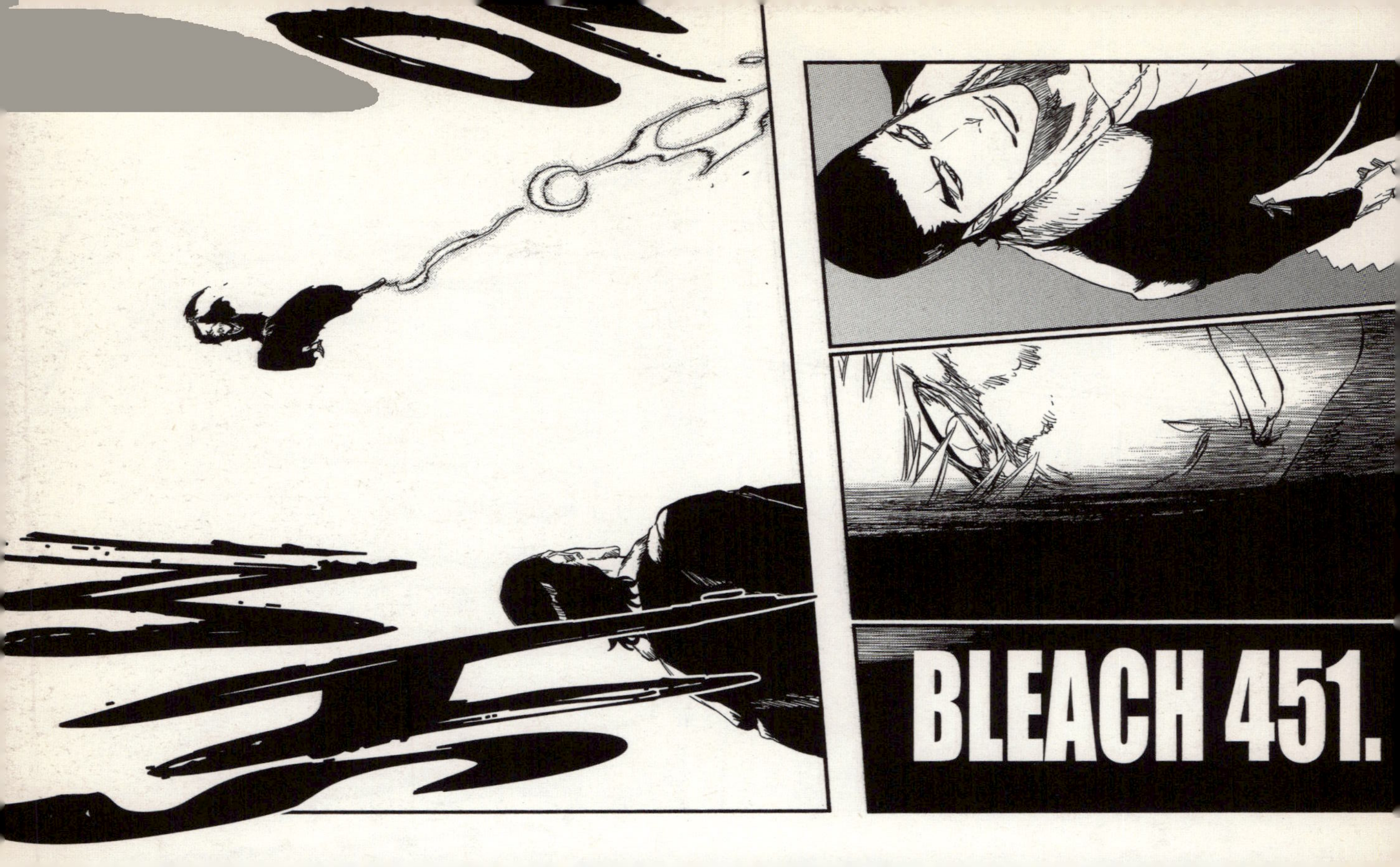
BLEACH 451.

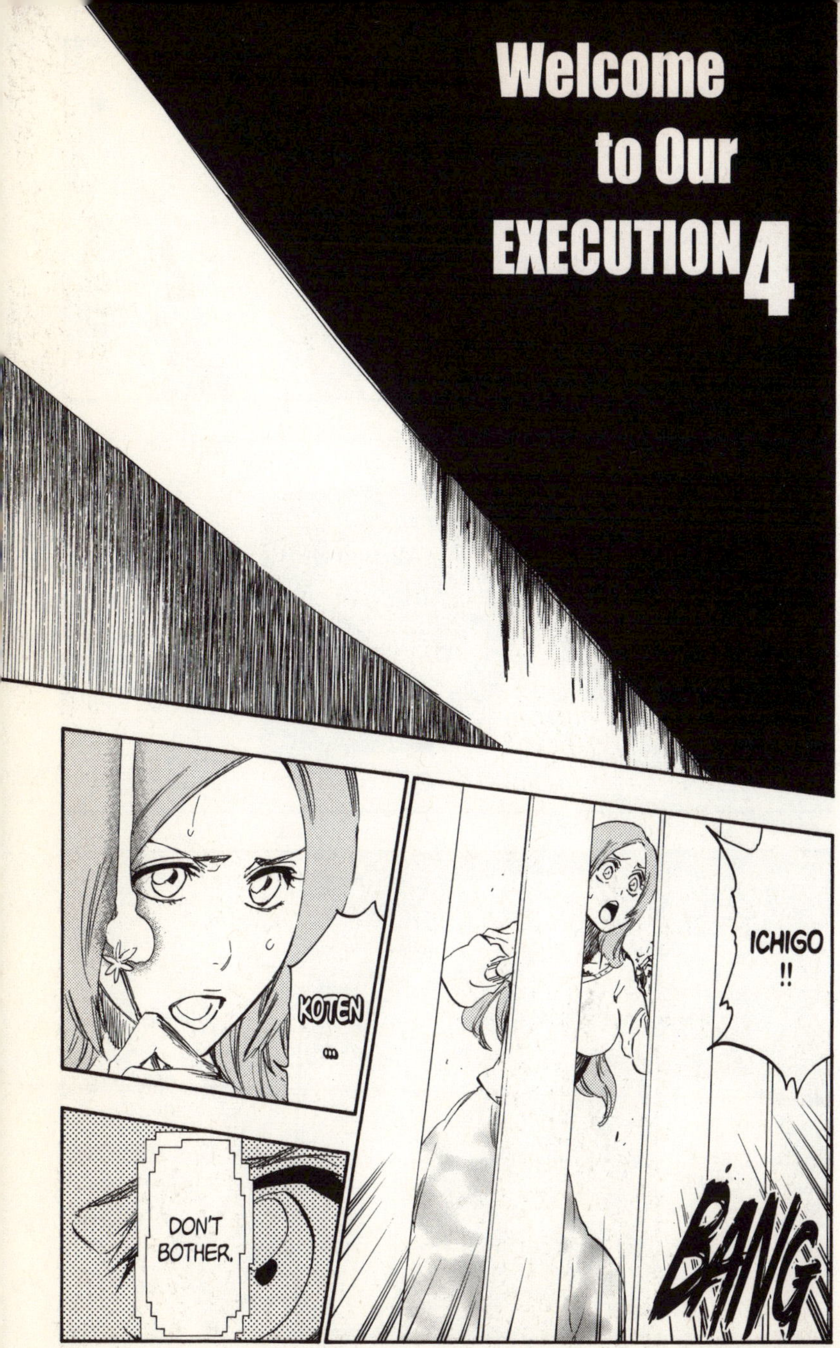
Welcome to Our EXECUTION 4
ICHIGO !!
BANG
KOTEN ...
DON'T BOTHER.

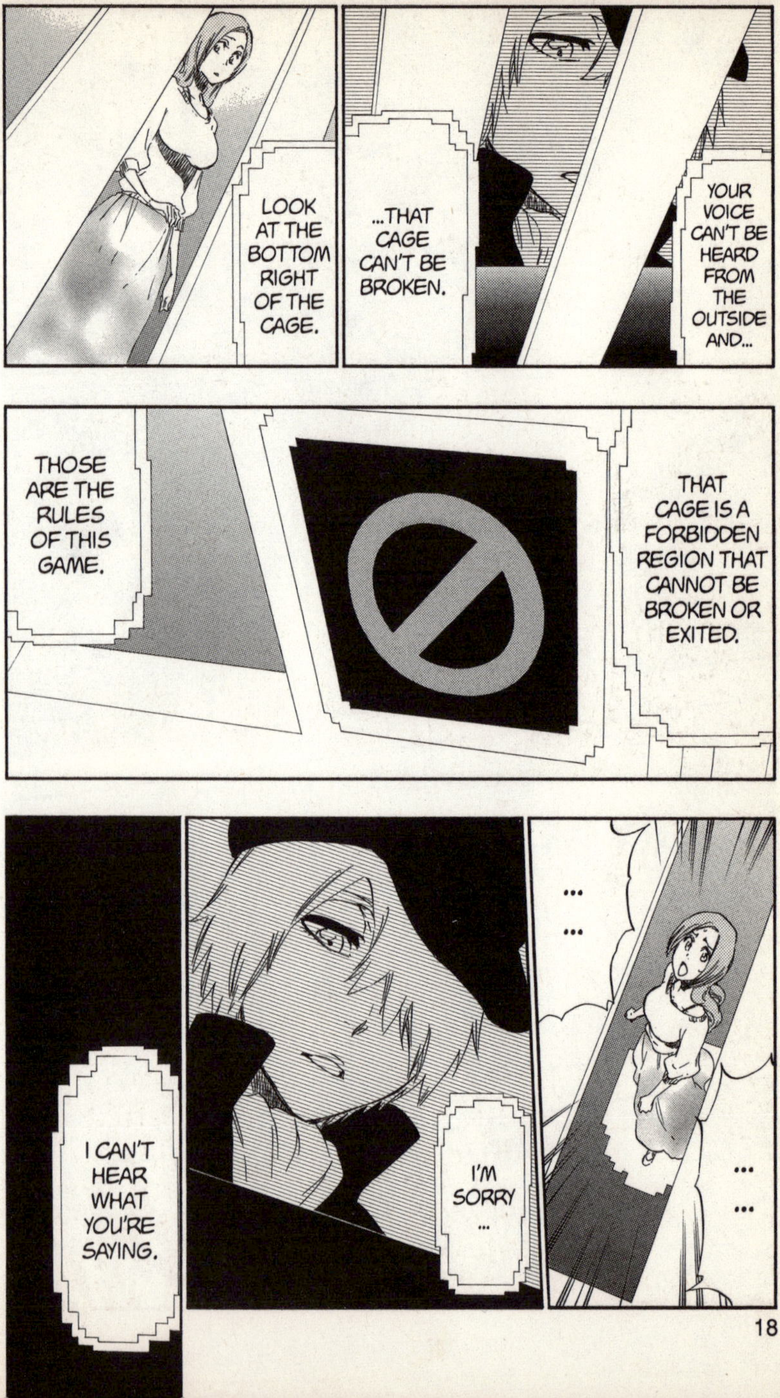
YOUR VOICE CAN'T BE HEARD FROM THE OUTSIDE AND...
...THAT CAGE CAN'T BE BROKEN.
LOOK AT THE BOTTOM RIGHT OF THE CAGE.
THAT CAGE IS A FORBIDDEN REGION THAT CANNOT BE BROKEN OR EXITED.
THOSE ARE THE RULES OF THIS GAME.
... ...
... ...
I'M SORRY ...
I CAN'T HEAR WHAT YOU'RE SAYING.

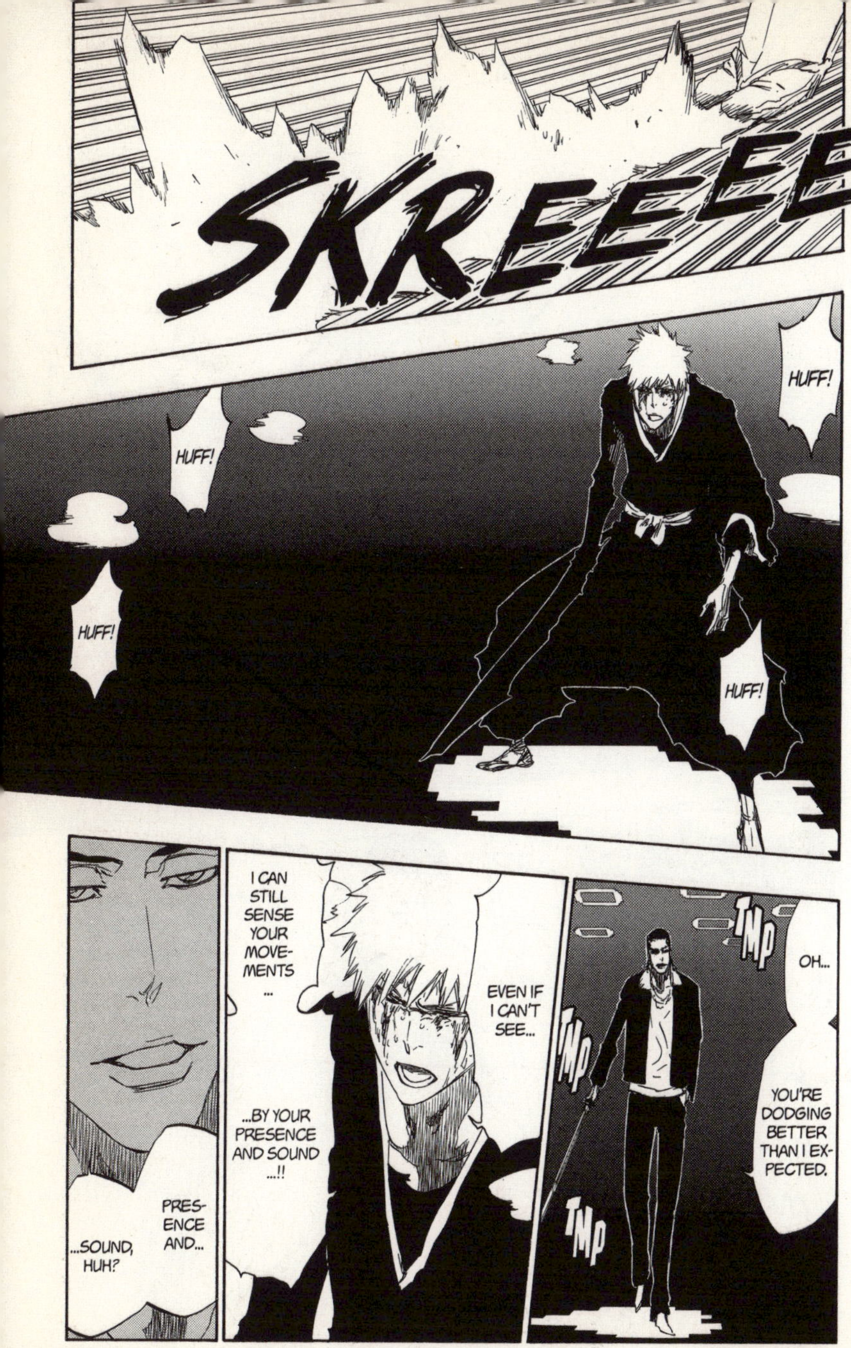
SKREEEEE
HUFF!
HUFF!
HUFF!
HUFF!
TMP
OH...
TMP
YOU'RE DODGING BETTER THAN I EXPECTED.
TMP
EVEN IF I CAN'T SEE...
I CAN STILL SENSE YOUR MOVEMENTS...
...BY YOUR PRESENCE AND SOUND...!!
PRESENCE AND...
...SOUND, HUH?

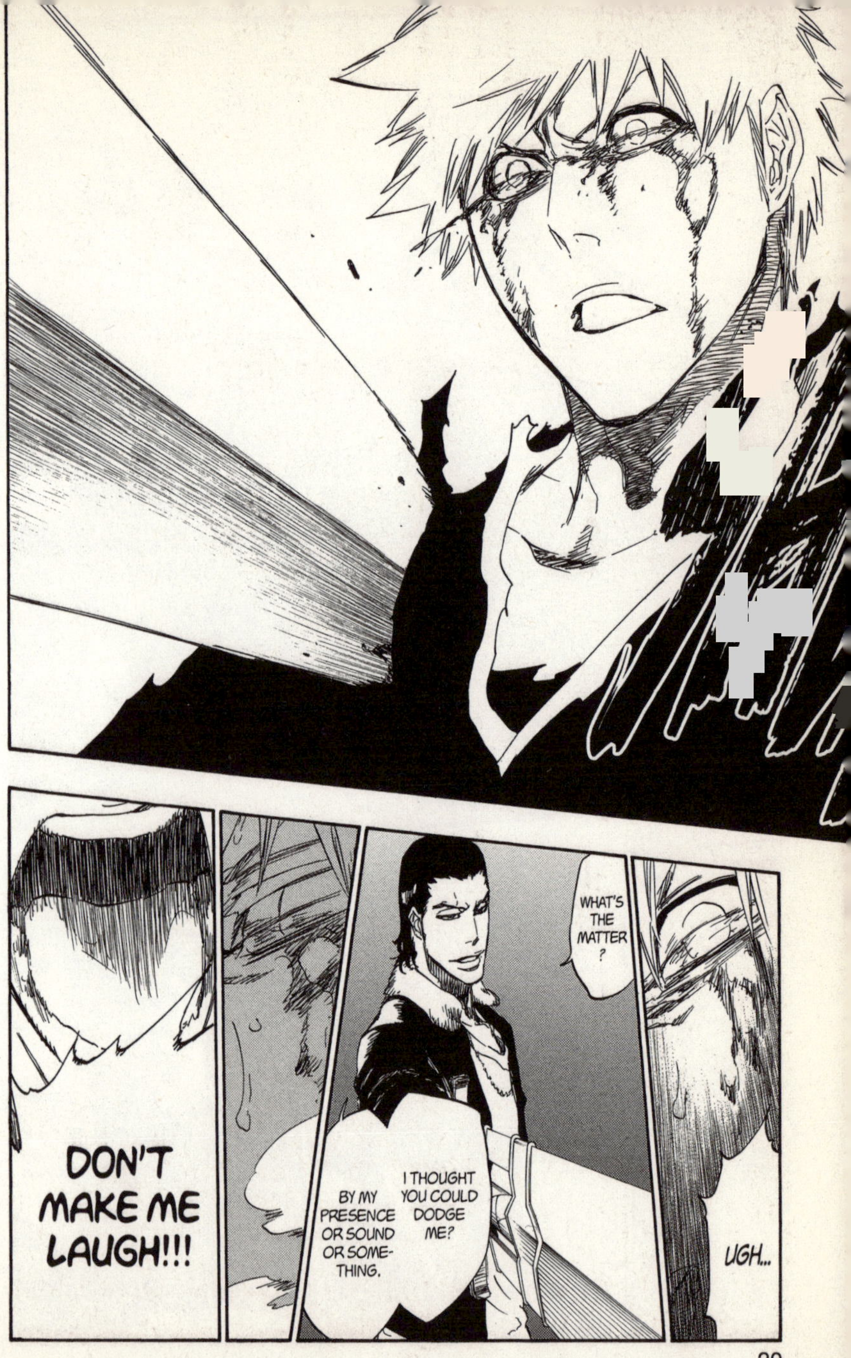
UGH...
WHAT'S THE MATTER?
I THOUGHT YOU COULD DODGE ME?
BY MY PRESENCE OR SOUND OR SOMETHING.
DON'T MAKE ME LAUGH!!!

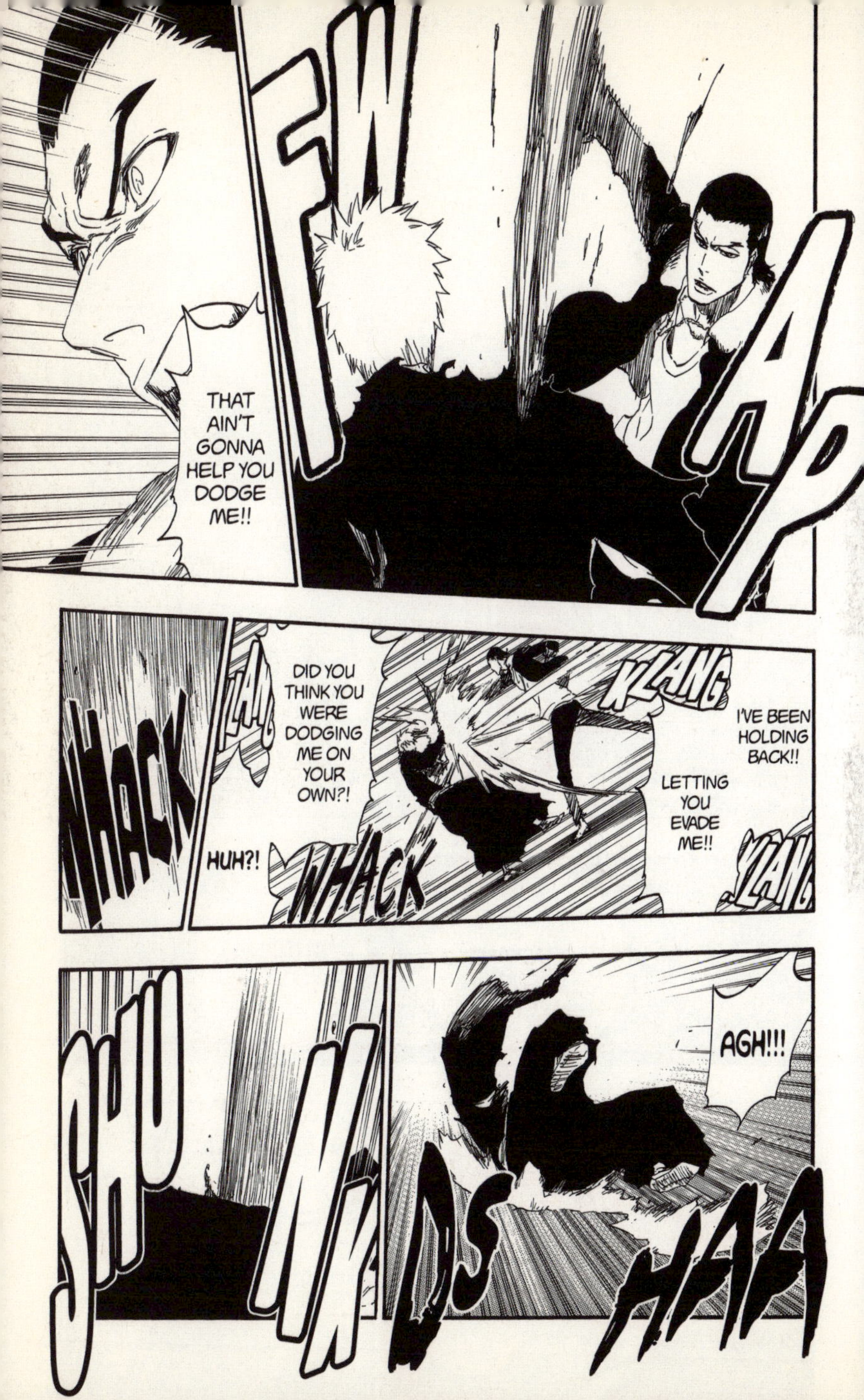
THAT AIN'T GONNA HELP YOU DODGE ME!!
KLANG
I'VE BEEN HOLDING BACK!!
LETTING YOU EVADE ME!!
DID YOU THINK YOU WERE DODGING ME ON YOUR OWN?!
WHACK
HUH?!
WHACK
AGH!!!
SHU

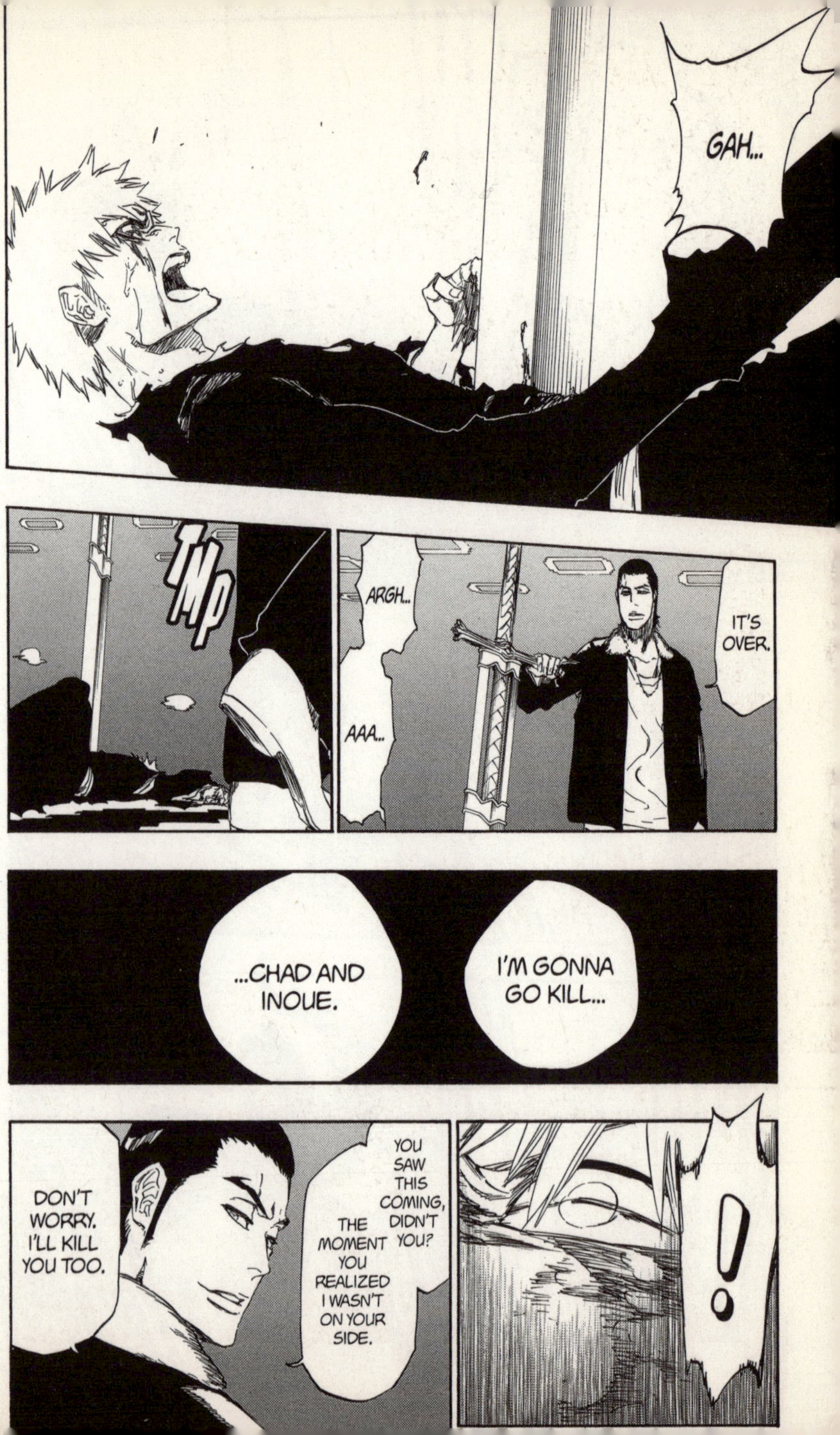
GAH...
IT'S OVER.
ARGH...
AAA...
TMP
I'M GONNA GO KILL...
...CHAD AND INOUE.
!
YOU SAW THIS COMING, DIDN'T YOU?
THE MOMENT YOU REALIZED I WASN'T ON YOUR SIDE.
DON'T WORRY. I'LL KILL YOU TOO.

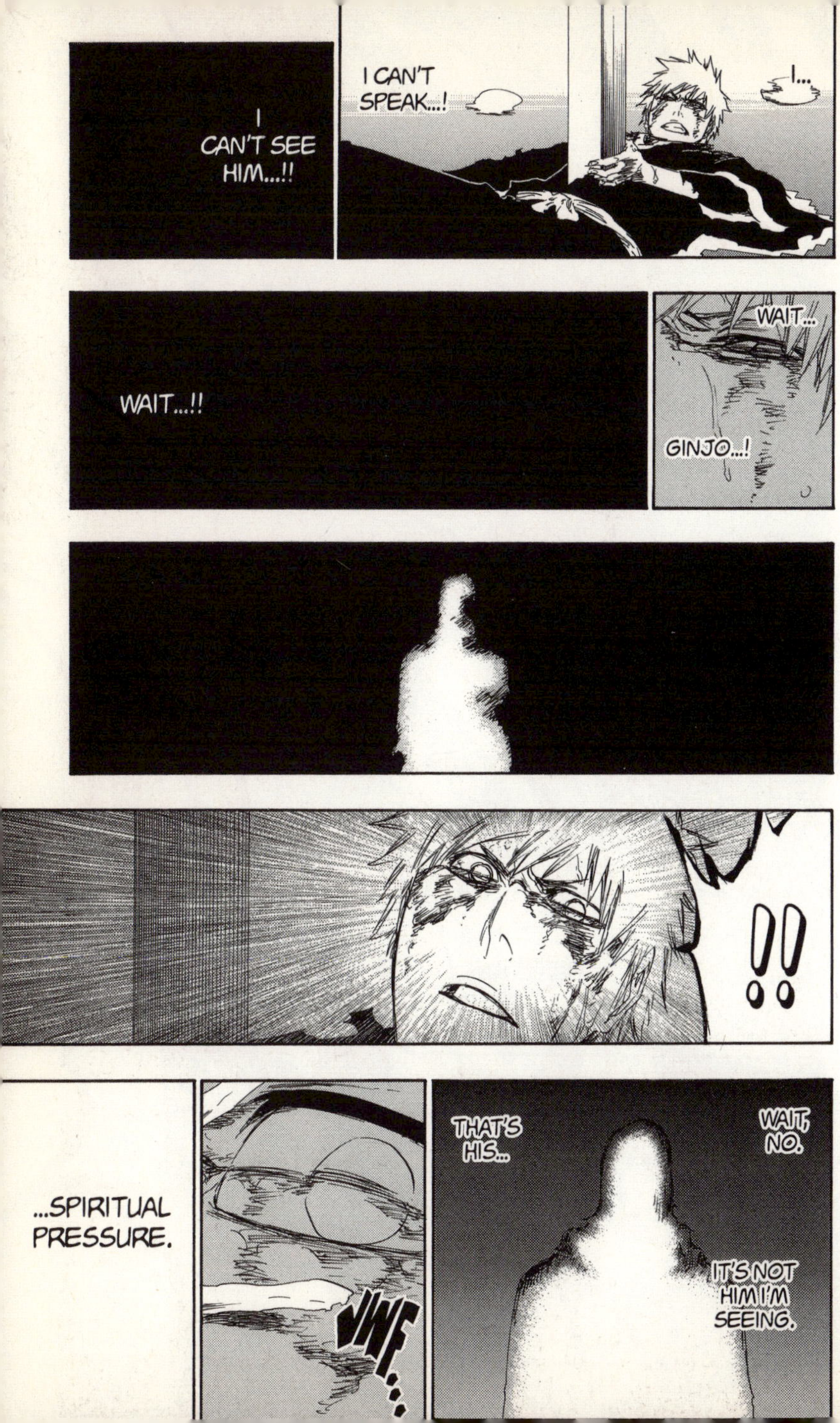
I...
I CAN'T SPEAK...!
I CAN'T SEE HIM...!!
WAIT...
GINJO...!
WAIT...!!
!!
WAIT, NO.
THAT'S HIS...
IT'S NOT HIM I'M SEEING.
VWF...
...SPIRITUAL PRESSURE.

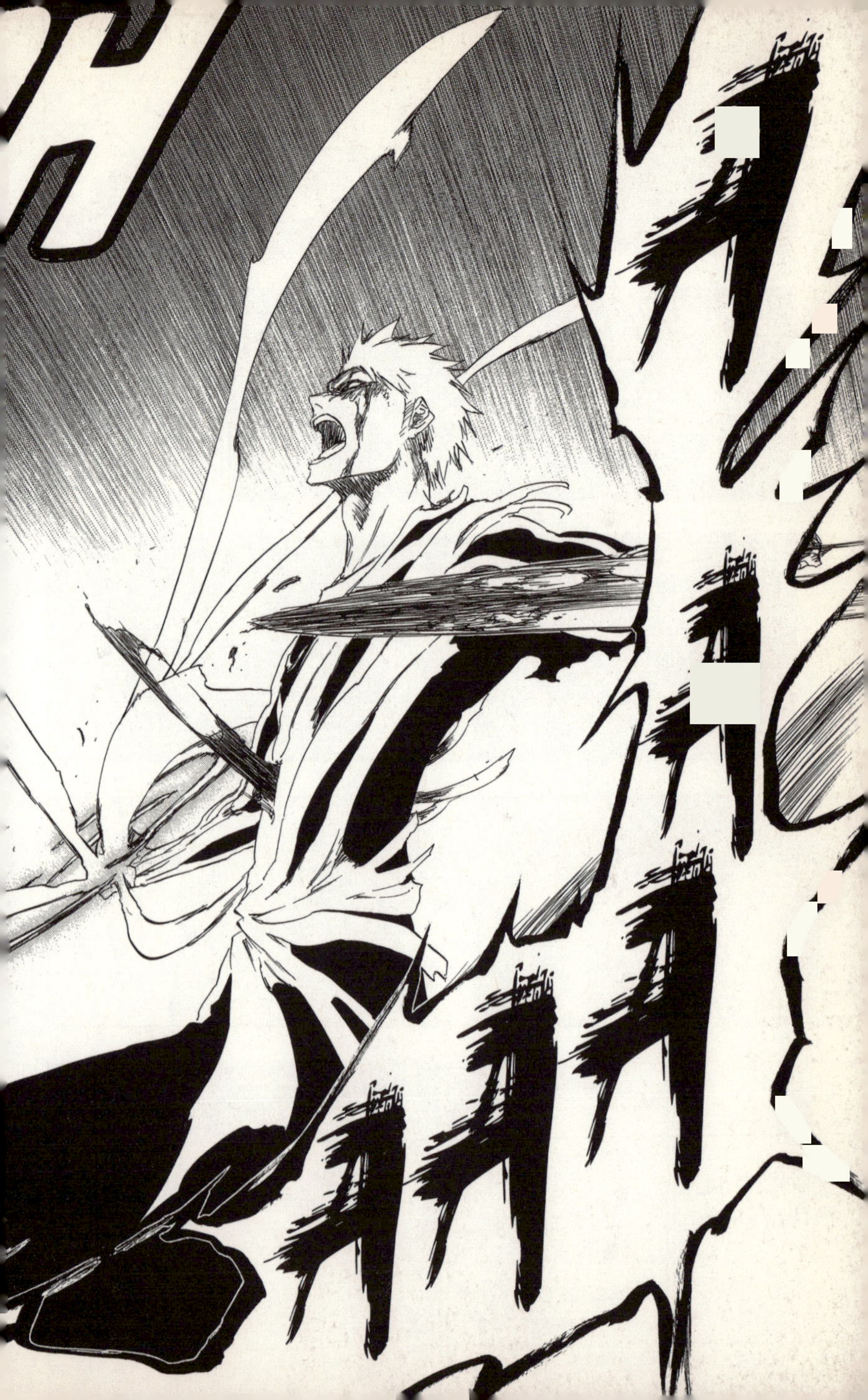

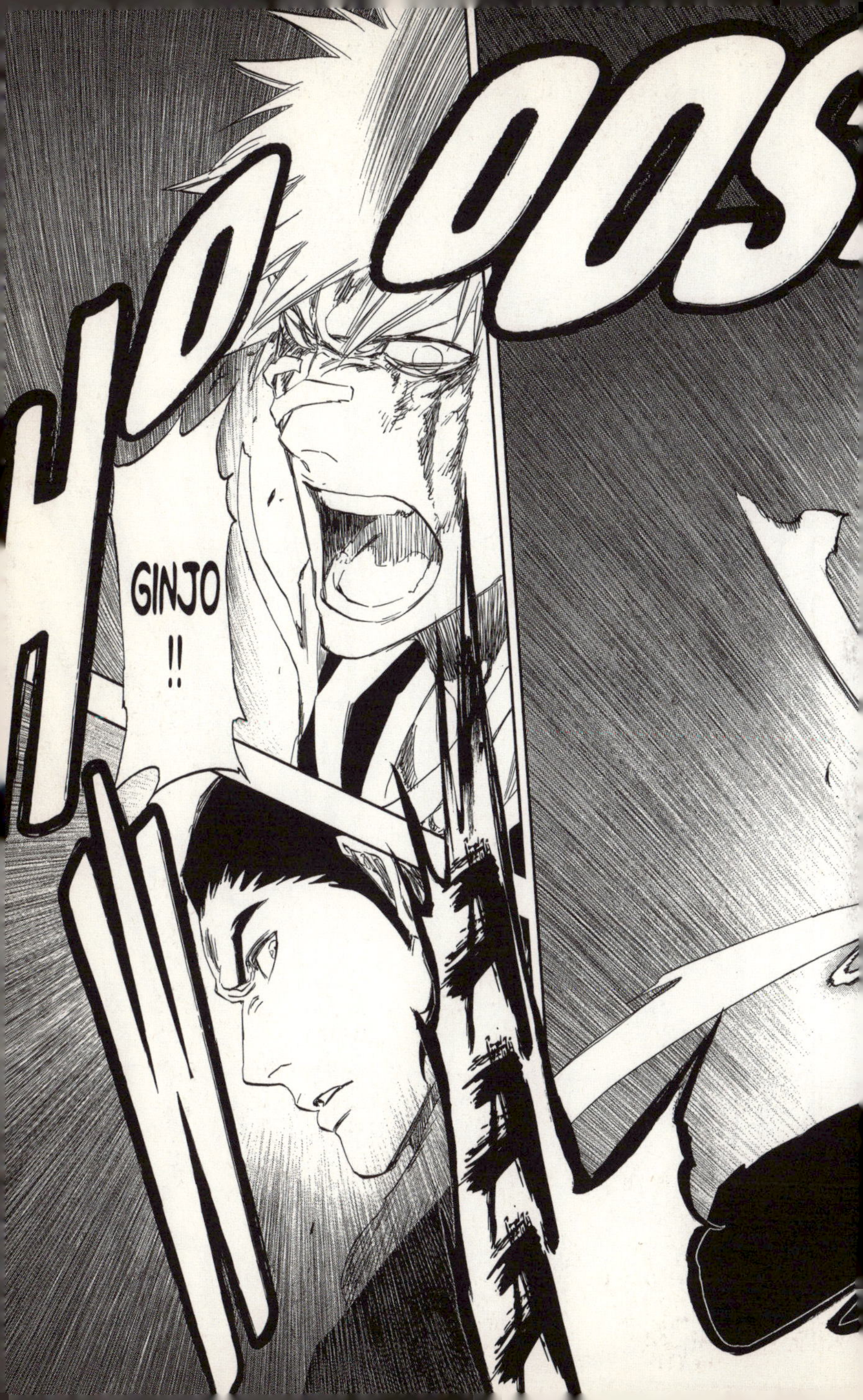
GINJO
!!

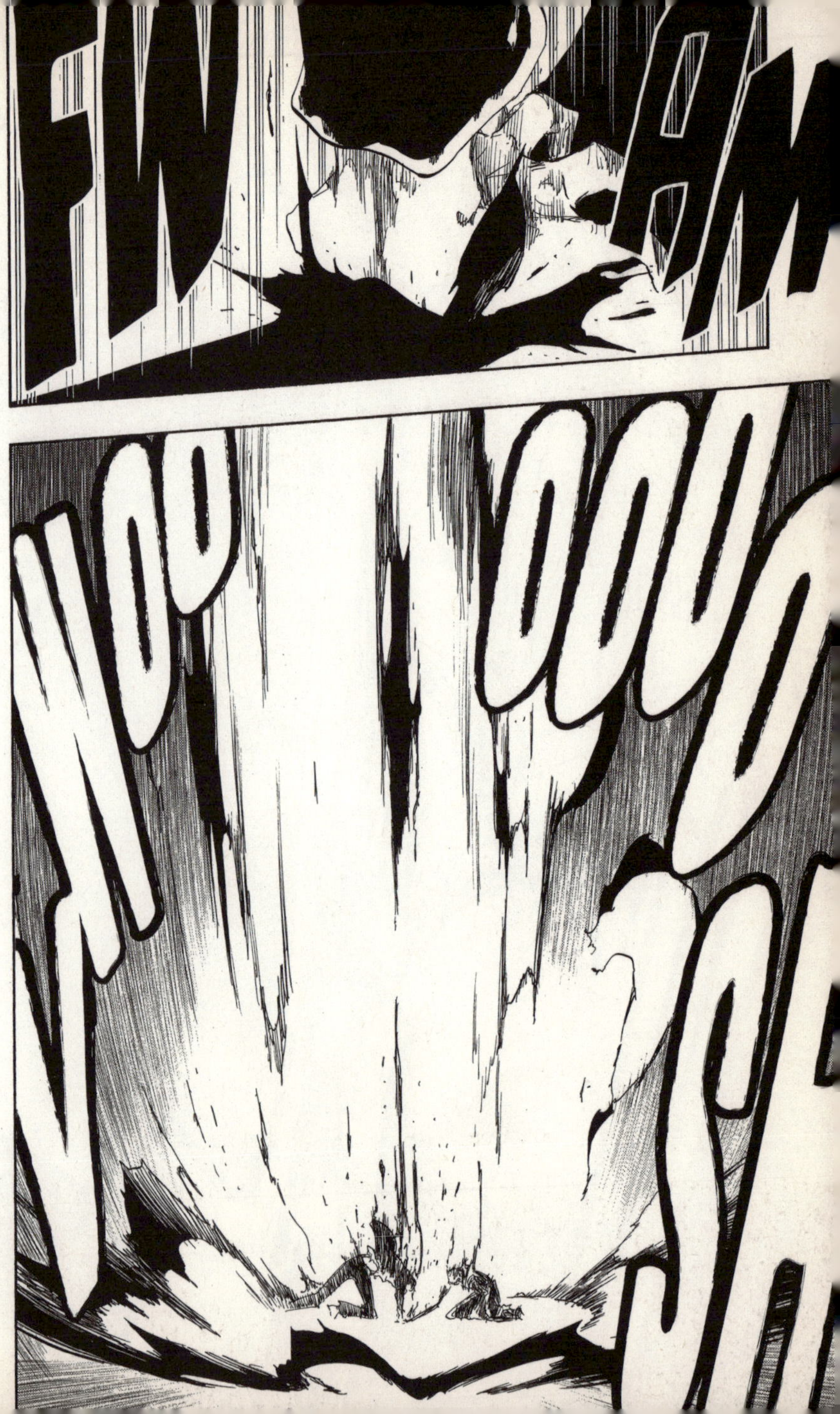

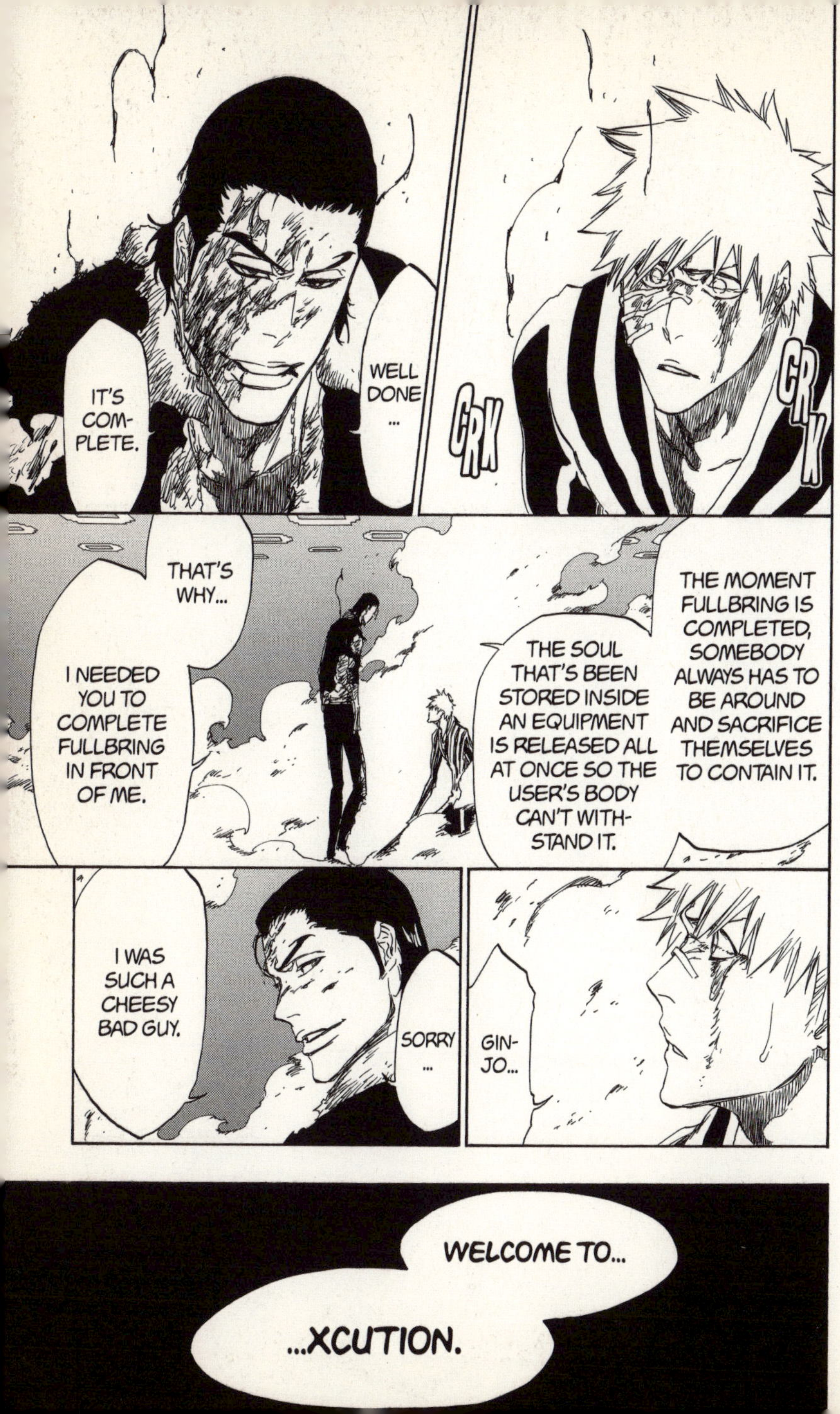
CRK
CRK
WELL DONE...
IT'S COM-PLETE.
THE MOMENT FULLBRING IS COMPLETED, SOMEBODY ALWAYS HAS TO BE AROUND AND SACRIFICE THEMSELVES TO CONTAIN IT.
THE SOUL THAT'S BEEN STORED INSIDE AN EQUIPMENT IS RELEASED ALL AT ONCE SO THE USER'S BODY CAN'T WITH-STAND IT.
THAT'S WHY...
I NEEDED YOU TO COMPLETE FULLBRING IN FRONT OF ME.
GIN-JO...
SORRY...
I WAS SUCH A CHEESY BAD GUY.
WELCOME TO...
...XCUTION.

THAT WAS
SOME
HORRIBLE
ACTING...

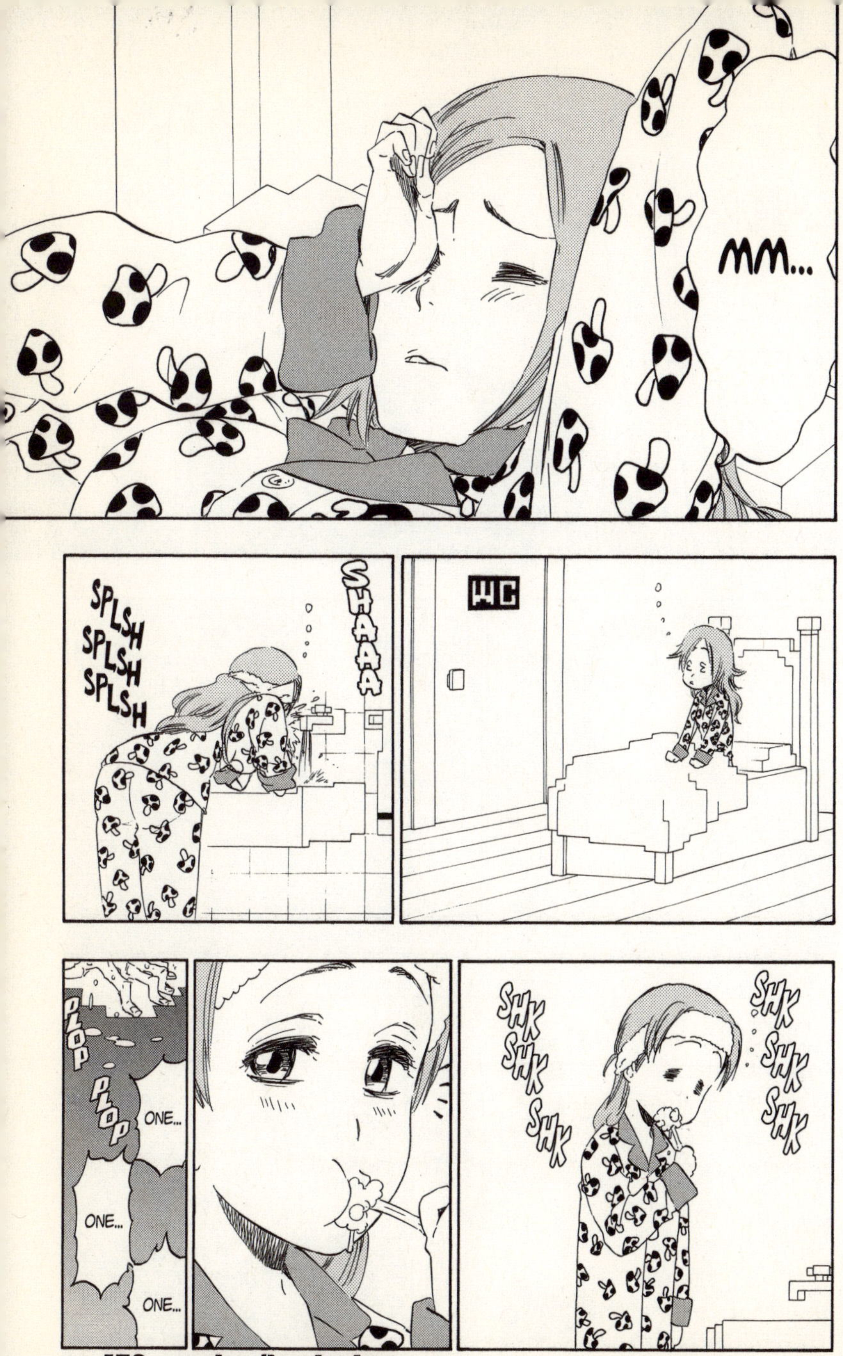
MM...
WC
SHAAA
SPLSH
SPLSH
SPLSH
SHK
SHK
SHK
SHK
SHK
SHK
PLOP
PLOP
ONE...
ONE...
ONE...

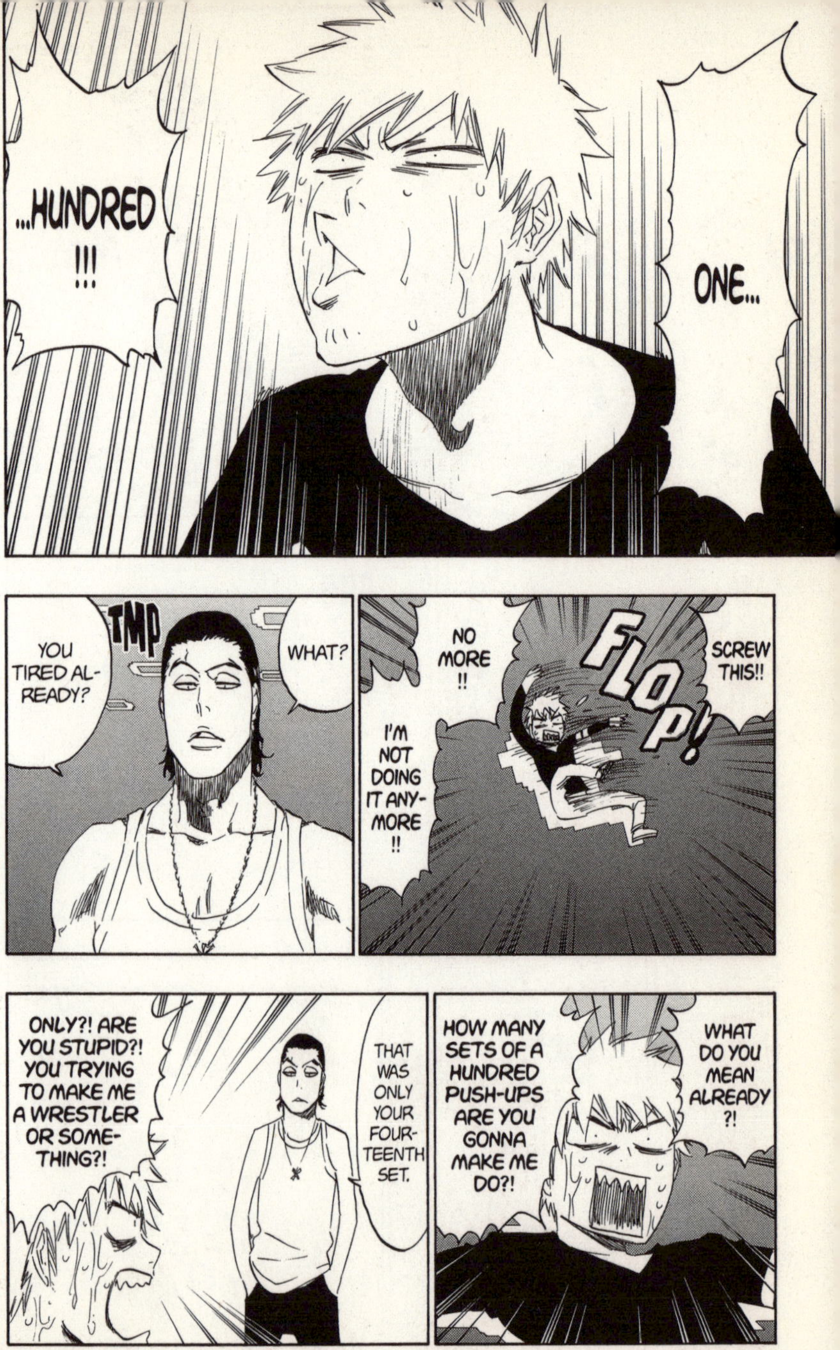
ONE...
...HUNDRED !!!
SCREW THIS!!
FLOP!
NO MORE !!
I'M NOT DOING IT ANYMORE !!
WHAT?
TMP
YOU TIRED ALREADY?
WHAT DO YOU MEAN ALREADY ?!
HOW MANY SETS OF A HUNDRED PUSH-UPS ARE YOU GONNA MAKE ME DO?!
THAT WAS ONLY YOUR FOURTEENTH SET.
ONLY?! ARE YOU STUPID?! YOU TRYING TO MAKE ME A WRESTLER OR SOMETHING?!

READ THIS WAY

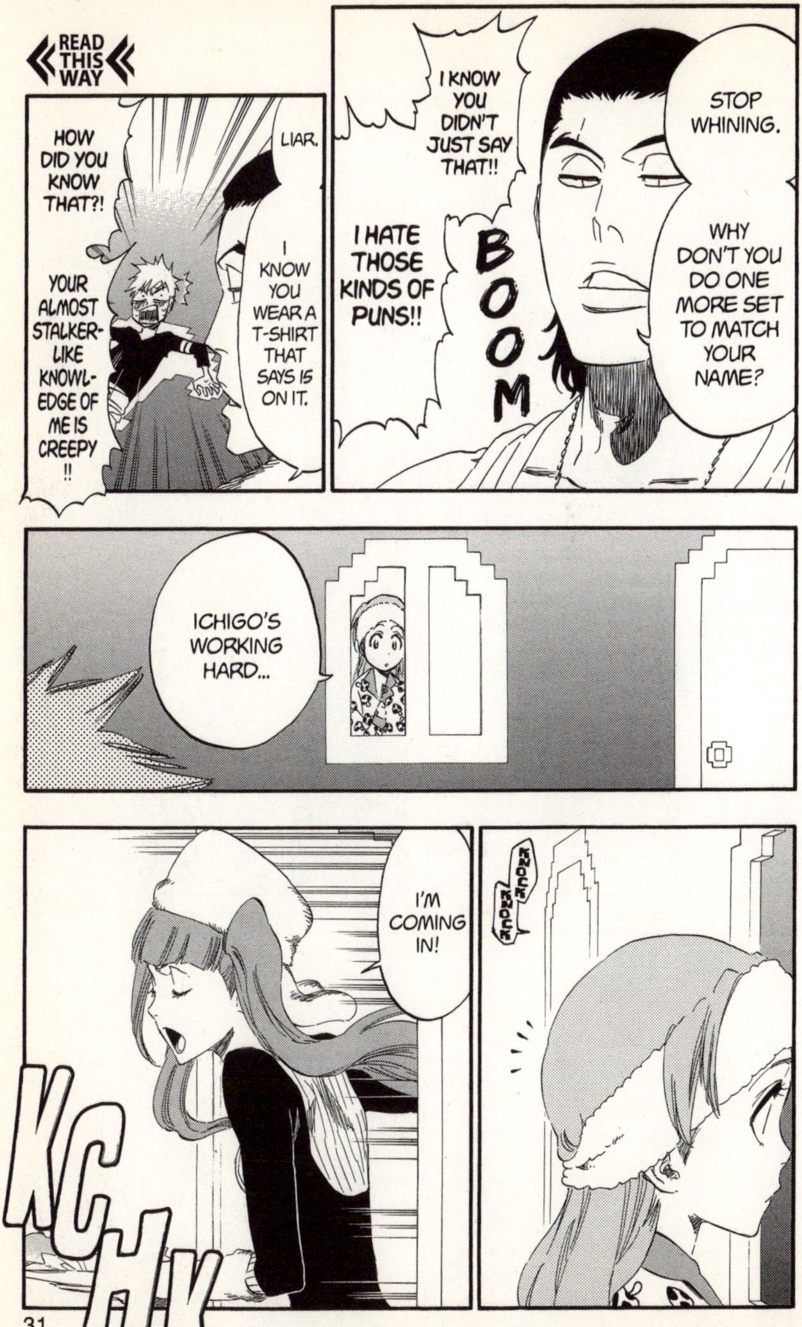

STOP WHINING.
WHY DON'T YOU DO ONE MORE SET TO MATCH YOUR NAME?
I KNOW YOU DIDN'T JUST SAY THAT!!
BOOM
I HATE THOSE KINDS OF PUNS!!
LIAR.
I KNOW YOU WEAR A T-SHIRT THAT SAYS 15 ON IT.
HOW DID YOU KNOW THAT?!
YOUR ALMOST STALKER-LIKE KNOWL-EDGE OF ME IS CREEPY!!
ICHIGO'S WORKING HARD...
KNOCK KNOCK
I'M COMING IN!
KCHK

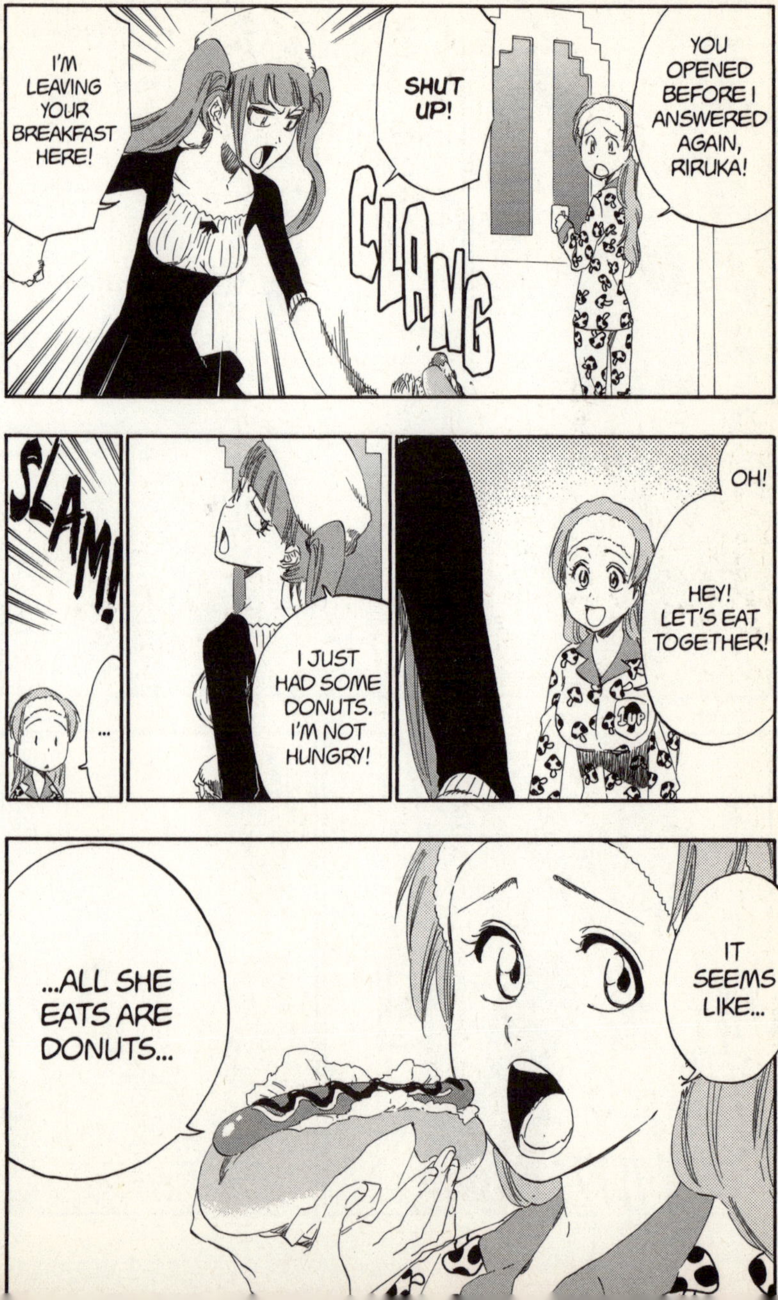
YOU OPENED BEFORE I ANSWERED AGAIN, RIRUKA!
SHUT UP!
CLANG
I'M LEAVING YOUR BREAKFAST HERE!
OH!
HEY! LET'S EAT TOGETHER!
I JUST HAD SOME DONUTS. I'M NOT HUNGRY!
SLAM!
...
IT SEEMS LIKE...
...ALL SHE EATS ARE DONUTS...

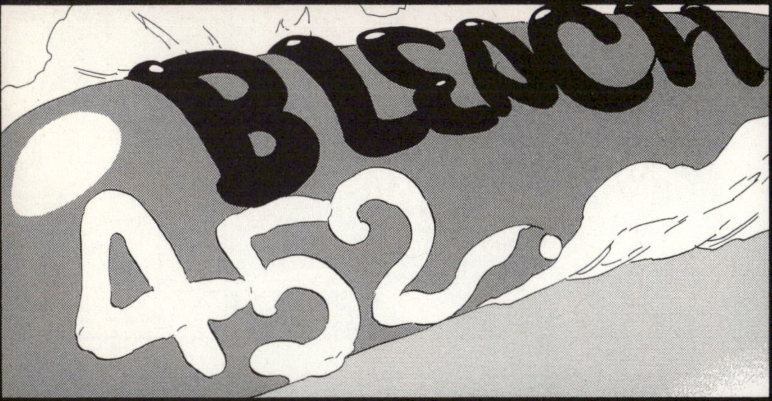
BLEACH
452

# erosion/implosion

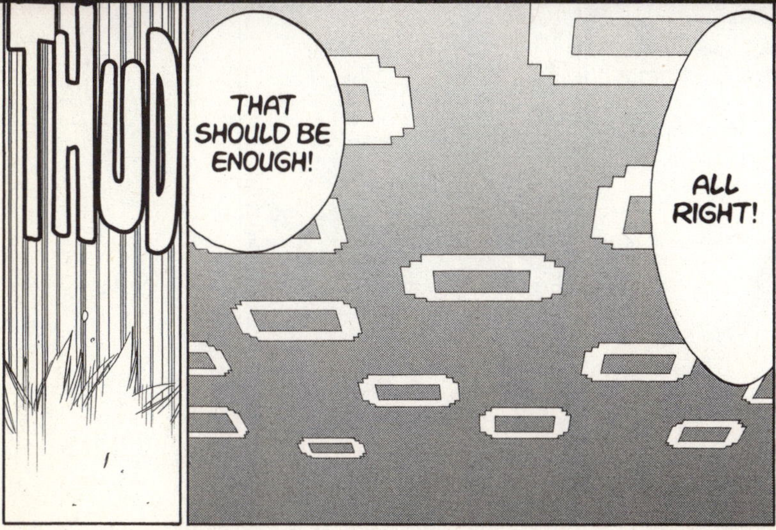
ALL RIGHT!
THAT SHOULD BE ENOUGH!
THUD

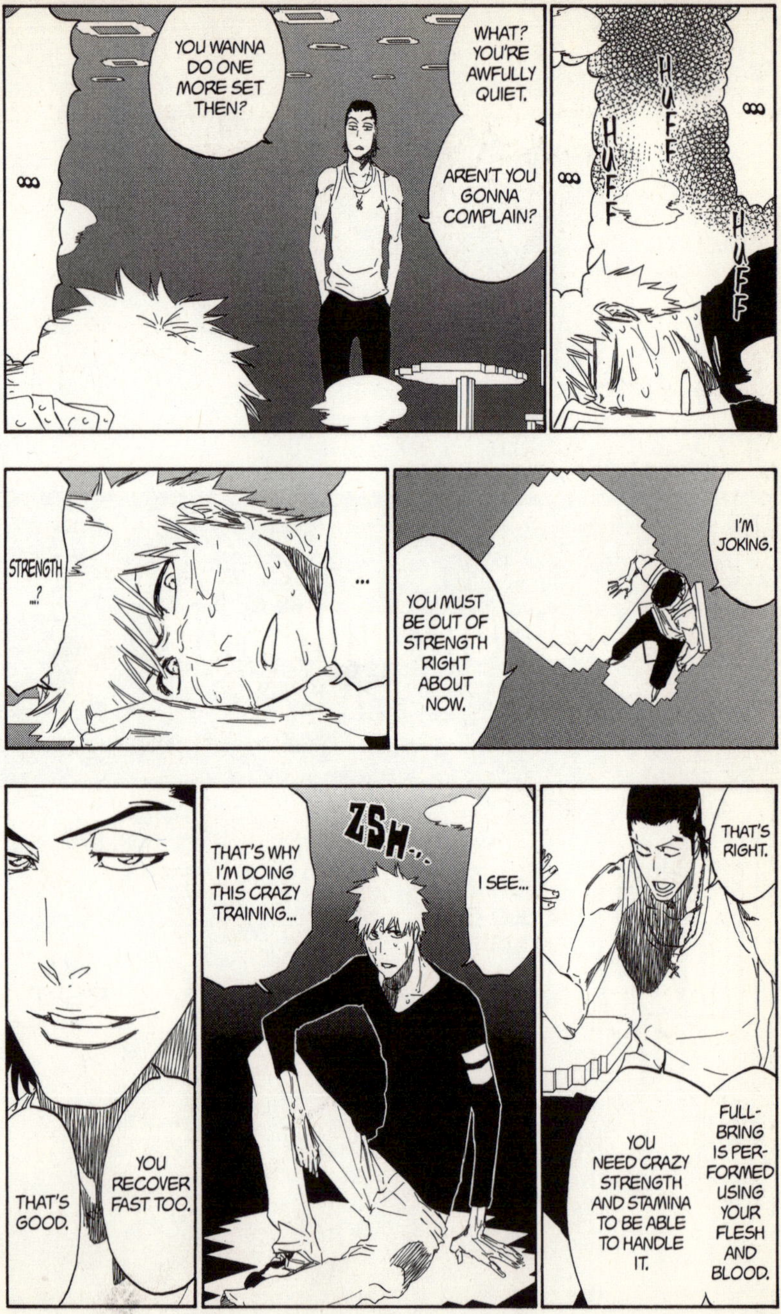
...
HUFF
HUFF
HUFF
...
WHAT? YOU'RE AWFULLY QUIET.
AREN'T YOU GONNA COMPLAIN?
YOU WANNA DO ONE MORE SET THEN?
...
I'M JOKING.
YOU MUST BE OUT OF STRENGTH RIGHT ABOUT NOW.
...
STRENGTH ...?
THAT'S RIGHT.
FULL-BRING IS PER-FORMED USING YOUR FLESH AND BLOOD.
YOU NEED CRAZY STRENGTH AND STAMINA TO BE ABLE TO HANDLE IT.
ZSH...
I SEE...
THAT'S WHY I'M DOING THIS CRAZY TRAINING...
YOU RECOVER FAST TOO.
THAT'S GOOD.

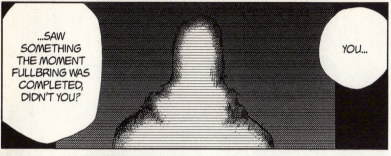

...SAW SOMETHING THE MOMENT FULLBRING WAS COMPLETED, DIDN'T YOU?

YOU...

YOU SHOULD'VE SEEN ME GLOWING AS A SPIRITUAL PRESSURE WITH YOUR SLASHED EYES.

I KNEW IT.

TWITCH

...FIGHT WITHOUT YOUR SIGHT TO MAKE SURE OF THAT.

I MADE YOU...

...PROOF THAT YOU'RE REGAINING YOUR SOUL REAPER POWERS.

THAT'S...

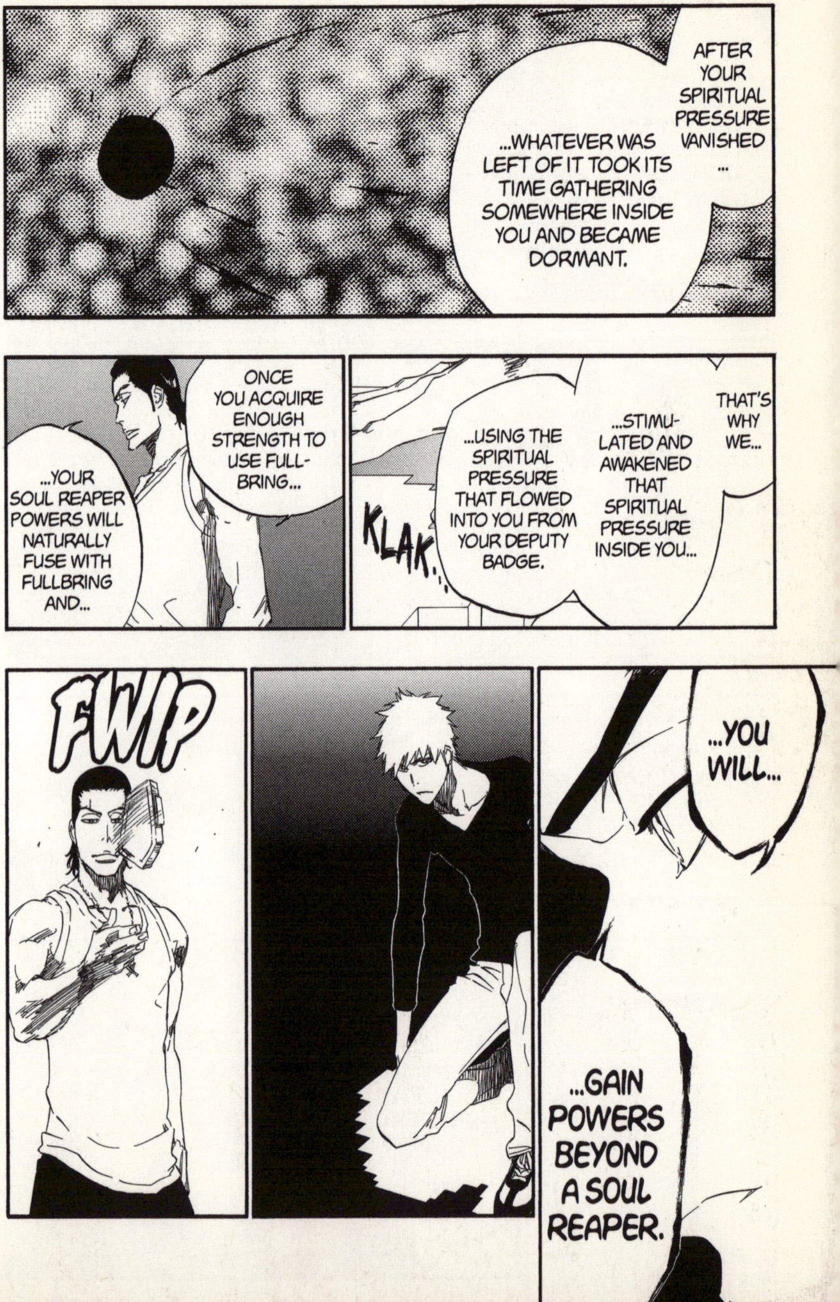
AFTER YOUR SPIRITUAL PRESSURE VANISHED...
...WHATEVER WAS LEFT OF IT TOOK ITS TIME GATHERING SOMEWHERE INSIDE YOU AND BECAME DORMANT.
THAT'S WHY WE...
...STIMU-LATED AND AWAKENED THAT SPIRITUAL PRESSURE INSIDE YOU...
...USING THE SPIRITUAL PRESSURE THAT FLOWED INTO YOU FROM YOUR DEPUTY BADGE.
KLAK...
ONCE YOU ACQUIRE ENOUGH STRENGTH TO USE FULL-BRING...
...YOUR SOUL REAPER POWERS WILL NATURALLY FUSE WITH FULLBRING AND...
...YOU WILL...
...GAIN POWERS BEYOND A SOUL REAPER.
FWIP

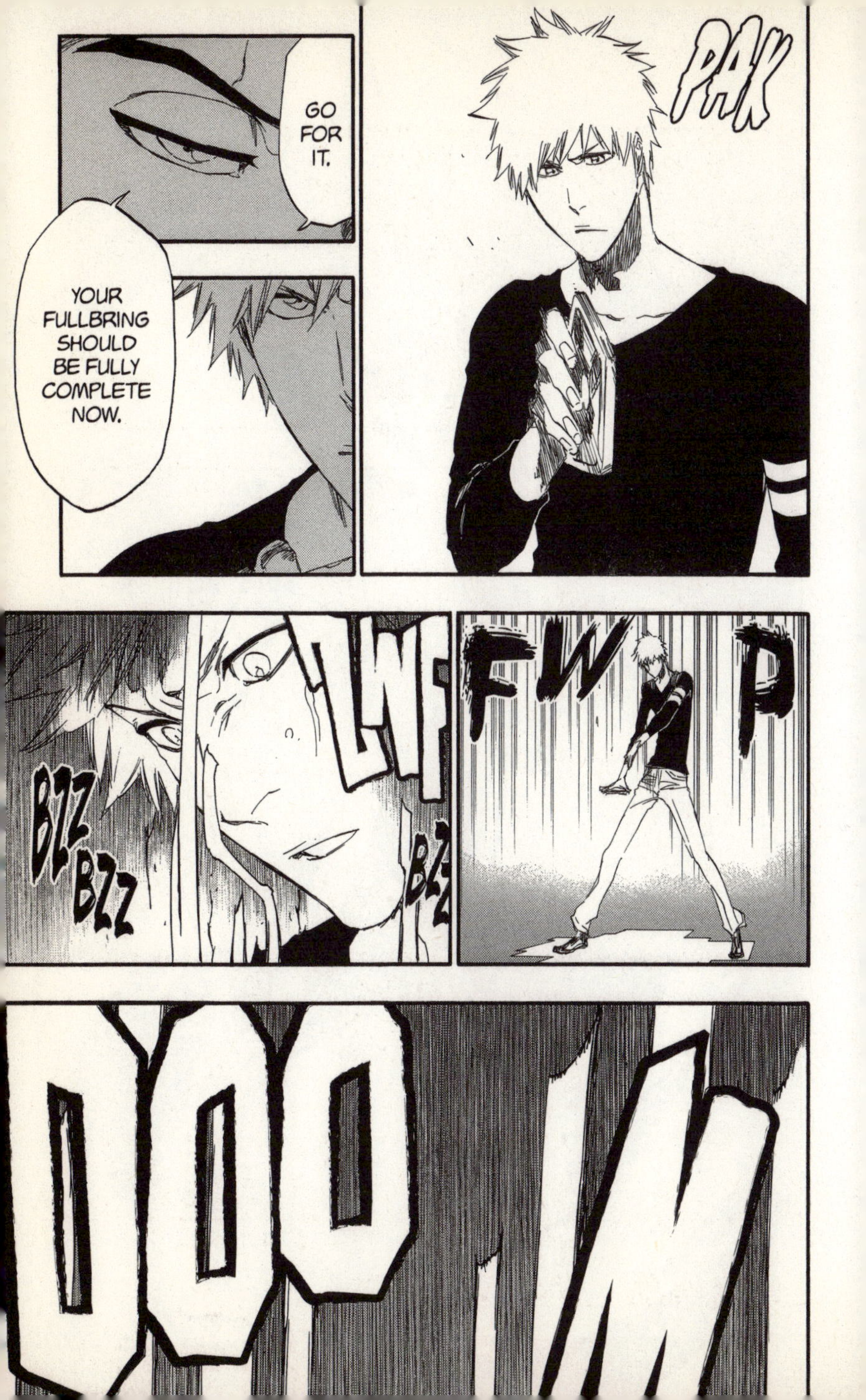
PAK
GO FOR IT.
YOUR FULLBRING SHOULD BE FULLY COMPLETE NOW.
FWP
BZZ BZZ
BZZ
DOOM

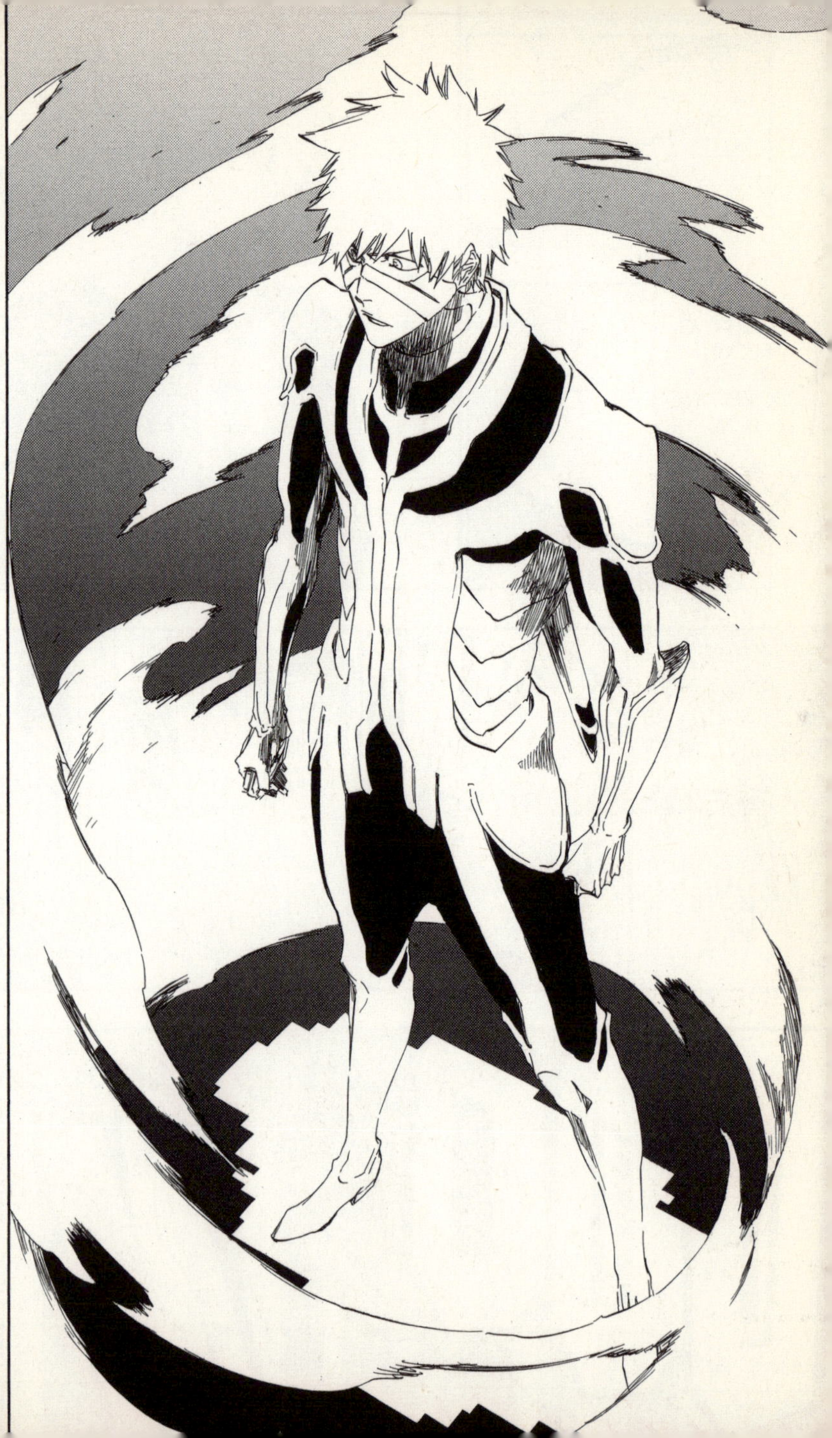

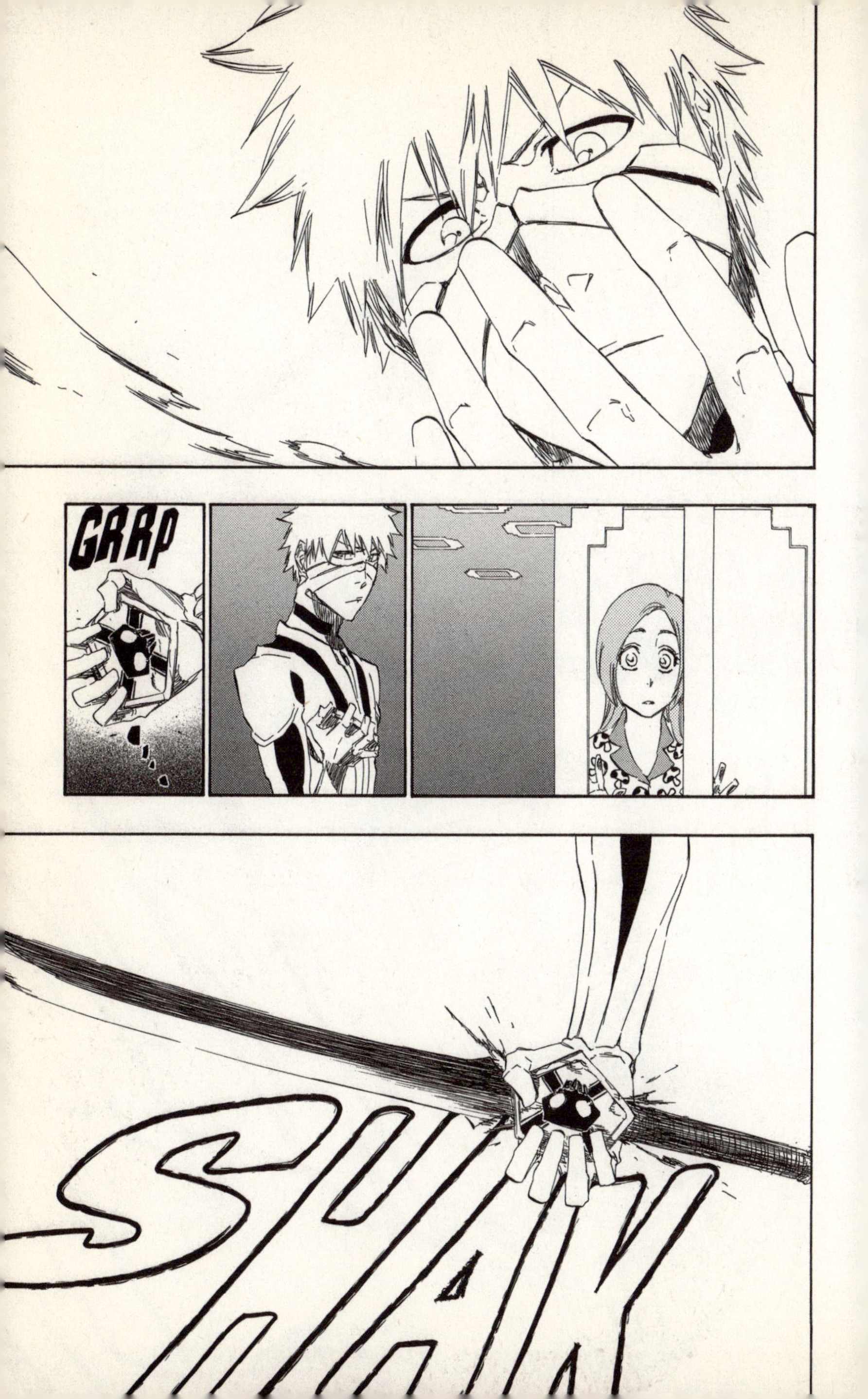
GRRP
SHAK

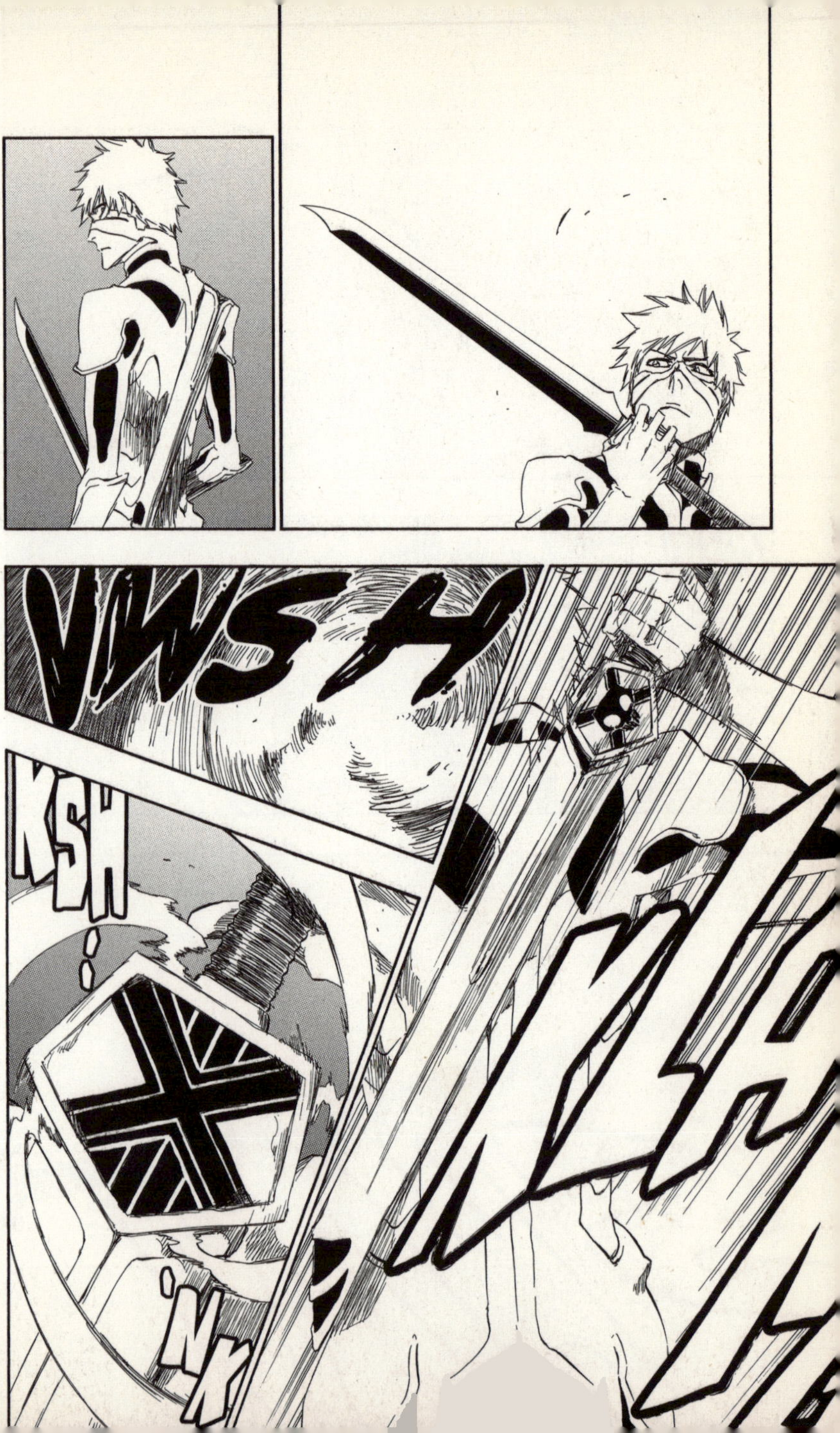
VWSH
KSH
'NK

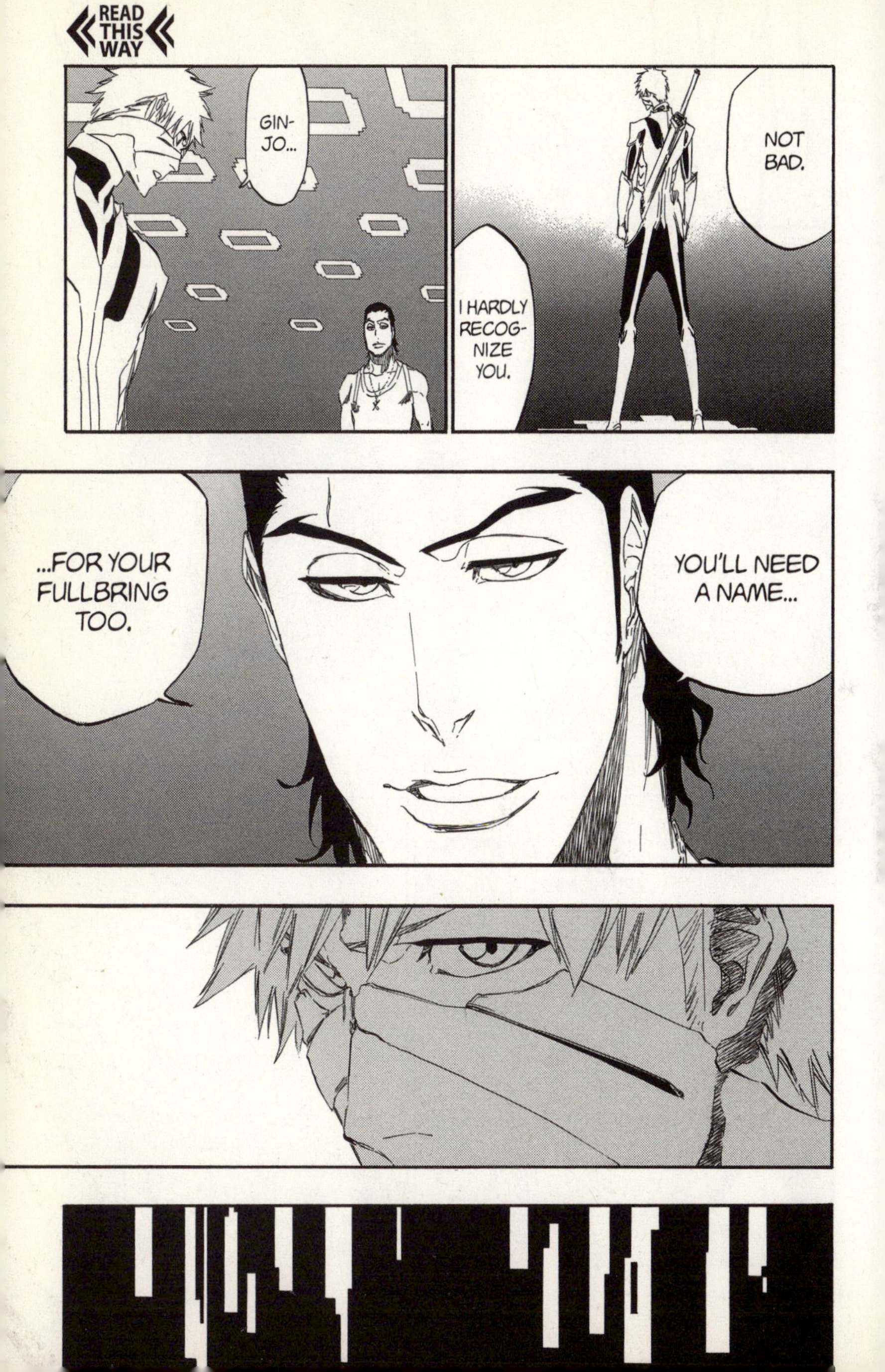
READ THIS WAY
NOT BAD.
I HARDLY RECOG-NIZE YOU.
GIN-JO...
YOU'LL NEED A NAME...
...FOR YOUR FULLBRING TOO.

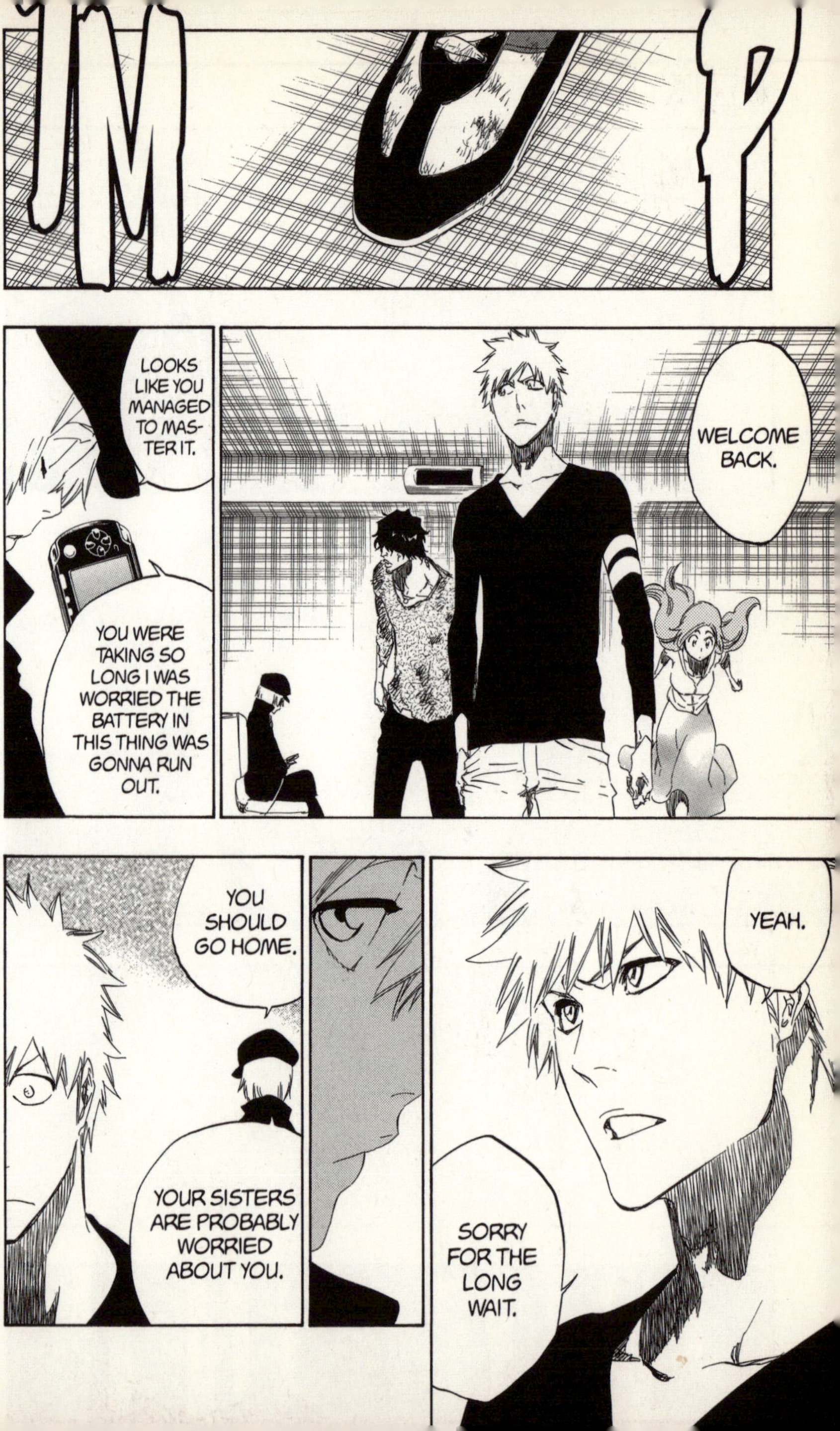
IMP
WELCOME BACK.
LOOKS LIKE YOU MANAGED TO MASTER IT.
YOU WERE TAKING SO LONG I WAS WORRIED THE BATTERY IN THIS THING WAS GONNA RUN OUT.
YEAH.
SORRY FOR THE LONG WAIT.
YOU SHOULD GO HOME.
YOUR SISTERS ARE PROBABLY WORRIED ABOUT YOU.

READ THIS WAY

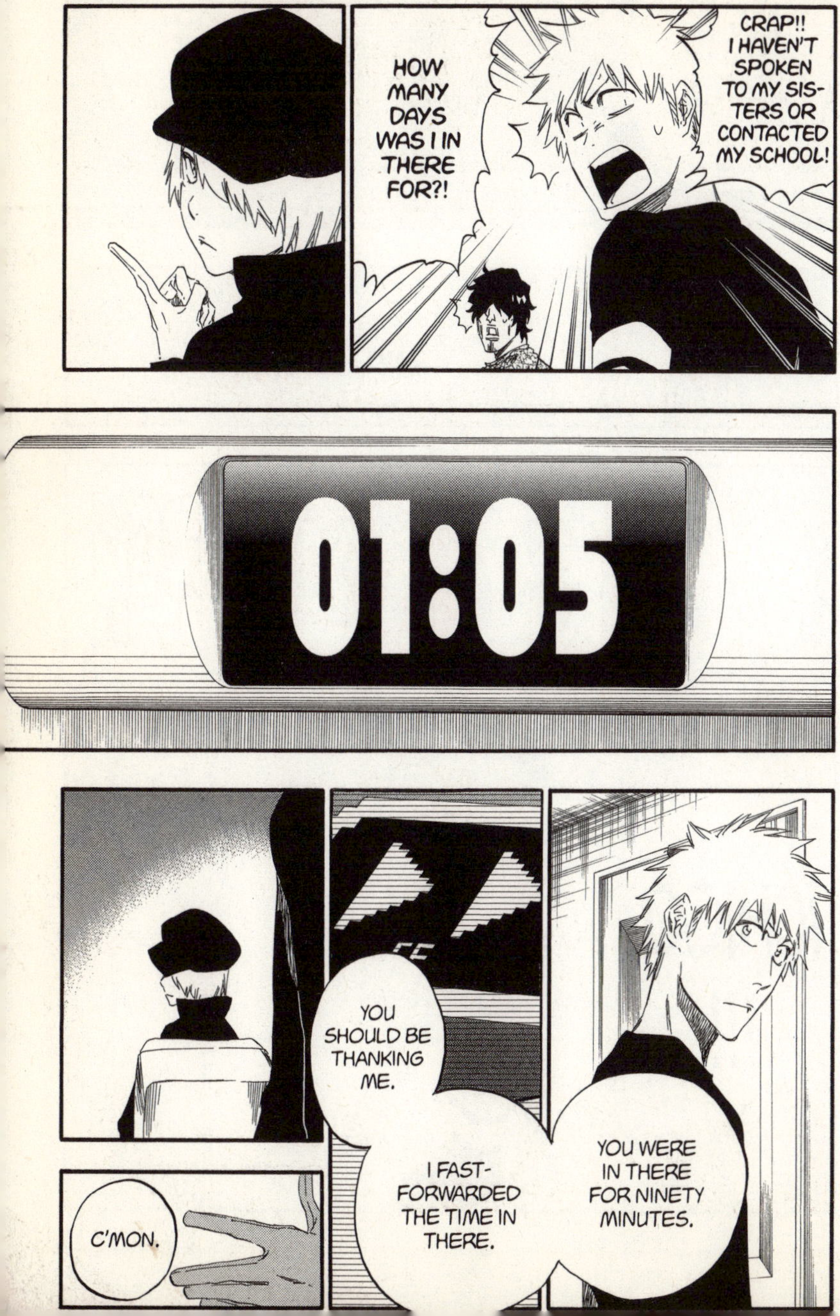

CRAP!! I HAVEN'T SPOKEN TO MY SIS-TERS OR CONTACTED MY SCHOOL!
HOW MANY DAYS WAS I IN THERE FOR?!
01:05
YOU WERE IN THERE FOR NINETY MINUTES.
I FAST-FORWARDED THE TIME IN THERE.
YOU SHOULD BE THANKING ME.
C'MON.

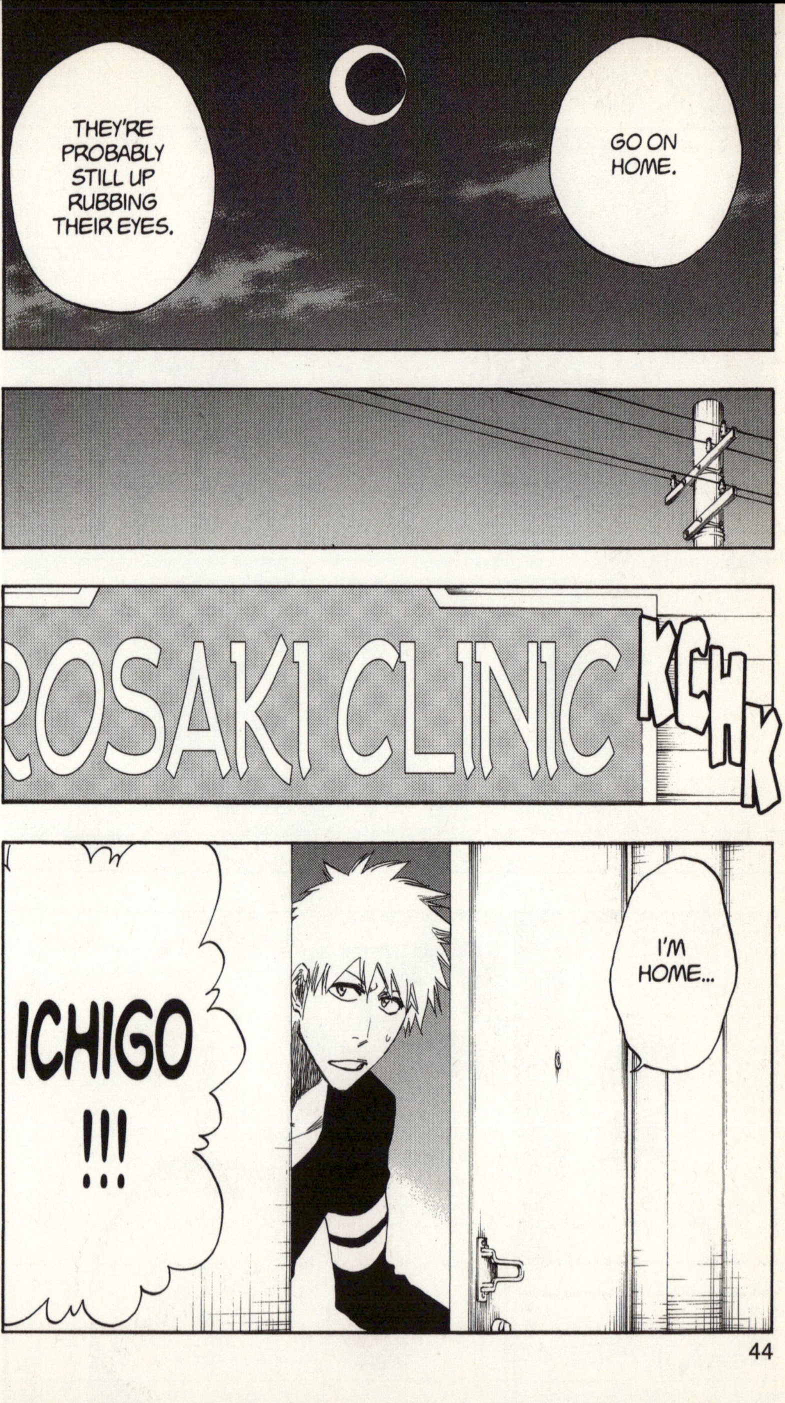
GO ON HOME.
THEY'RE PROBABLY STILL UP RUBBING THEIR EYES.
ROSAKI CLINIC
KCHK
I'M HOME...
ICHIGO !!!

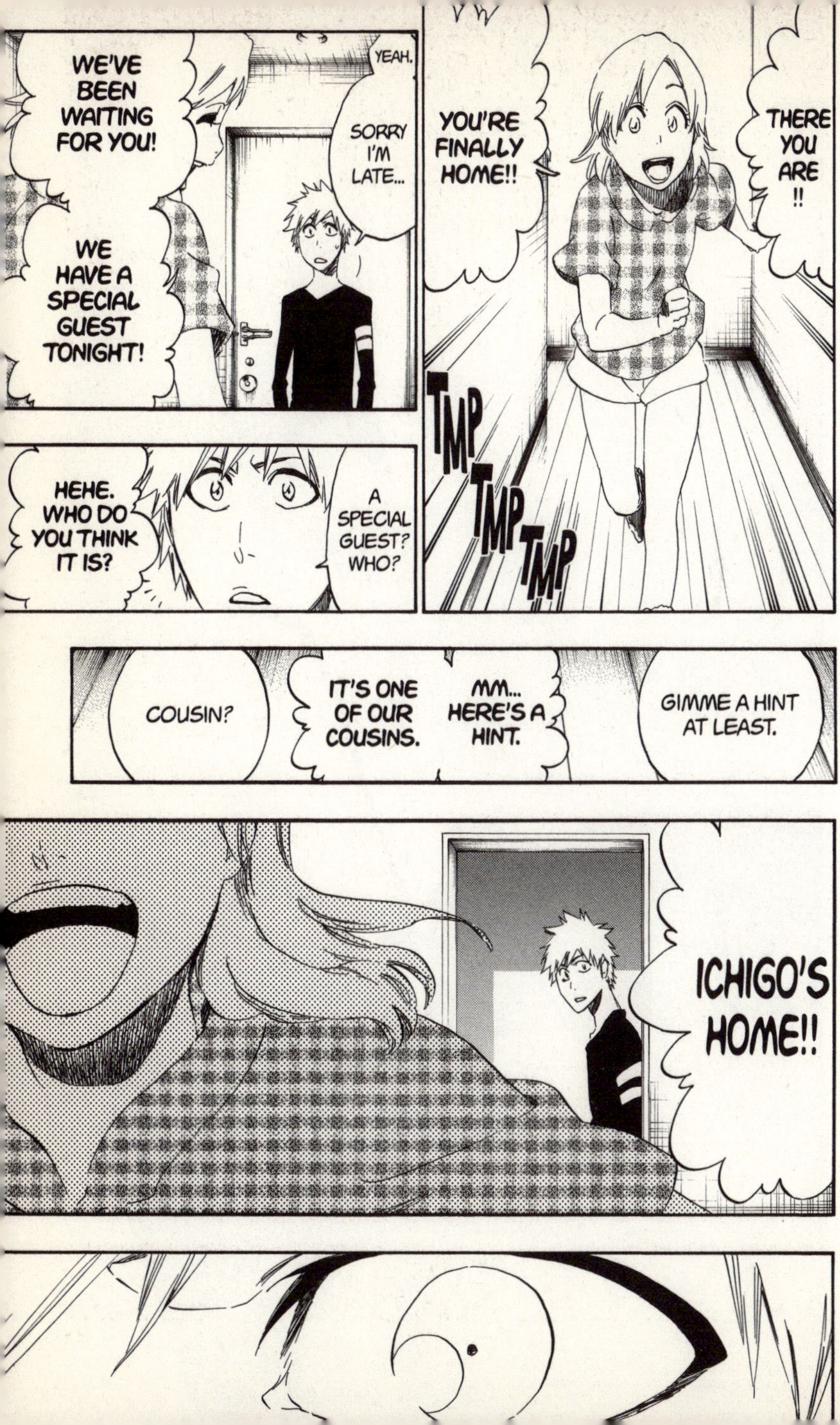
THERE YOU ARE !!
YOU'RE FINALLY HOME!!
TMP TMP TMP
YEAH.
SORRY I'M LATE...
WE'VE BEEN WAITING FOR YOU!
WE HAVE A SPECIAL GUEST TONIGHT!
A SPECIAL GUEST? WHO?
HEHE. WHO DO YOU THINK IT IS?
GIMME A HINT AT LEAST.
MM... HERE'S A HINT.
IT'S ONE OF OUR COUSINS.
COUSIN?
ICHIGO'S HOME!!

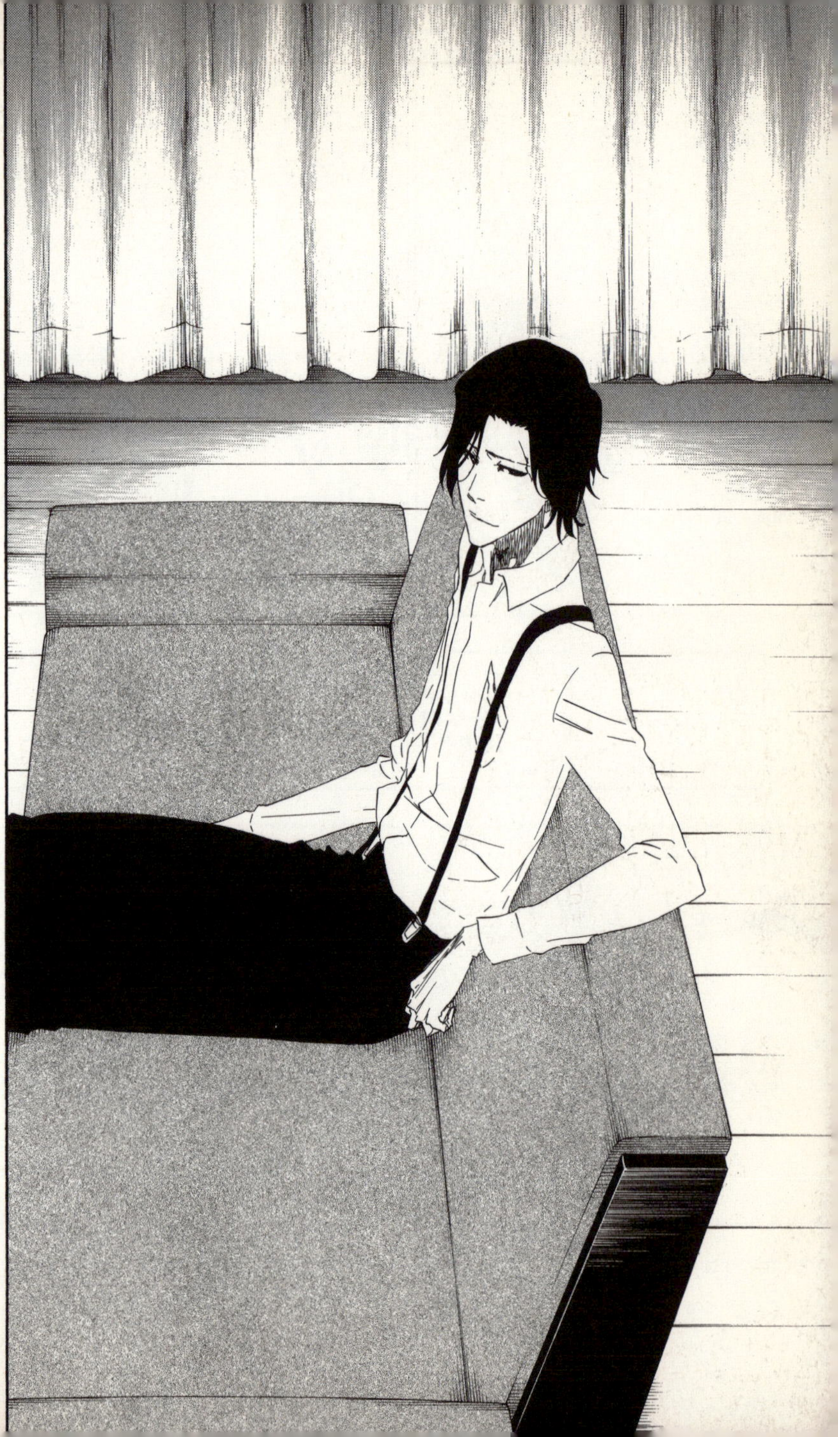

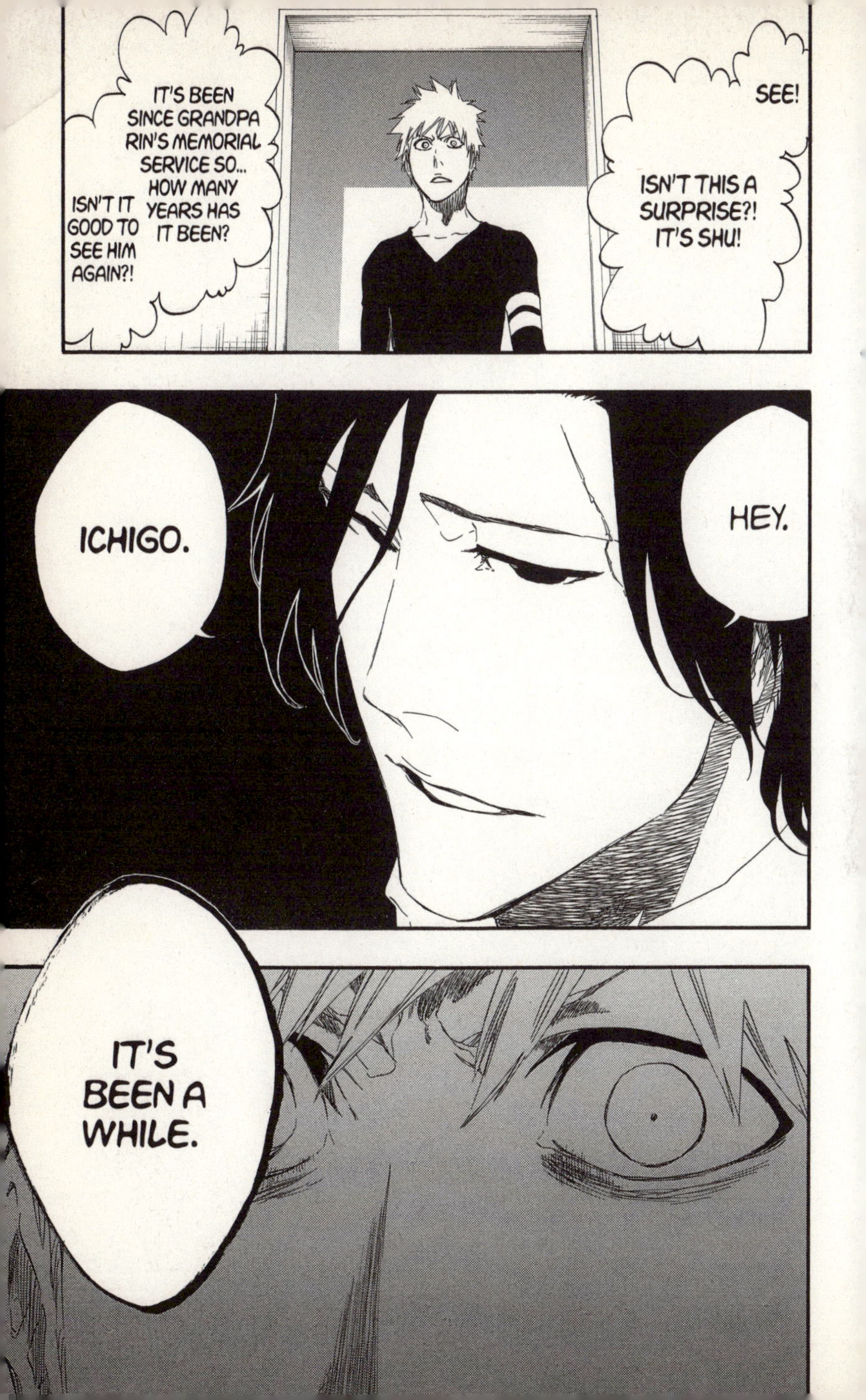
SEE!
ISN'T THIS A SURPRISE?! IT'S SHU!
IT'S BEEN SINCE GRANDPA RIN'S MEMORIAL SERVICE SO... HOW MANY YEARS HAS IT BEEN?
ISN'T IT GOOD TO SEE HIM AGAIN?!
HEY.
ICHIGO.
IT'S BEEN A WHILE.

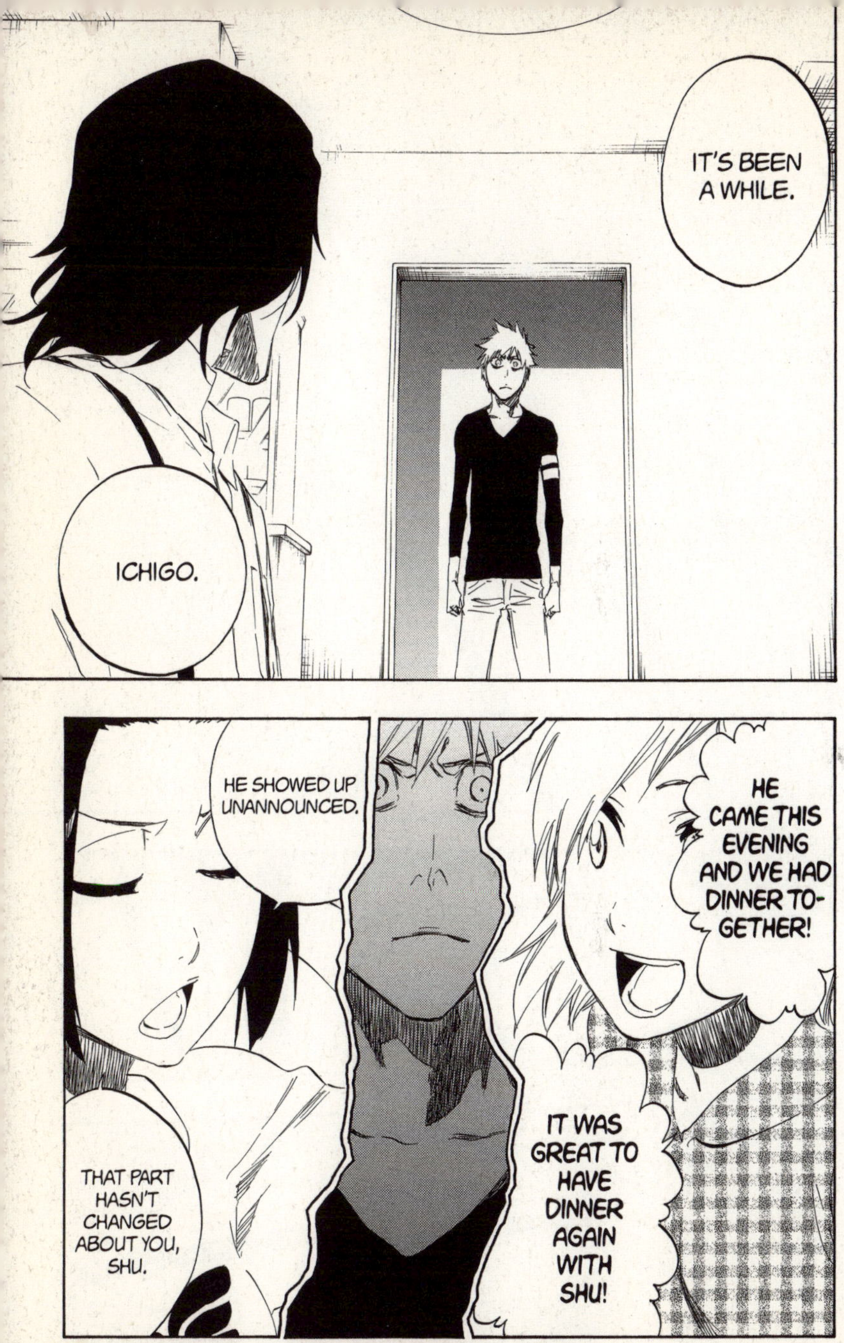
IT'S BEEN A WHILE.
ICHIGO.
HE CAME THIS EVENING AND WE HAD DINNER TO-GETHER!
IT WAS GREAT TO HAVE DINNER AGAIN WITH SHU!
HE SHOWED UP UNANNOUNCED.
THAT PART HASN'T CHANGED ABOUT YOU, SHU.

**BLEACH 453. Mute Your Breathe Friendship**

DID I CAUSE YOU GUYS TROUBLE?

SORRY.

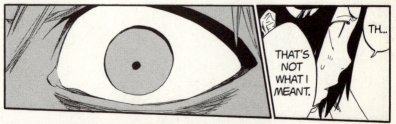

TH...

THAT'S NOT WHAT I MEANT.

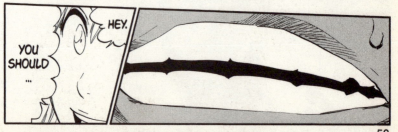

HEY.

YOU SHOULD...

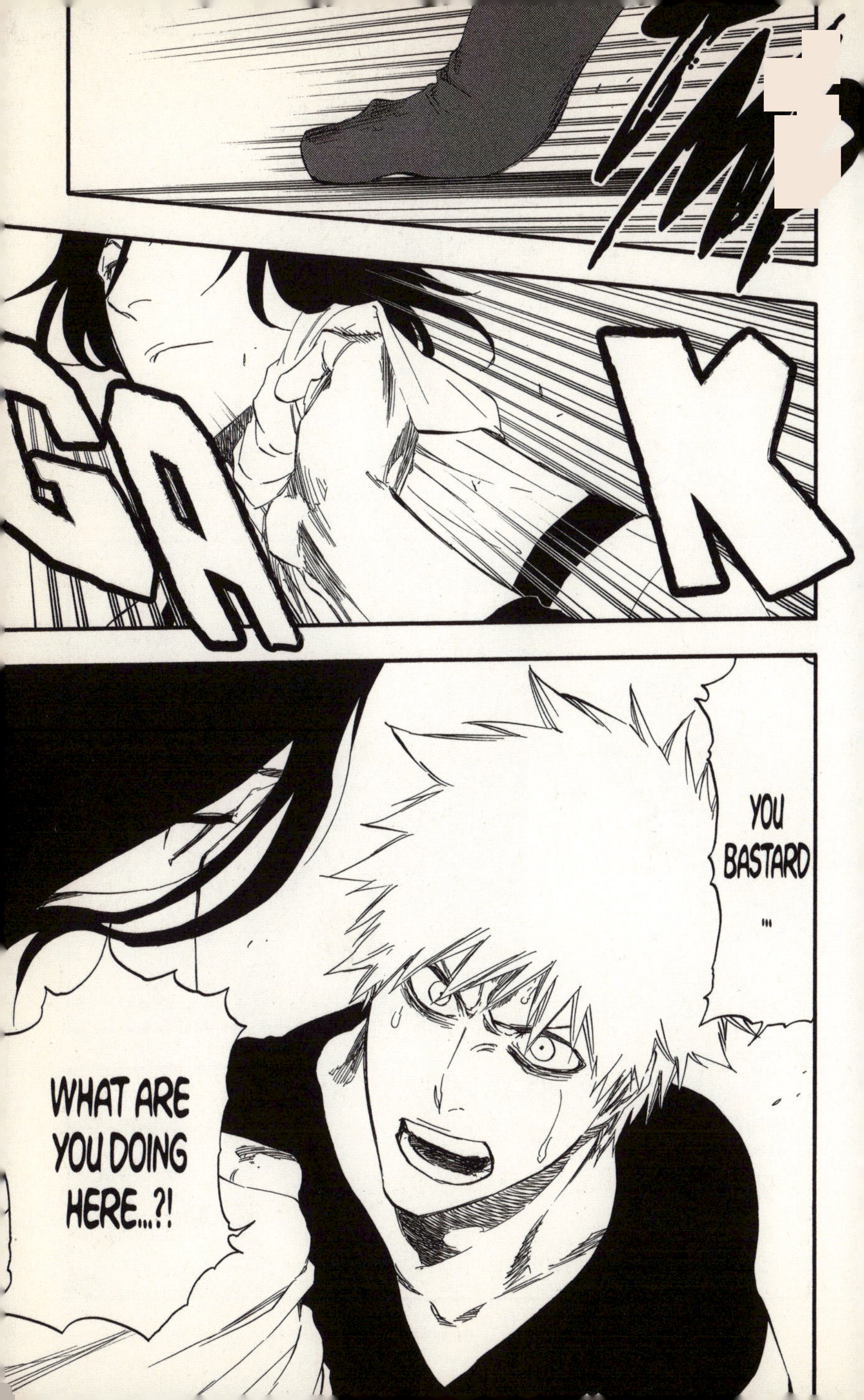
YOU BASTARD...
WHAT ARE YOU DOING HERE...?!

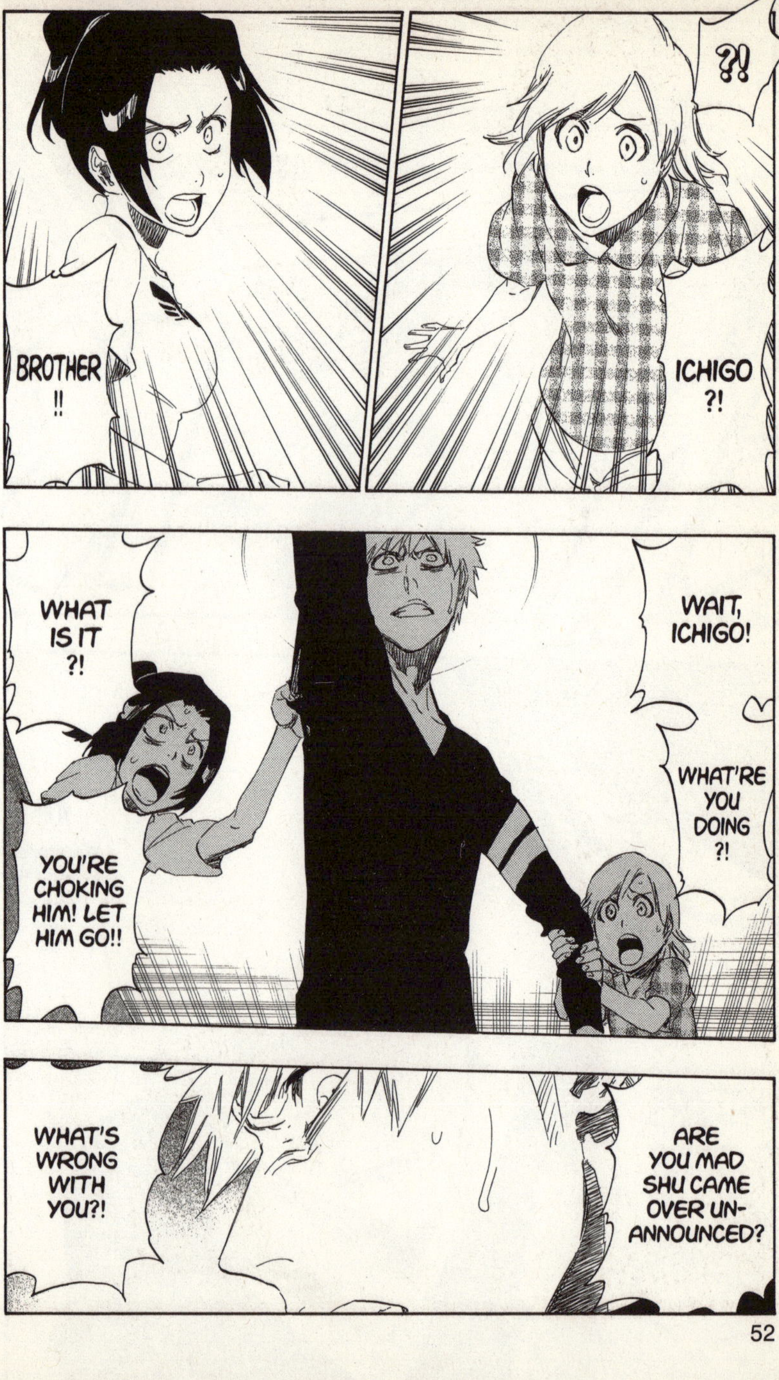
?!
ICHIGO ?!
BROTHER !!
WAIT, ICHIGO!
WHAT'RE YOU DOING ?!
WHAT IS IT ?!
YOU'RE CHOKING HIM! LET HIM GO!!
ARE YOU MAD SHU CAME OVER UN-ANNOUNCED?
WHAT'S WRONG WITH YOU?!

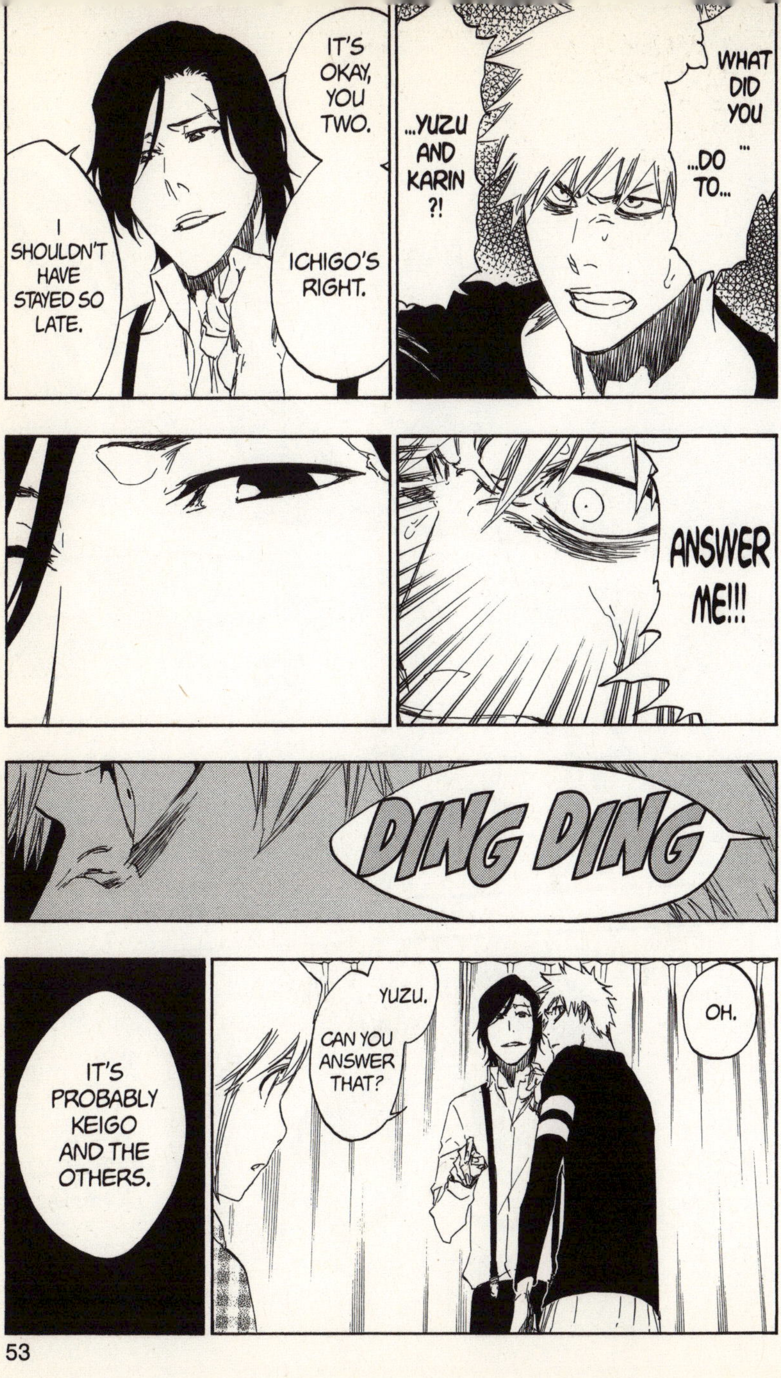
WHAT DID YOU ... ...DO TO...
...YUZU AND KARIN ?!
IT'S OKAY, YOU TWO.
ICHIGO'S RIGHT.
I SHOULDN'T HAVE STAYED SO LATE.
ANSWER ME!!!
DING DING
OH.
YUZU.
CAN YOU ANSWER THAT?
IT'S PROBABLY KEIGO AND THE OTHERS.

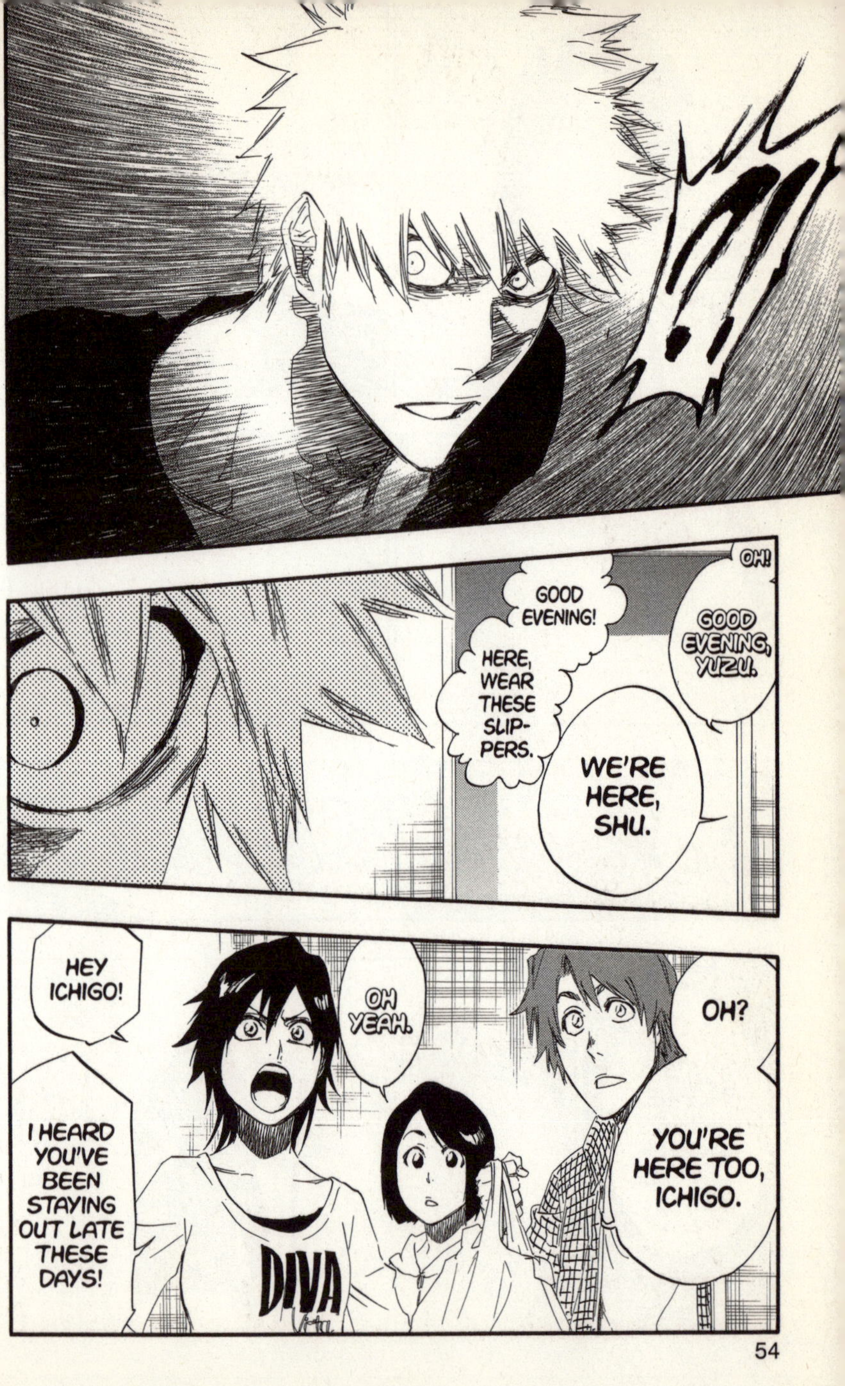
OH!
GOOD EVENING, YUZU.
GOOD EVENING!
HERE, WEAR THESE SLIP-PERS.
WE'RE HERE, SHU.
OH?
YOU'RE HERE TOO, ICHIGO.
OH YEAH.
HEY ICHIGO!
I HEARD YOU'VE BEEN STAYING OUT LATE THESE DAYS!
DIVA

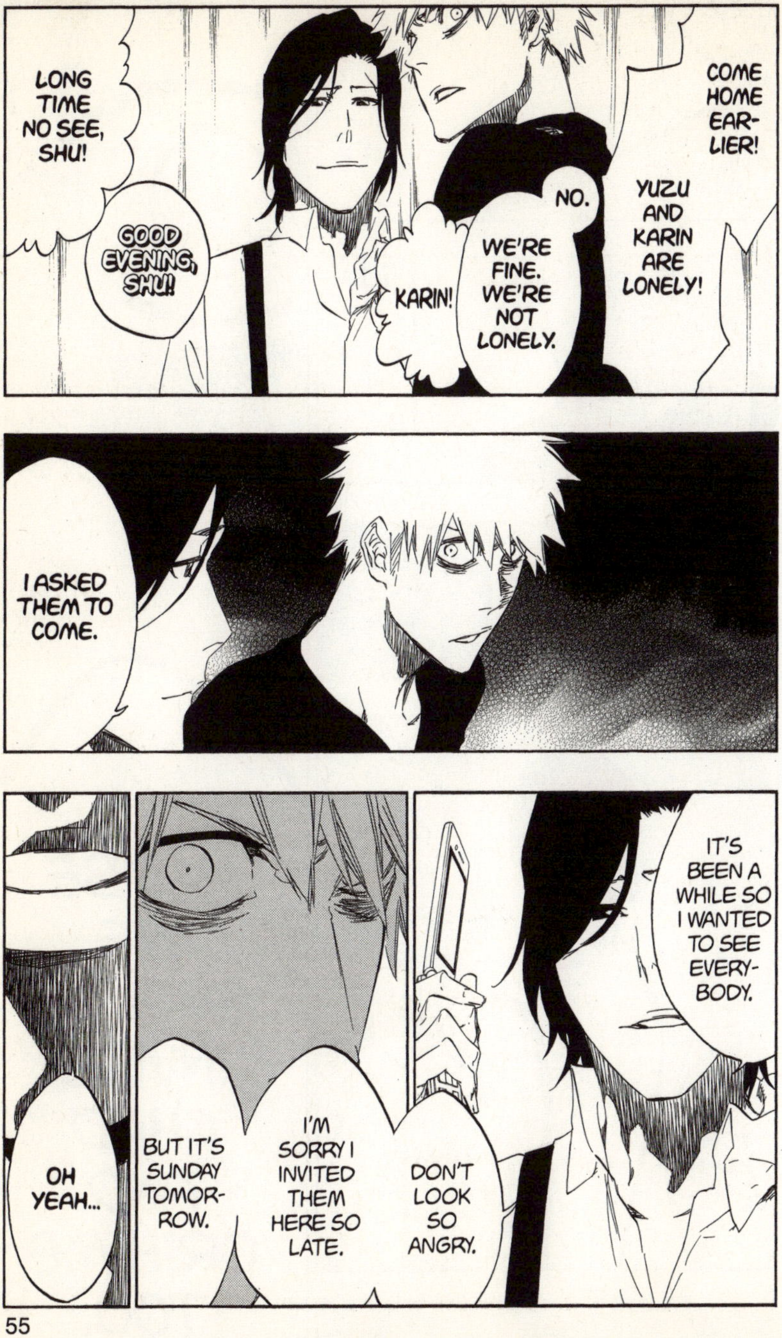
COME HOME EARLIER!
YUZU AND KARIN ARE LONELY!
NO.
WE'RE FINE. WE'RE NOT LONELY.
KARIN!
LONG TIME NO SEE, SHU!
GOOD EVENING, SHU!
I ASKED THEM TO COME.
IT'S BEEN A WHILE SO I WANTED TO SEE EVERYBODY.
DON'T LOOK SO ANGRY.
I'M SORRY I INVITED THEM HERE SO LATE.
BUT IT'S SUNDAY TOMORROW.
OH YEAH...

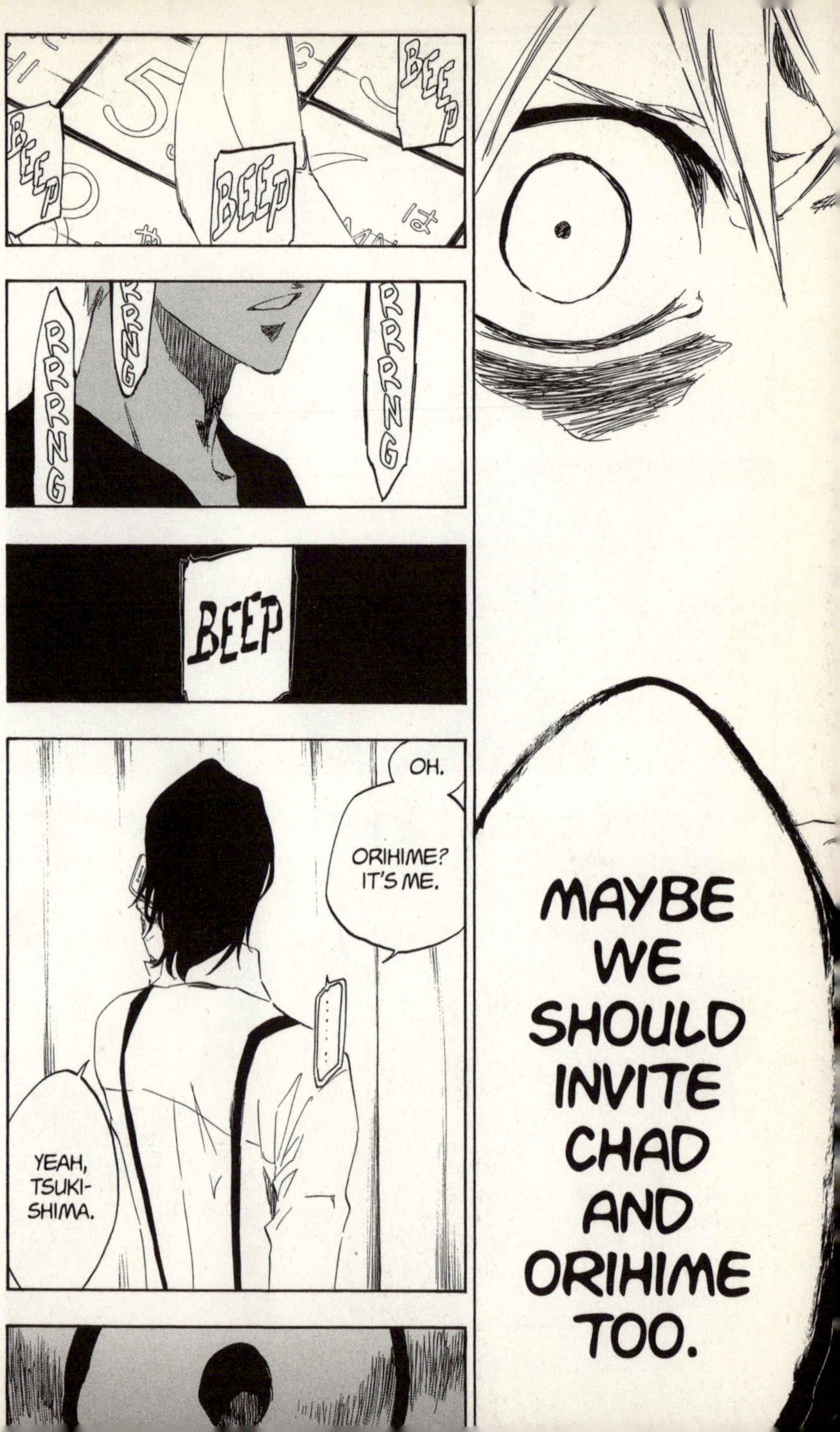
MAYBE WE SHOULD INVITE CHAD AND ORIHIME TOO.
BEEP
BEEP
BEEP
RRRRNG
RRRNG
RRRRNG
BEEP
OH.
ORIHIME? IT'S ME.
......
YEAH, TSUKI-SHIMA.

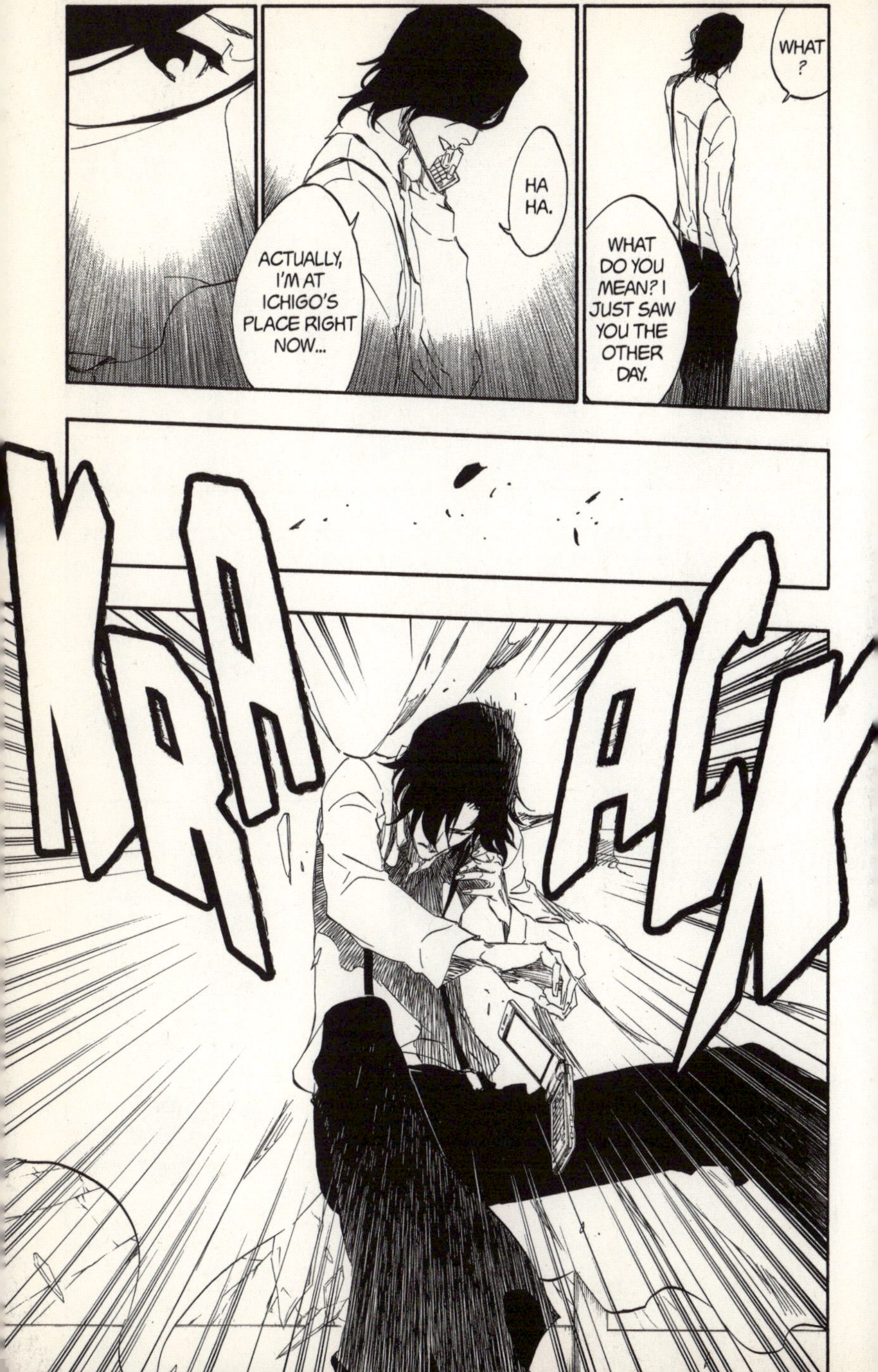
WHAT ?
WHAT DO YOU MEAN? I JUST SAW YOU THE OTHER DAY.
HA HA.
ACTUALLY, I'M AT ICHIGO'S PLACE RIGHT NOW...
KRAACK

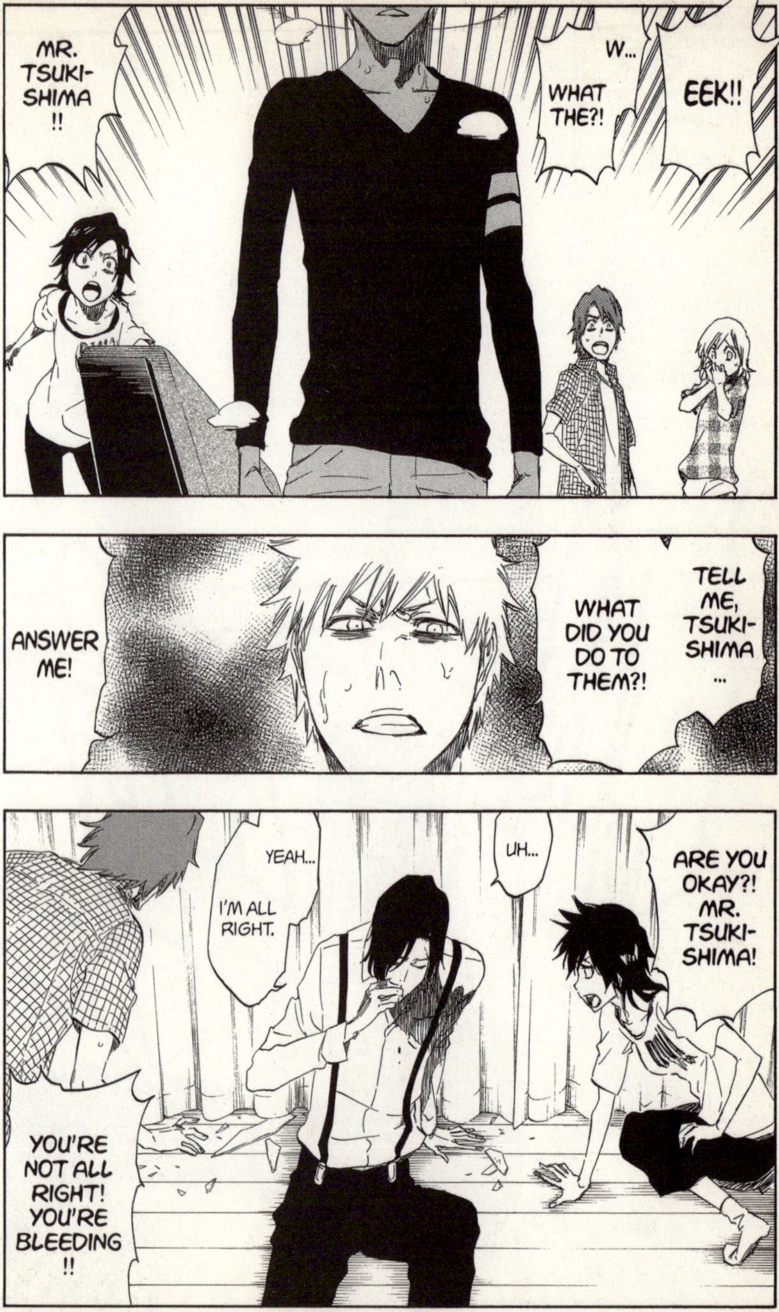
EEK!!
W... WHAT THE?!
MR. TSUKI-SHIMA !!
TELL ME, TSUKI-SHIMA ...
WHAT DID YOU DO TO THEM?!
ANSWER ME!
ARE YOU OKAY?! MR. TSUKI-SHIMA!
UH...
YEAH...
I'M ALL RIGHT.
YOU'RE NOT ALL RIGHT! YOU'RE BLEEDING !!

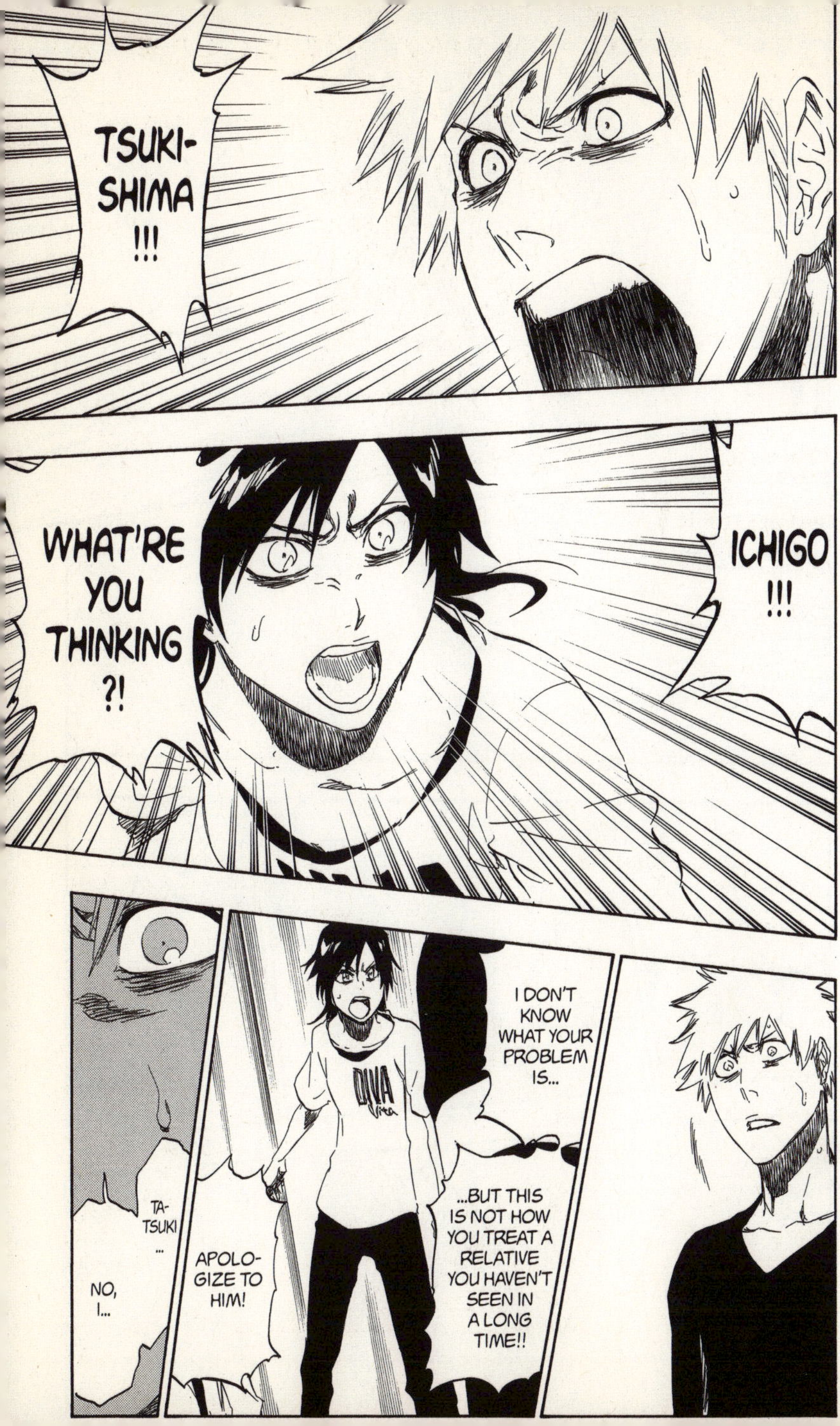
TSUKI-SHIMA !!!
ICHIGO !!!
WHAT'RE YOU THINKING ?!
I DON'T KNOW WHAT YOUR PROBLEM IS...
...BUT THIS IS NOT HOW YOU TREAT A RELATIVE YOU HAVEN'T SEEN IN A LONG TIME!!
APOLO-GIZE TO HIM!
TA-TSUKI ...
NO, I...

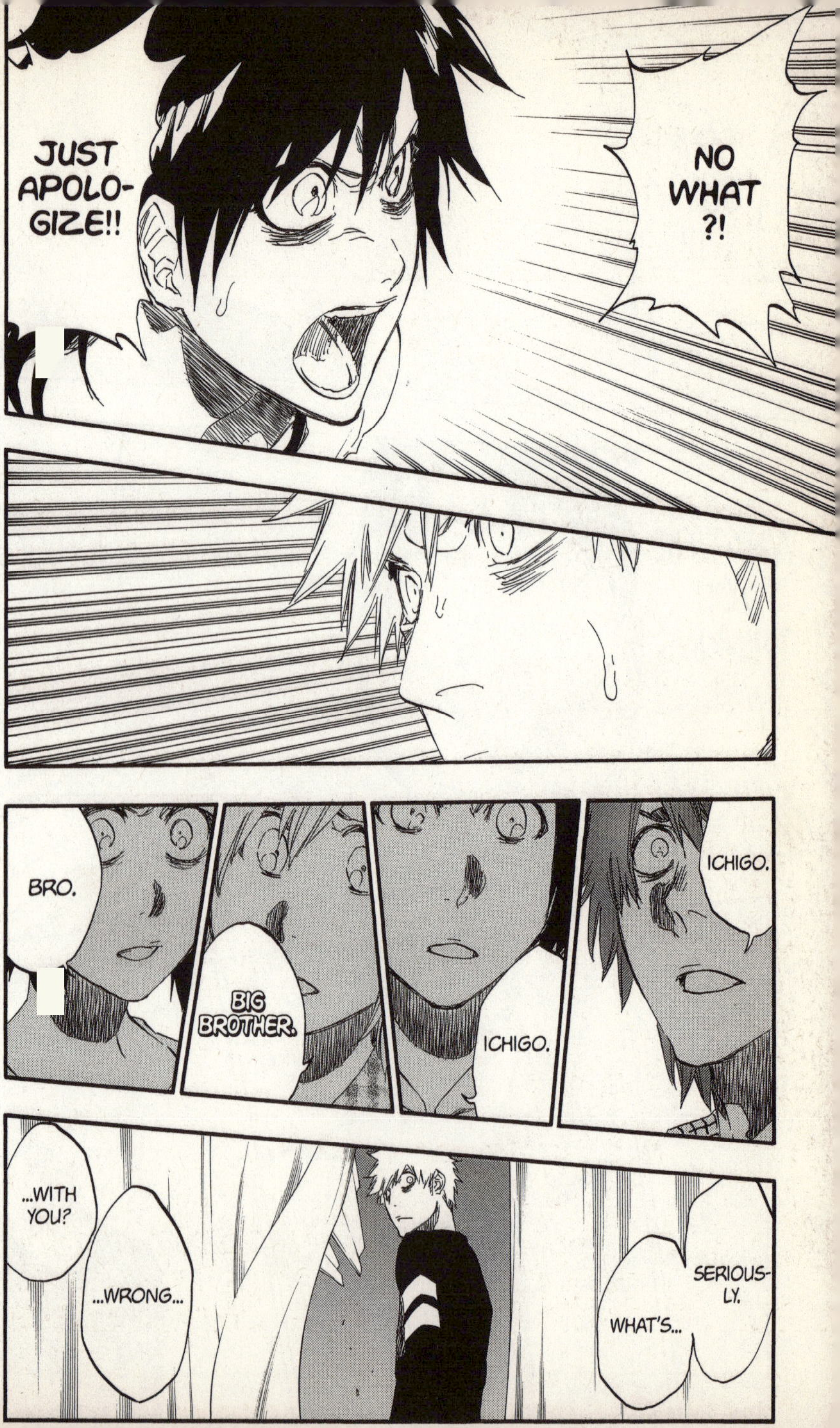
NO WHAT ?!
JUST APOLO-GIZE!!
ICHIGO.
ICHIGO.
BIG BROTHER.
BRO.
SERIOUS-LY.
WHAT'S...
...WRONG...
...WITH YOU?

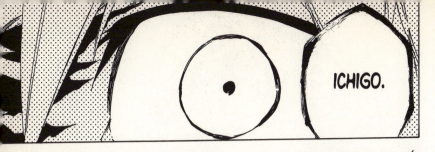

ICHIGO.

HEY!!

TMP

SKREE

WHAT'S GOING ON...?

ICHIGO, WAIT!!

IS THIS...

HEY!!

...TSUKISHIMA'S ABILITY...?!

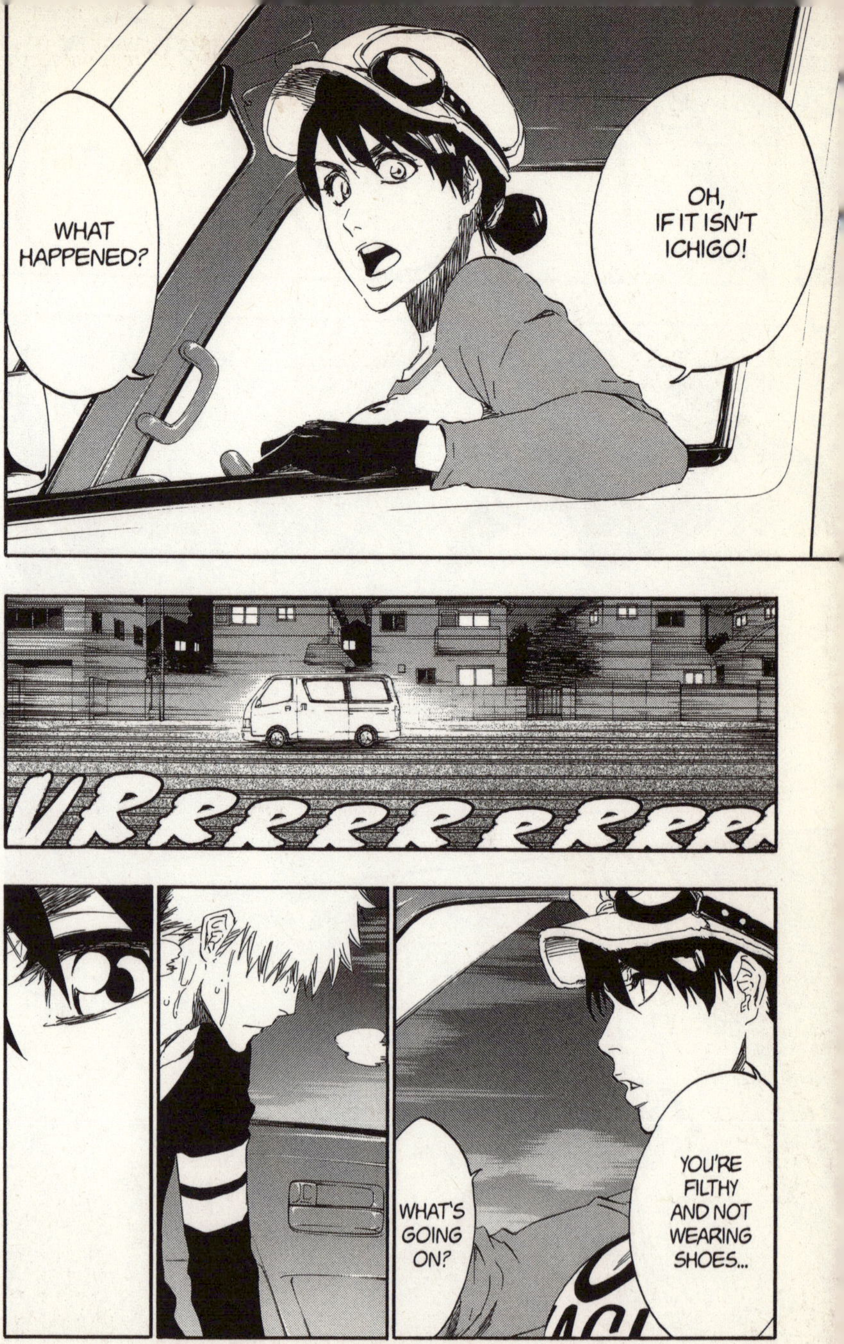
OH, IF IT ISN'T ICHIGO!
WHAT HAPPENED?
VRRRRRRRRRRR
YOU'RE FILTHY AND NOT WEARING SHOES...
WHAT'S GOING ON?

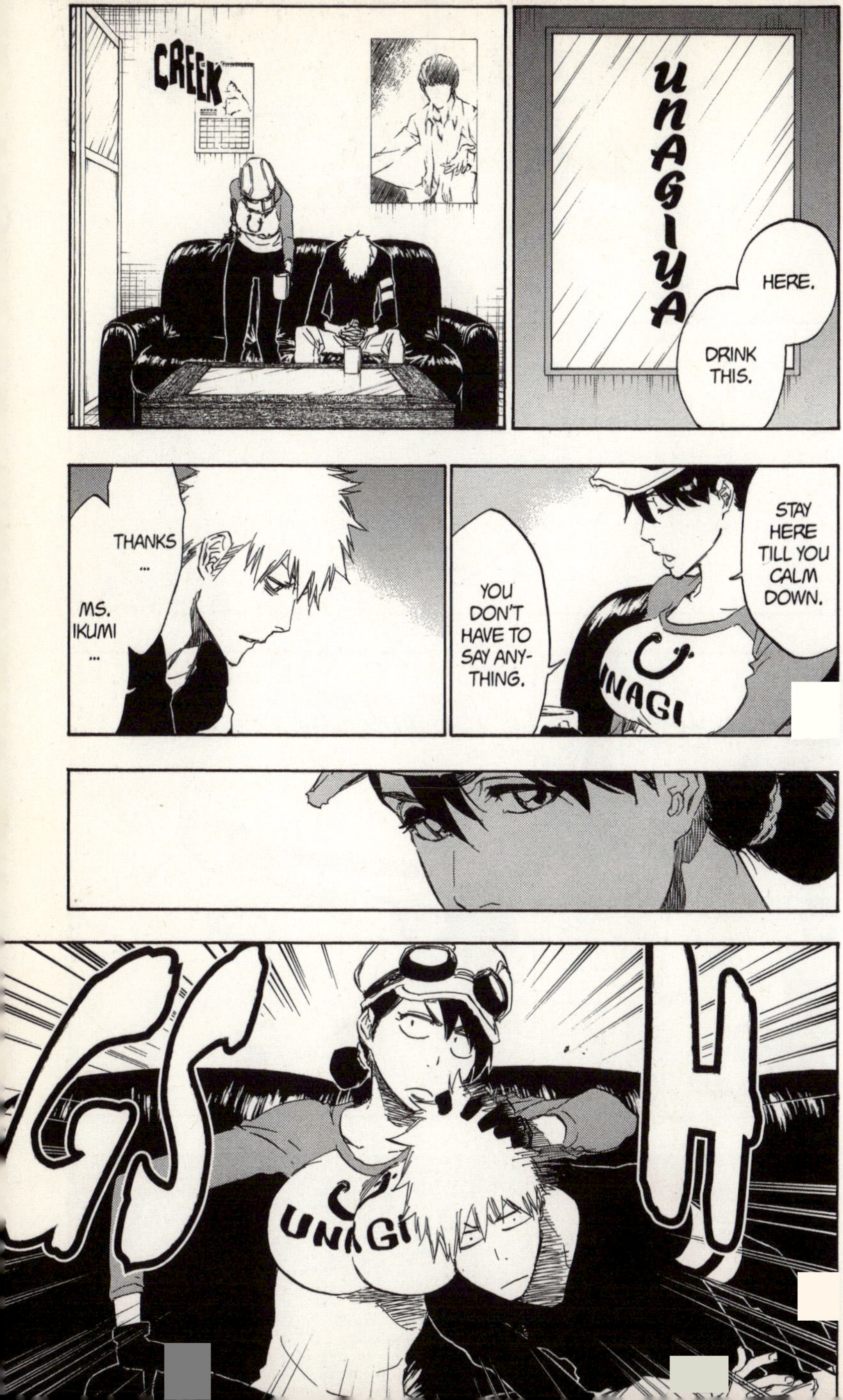
UNAGIYA
CREEK
HERE.
DRINK THIS.
STAY HERE TILL YOU CALM DOWN.
YOU DON'T HAVE TO SAY ANYTHING.
THANKS... MS. IKUMI...
UNAGI
GSH

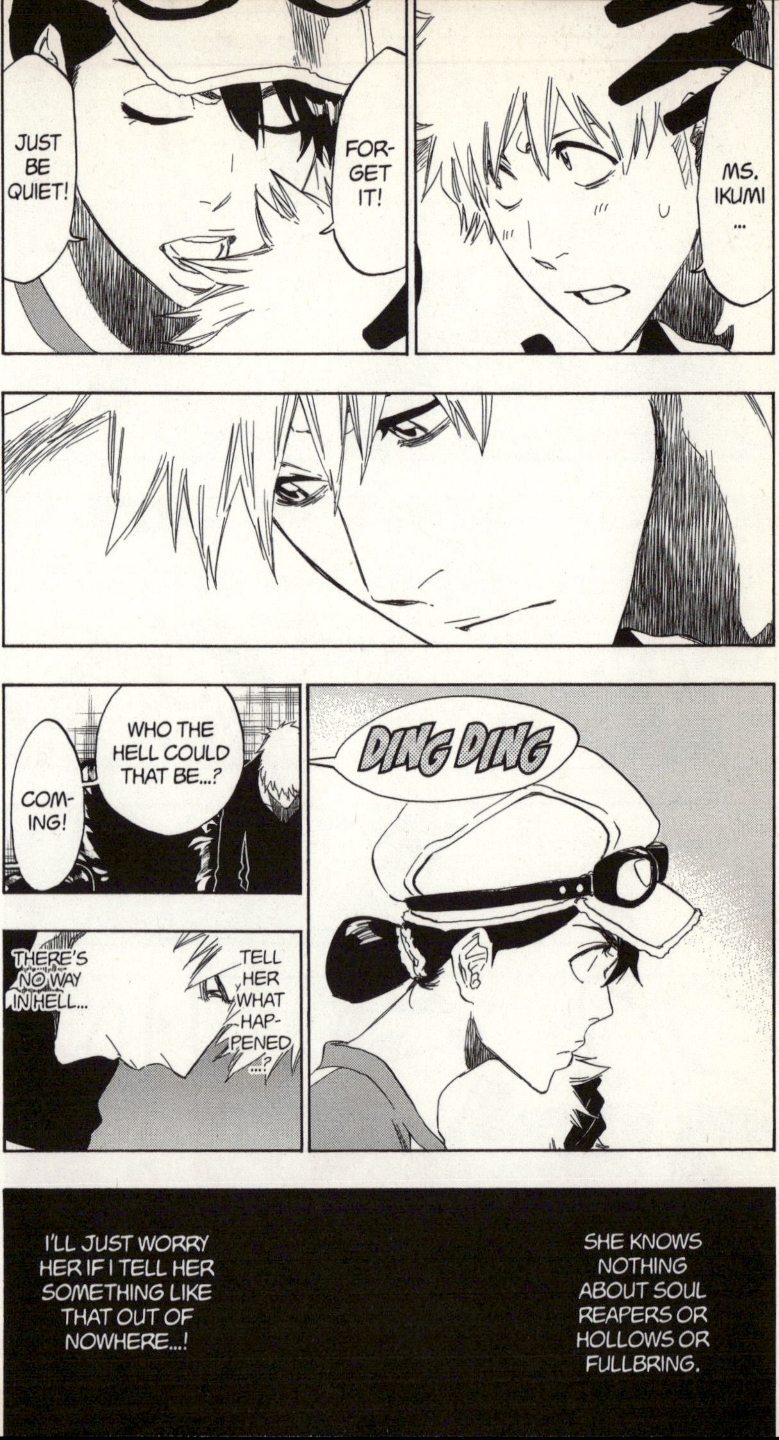
MS. IKUMI...
FORGET IT!
JUST BE QUIET!
DING DING
WHO THE HELL COULD THAT BE...?
COMING!
TELL HER WHAT HAPPENED...?
THERE'S NO WAY IN HELL...
SHE KNOWS NOTHING ABOUT SOUL REAPERS OR HOLLOWS OR FULLBRING.
I'LL JUST WORRY HER IF I TELL HER SOMETHING LIKE THAT OUT OF NOWHERE...!

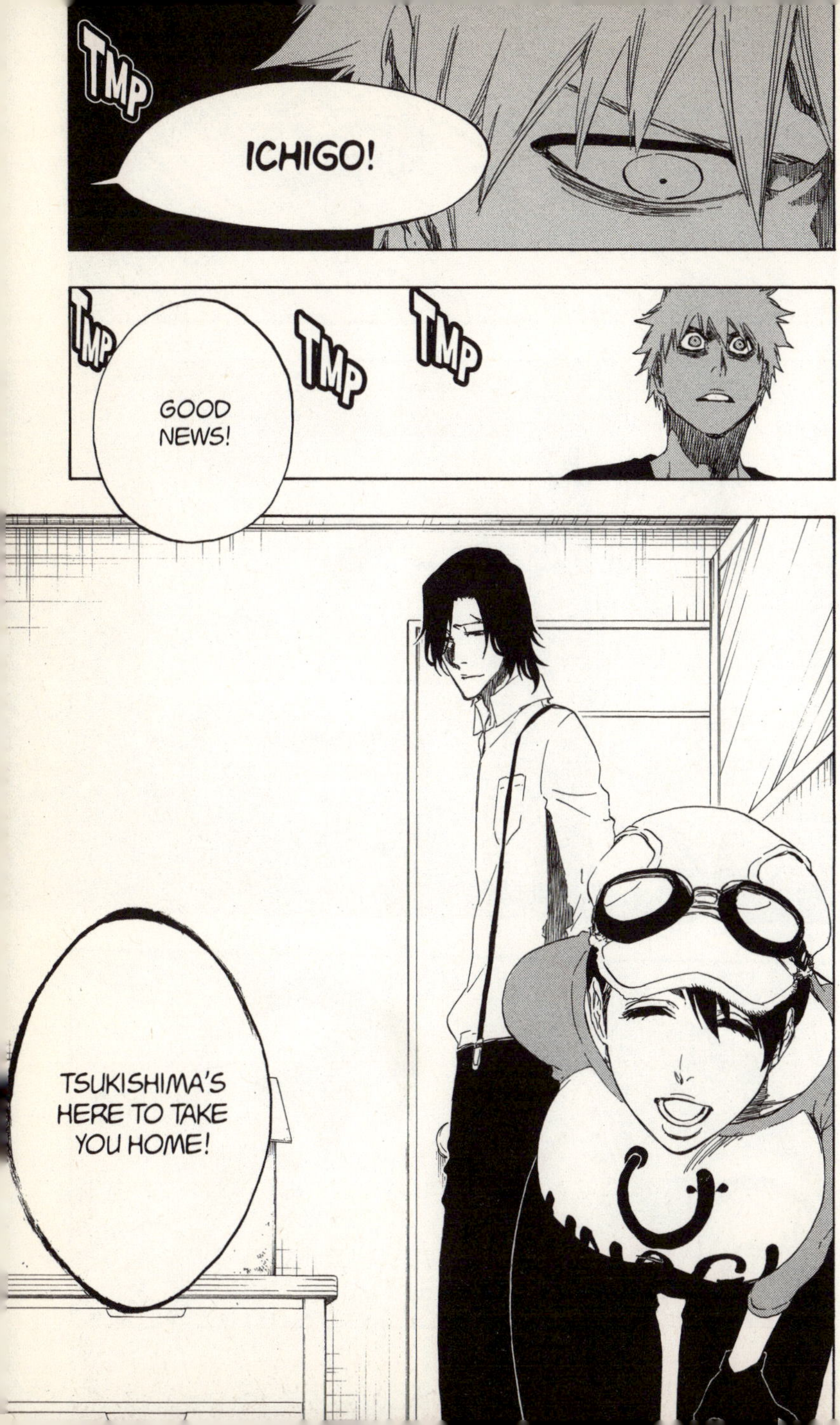
TMP
ICHIGO!
TMP
TMP
TMP
GOOD NEWS!
TSUKISHIMA'S HERE TO TAKE YOU HOME!

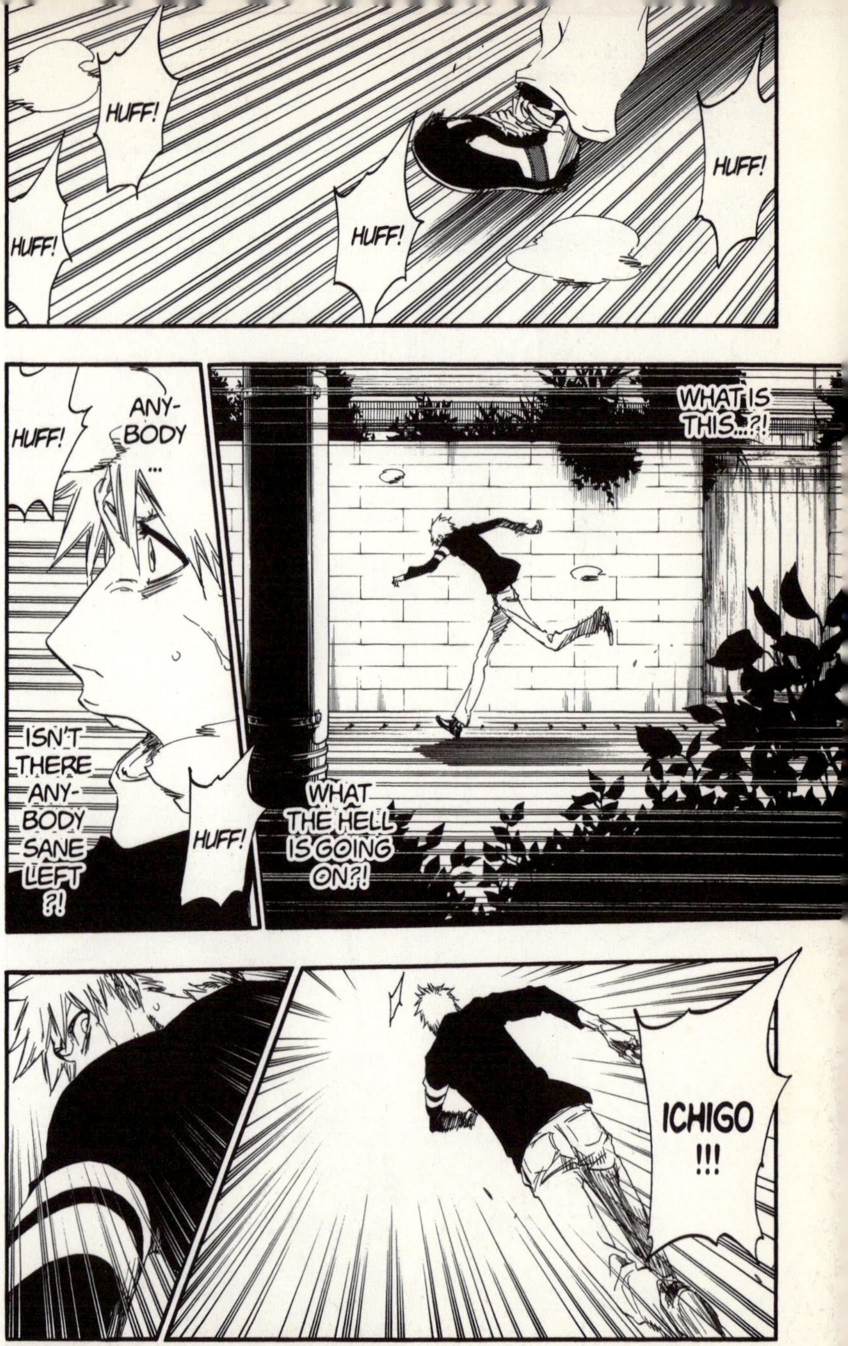
HUFF!
HUFF!
HUFF!
HUFF!
WHAT IS THIS...?!
ANY-BODY ...
HUFF!
WHAT THE HELL IS GOING ON?!
HUFF!
ISN'T THERE ANY-BODY SANE LEFT ?!
ICHIGO !!!

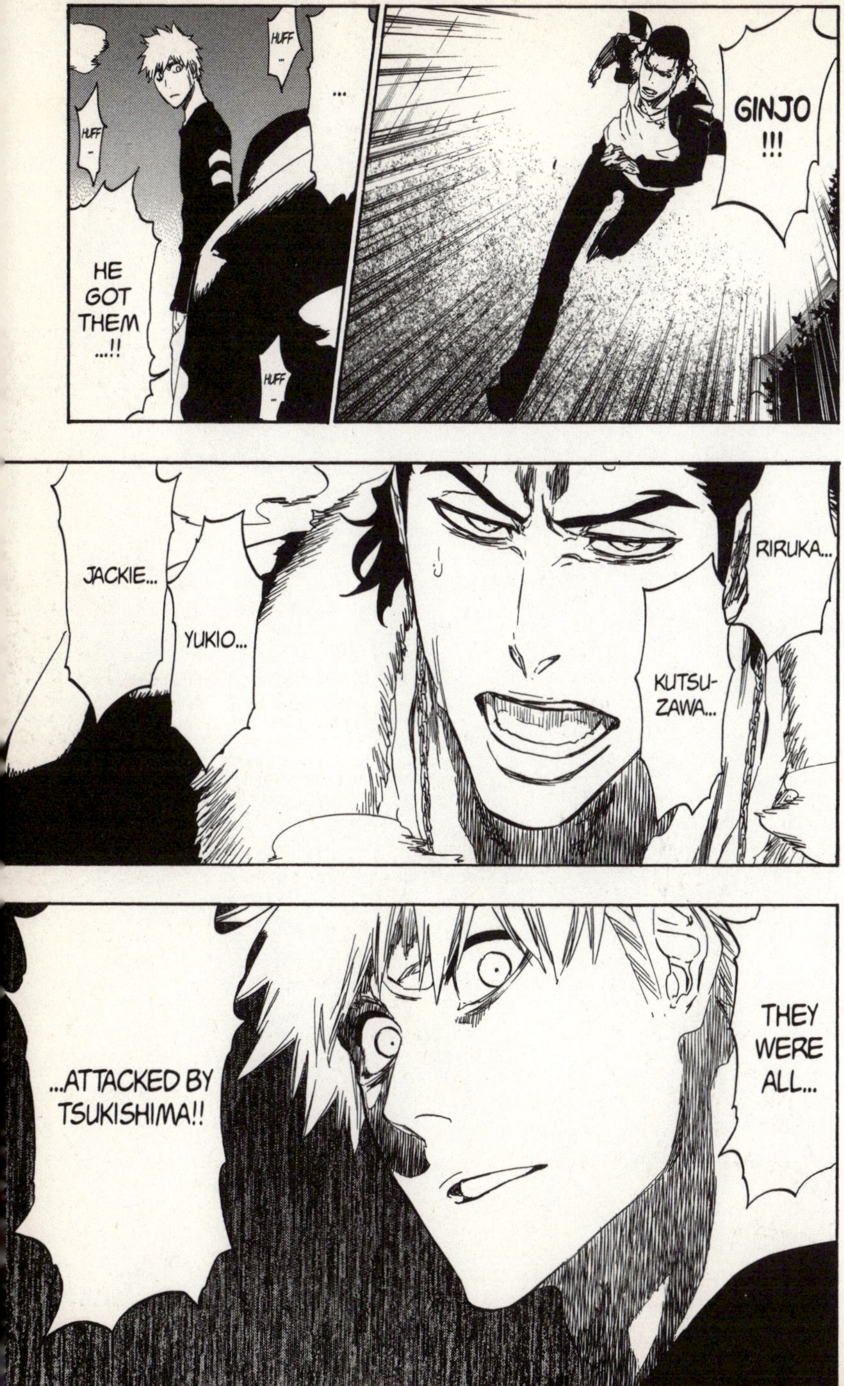
GINJO !!!
...
HUFF ...
HUFF ...
HE GOT THEM ...!!
HUFF ...
RIRUKA...
KUTSU-ZAWA...
YUKIO...
JACKIE...
THEY WERE ALL...
...ATTACKED BY TSUKISHIMA!!

d reaD

## 454. Sheathebreaker

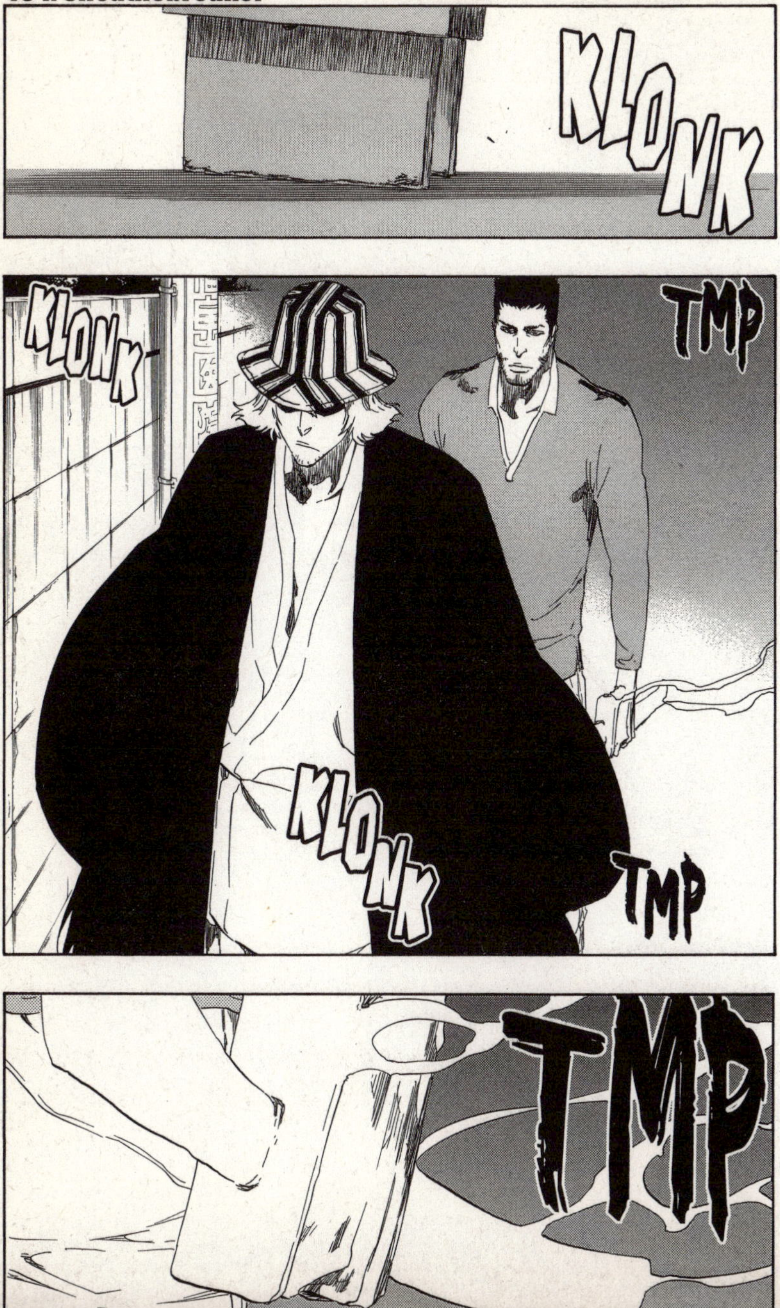
KLONK
KLONK
TMP
KLONK
TMP
TMP

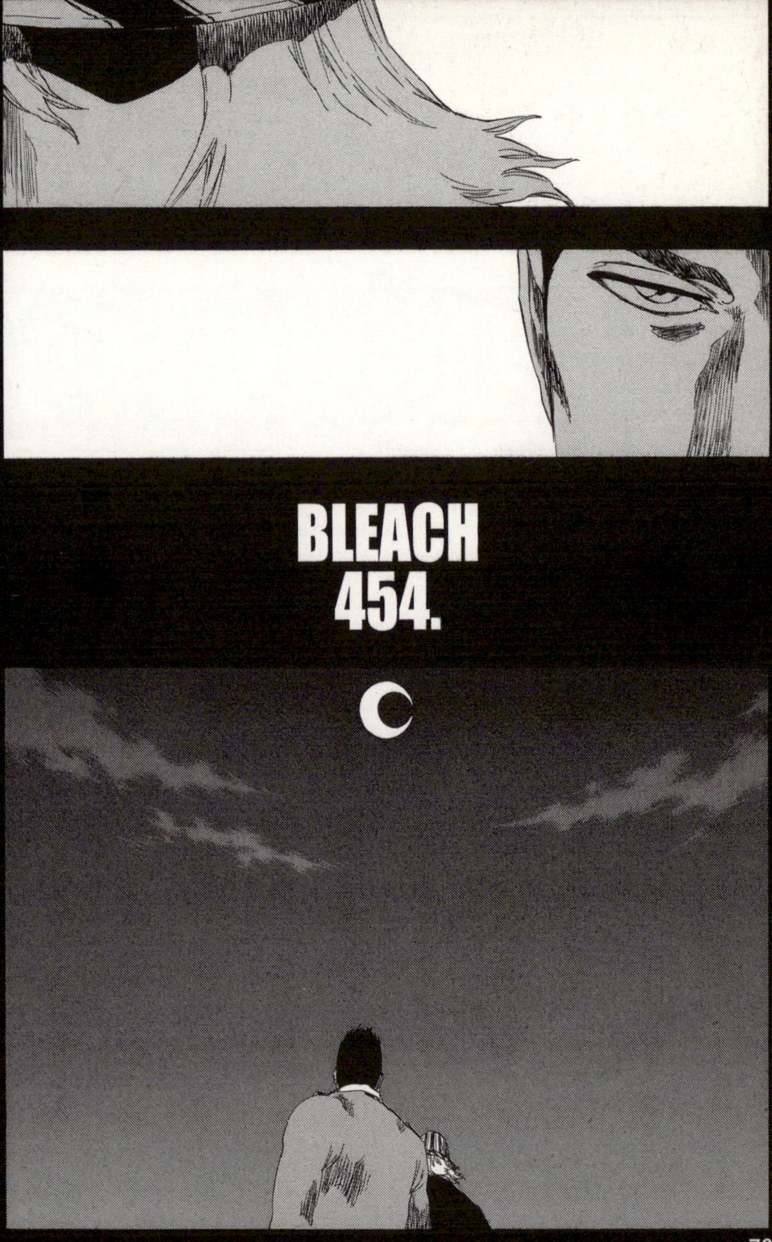
BLEACH
454.

# Sheathebreaker

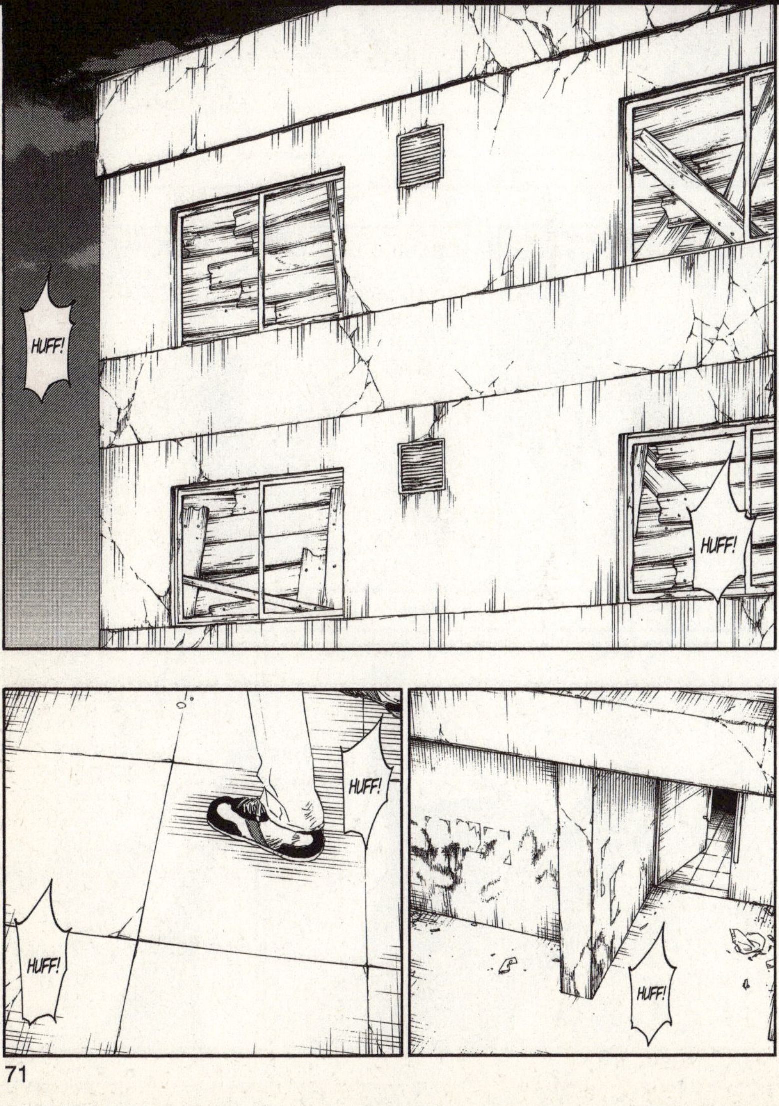
HUFF!
HUFF!
HUFF!
HUFF!
HUFF!
HUFF!

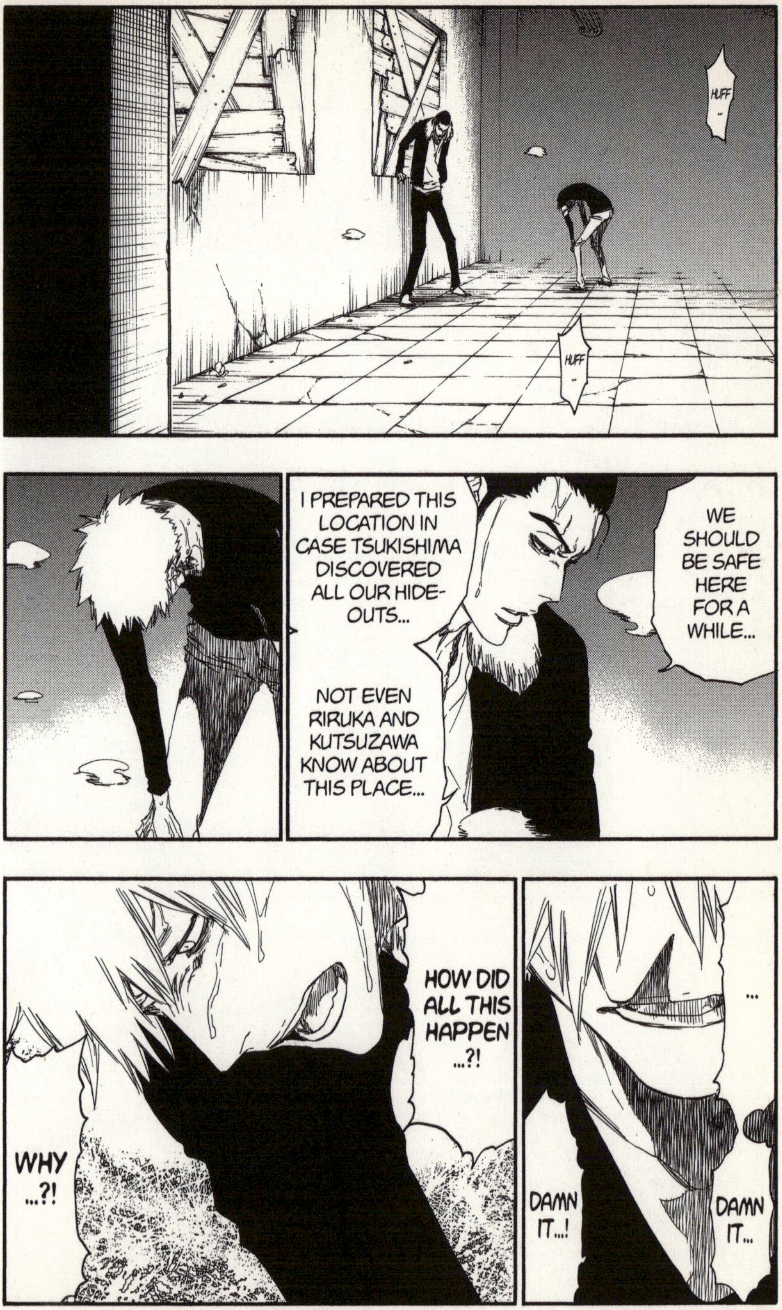
HUFF...
HUFF...
WE SHOULD BE SAFE HERE FOR A WHILE...
I PREPARED THIS LOCATION IN CASE TSUKISHIMA DISCOVERED ALL OUR HIDE-OUTS...
NOT EVEN RIRUKA AND KUTSUZAWA KNOW ABOUT THIS PLACE...
...
DAMN IT...
DAMN IT...!
HOW DID ALL THIS HAPPEN...?!
WHY...?!

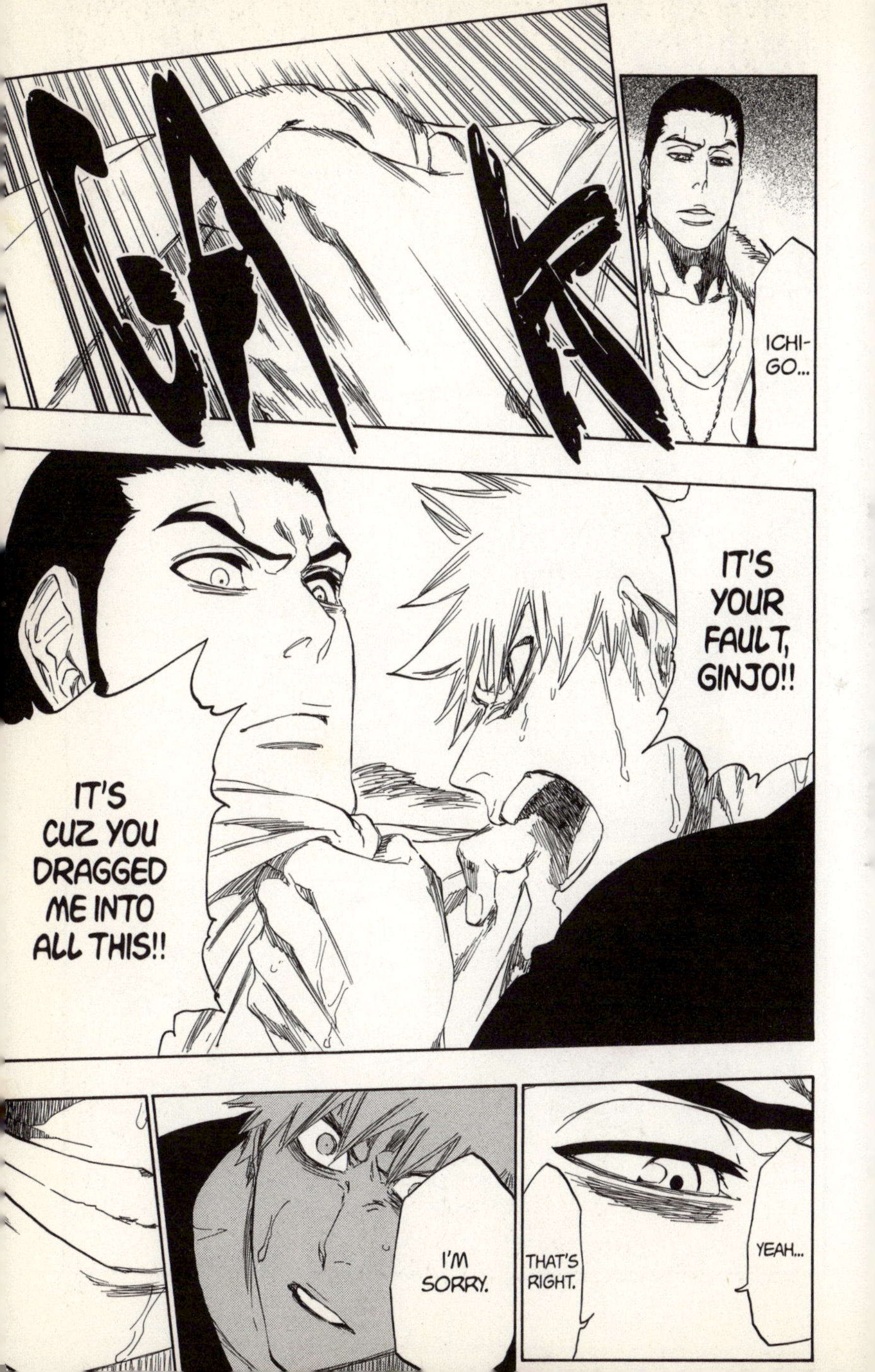
ICHI-
GO...
CAK
IT'S YOUR FAULT, GINJO!!
IT'S CUZ YOU DRAGGED ME INTO ALL THIS!!
YEAH...
THAT'S RIGHT.
I'M SORRY.

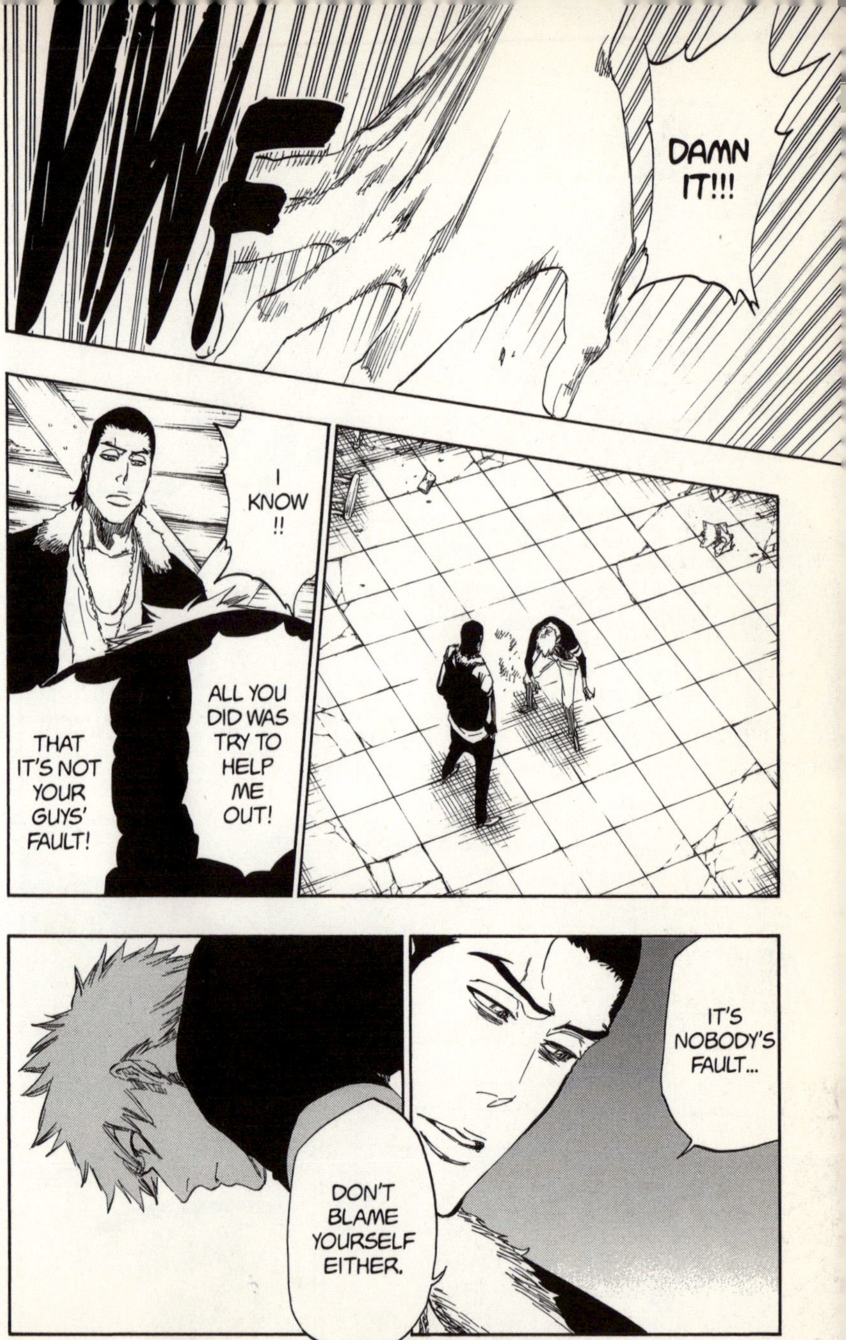
VWF
DAMN IT!!!
I KNOW !!
ALL YOU DID WAS TRY TO HELP ME OUT!
THAT IT'S NOT YOUR GUYS' FAULT!
IT'S NOBODY'S FAULT...
DON'T BLAME YOURSELF EITHER.

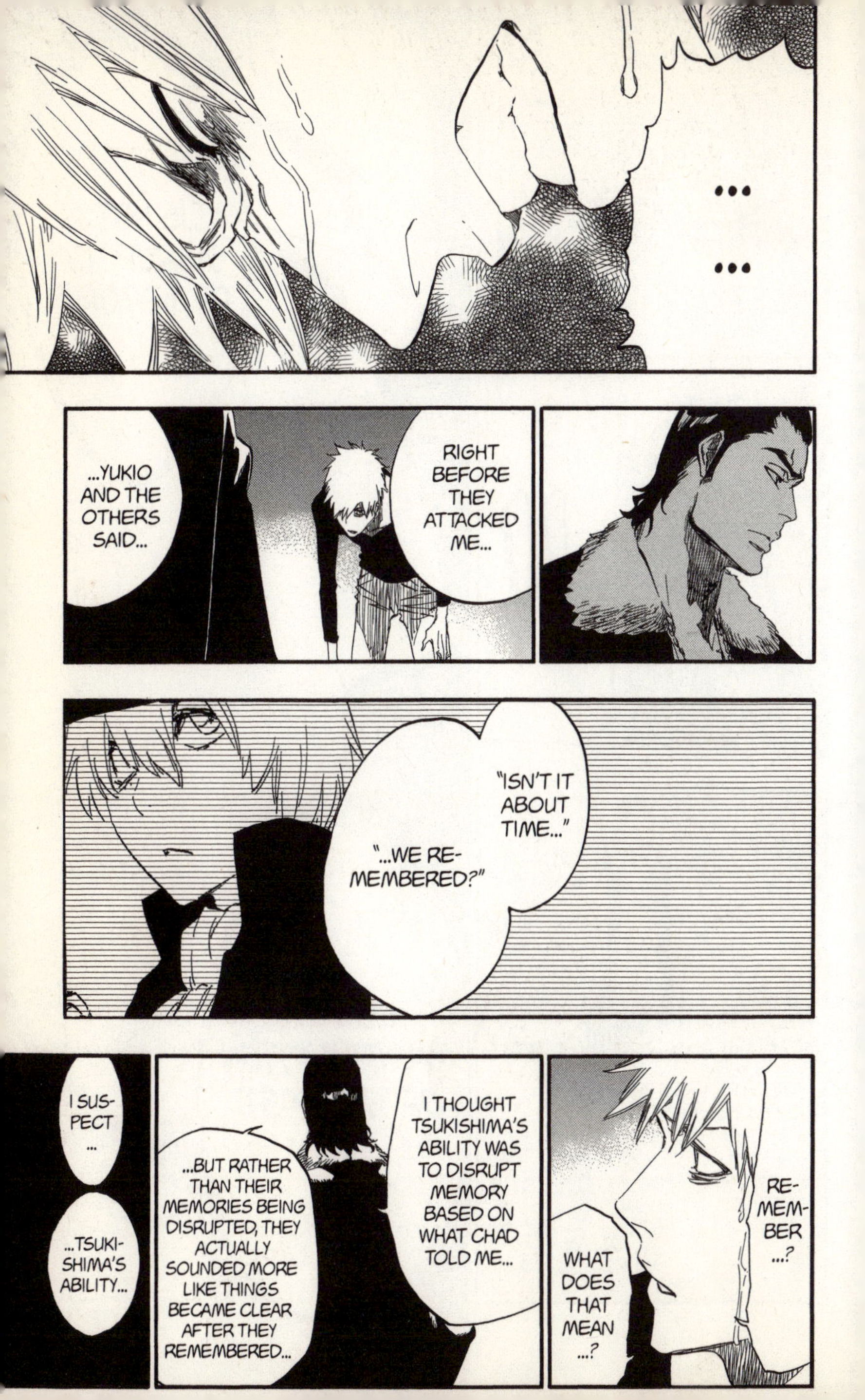
...
...
RIGHT BEFORE THEY ATTACKED ME...
...YUKIO AND THE OTHERS SAID...
"ISN'T IT ABOUT TIME..."
"...WE REMEMBERED?"
REMEMBER...?
WHAT DOES THAT MEAN...?
I THOUGHT TSUKISHIMA'S ABILITY WAS TO DISRUPT MEMORY BASED ON WHAT CHAD TOLD ME...
...BUT RATHER THAN THEIR MEMORIES BEING DISRUPTED, THEY ACTUALLY SOUNDED MORE LIKE THINGS BECAME CLEAR AFTER THEY REMEMBERED...
I SUSPECT...
...TSUKISHIMA'S ABILITY...

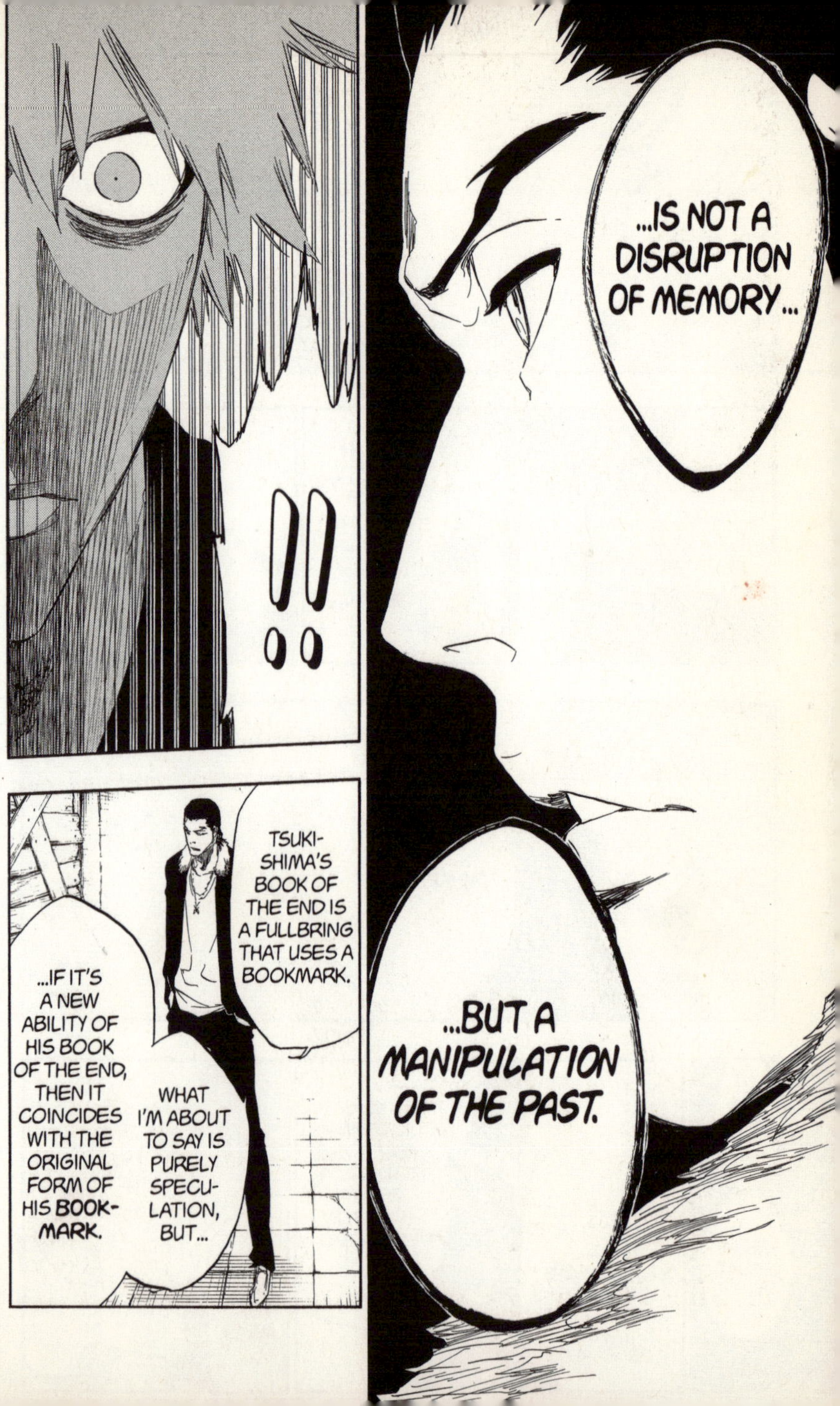
TSUKI-SHIMA'S BOOK OF THE END IS A FULLBRING THAT USES A BOOKMARK.
...IF IT'S A NEW ABILITY OF HIS BOOK OF THE END, THEN IT COINCIDES WITH THE ORIGINAL FORM OF HIS **BOOK-MARK.**
WHAT I'M ABOUT TO SAY IS PURELY SPECU-LATION, BUT...
...IS NOT A DISRUPTION OF MEMORY...
...BUT A *MANIPULATION OF THE PAST.*
!!

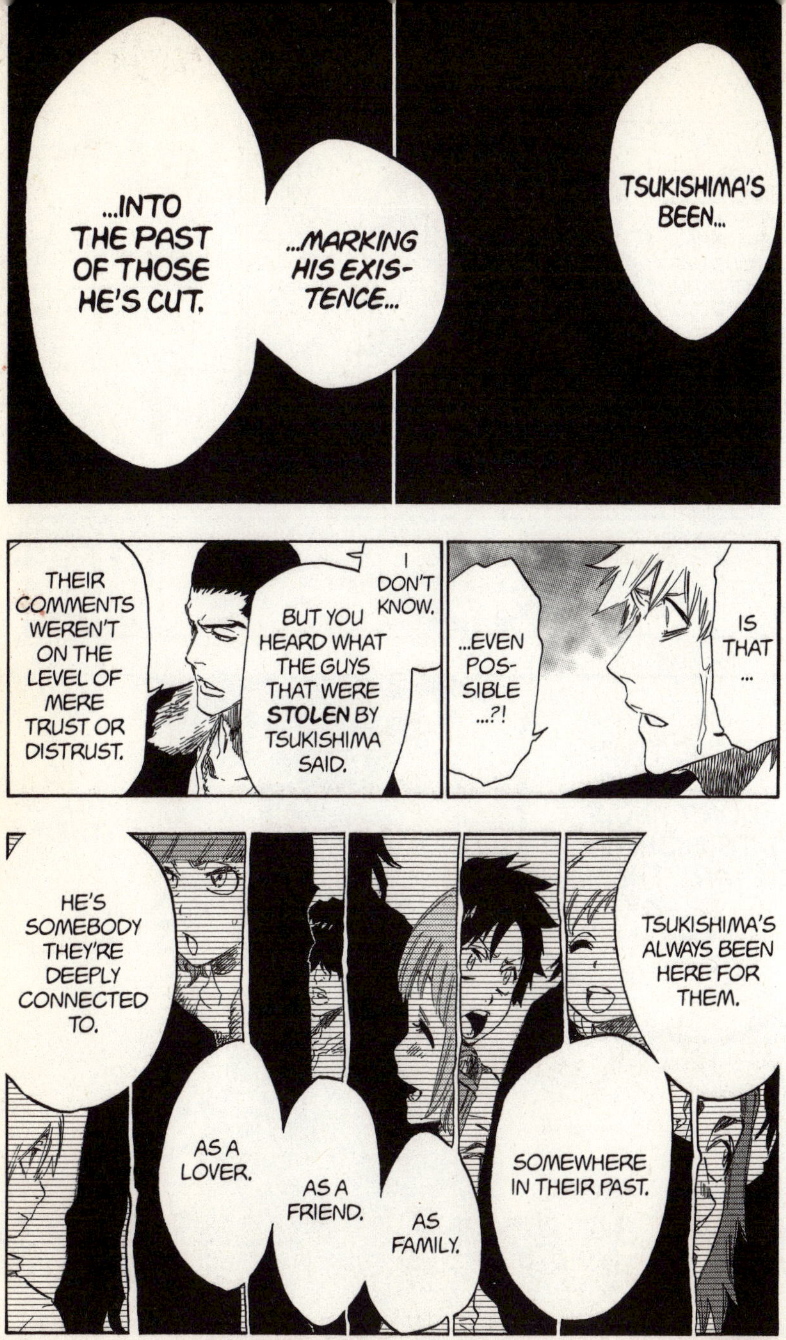
TSUKISHIMA'S BEEN...
...MARKING HIS EXIS-TENCE...
...INTO THE PAST OF THOSE HE'S CUT.
IS THAT ...
...EVEN POS-SIBLE ...?!
I DON'T KNOW.
BUT YOU HEARD WHAT THE GUYS THAT WERE **STOLEN** BY TSUKISHIMA SAID.
THEIR COMMENTS WEREN'T ON THE LEVEL OF MERE TRUST OR DISTRUST.
TSUKISHIMA'S ALWAYS BEEN HERE FOR THEM.
HE'S SOMEBODY THEY'RE DEEPLY CONNECTED TO.
SOMEWHERE IN THEIR PAST.
AS FAMILY.
AS A FRIEND.
AS A LOVER.

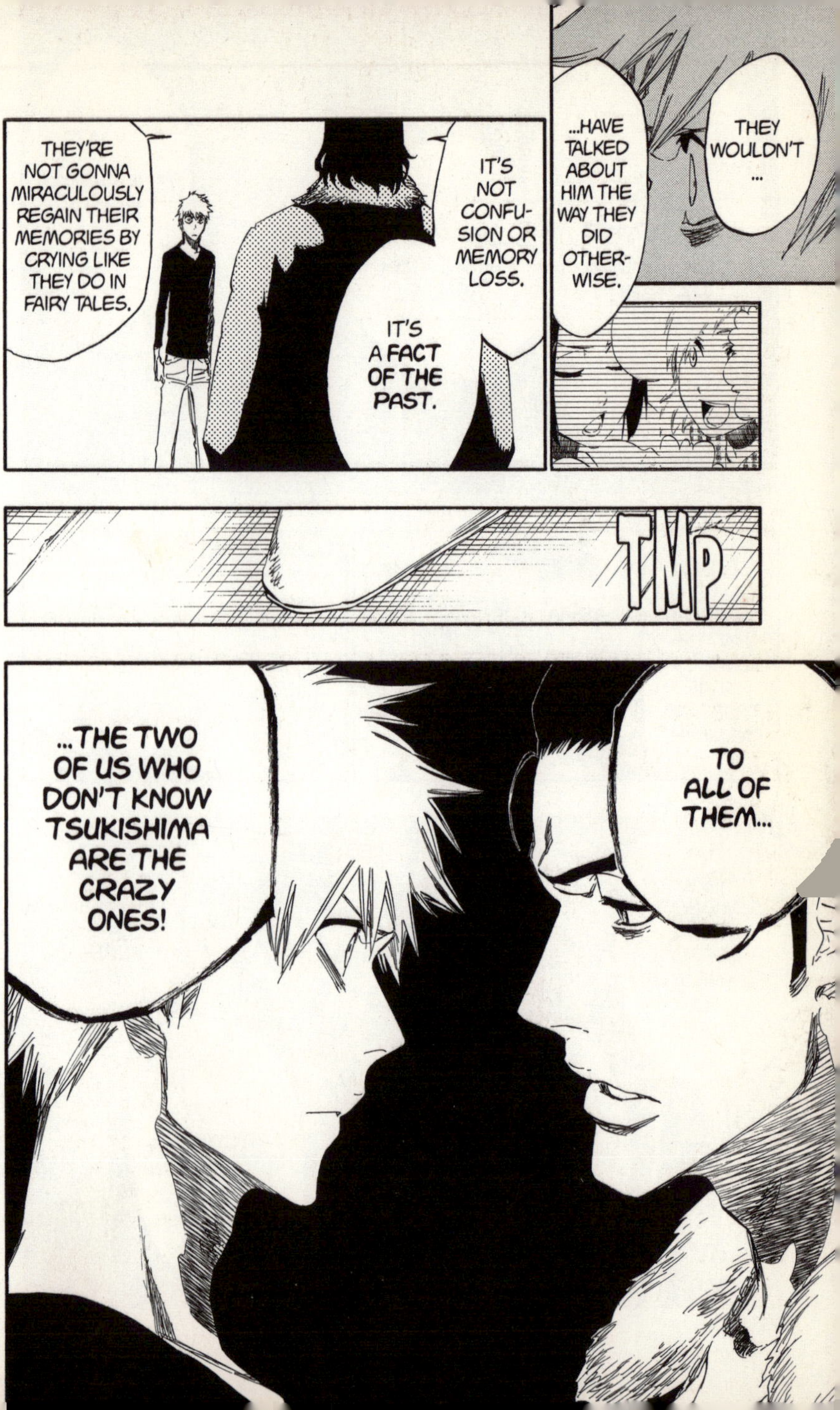
THEY WOULDN'T ...
...HAVE TALKED ABOUT HIM THE WAY THEY DID OTHER-WISE.
IT'S NOT CONFU-SION OR MEMORY LOSS.
IT'S A FACT OF THE PAST.
THEY'RE NOT GONNA MIRACULOUSLY REGAIN THEIR MEMORIES BY CRYING LIKE THEY DO IN FAIRY TALES.
TMP
TO ALL OF THEM...
...THE TWO OF US WHO DON'T KNOW TSUKISHIMA ARE THE CRAZY ONES!

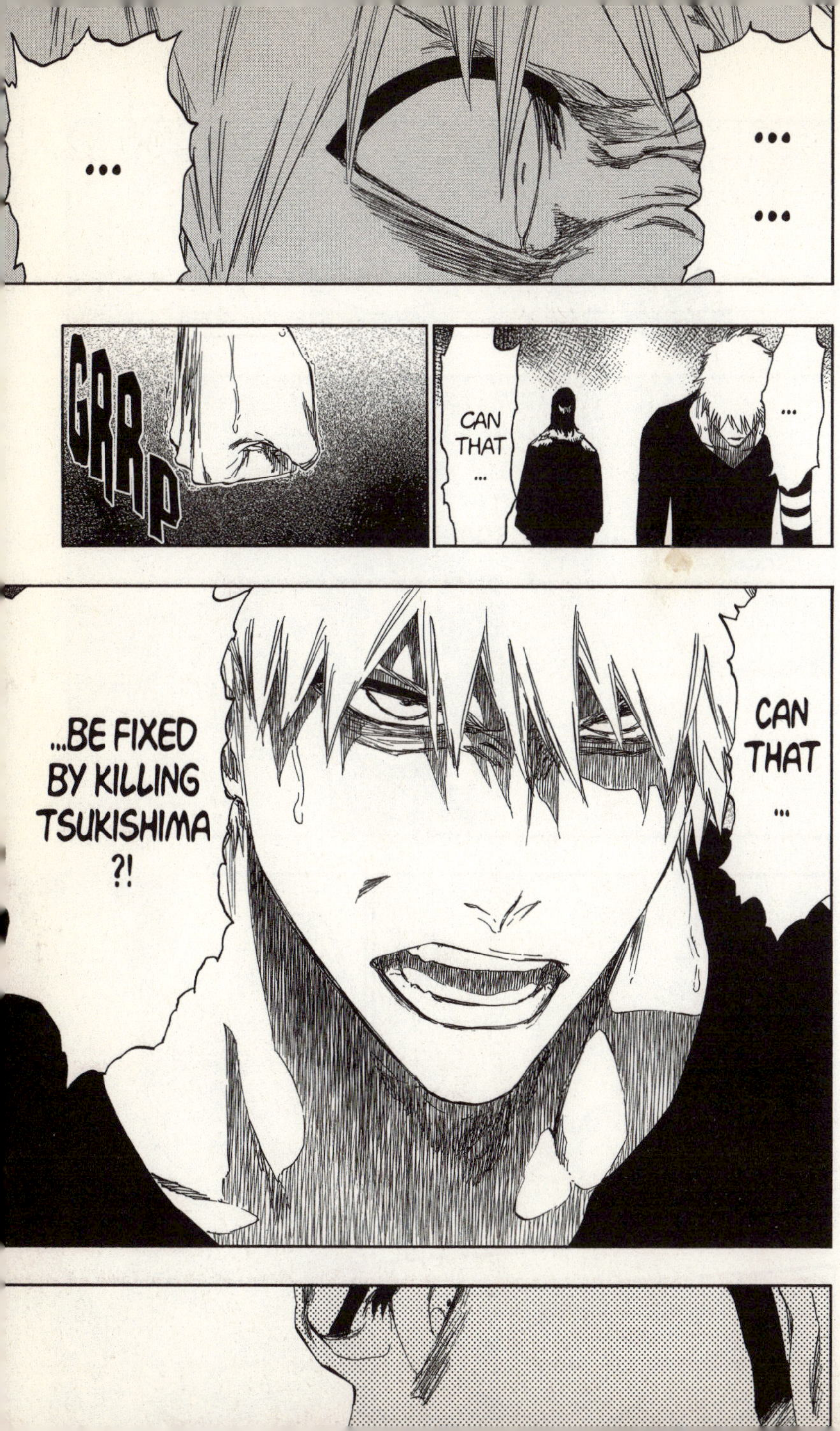
...
...
...
...
CAN THAT ...
GRRP
CAN THAT ...
...BE FIXED BY KILLING TSUKISHIMA ?!

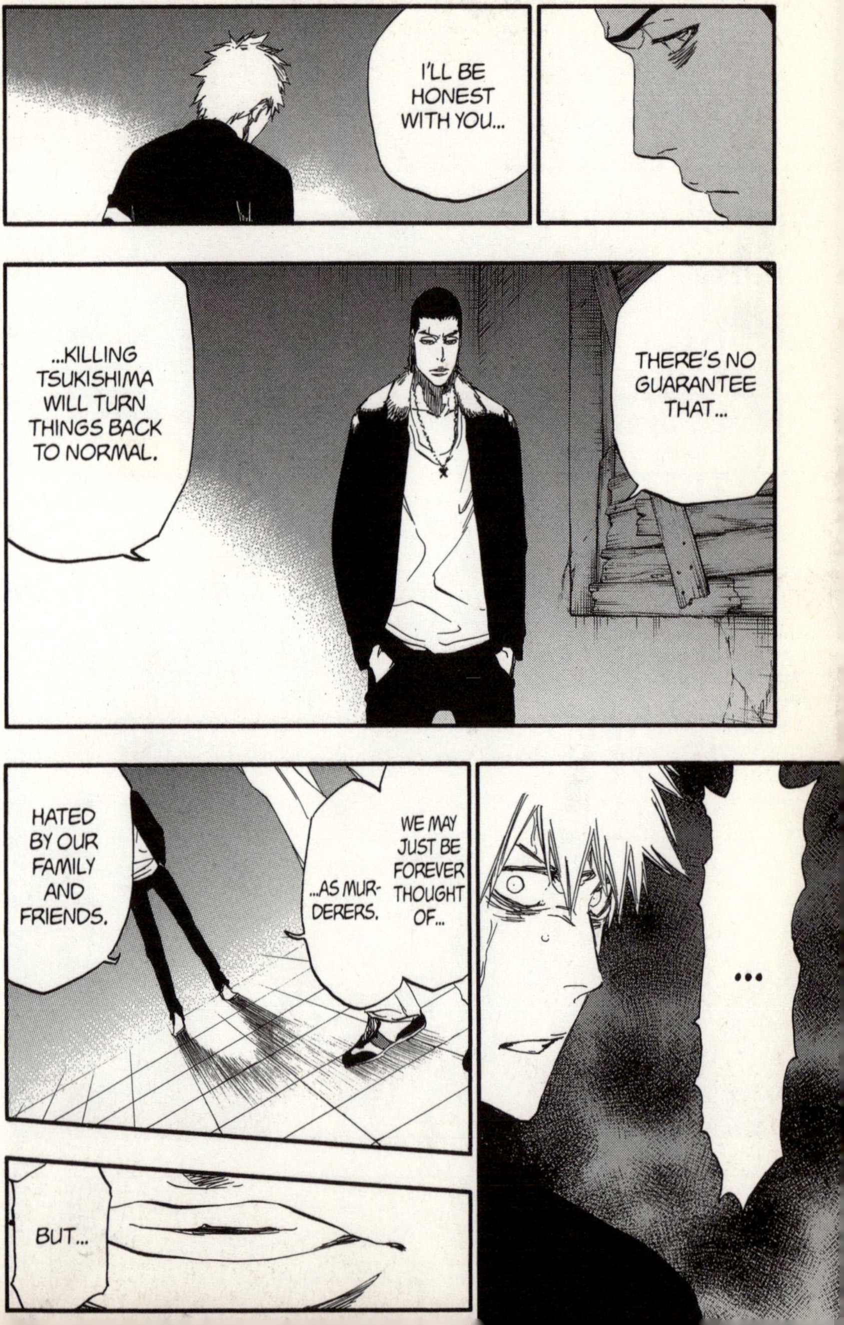
I'LL BE HONEST WITH YOU...
THERE'S NO GUARANTEE THAT...
...KILLING TSUKISHIMA WILL TURN THINGS BACK TO NORMAL.
WE MAY JUST BE FOREVER THOUGHT OF...
...AS MURDERERS.
HATED BY OUR FAMILY AND FRIENDS.
...
BUT...

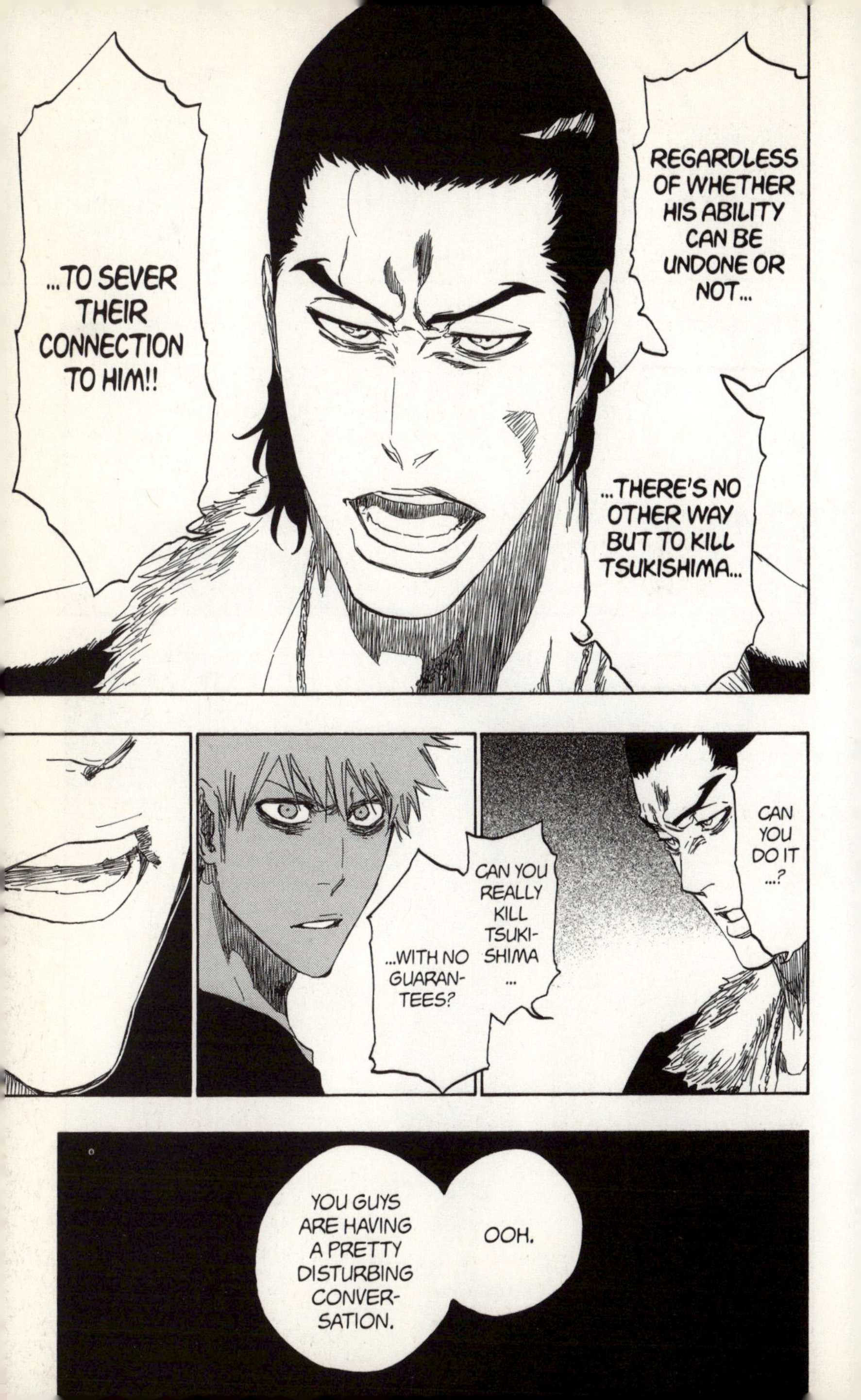
REGARDLESS OF WHETHER HIS ABILITY CAN BE UNDONE OR NOT...
...THERE'S NO OTHER WAY BUT TO KILL TSUKISHIMA...
...TO SEVER THEIR CONNECTION TO HIM!!
CAN YOU DO IT ...?
CAN YOU REALLY KILL TSUKI-SHIMA ...
...WITH NO GUARAN-TEES?
OOH.
YOU GUYS ARE HAVING A PRETTY DISTURBING CONVER-SATION.

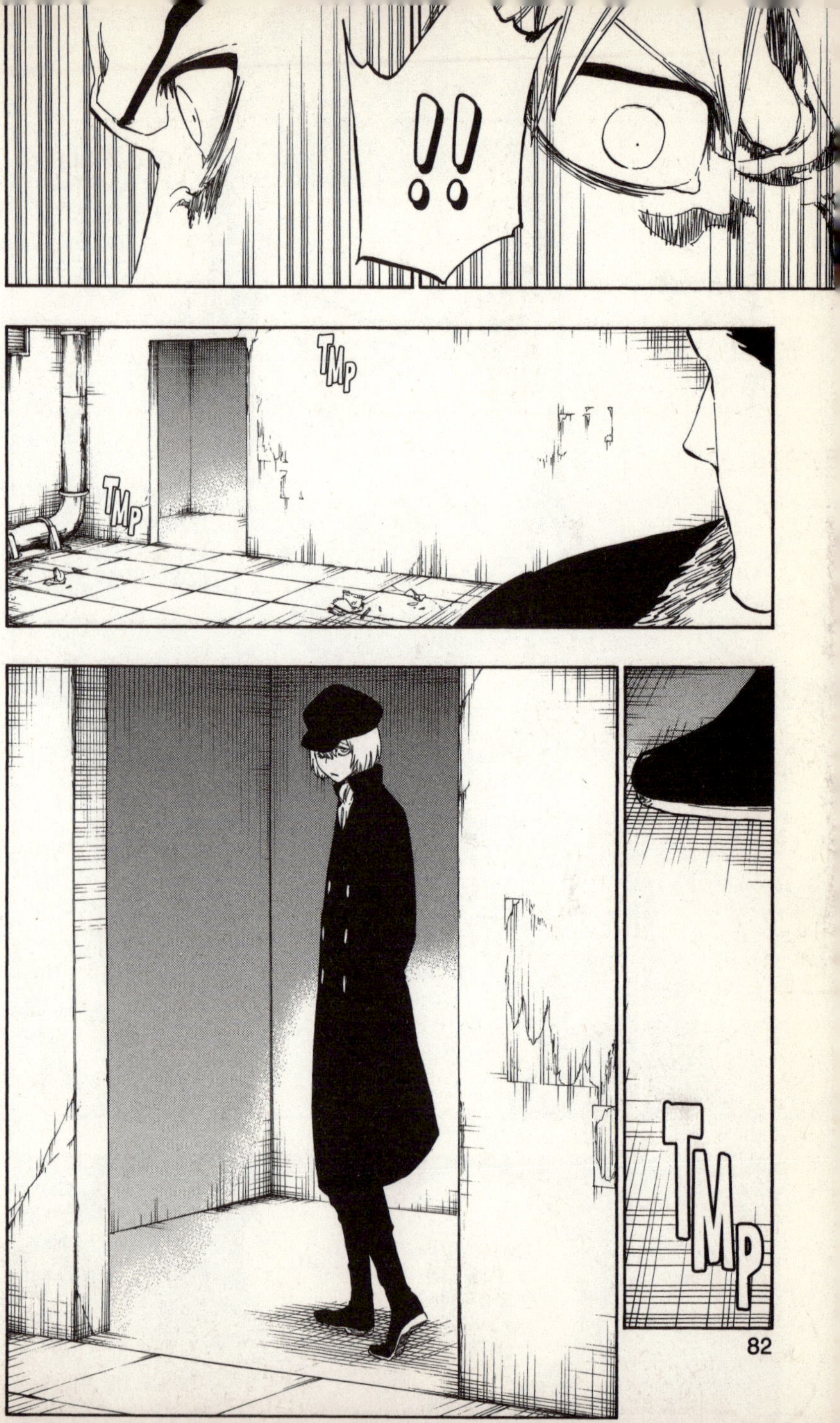
!!
TMP
TMP
TMP

READ THIS WAY

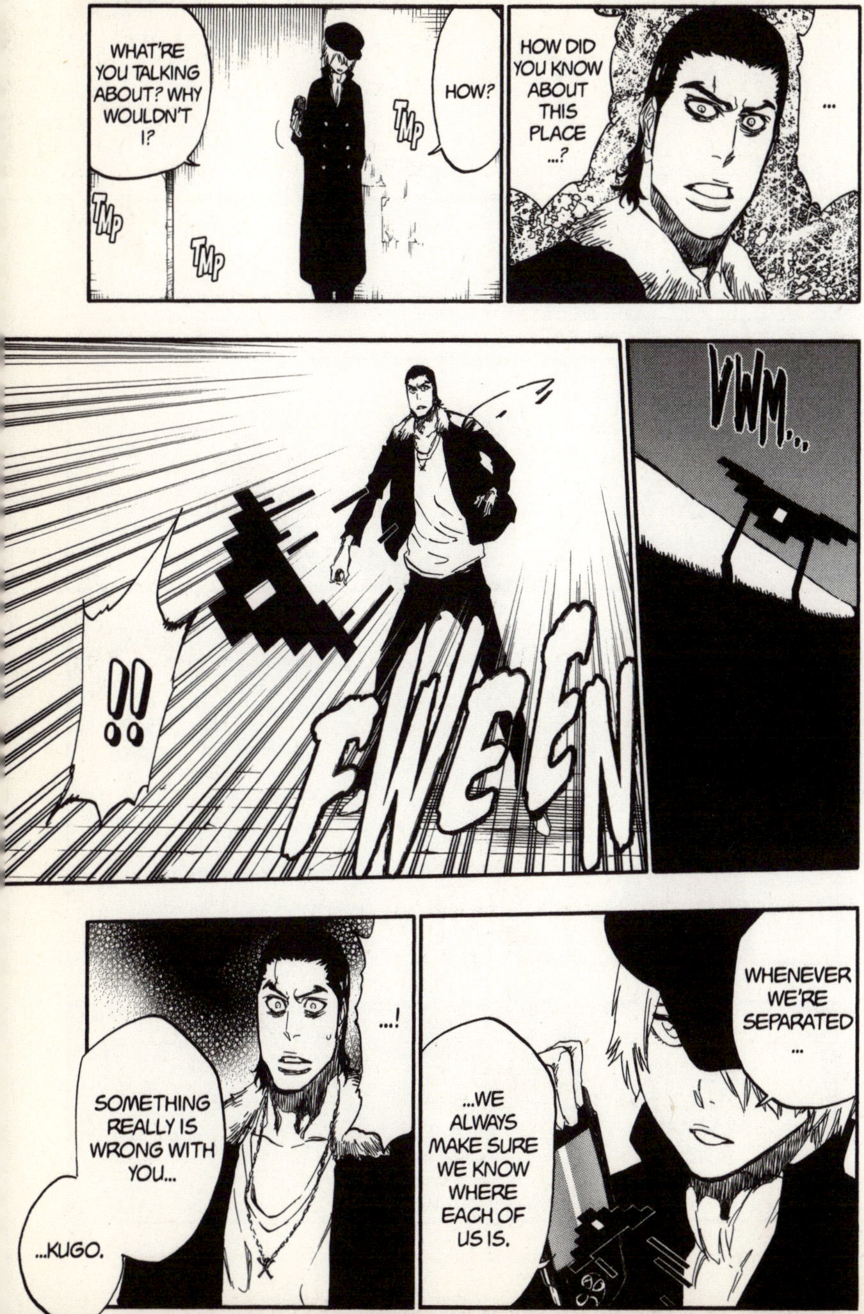
...
HOW DID YOU KNOW ABOUT THIS PLACE ...?
HOW?
TMP
WHAT'RE YOU TALKING ABOUT? WHY WOULDN'T I?
TMP
TMP
VWM...
FWEEN
!!
WHENEVER WE'RE SEPARATED ...
...WE ALWAYS MAKE SURE WE KNOW WHERE EACH OF US IS.
...!
SOMETHING REALLY IS WRONG WITH YOU...
...KUGO.

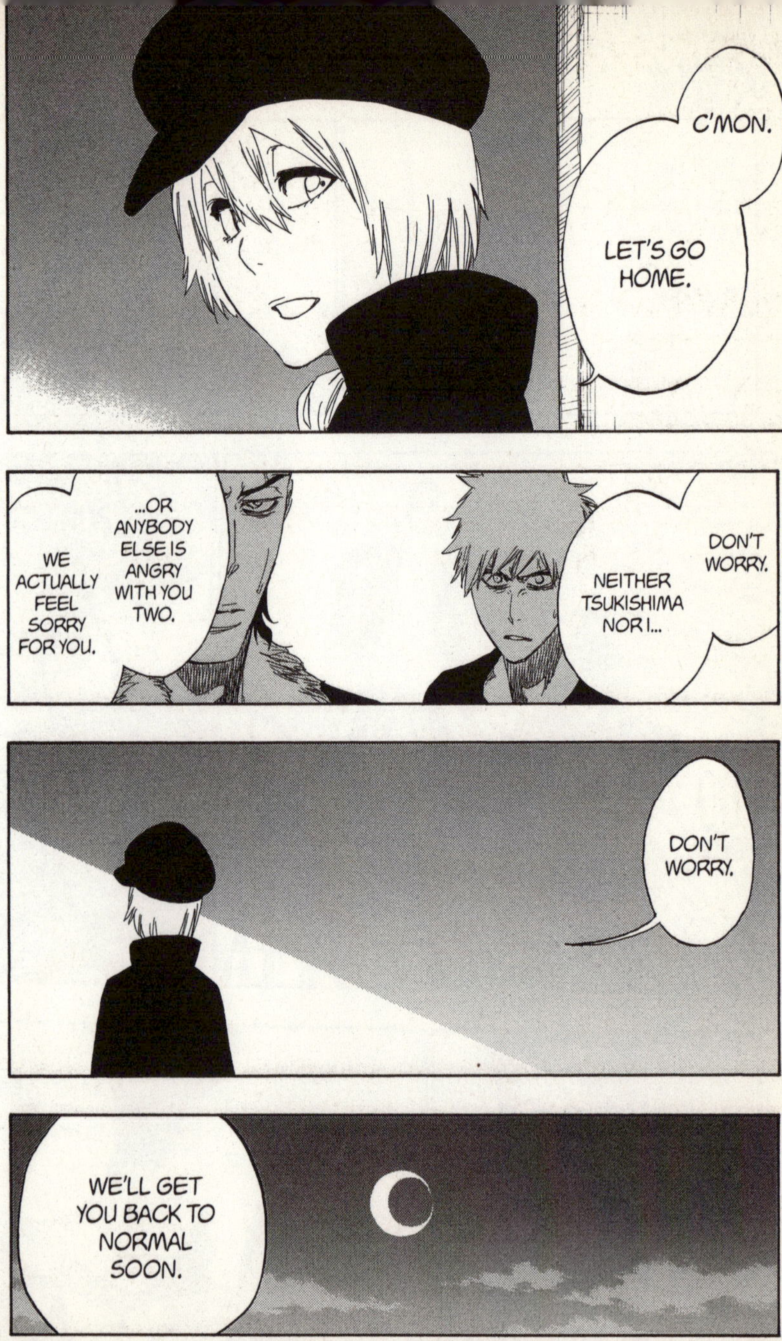
C'MON.
LET'S GO HOME.
DON'T WORRY.
NEITHER TSUKISHIMA NOR I...
...OR ANYBODY ELSE IS ANGRY WITH YOU TWO.
WE ACTUALLY FEEL SORRY FOR YOU.
DON'T WORRY.
WE'LL GET YOU BACK TO NORMAL SOON.

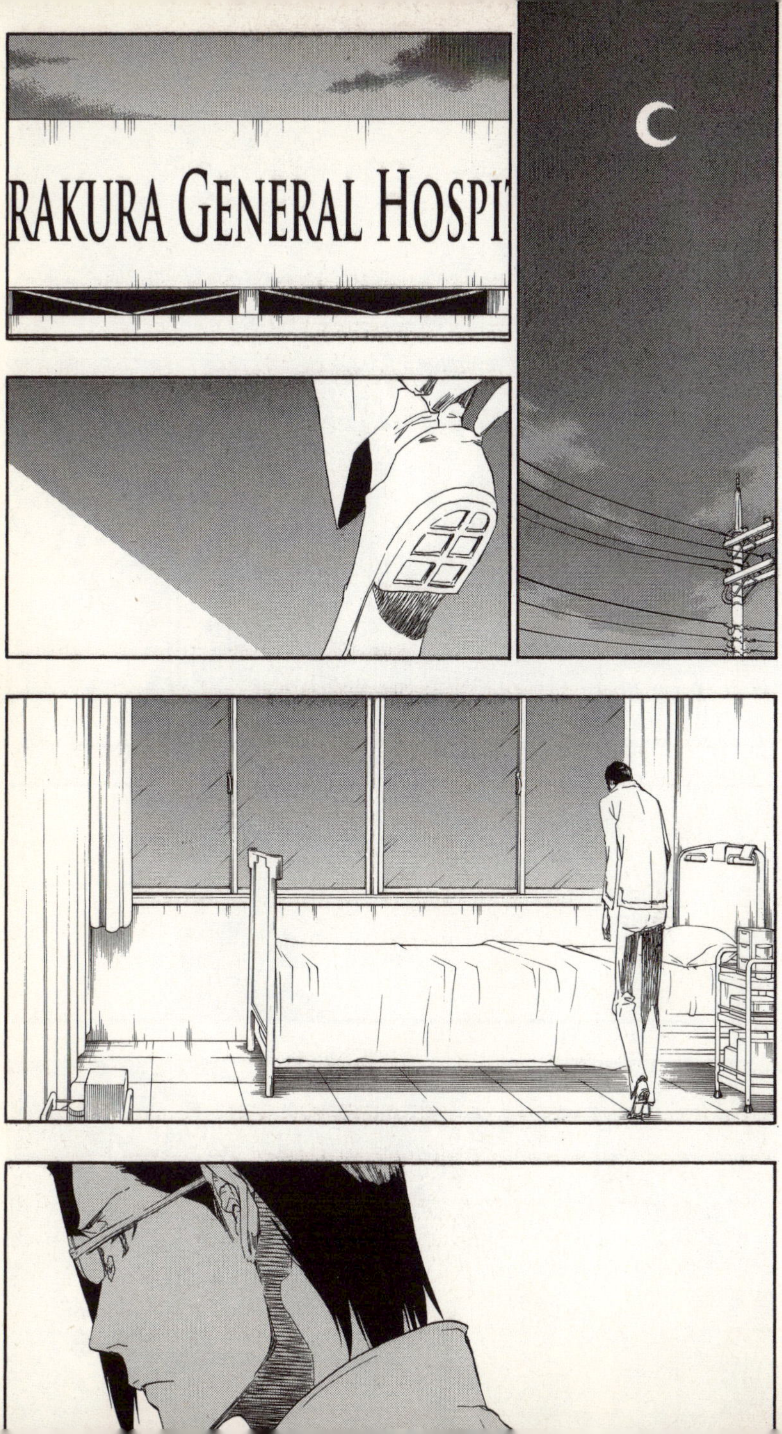
RAKURA GENERAL HOSPIT

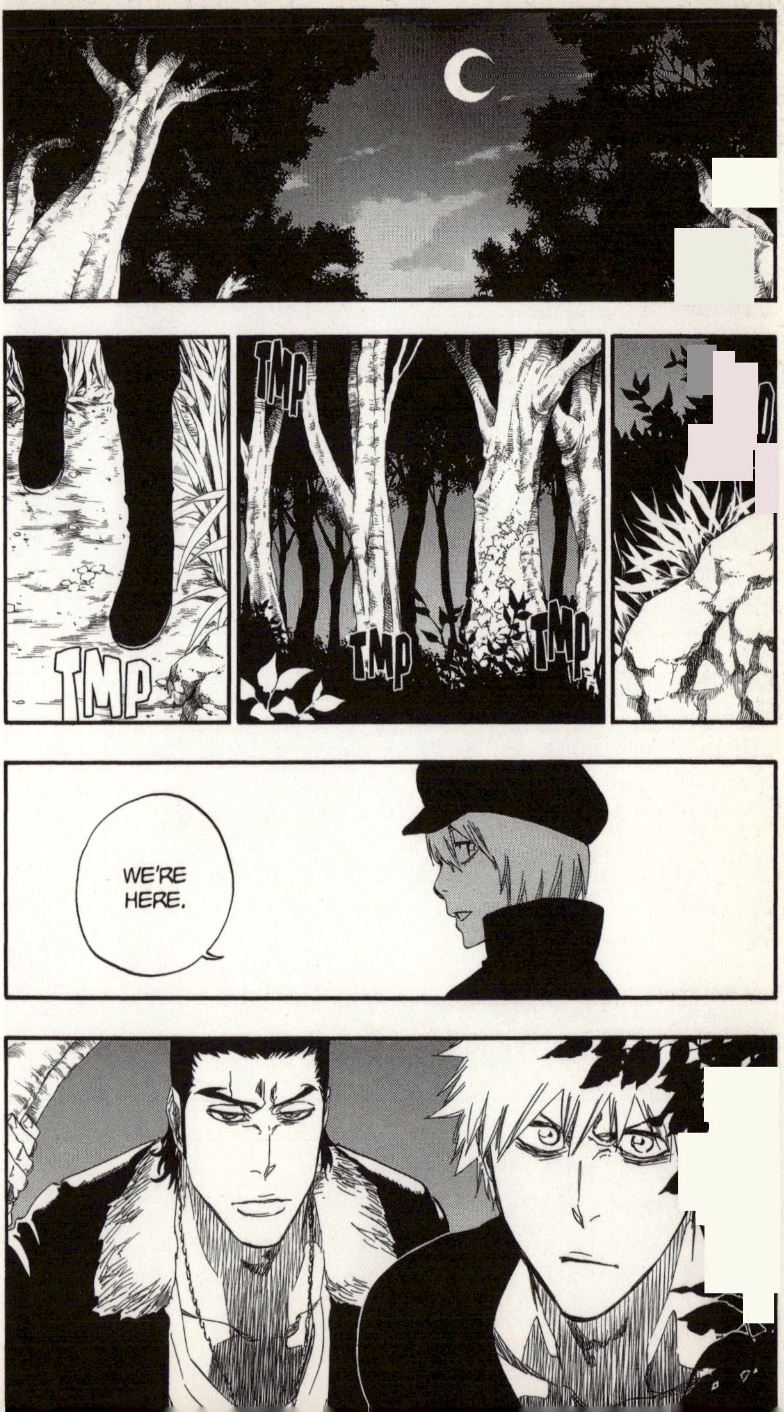
TMP
TMP
TMP
TMP
WE'RE HERE.

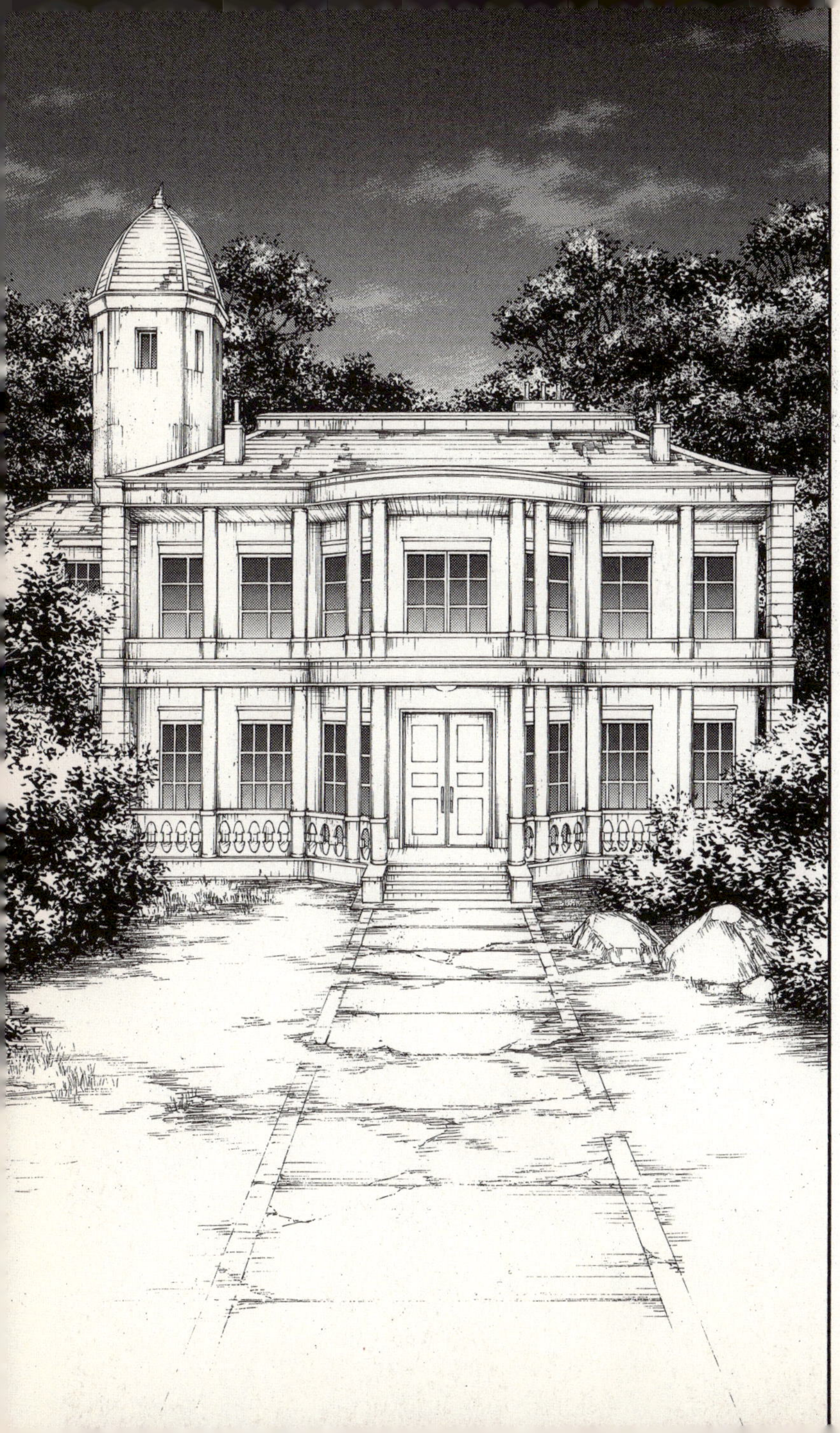

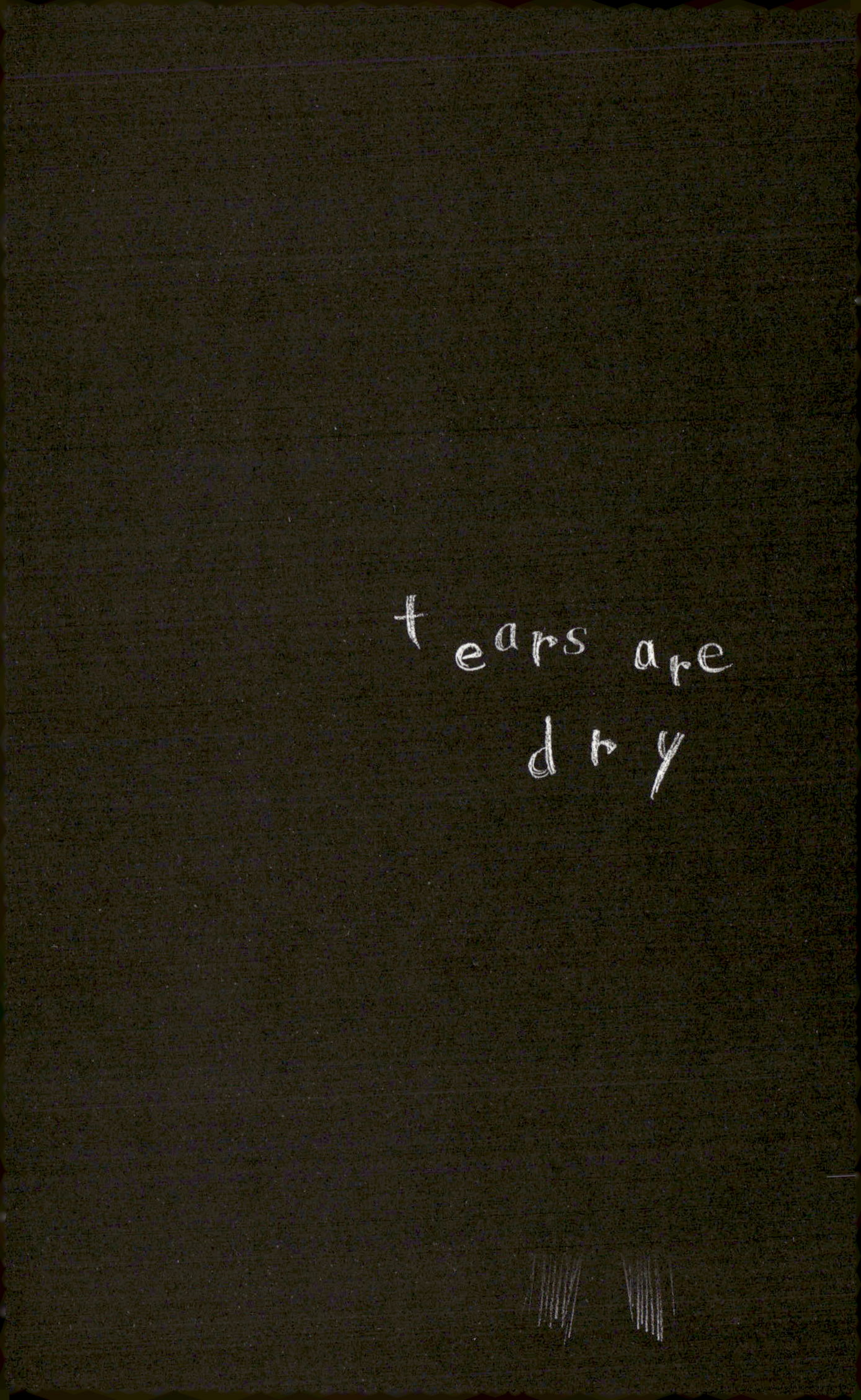
tears are dry

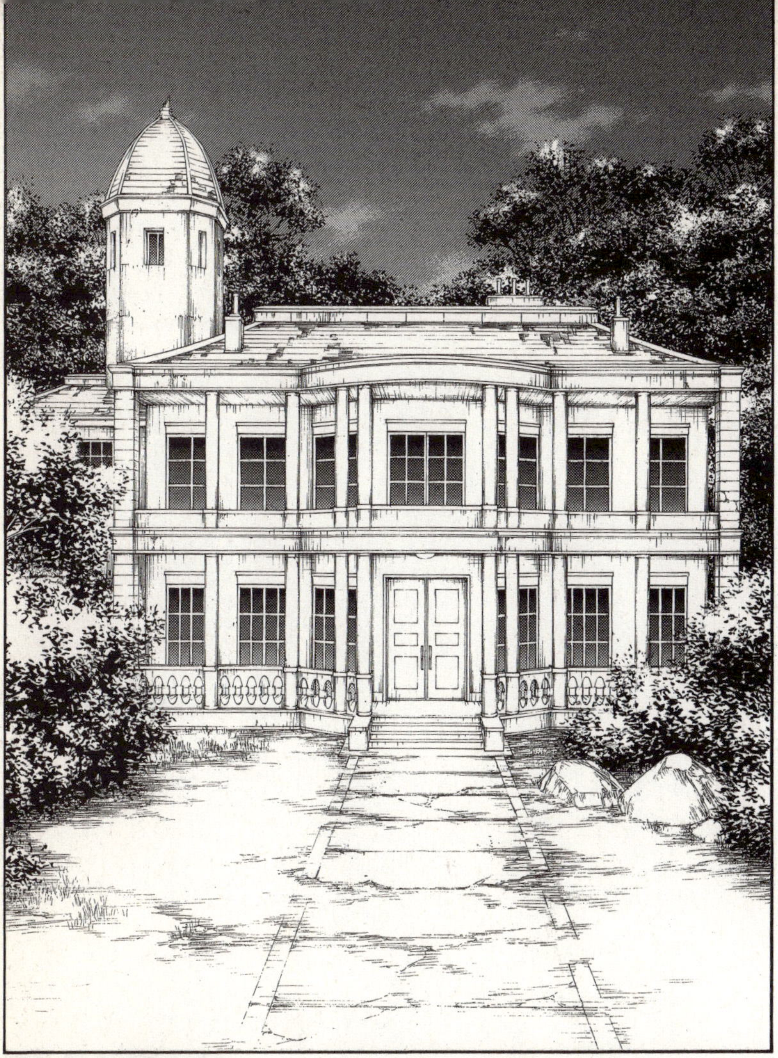

## 455. End of Bond 1

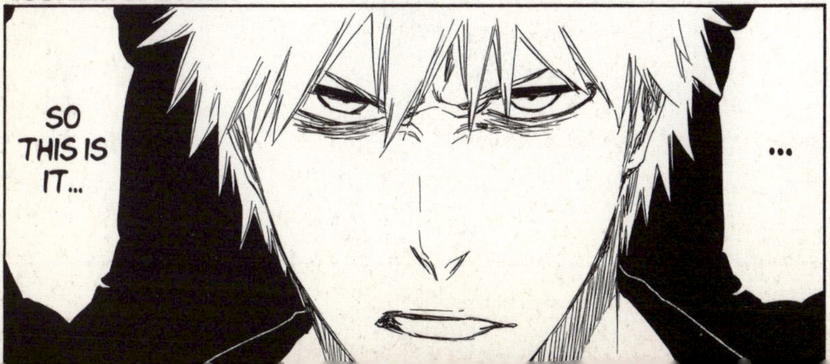
…
SO THIS IS IT…

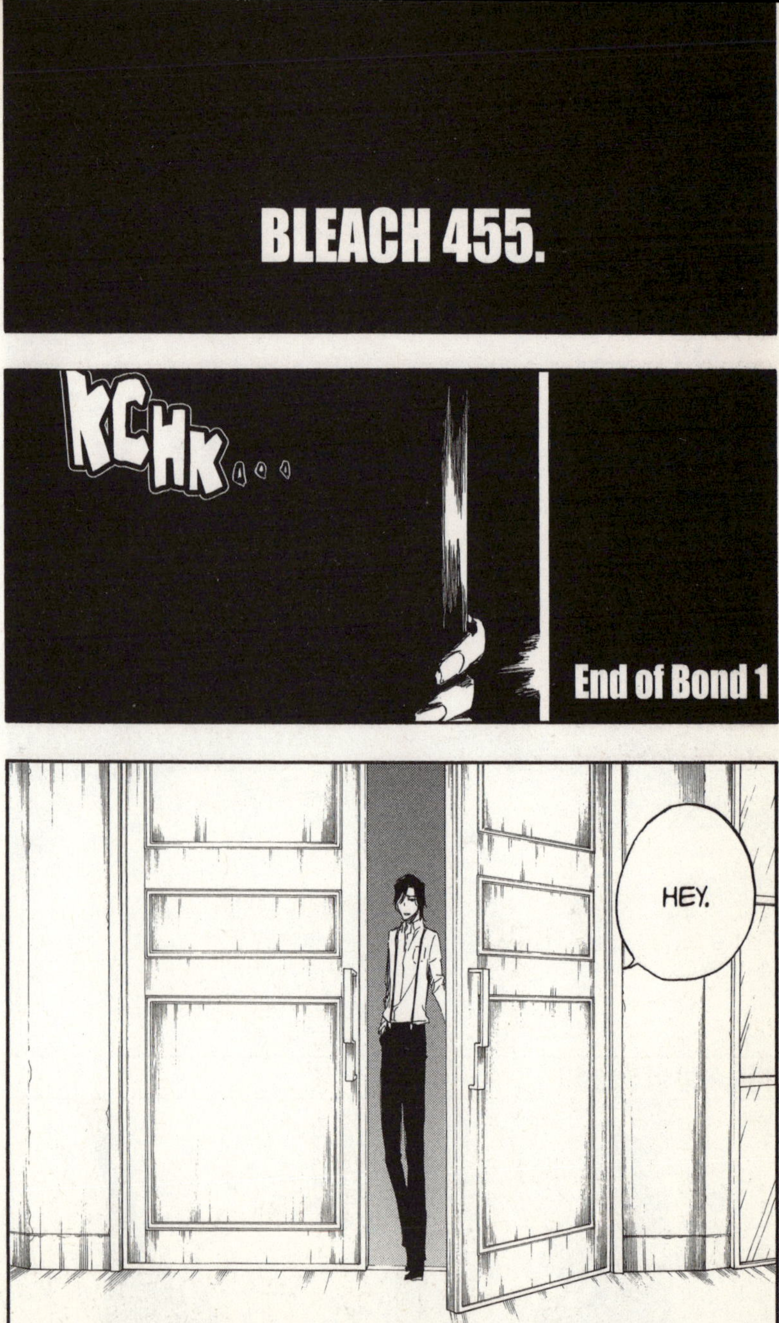
BLEACH 455.
End of Bond 1
KCHK...
HEY.

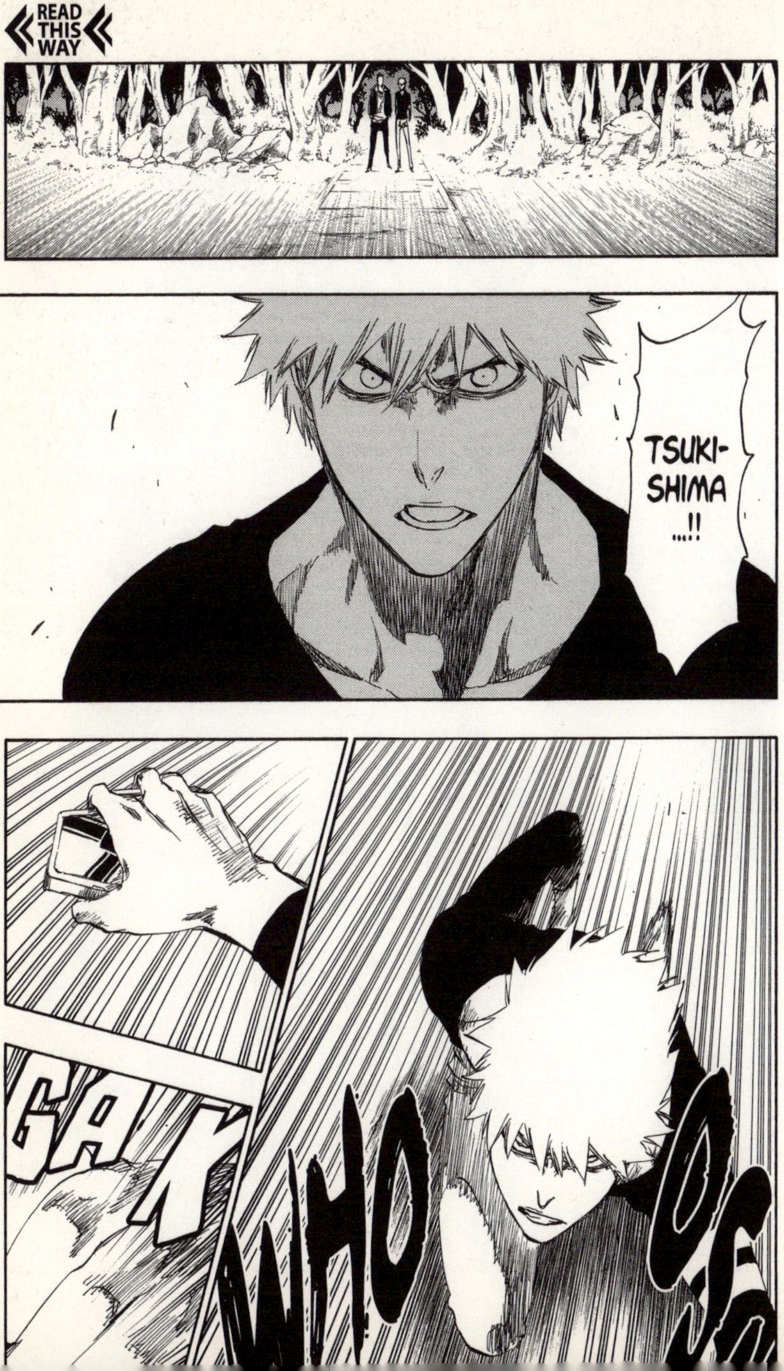
READ THIS WAY
TSUKI-SHIMA ...!!
GAK
WHOOSH

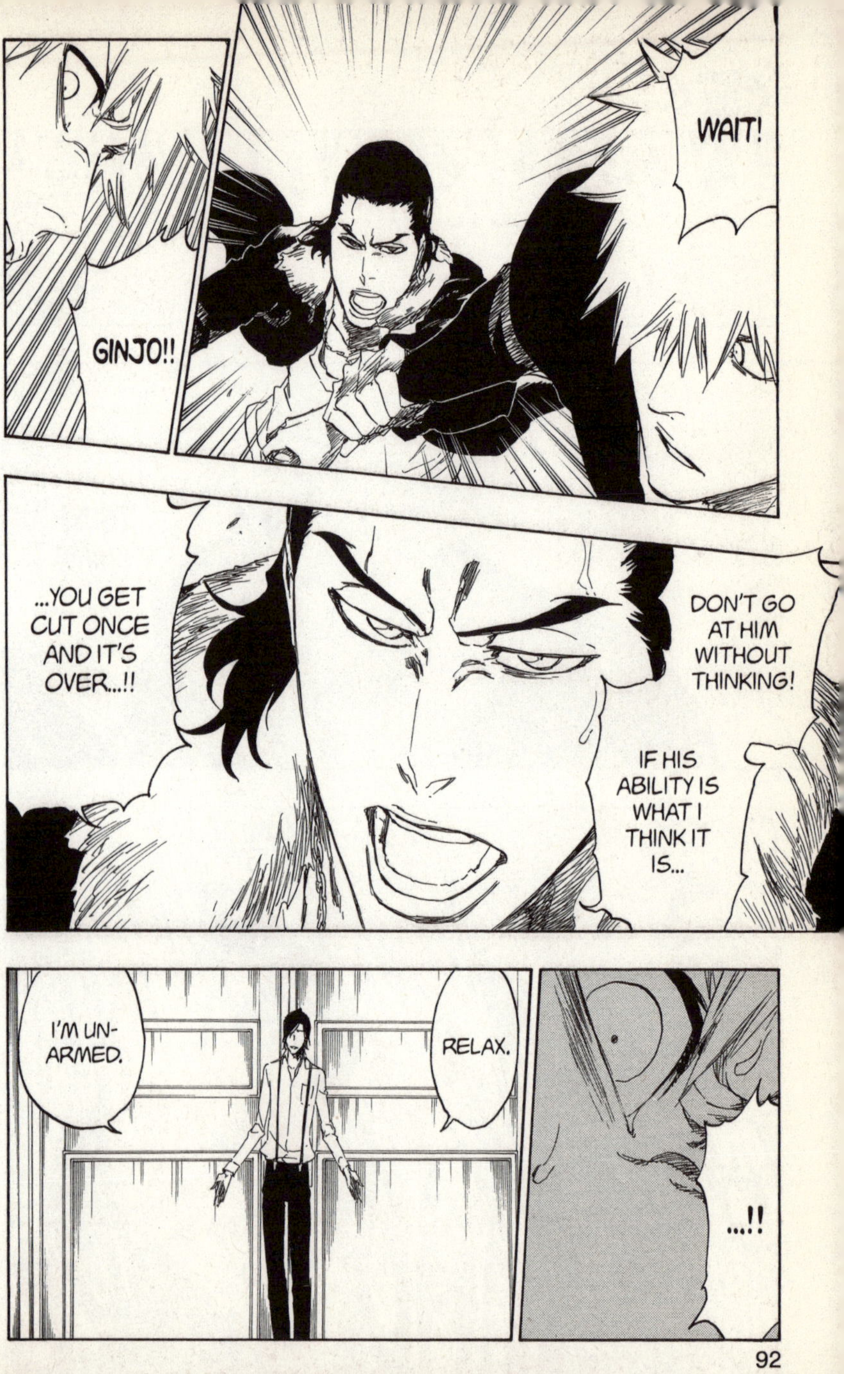
WAIT!
GINJO!!
DON'T GO AT HIM WITHOUT THINKING!
IF HIS ABILITY IS WHAT I THINK IT IS...
...YOU GET CUT ONCE AND IT'S OVER...!!
...!!
RELAX.
I'M UN-ARMED.

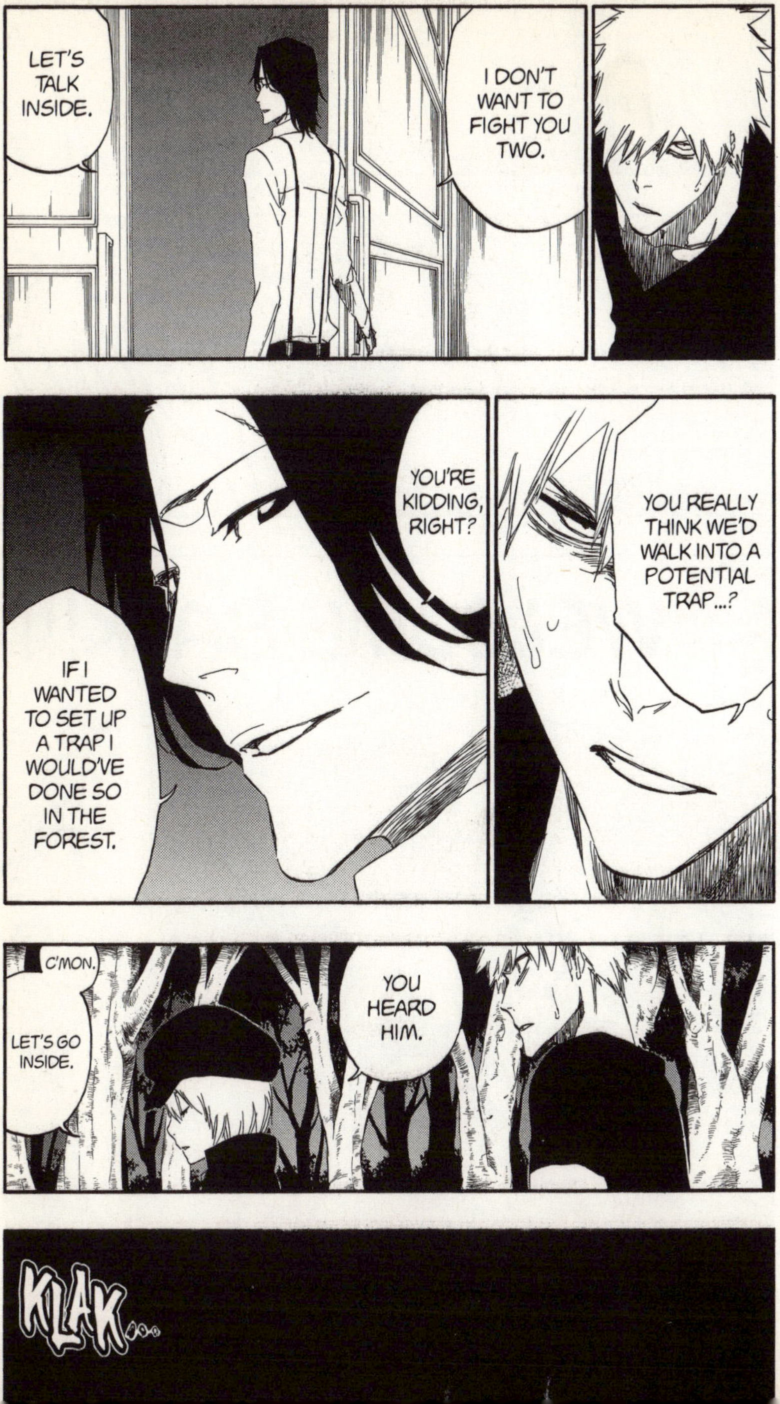
LET'S TALK INSIDE.
I DON'T WANT TO FIGHT YOU TWO.
YOU'RE KIDDING, RIGHT?
YOU REALLY THINK WE'D WALK INTO A POTENTIAL TRAP...?
IF I WANTED TO SET UP A TRAP I WOULD'VE DONE SO IN THE FOREST.
C'MON.
LET'S GO INSIDE.
YOU HEARD HIM.
KLAK...

POP
POP
POP
WELCOME BACK!!!
DIVA

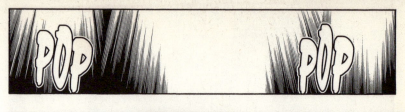

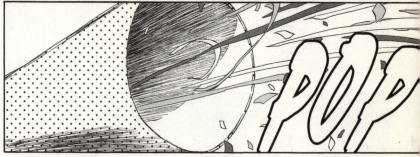

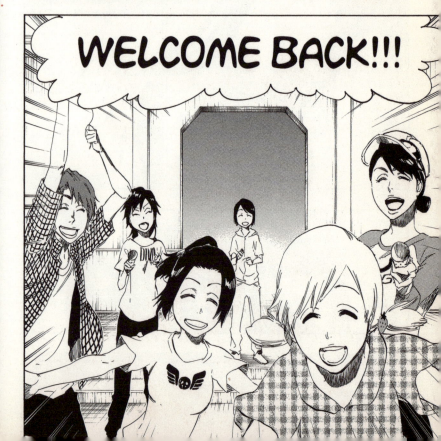

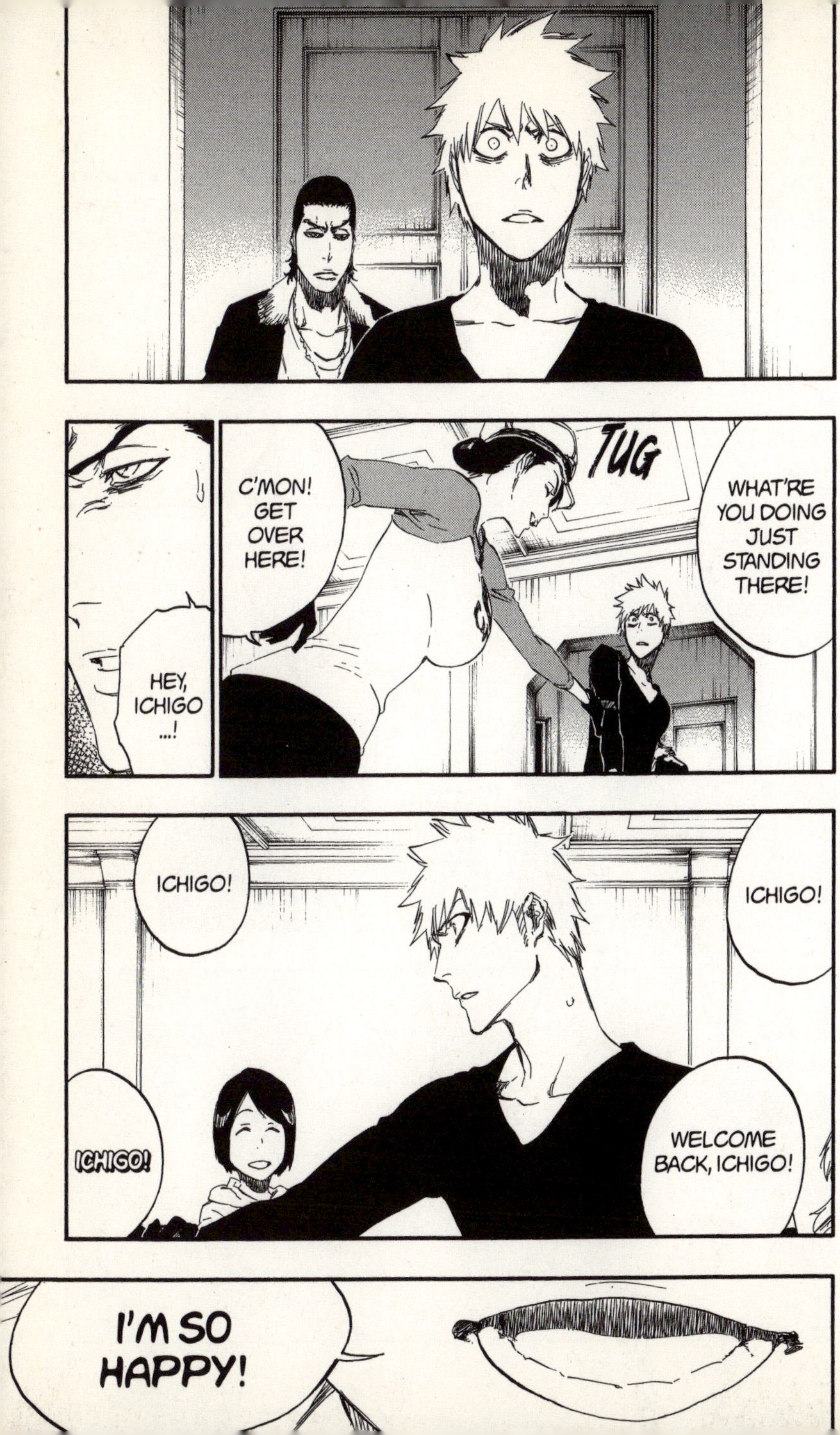
TUG
WHAT'RE YOU DOING JUST STANDING THERE!
C'MON! GET OVER HERE!
HEY, ICHIGO ...!
ICHIGO!
ICHIGO!
WELCOME BACK, ICHIGO!
ICHIGO!
I'M SO HAPPY!

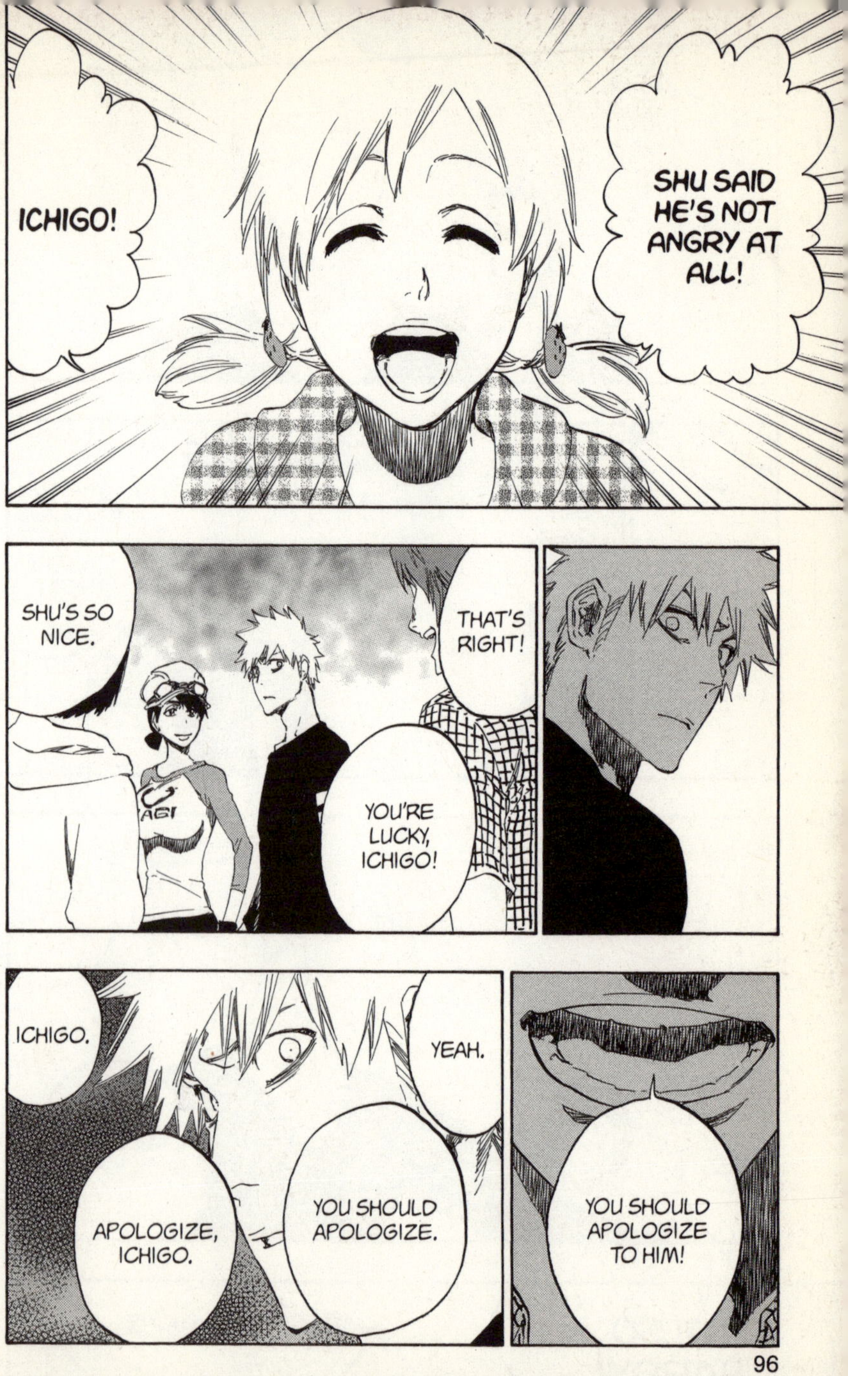
SHU SAID HE'S NOT ANGRY AT ALL!
ICHIGO!
THAT'S RIGHT!
YOU'RE LUCKY, ICHIGO!
SHU'S SO NICE.
YOU SHOULD APOLOGIZE TO HIM!
YEAH.
YOU SHOULD APOLOGIZE.
ICHIGO.
APOLOGIZE, ICHIGO.

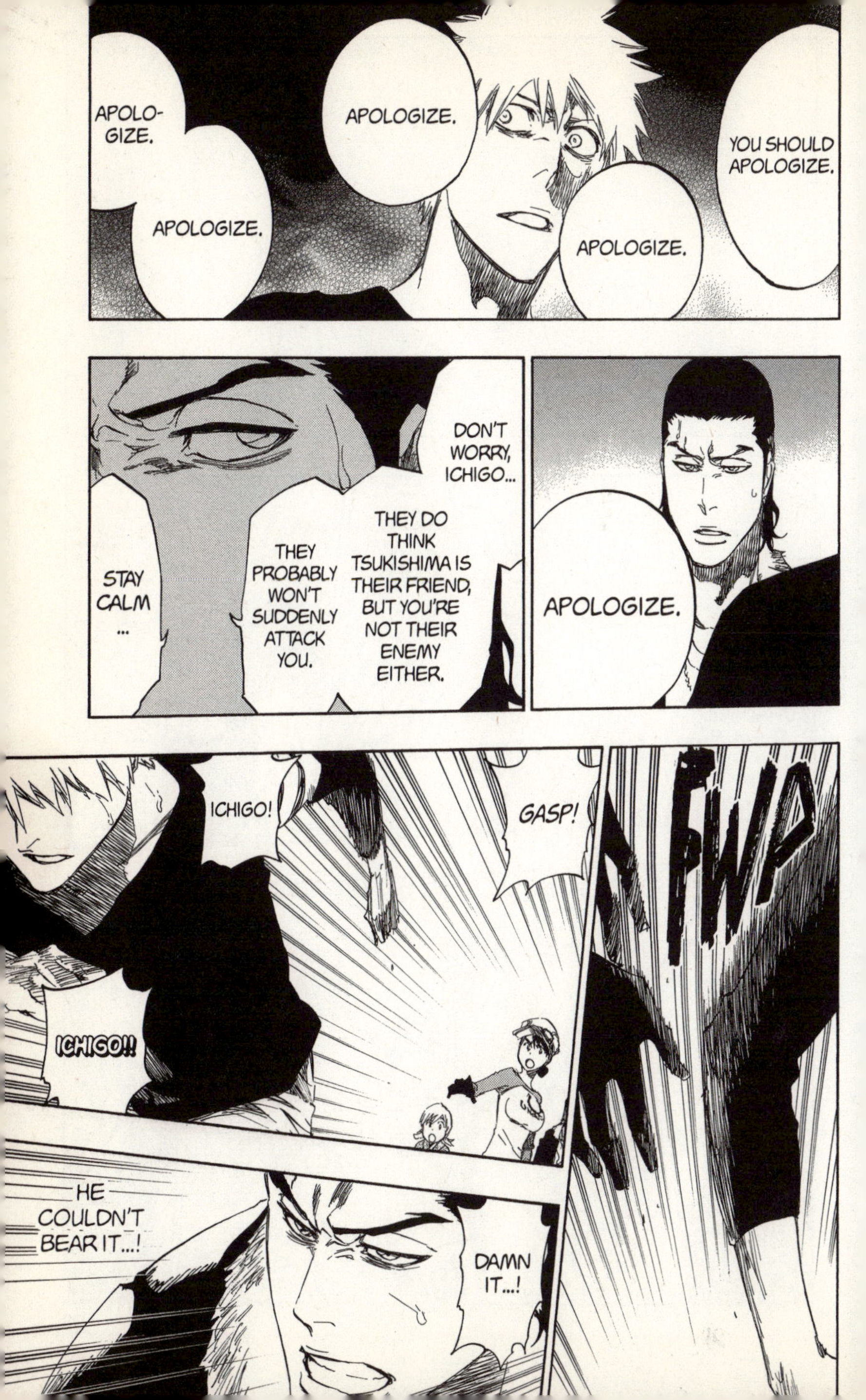
APOLO-GIZE.
APOLOGIZE.
APOLOGIZE.
APOLOGIZE.
YOU SHOULD APOLOGIZE.
STAY CALM ...
THEY PROBABLY WON'T SUDDENLY ATTACK YOU.
THEY DO THINK TSUKISHIMA IS THEIR FRIEND, BUT YOU'RE NOT THEIR ENEMY EITHER.
DON'T WORRY, ICHIGO...
APOLOGIZE.
ICHIGO!
GASP!
FWP
ICHIGO!!
HE COULDN'T BEAR IT...!
DAMN IT...!

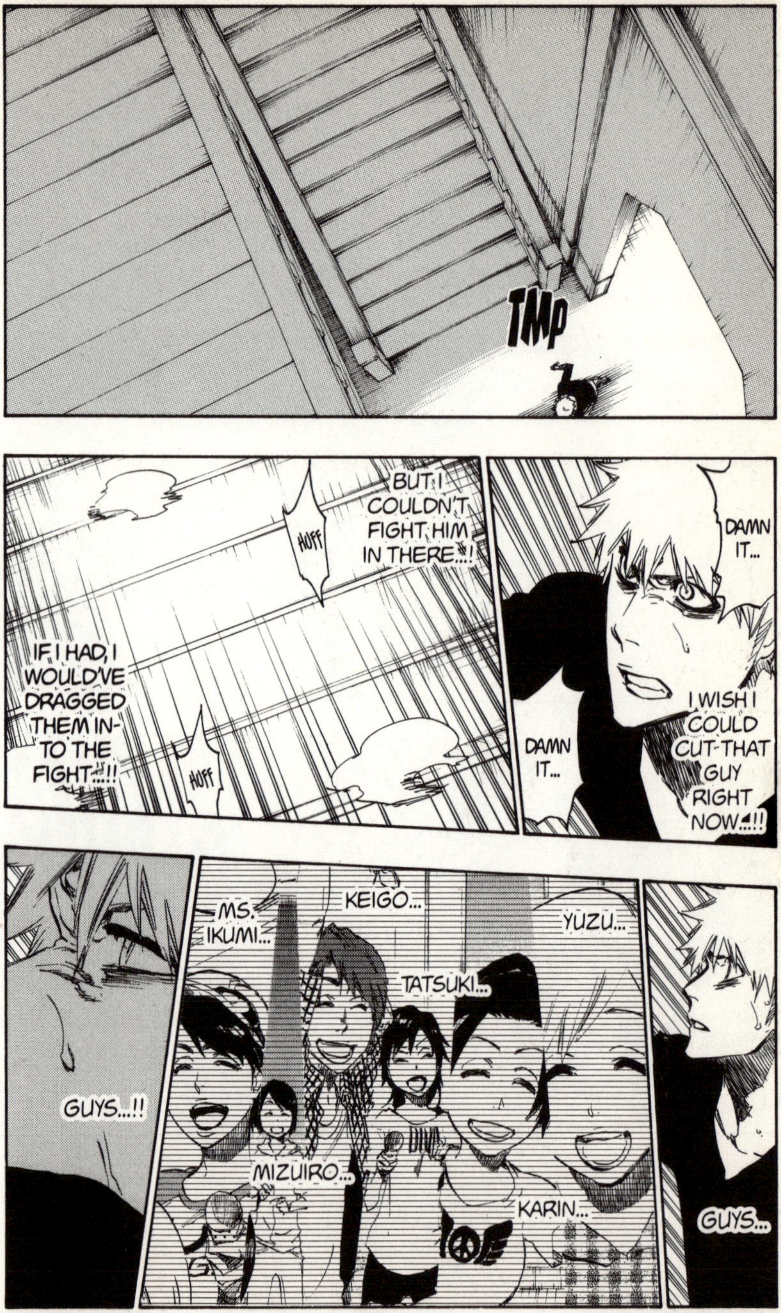
TMP
DAMN IT...
BUT I COULDN'T FIGHT HIM IN THERE...!
HUFF
IF I HAD, I WOULD'VE DRAGGED THEM INTO THE FIGHT...!!
HUFF
DAMN IT...
I WISH I COULD CUT THAT GUY RIGHT NOW...!!
YUZU...
KEIGO...
MS. IKUMI...
TATSUKI...
GUYS...!!
KARIN...
MIZUIRO...
GUYS...

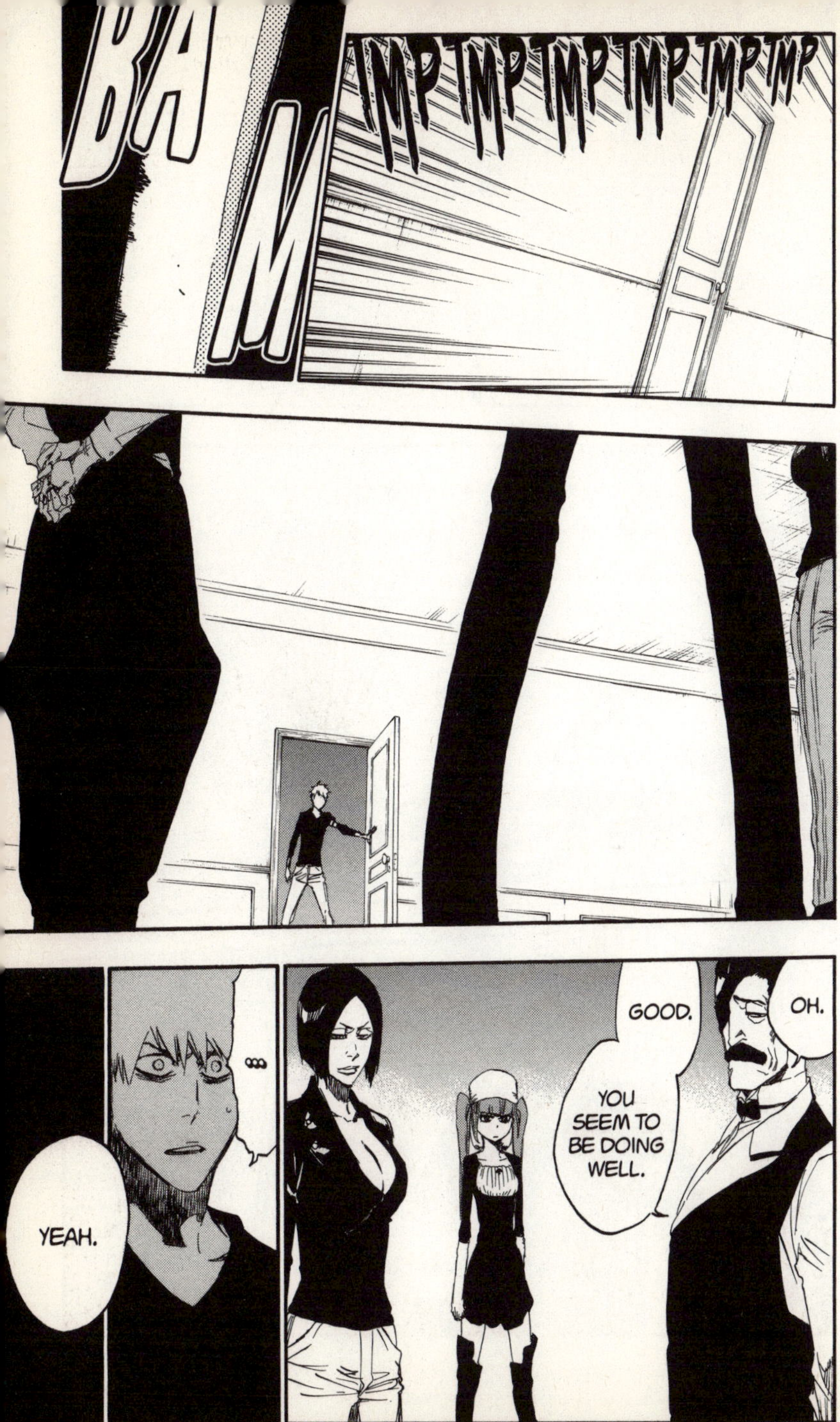
BAM
TMP TMP TMP TMP TMP TMP
OH.
GOOD.
YOU SEEM TO BE DOING WELL.
...
YEAH.

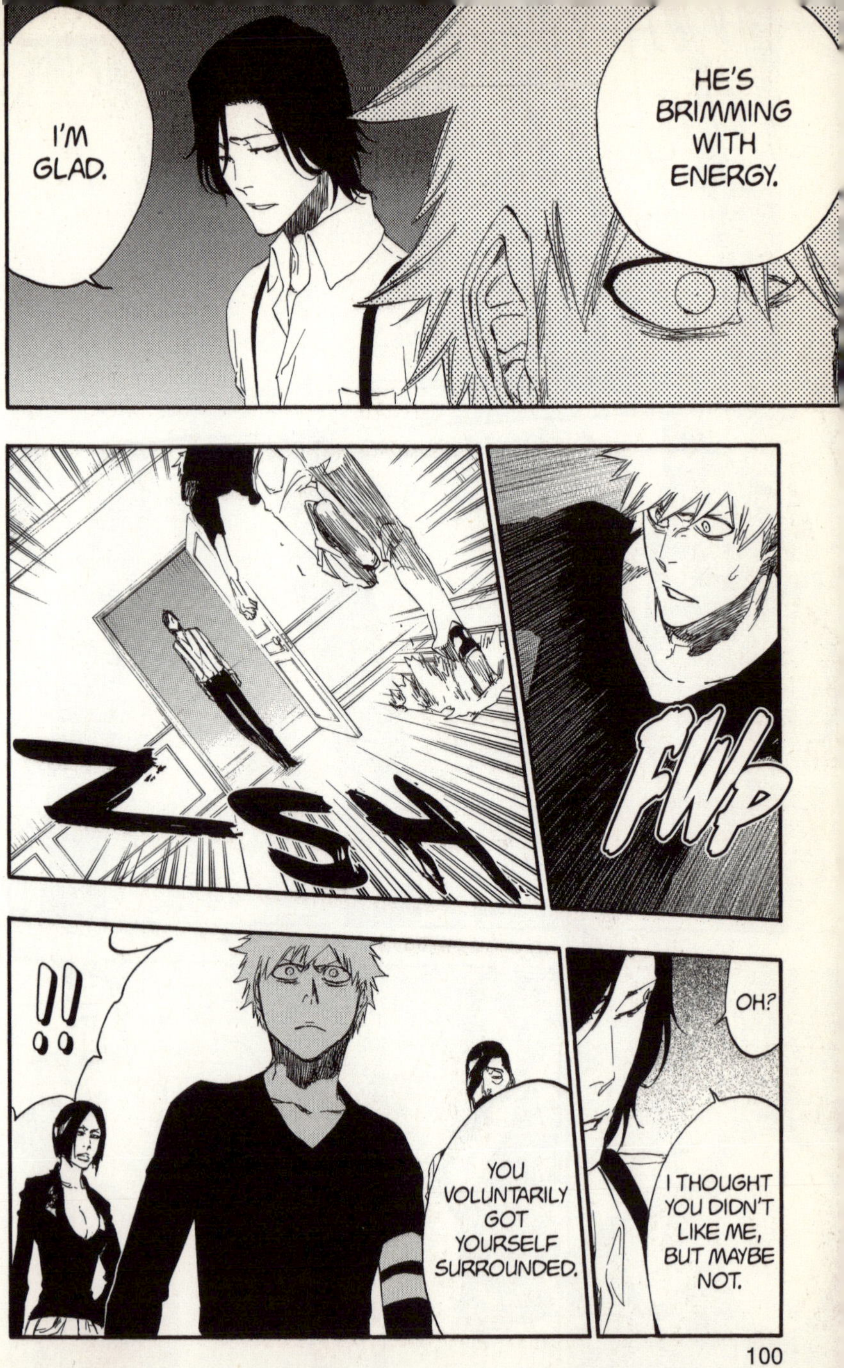
HE'S BRIMMING WITH ENERGY.
I'M GLAD.
FWP
ZSH
OH?
I THOUGHT YOU DIDN'T LIKE ME, BUT MAYBE NOT.
YOU VOLUNTARILY GOT YOURSELF SURROUNDED.
!!

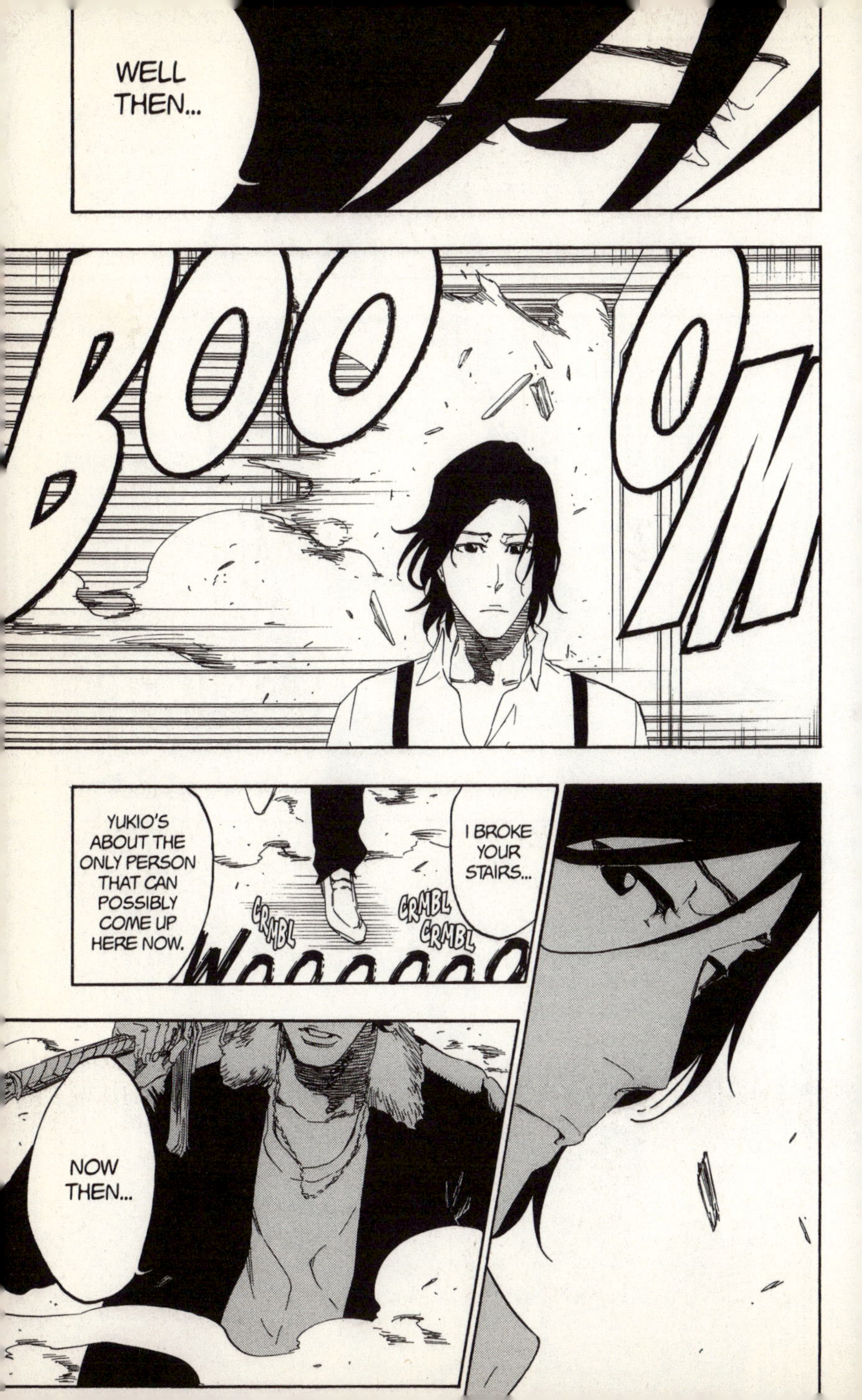
WELL THEN...
BOOOM
YUKIO'S ABOUT THE ONLY PERSON THAT CAN POSSIBLY COME UP HERE NOW.
I BROKE YOUR STAIRS...
CRMBL
CRMBL
CRMBL
NOW THEN...

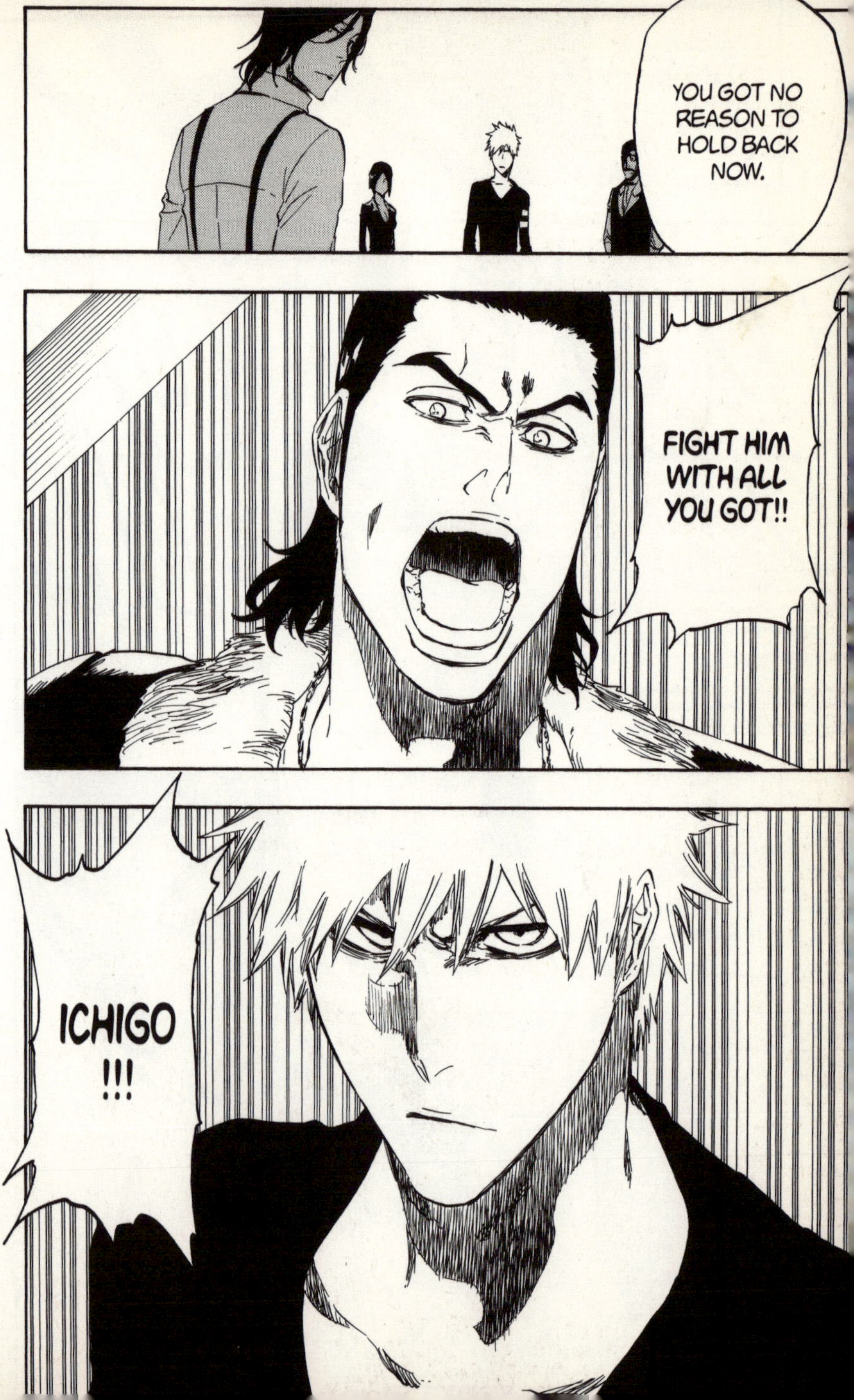
YOU GOT NO REASON TO HOLD BACK NOW.
FIGHT HIM WITH ALL YOU GOT!!
ICHIGO !!!

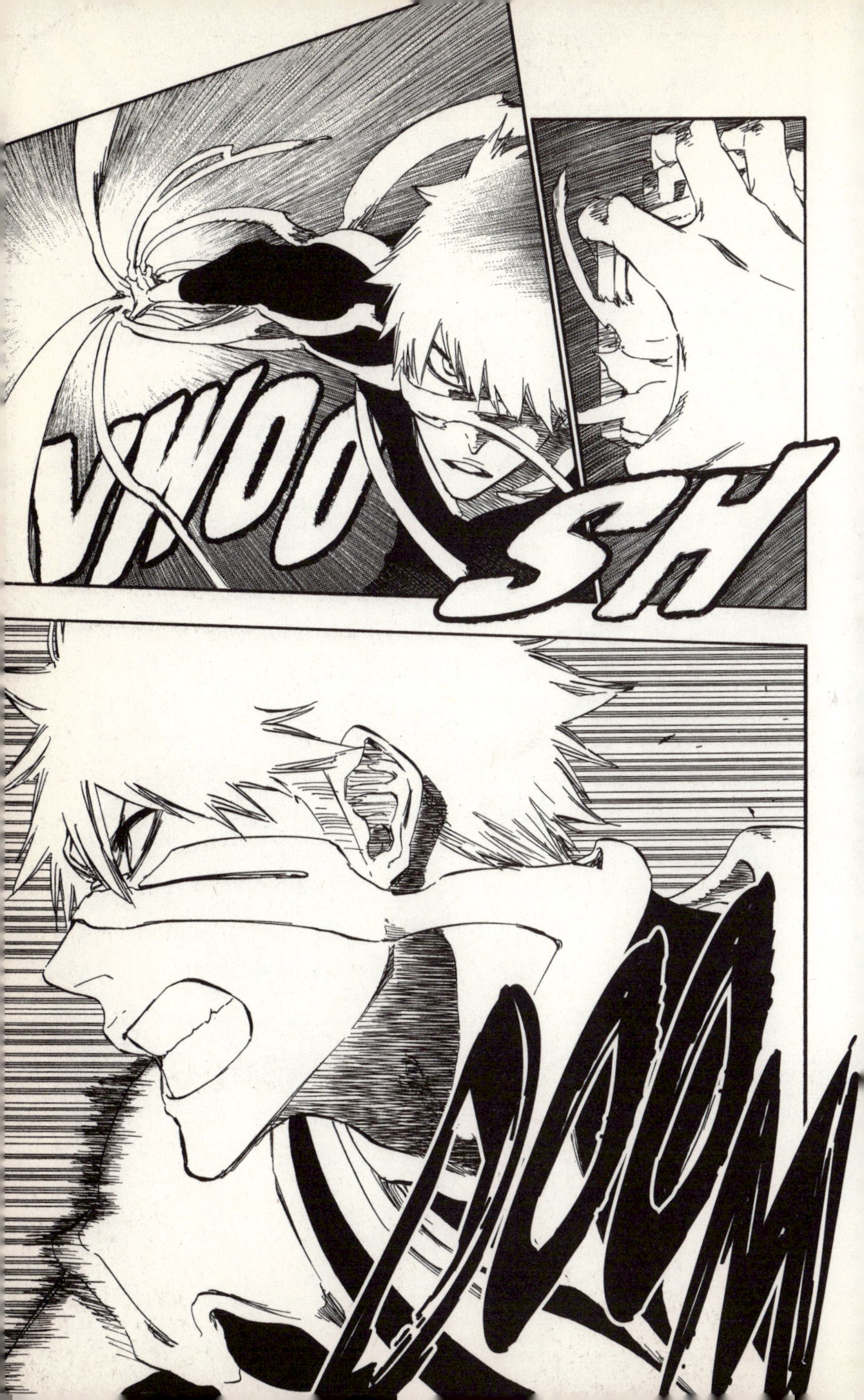
VWOOSH

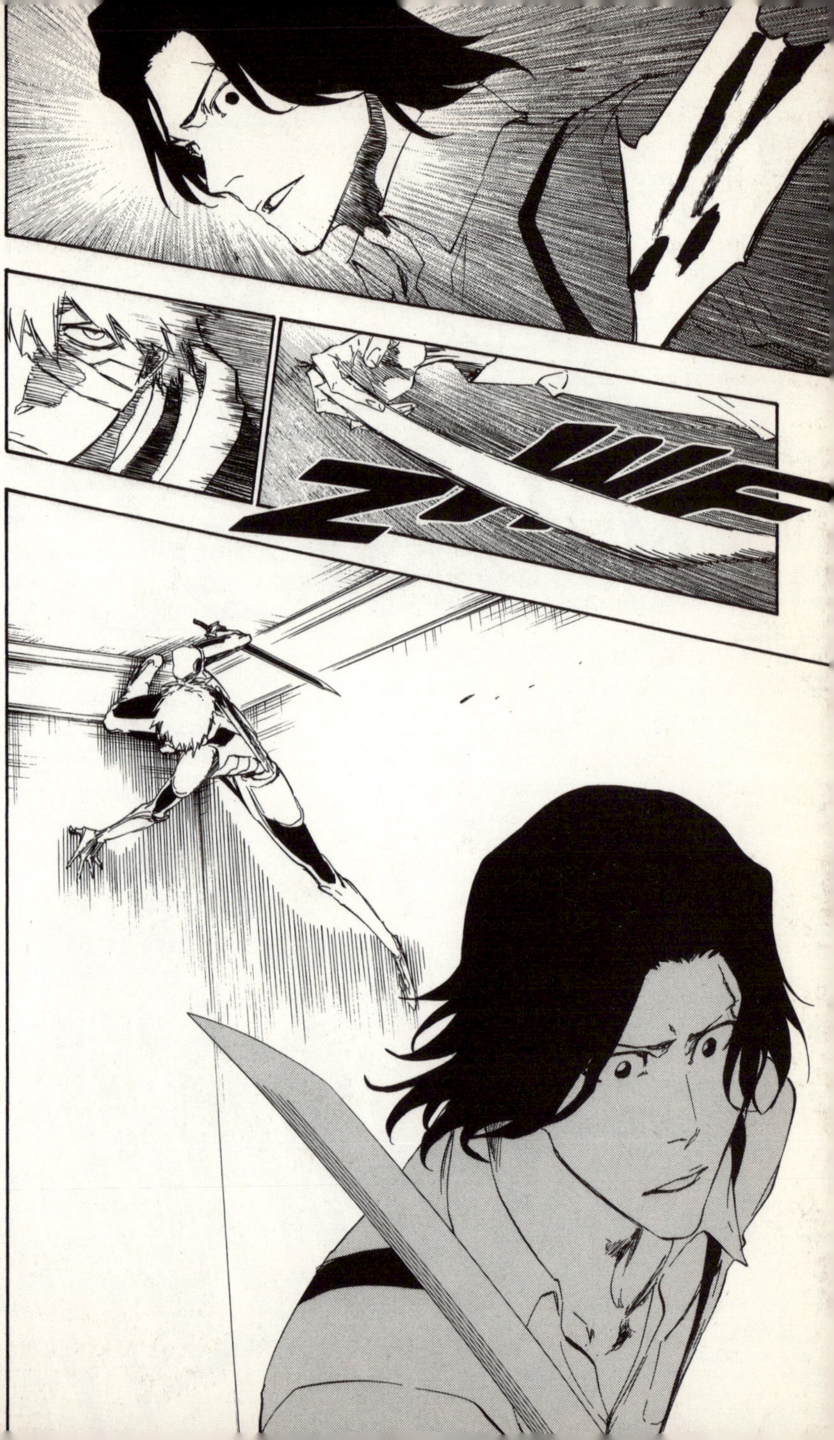
ZWIF

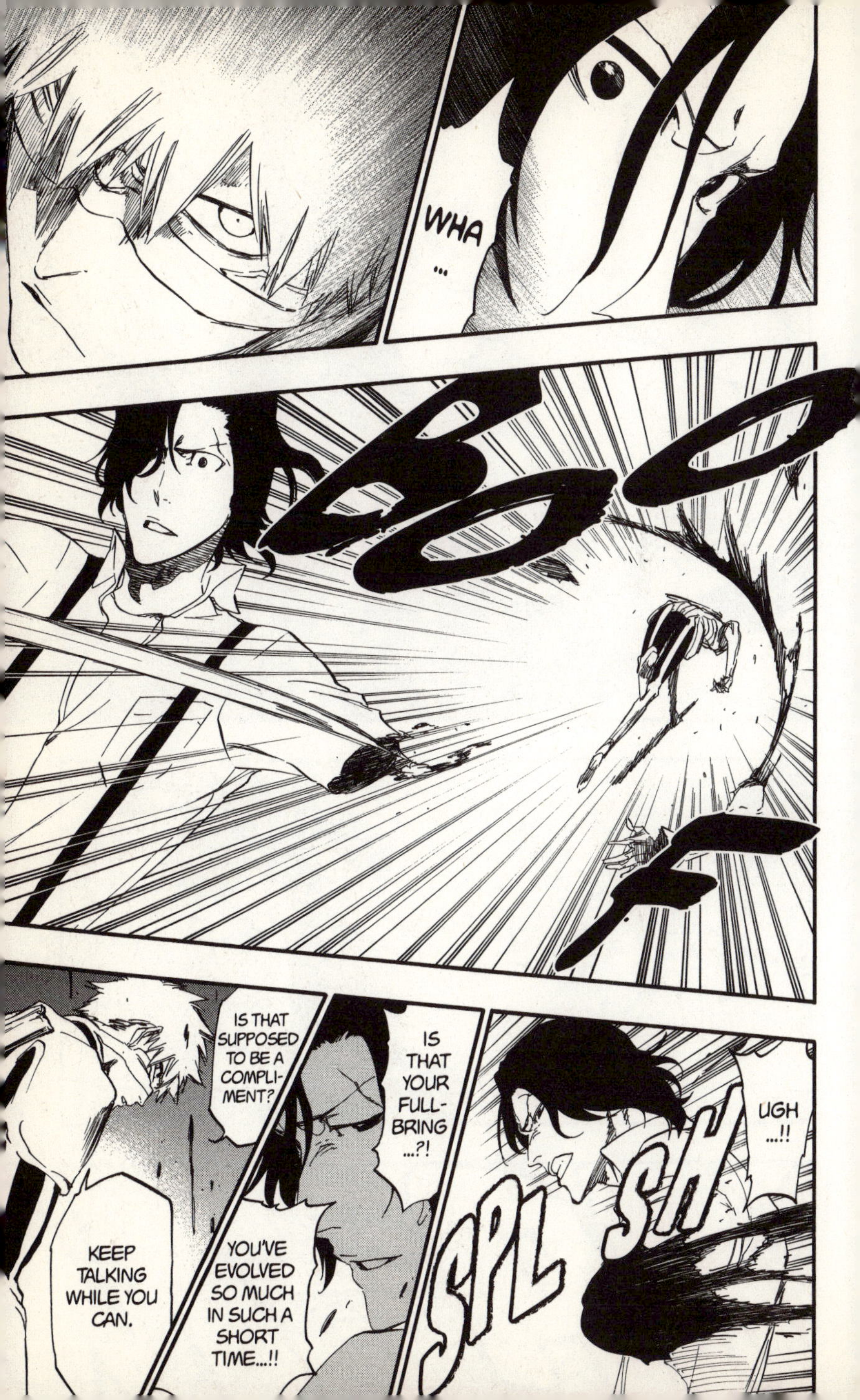

WHA
...
BOOF
UGH
...!!
SPLSH
IS THAT YOUR FULL-BRING ...?!
YOU'VE EVOLVED SO MUCH IN SUCH A SHORT TIME...!!
IS THAT SUPPOSED TO BE A COMPLI-MENT?
KEEP TALKING WHILE YOU CAN.

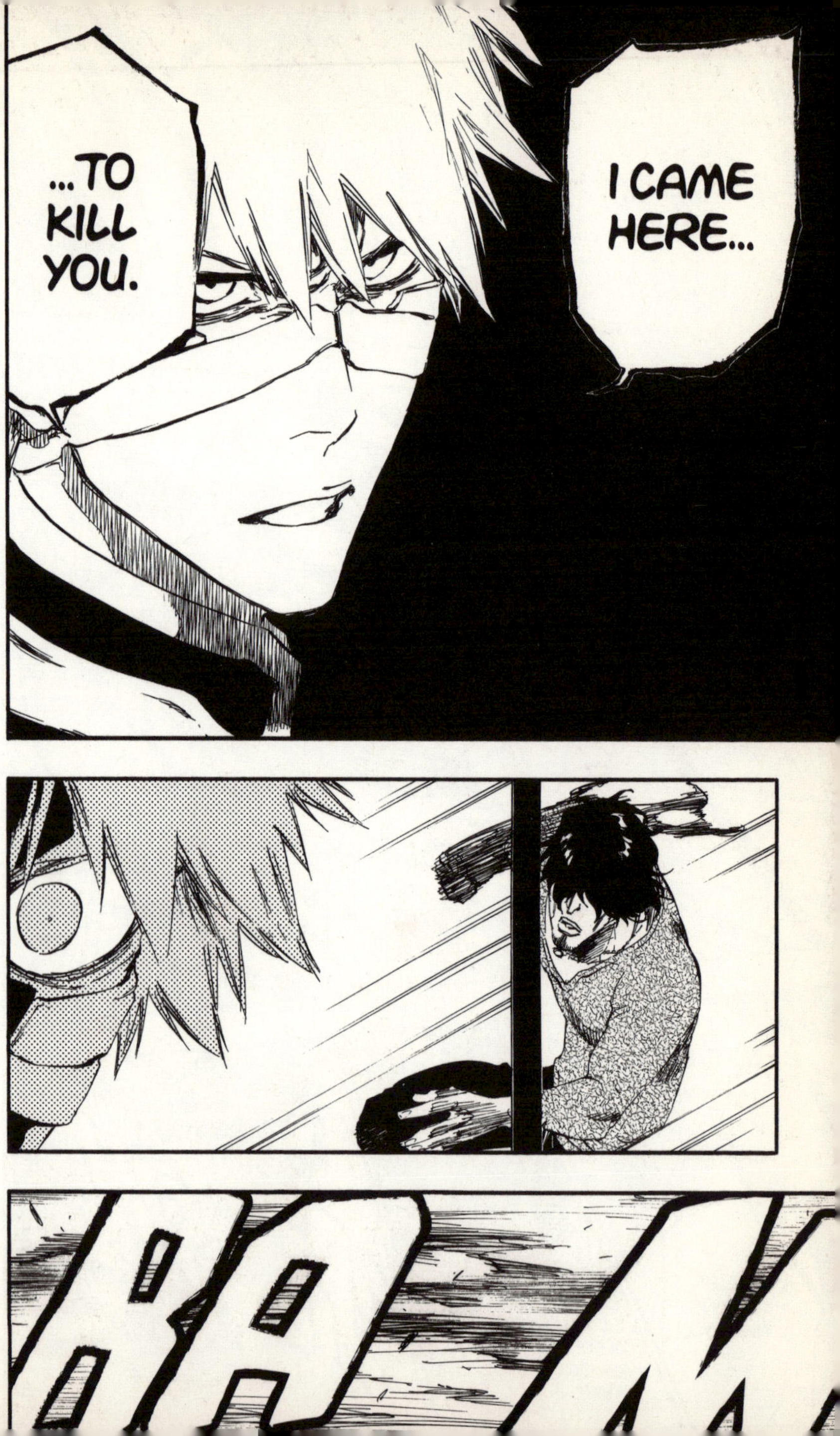
I CAME HERE...
...TO KILL YOU.

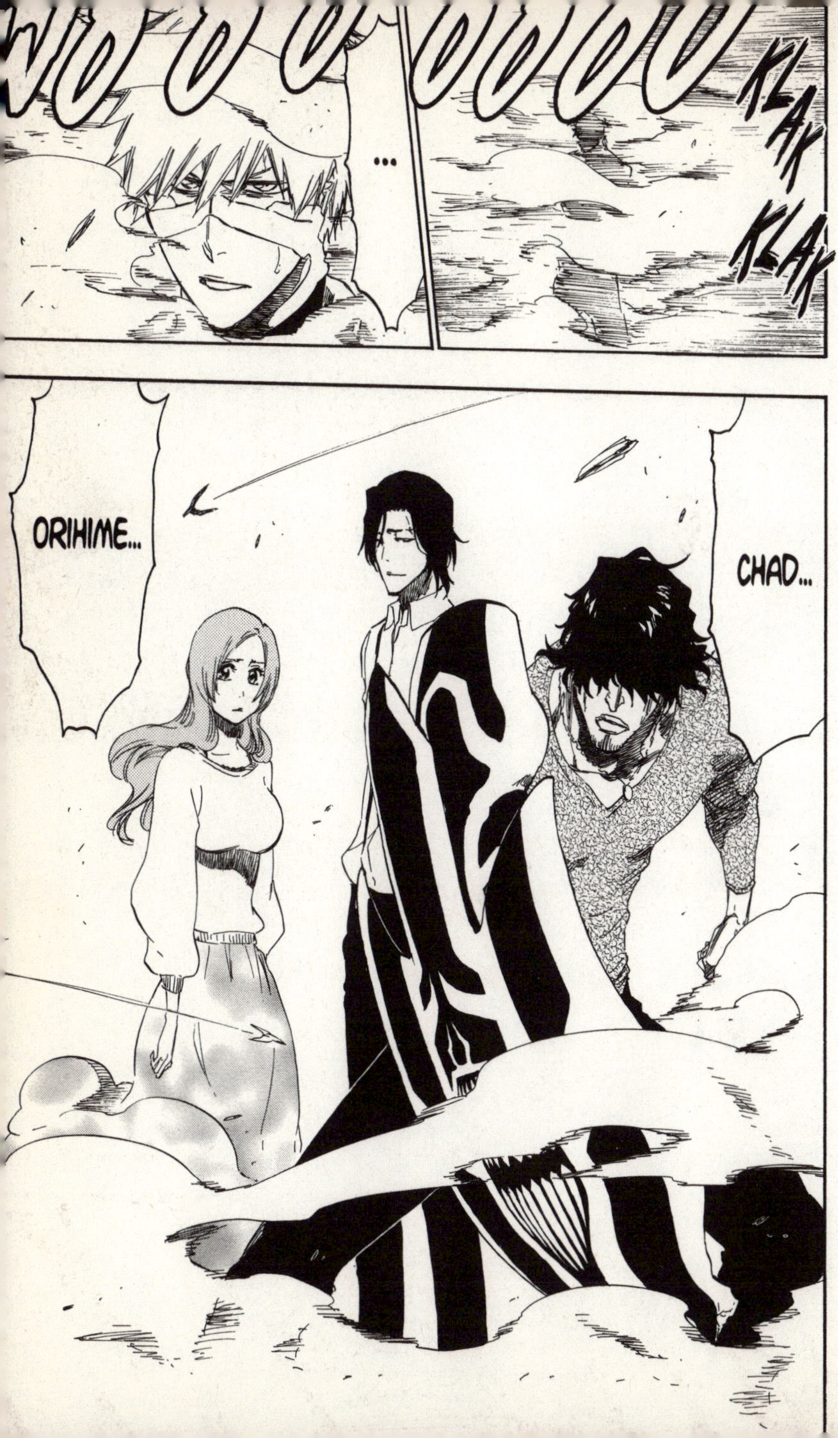
WHOOOOOOOOOOOO
...
KLAK KLAK
ORIHIME...
CHAD...

why

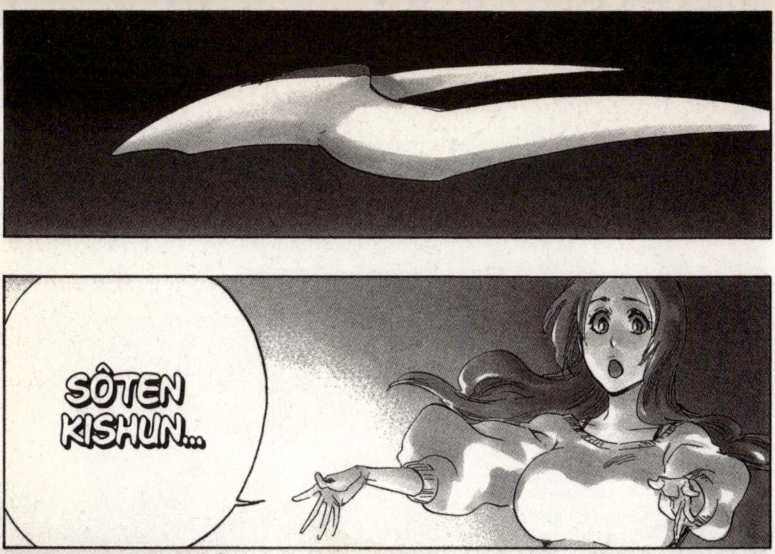
SÔTEN KISHUN...

## 456. End of Bond 2

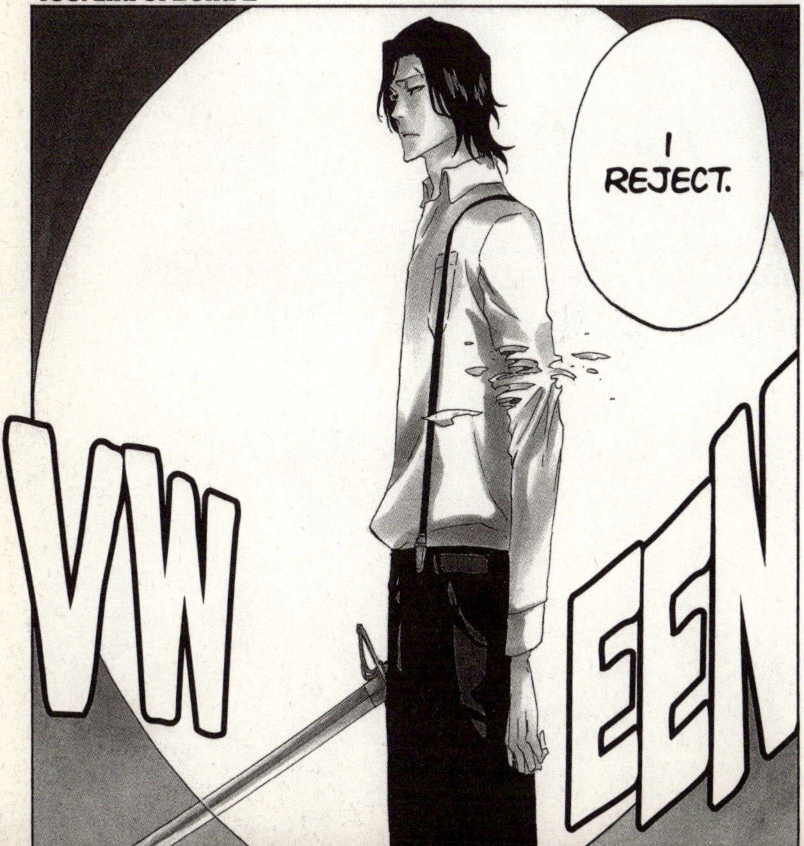
I REJECT.
VWEEN

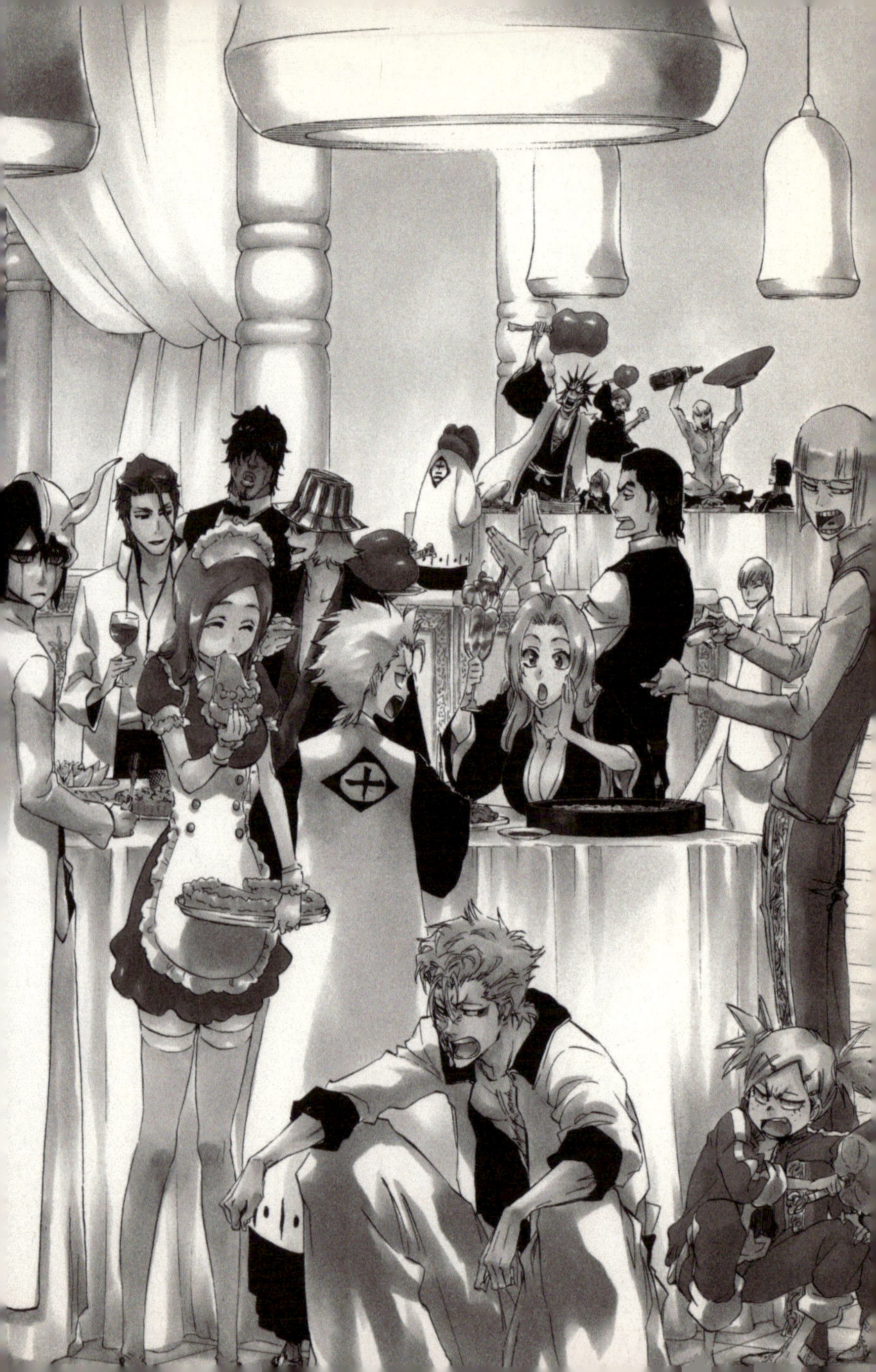

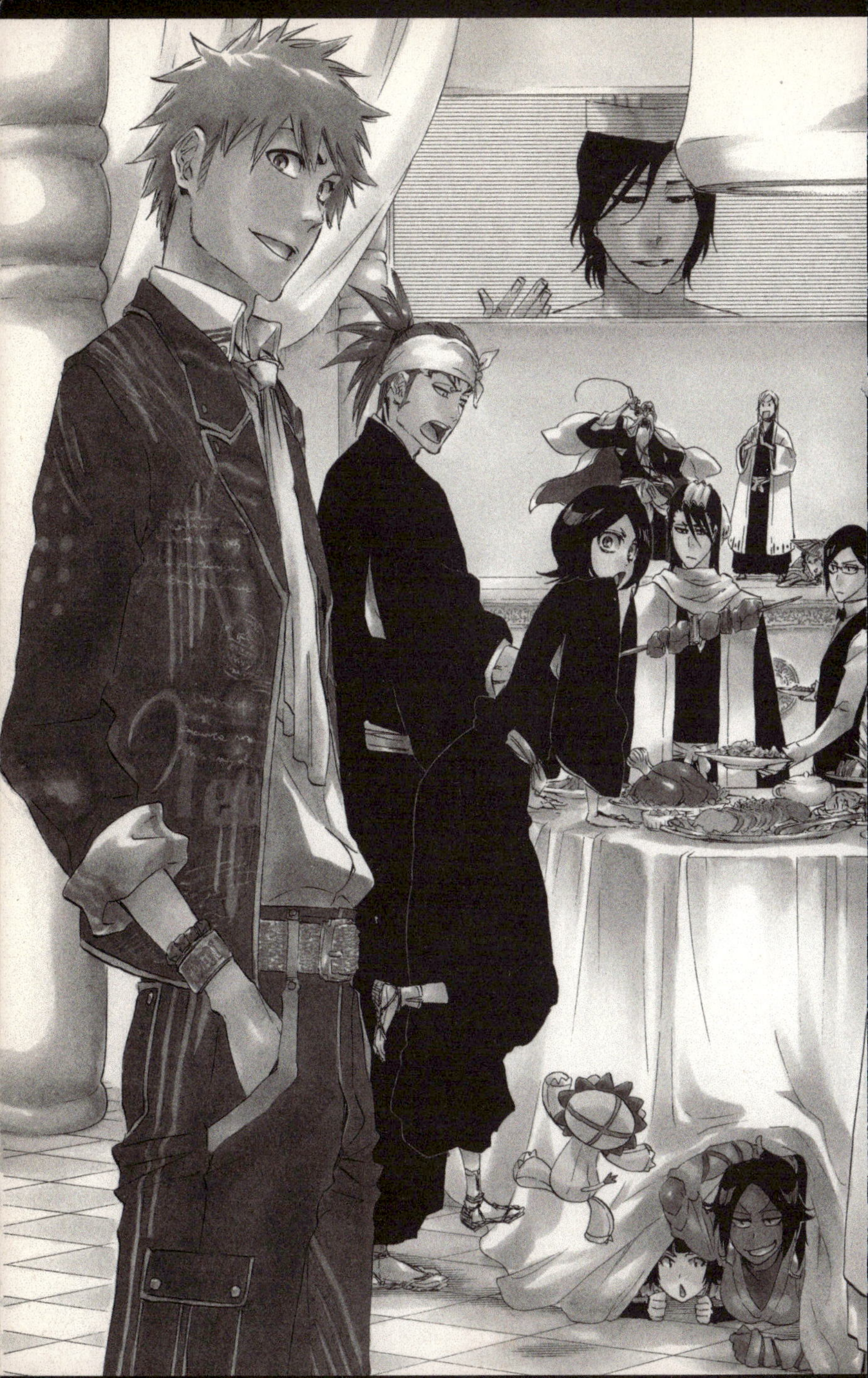

BLEACH
ブリーチ

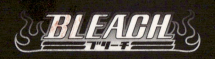

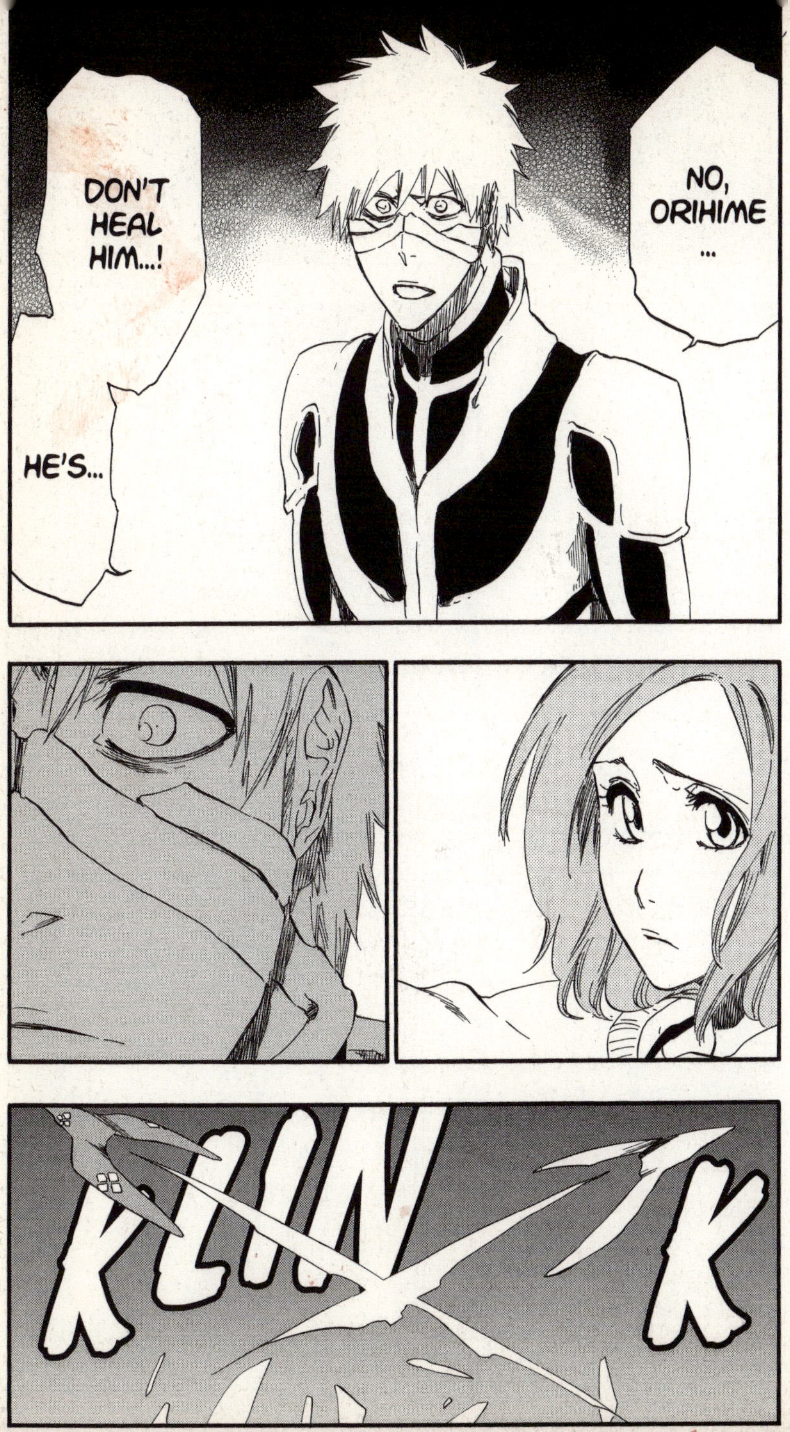
NO, ORIHIME ...
DON'T HEAL HIM...!
HE'S...
KLIN K

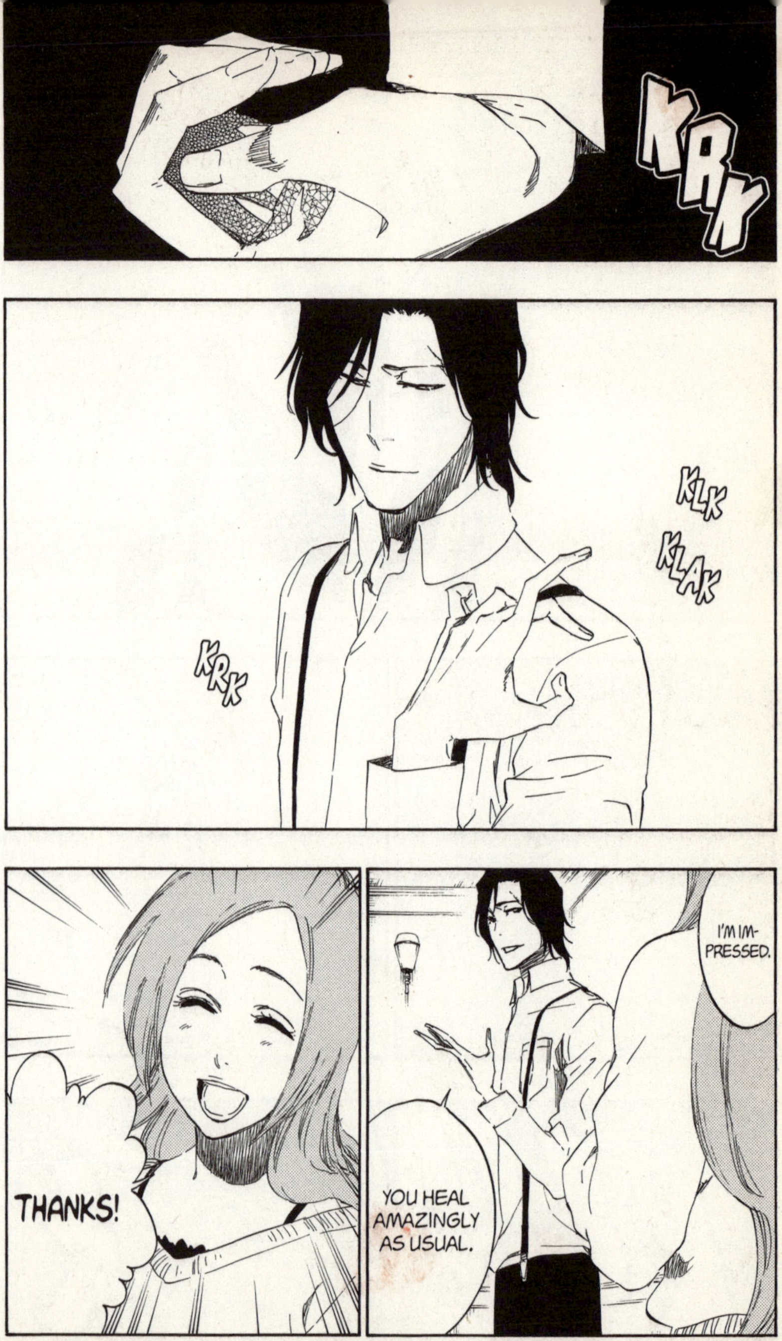
KRK
KLK
KLAK
KRK
I'M IM-PRESSED.
YOU HEAL AMAZINGLY AS USUAL.
THANKS!

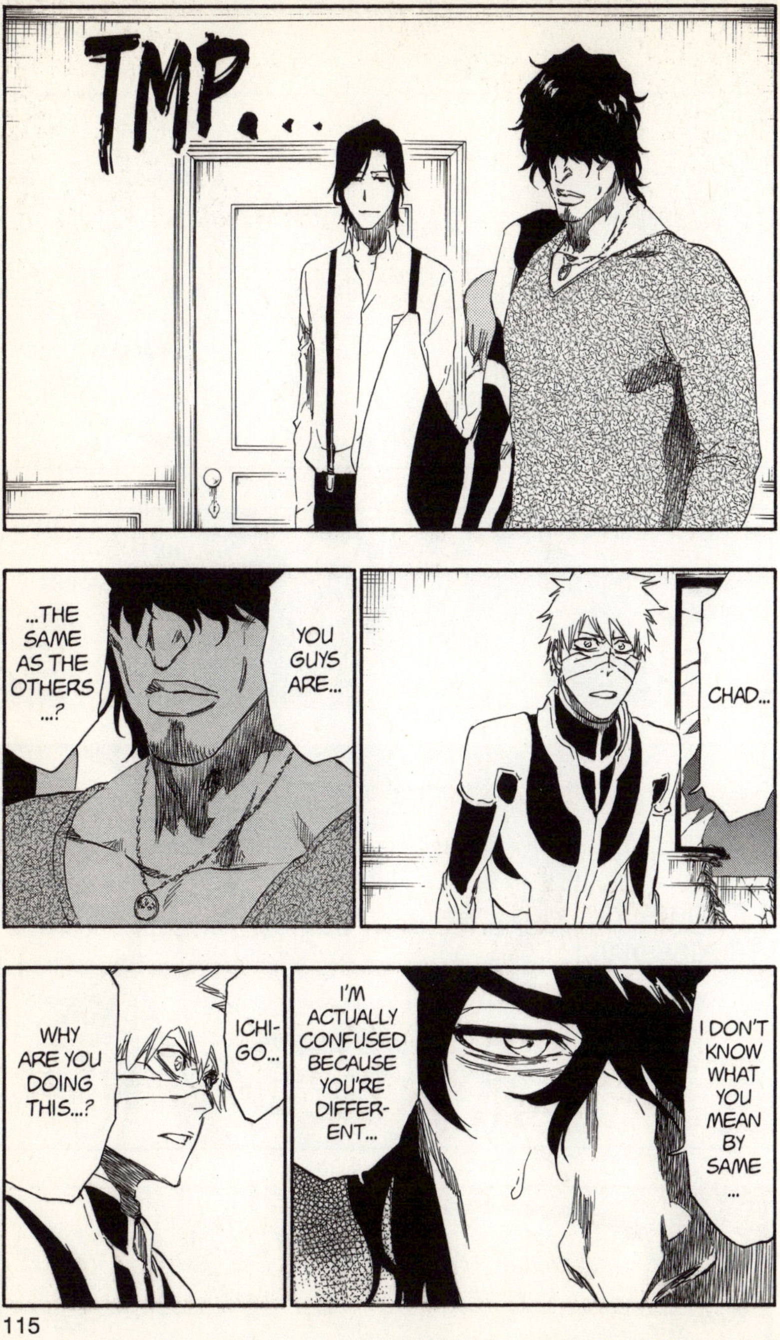
TMP...
CHAD...
YOU GUYS ARE...
...THE SAME AS THE OTHERS ...?
I DON'T KNOW WHAT YOU MEAN BY SAME ...
I'M ACTUALLY CONFUSED BECAUSE YOU'RE DIFFER-ENT...
ICHI-GO...
WHY ARE YOU DOING THIS...?

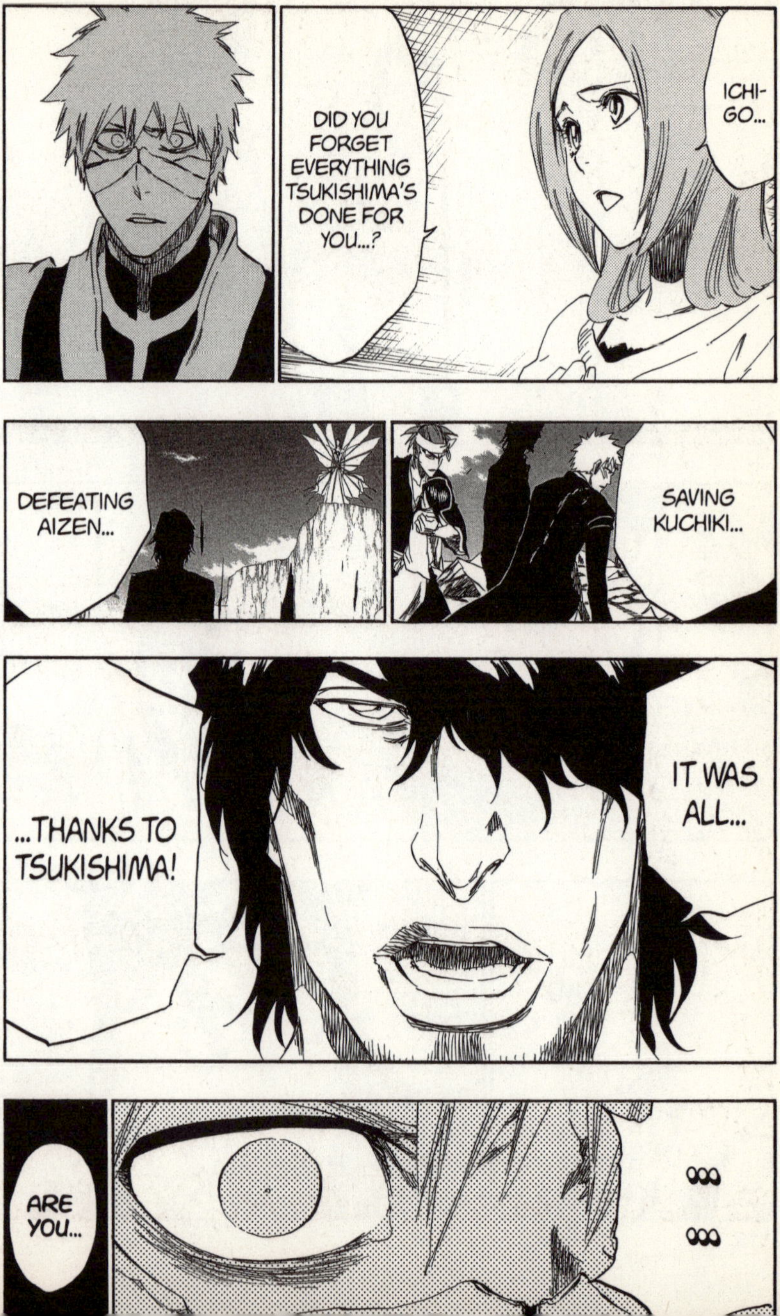
ICHI-GO...
DID YOU FORGET EVERYTHING TSUKISHIMA'S DONE FOR YOU...?
SAVING KUCHIKI...
DEFEATING AIZEN...
IT WAS ALL...
...THANKS TO TSUKISHIMA!
ARE YOU...

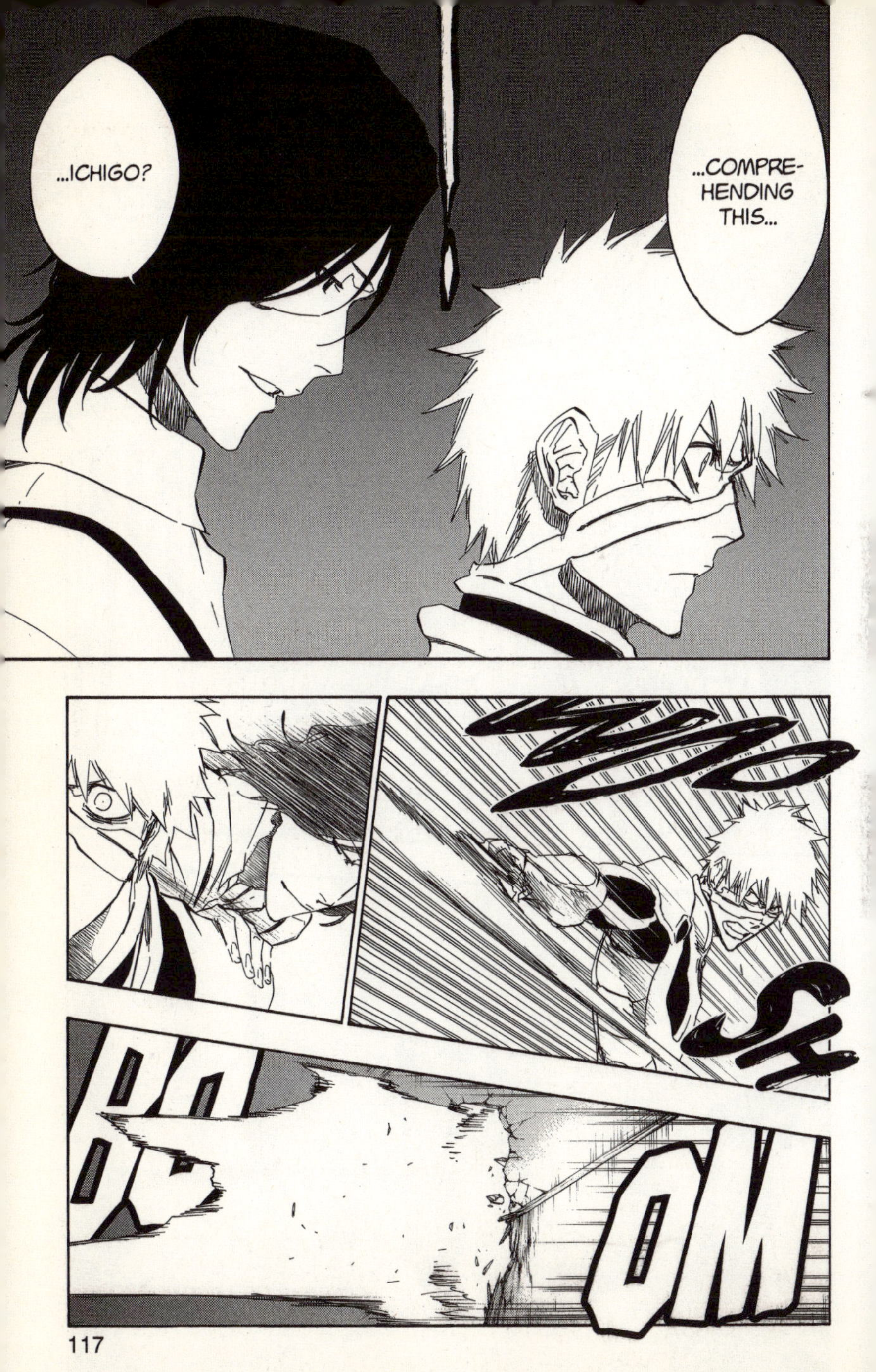
...COMPRE-
HENDING
THIS...
...ICHIGO?
SH
BOOM

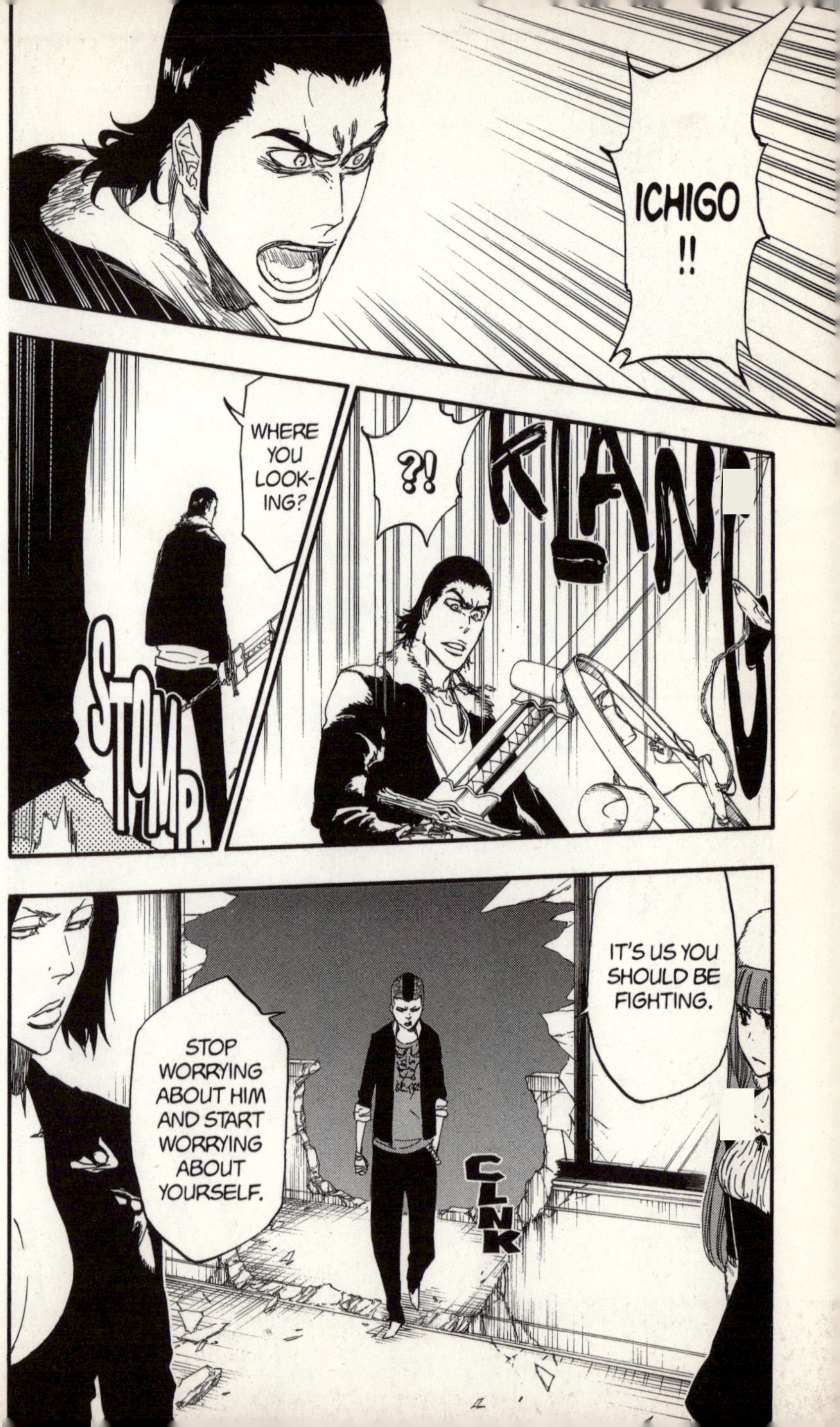
ICHIGO !!
?!
KLANG
WHERE YOU LOOKING?
STOMP
IT'S US YOU SHOULD BE FIGHTING.
CLNK
STOP WORRYING ABOUT HIM AND START WORRYING ABOUT YOURSELF.

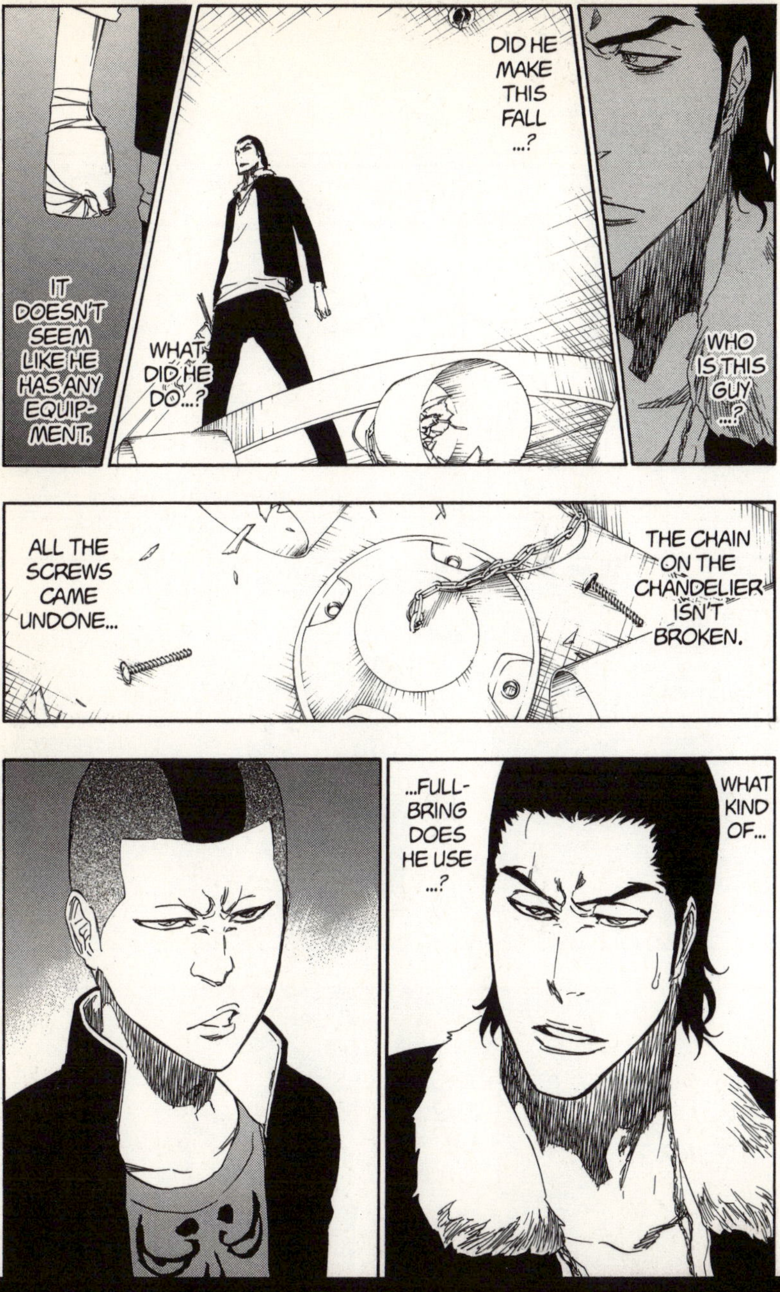
WHO IS THIS GUY ...?
DID HE MAKE THIS FALL ...?
WHAT DID HE DO...?
IT DOESN'T SEEM LIKE HE HAS ANY EQUIP-MENT.
THE CHAIN ON THE CHANDELIER ISN'T BROKEN.
ALL THE SCREWS CAME UNDONE...
WHAT KIND OF...
...FULL-BRING DOES HE USE ...?

# BLEACH 456.

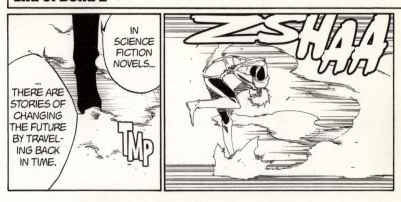

End of Bond 2
ZSHAA
IN SCIENCE FICTION NOVELS...
...THERE ARE STORIES OF CHANGING THE FUTURE BY TRAVELING BACK IN TIME.
TMP
WOOOOO
IT'S ALWAYS THE FUTURE THAT CHANGES WHEN SOMETHING IS ALTERED.
THAT IS BECAUSE IT IS BELIEVED THAT TIME FLOWS FROM THE PAST TO THE FUTURE.
TMP
TMP
BUT MY BOOK OF THE END...
...CHANGES THE PAST.
KLINK

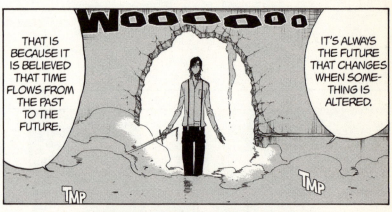

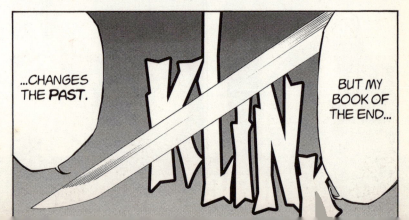

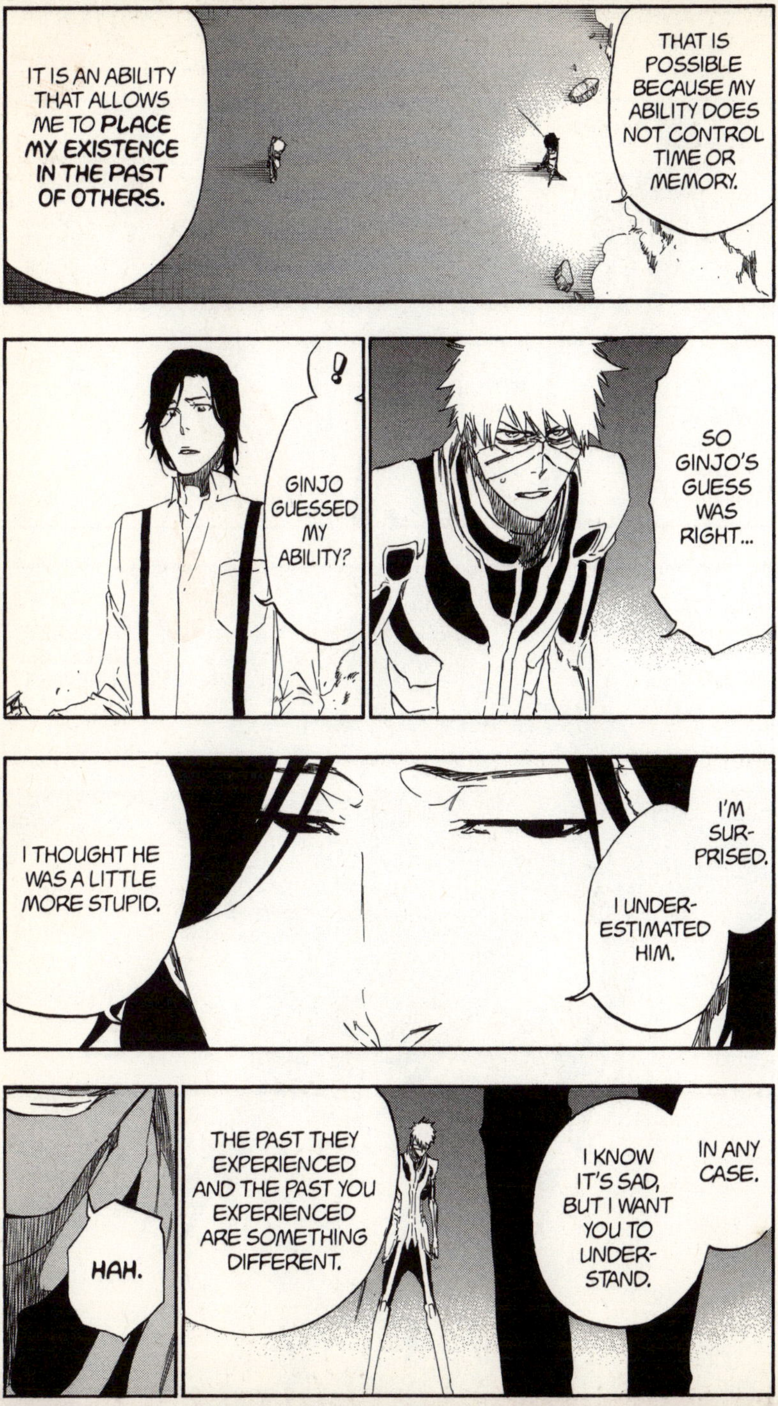
THAT IS POSSIBLE BECAUSE MY ABILITY DOES NOT CONTROL TIME OR MEMORY.
IT IS AN ABILITY THAT ALLOWS ME TO PLACE MY EXISTENCE IN THE PAST OF OTHERS.
SO GINJO'S GUESS WAS RIGHT...
!
GINJO GUESSED MY ABILITY?
I'M SURPRISED.
I UNDERESTIMATED HIM.
I THOUGHT HE WAS A LITTLE MORE STUPID.
IN ANY CASE.
I KNOW IT'S SAD, BUT I WANT YOU TO UNDERSTAND.
THE PAST THEY EXPERIENCED AND THE PAST YOU EXPERIENCED ARE SOMETHING DIFFERENT.
HAH.

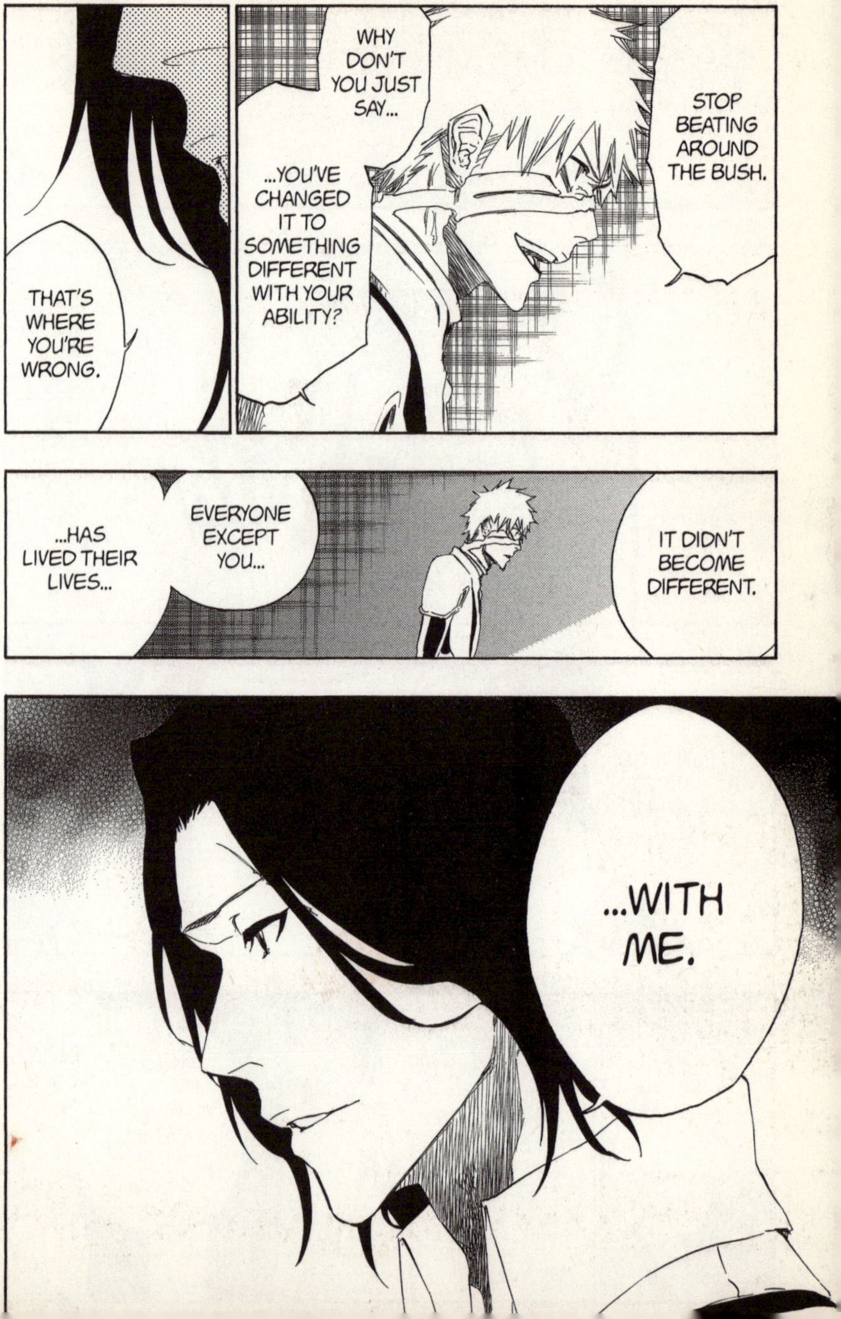
STOP BEATING AROUND THE BUSH.
WHY DON'T YOU JUST SAY...
...YOU'VE CHANGED IT TO SOMETHING DIFFERENT WITH YOUR ABILITY?
THAT'S WHERE YOU'RE WRONG.
IT DIDN'T BECOME DIFFERENT.
EVERYONE EXCEPT YOU...
...HAS LIVED THEIR LIVES...
...WITH ME.

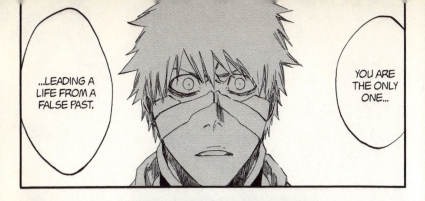

YOU ARE THE ONLY ONE...
...LEADING A LIFE FROM A FALSE PAST.
YOU MUST BE SAD THAT IT'S ONLY DIFFERENT FOR YOU.
BUT YOU DON'T HAVE TO WORRY.
SOON...
...THAT SADNESS WILL HAVE NEVER EXISTED IN THE FIRST PLACE.

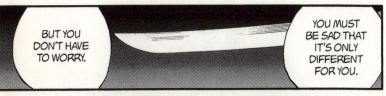

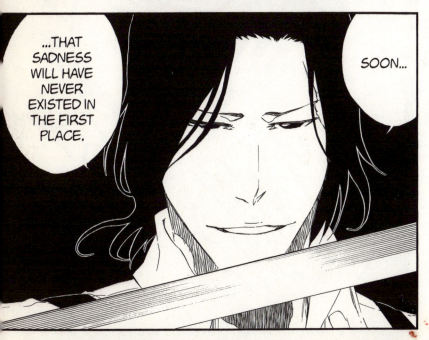

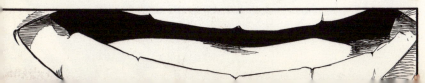

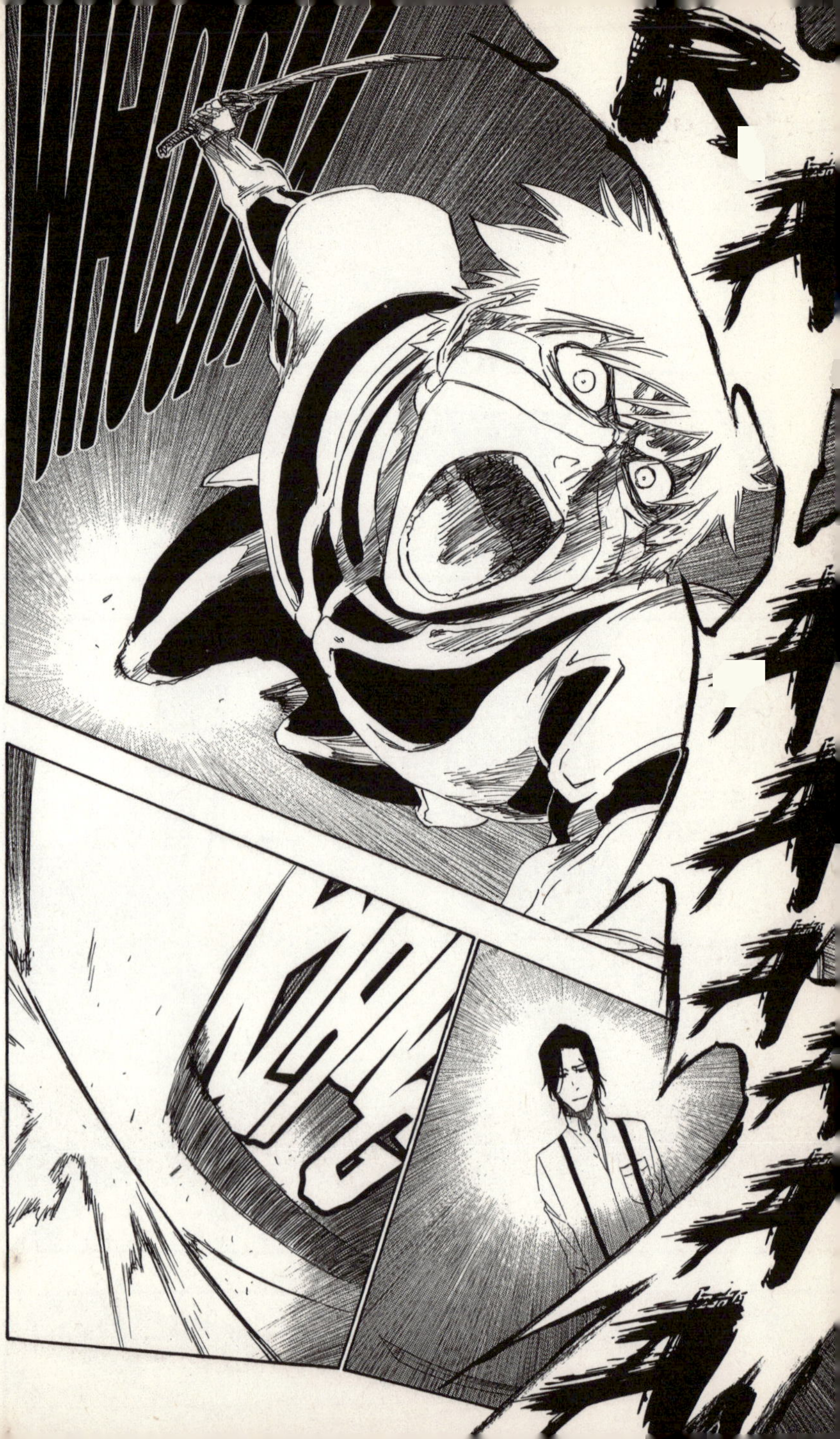

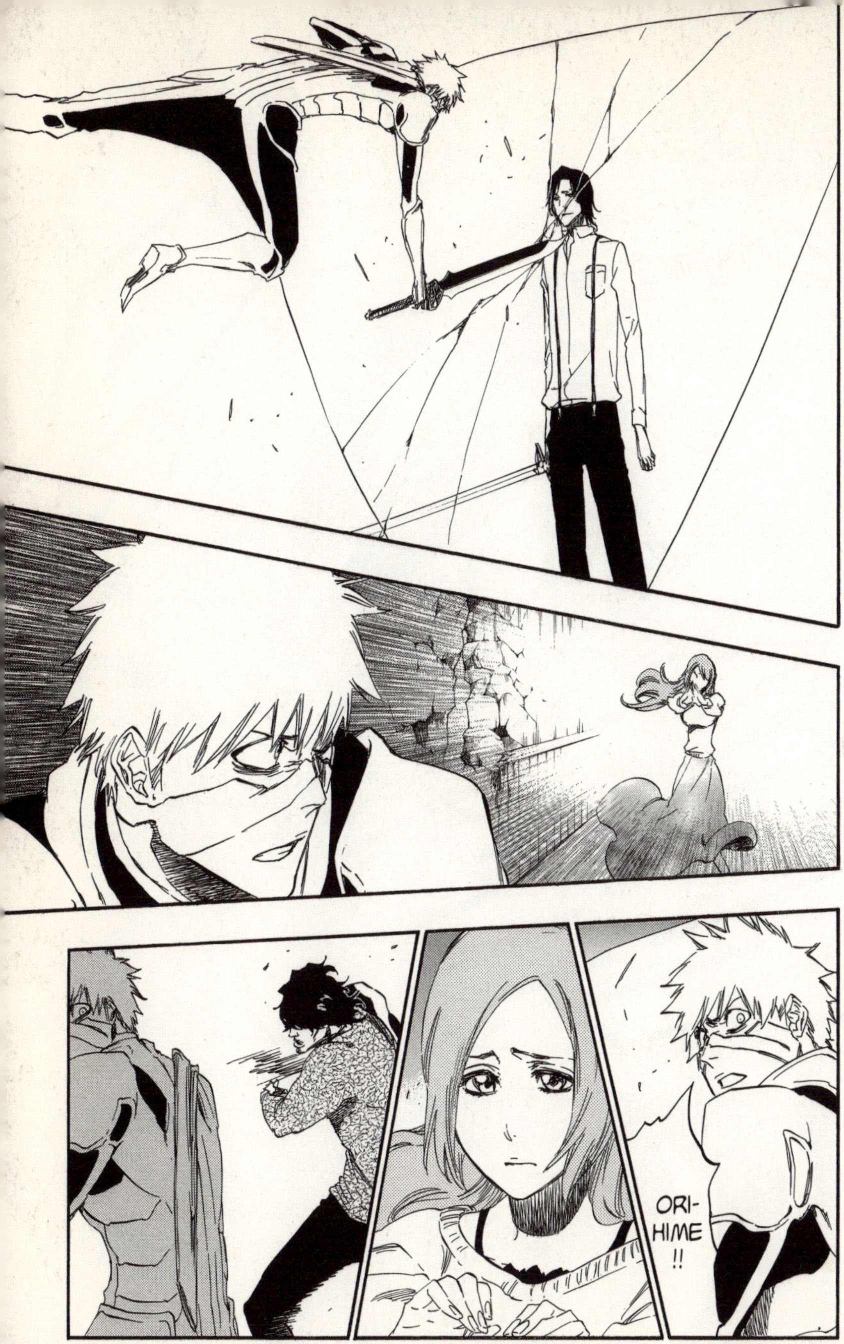
ORI-
HIME
!!

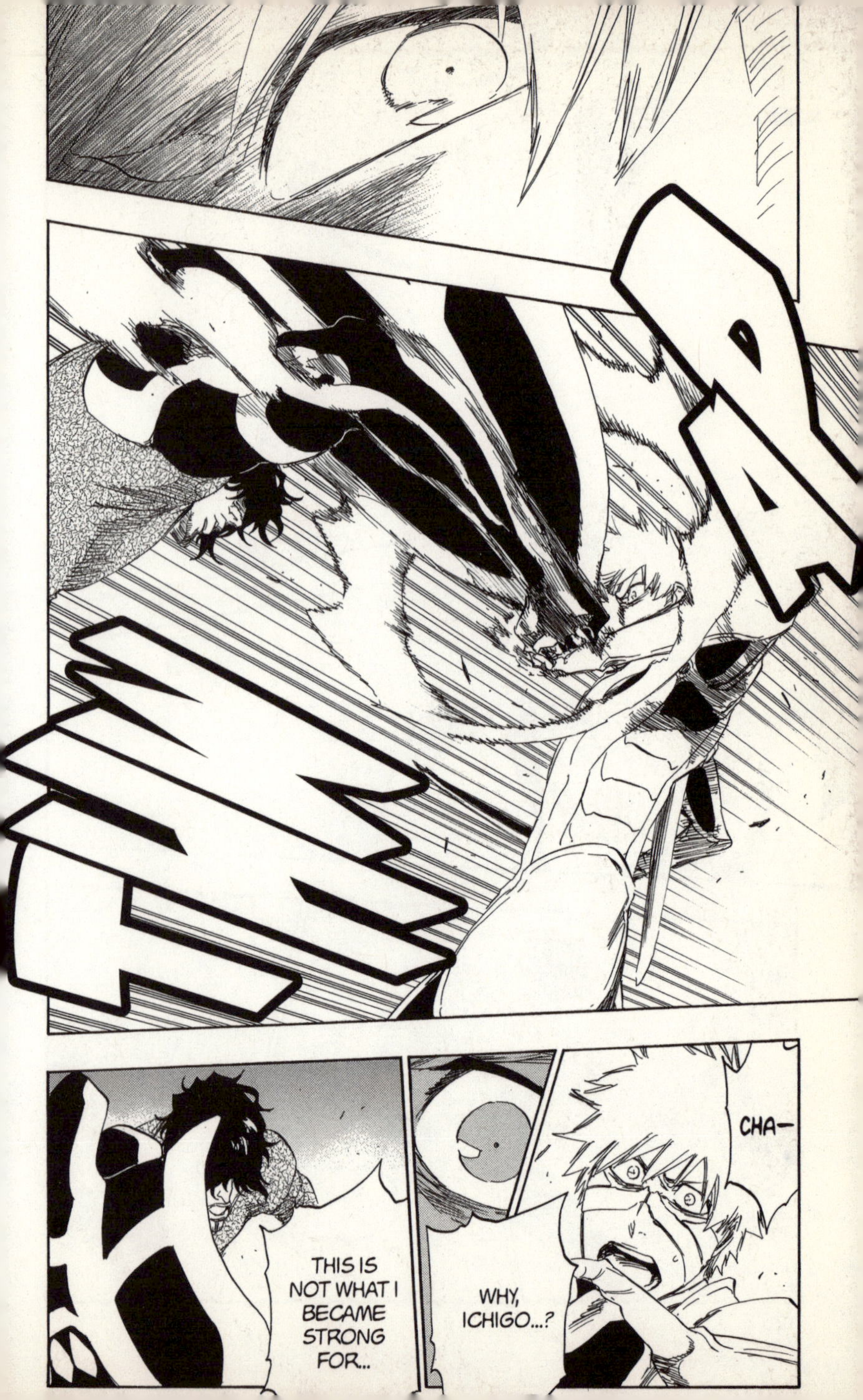
CHA—
WHY, ICHIGO...?
THIS IS NOT WHAT I BECAME STRONG FOR...

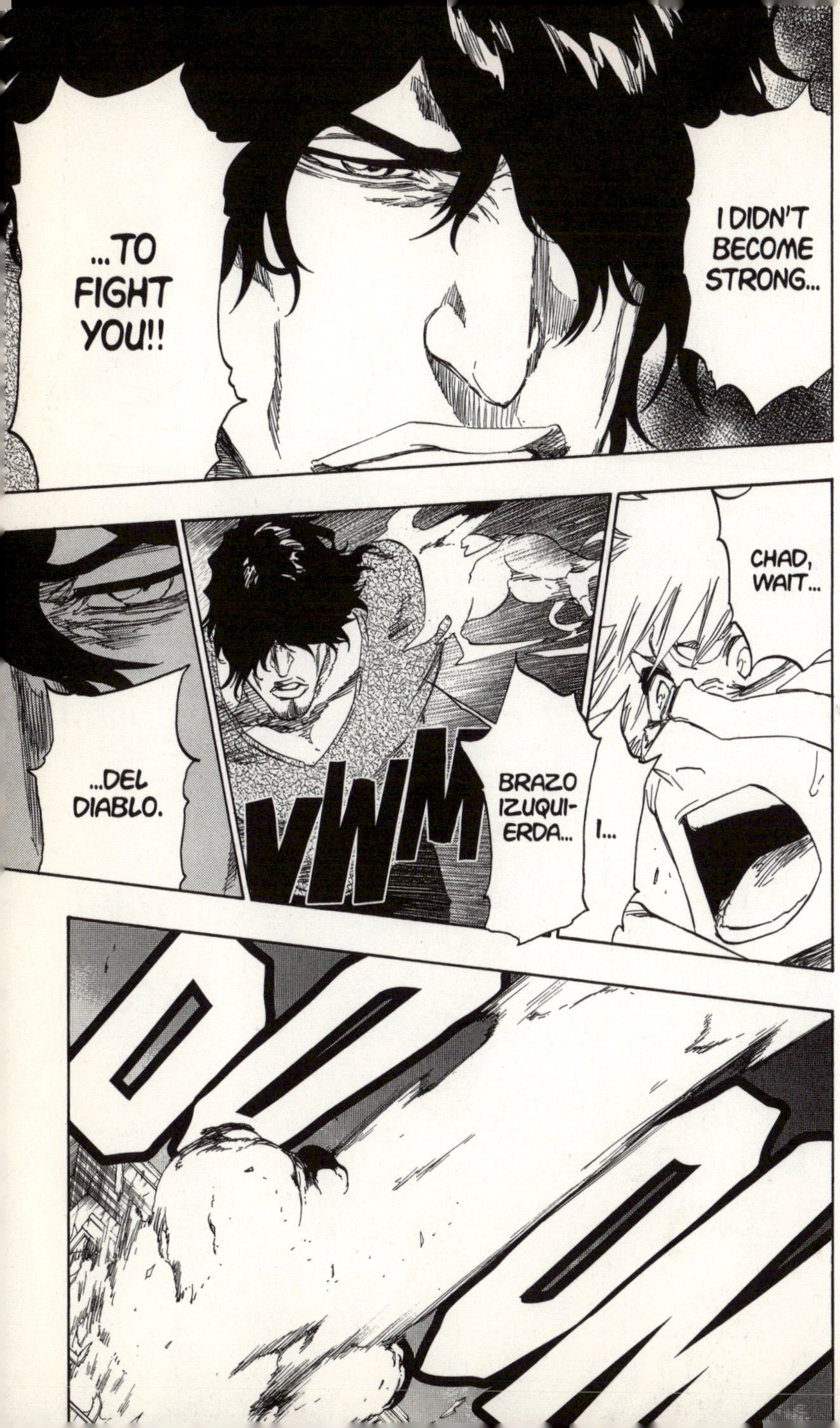
I DIDN'T BECOME STRONG...
...TO FIGHT YOU!!
CHAD, WAIT...
I...
BRAZO IZUQUIERDA...
VWM
...DEL DIABLO.

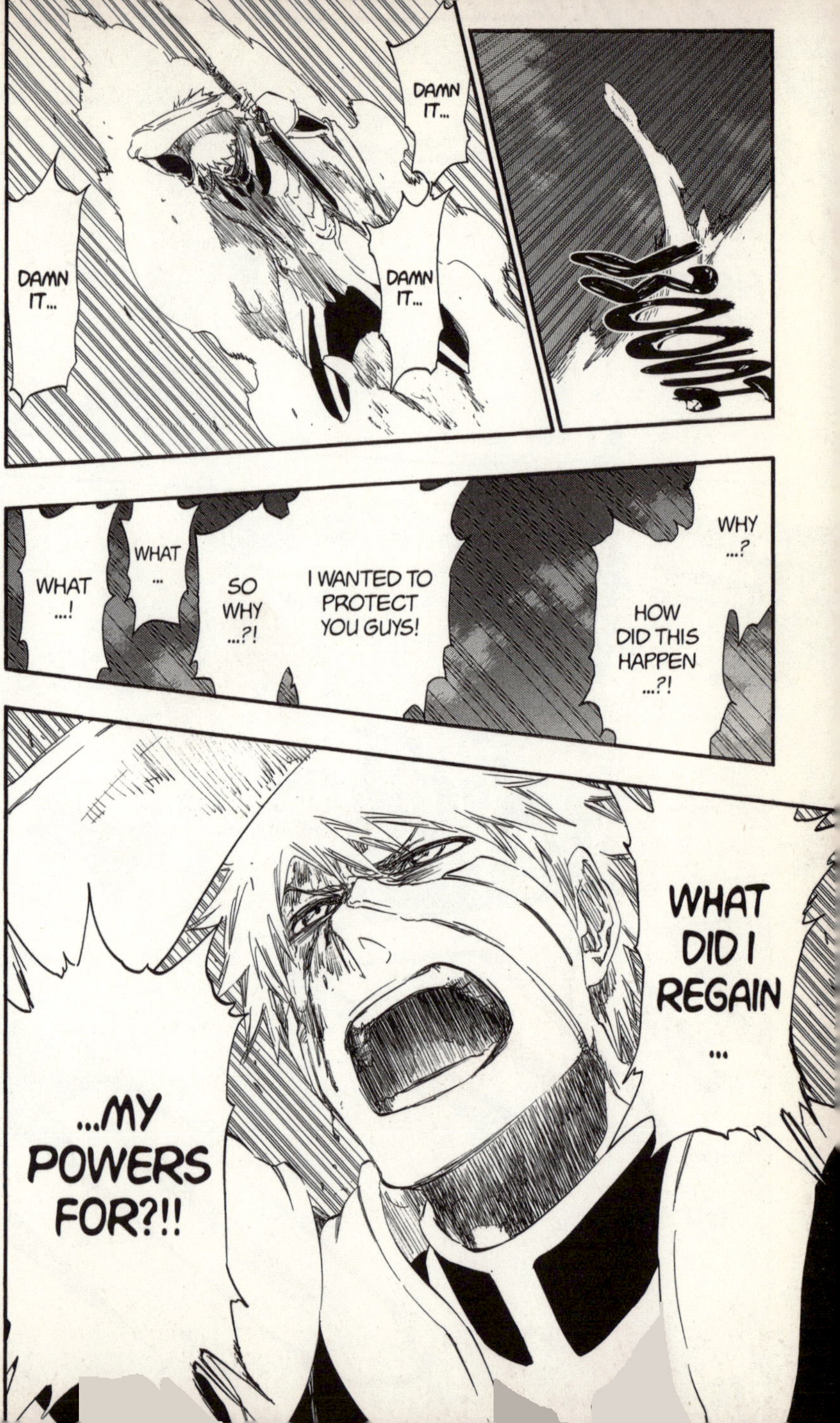
DAMN IT...
DAMN IT...
DAMN IT...
WHY ...?
HOW DID THIS HAPPEN ...?!
I WANTED TO PROTECT YOU GUYS!
SO WHY ...?!
WHAT ...
WHAT ...!
WHAT DID I REGAIN ...
...MY POWERS FOR?!!

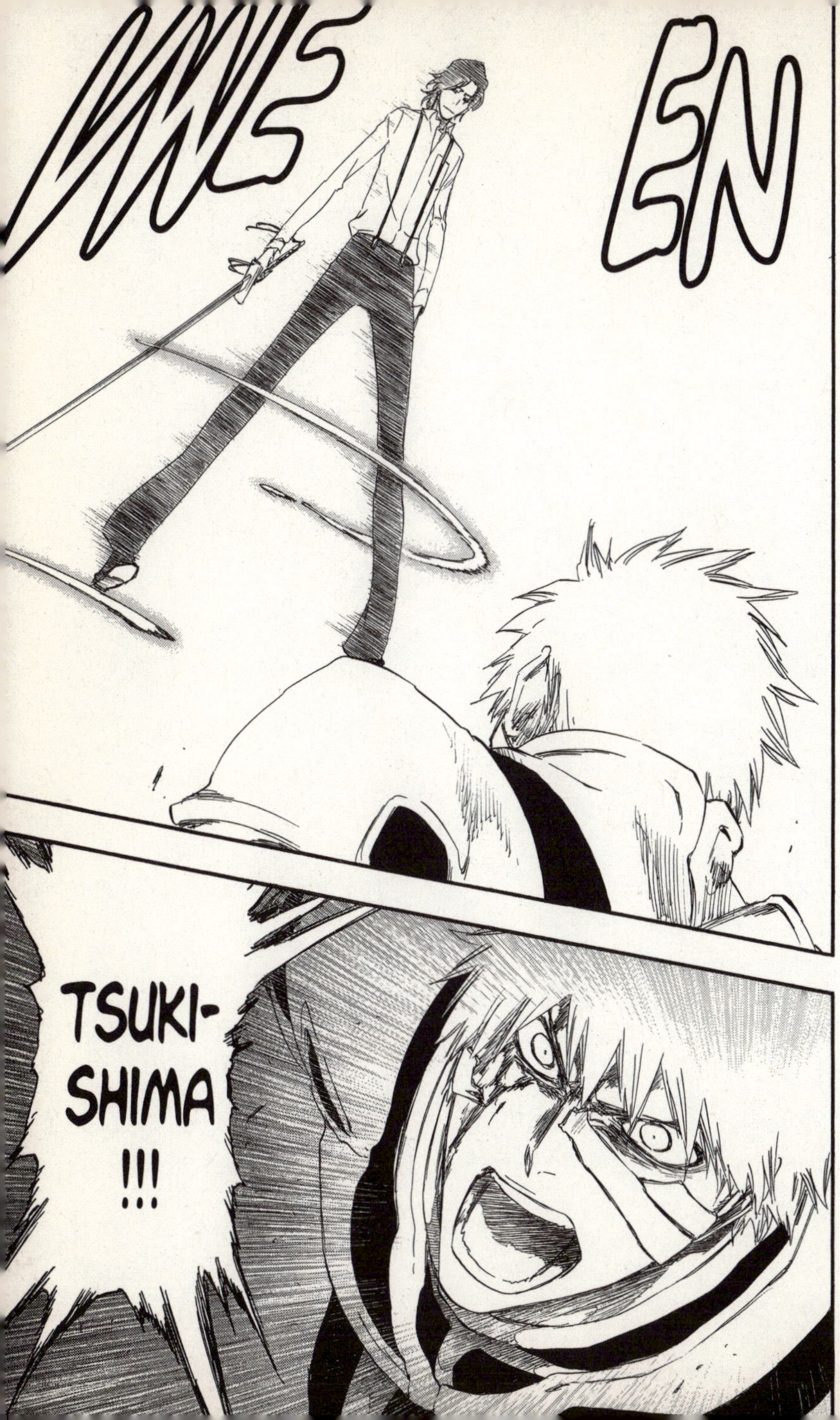
EN
WAVE
TSUKI-
SHIMA
!!!

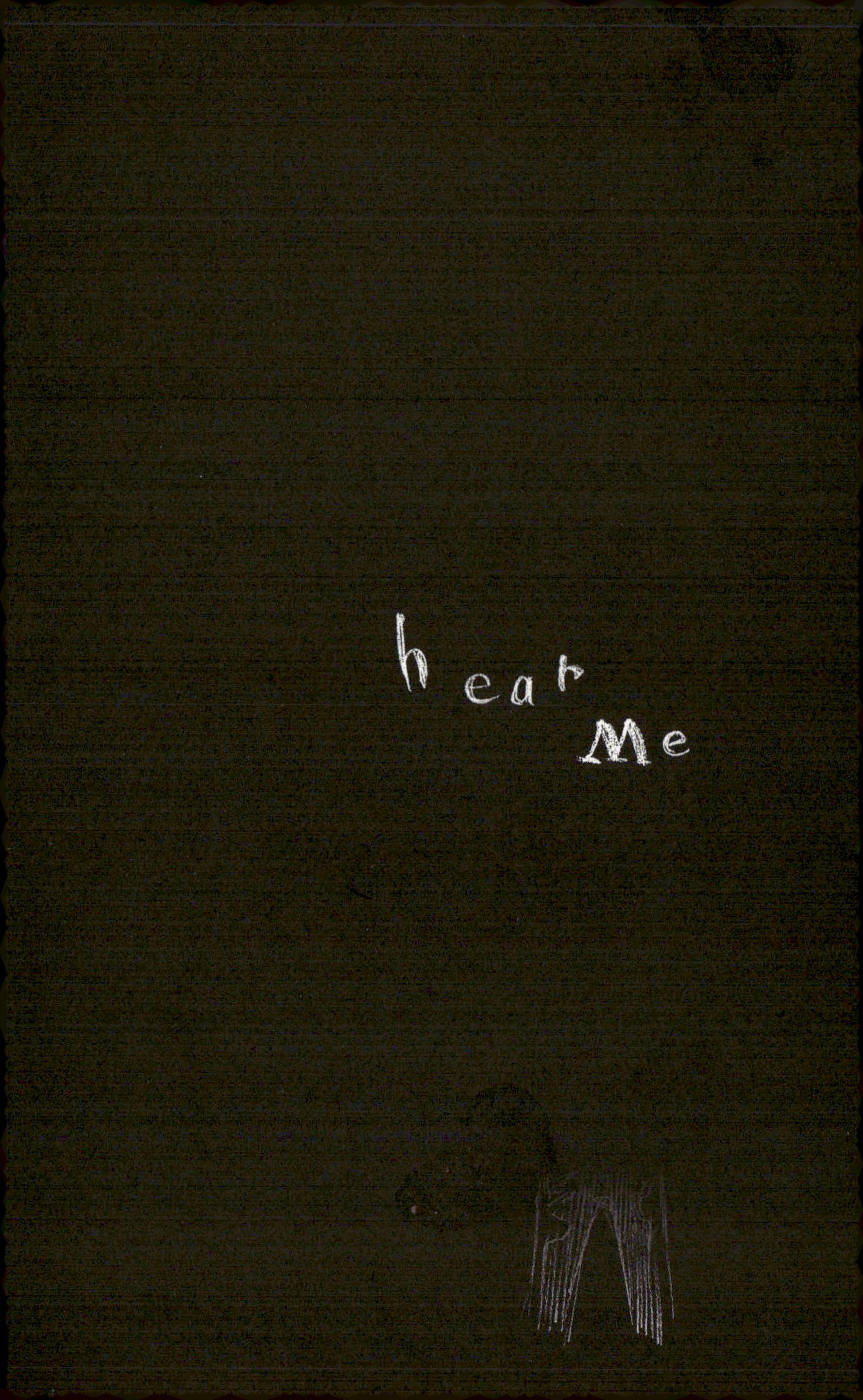
hear Me

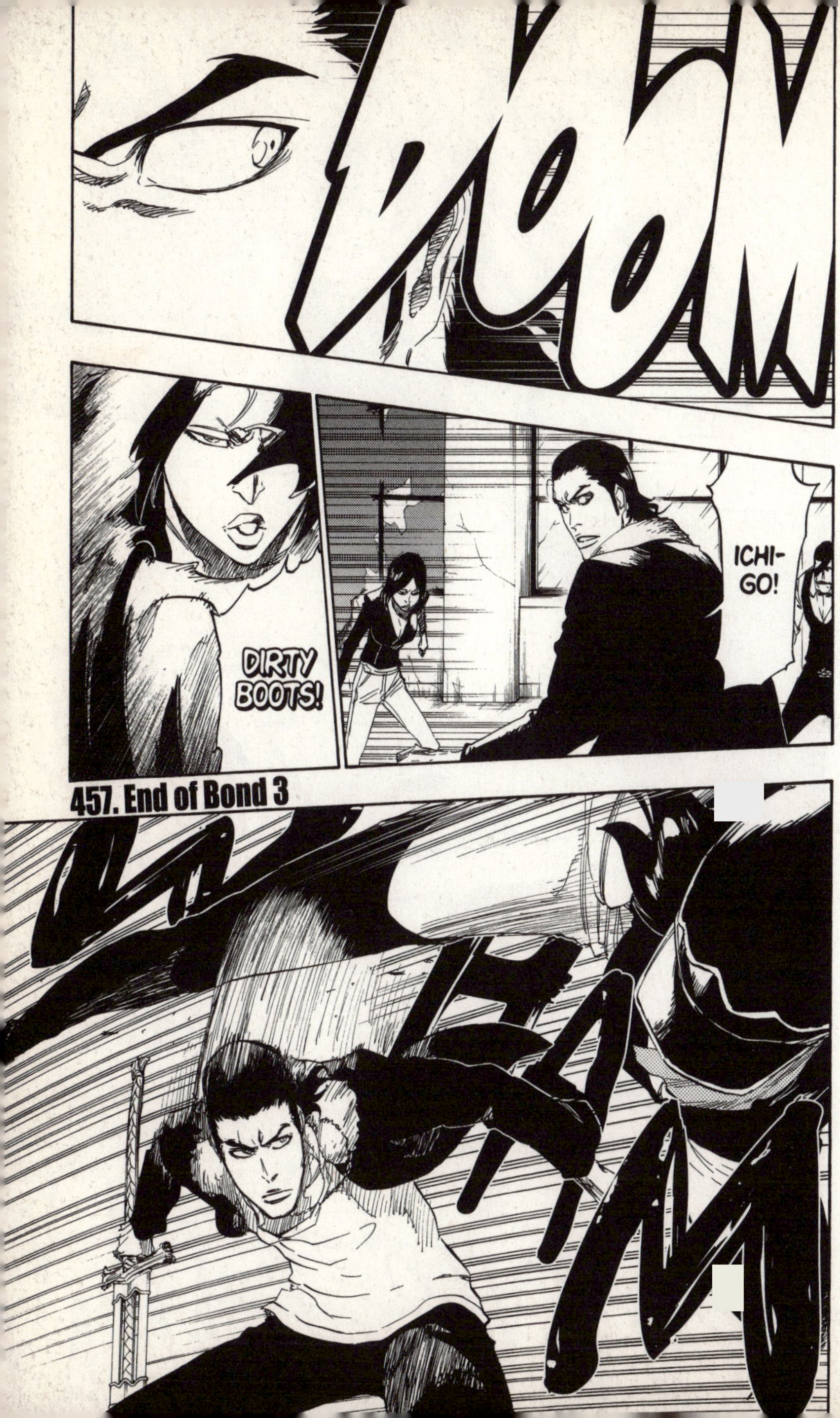
ICHI-GO!
DIRTY BOOTS!
457. End of Bond 3

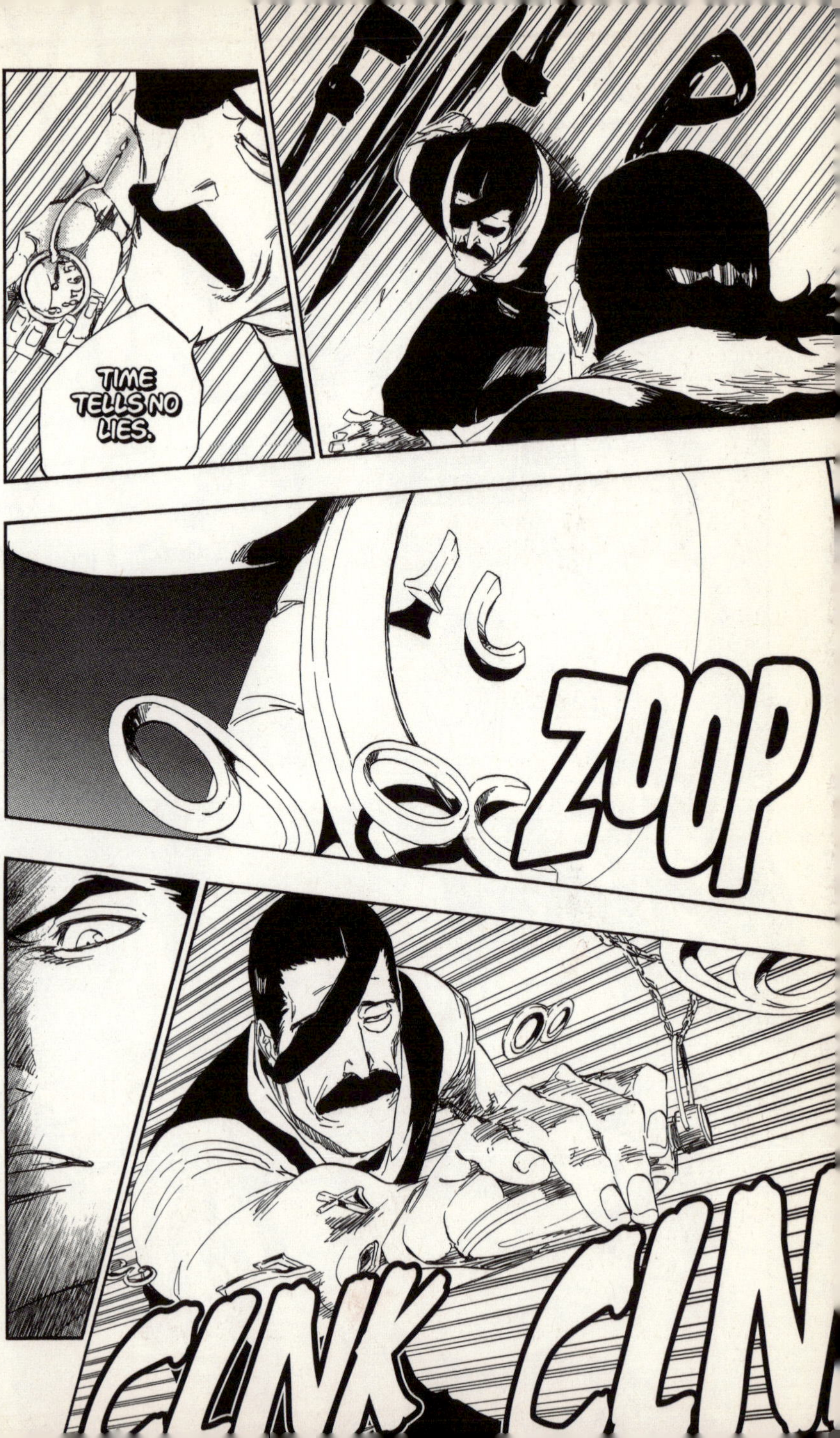

TIME TELLS NO LIES.
ZOOP
CLINK CLIN

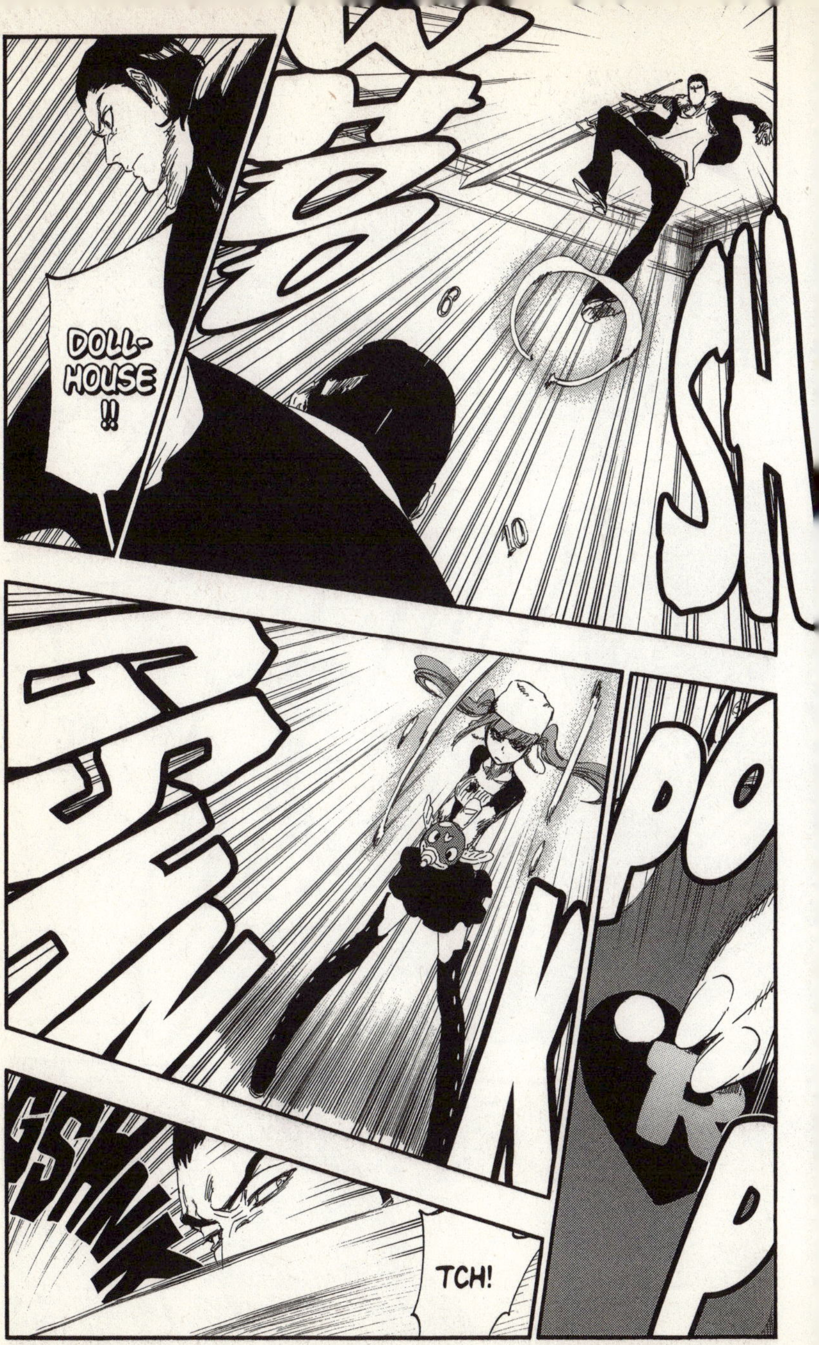
DOLL-
HOUSE
!!
TCH!

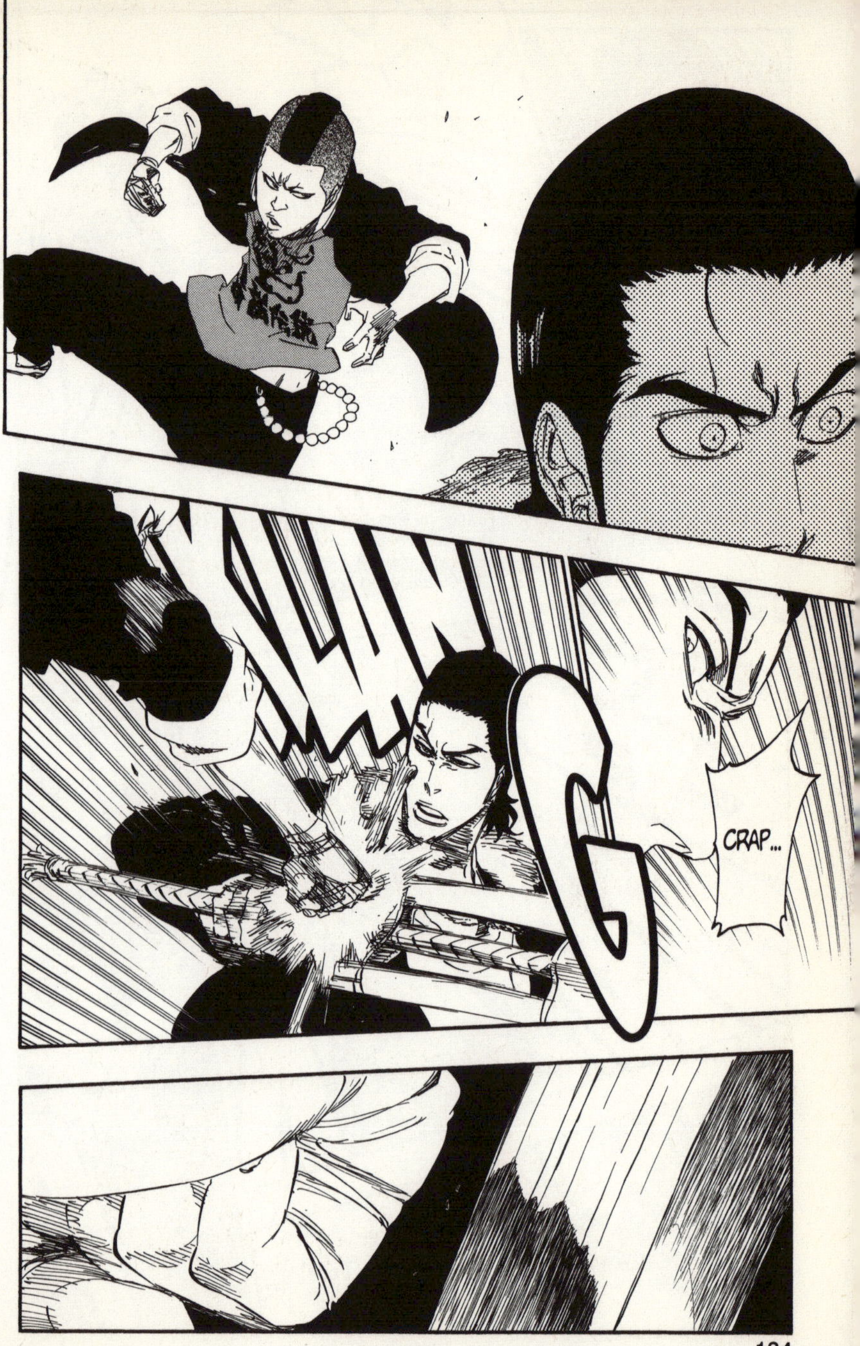
CRAP...

READ THIS WAY

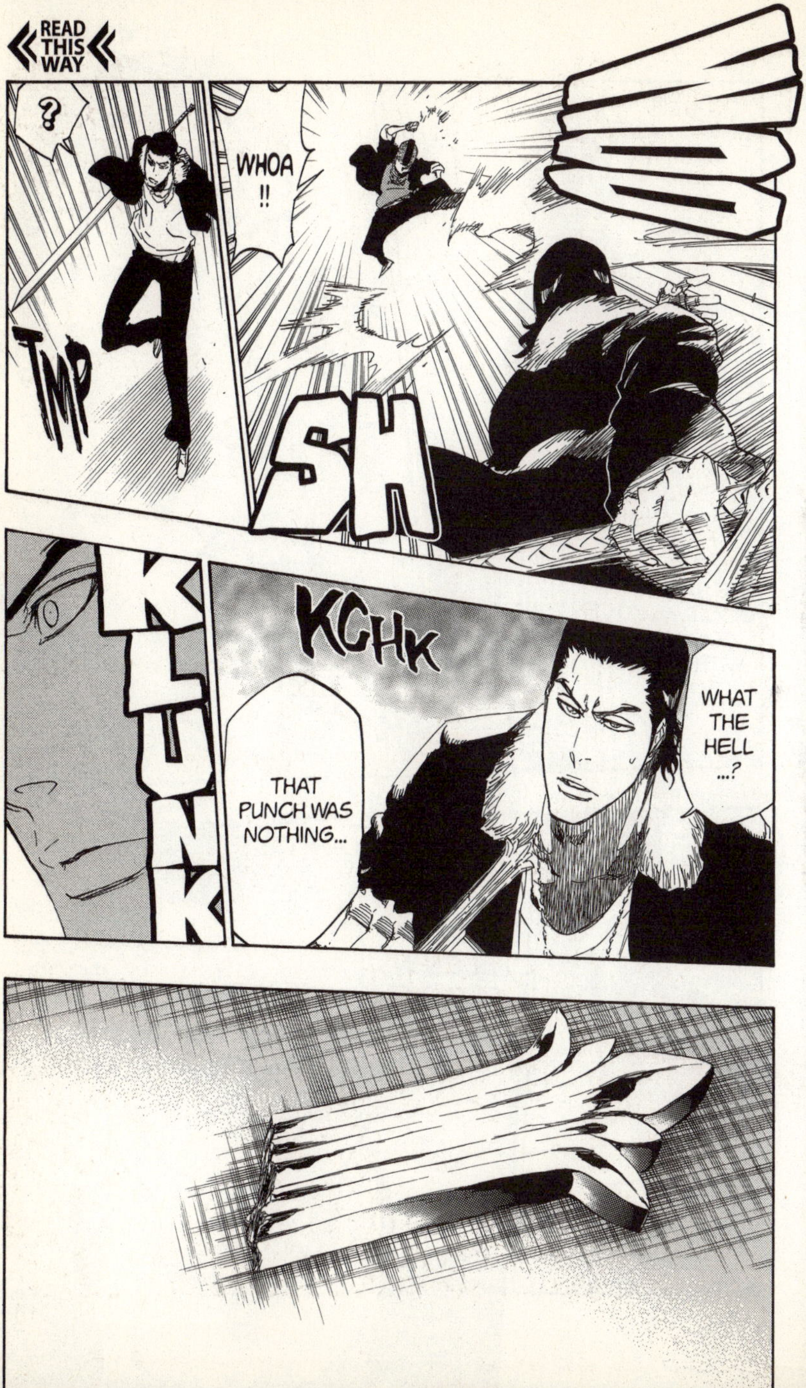
WHOA !!
SH
?
TMP
KCHK
WHAT THE HELL ...?
THAT PUNCH WAS NOTHING...
KLUNK

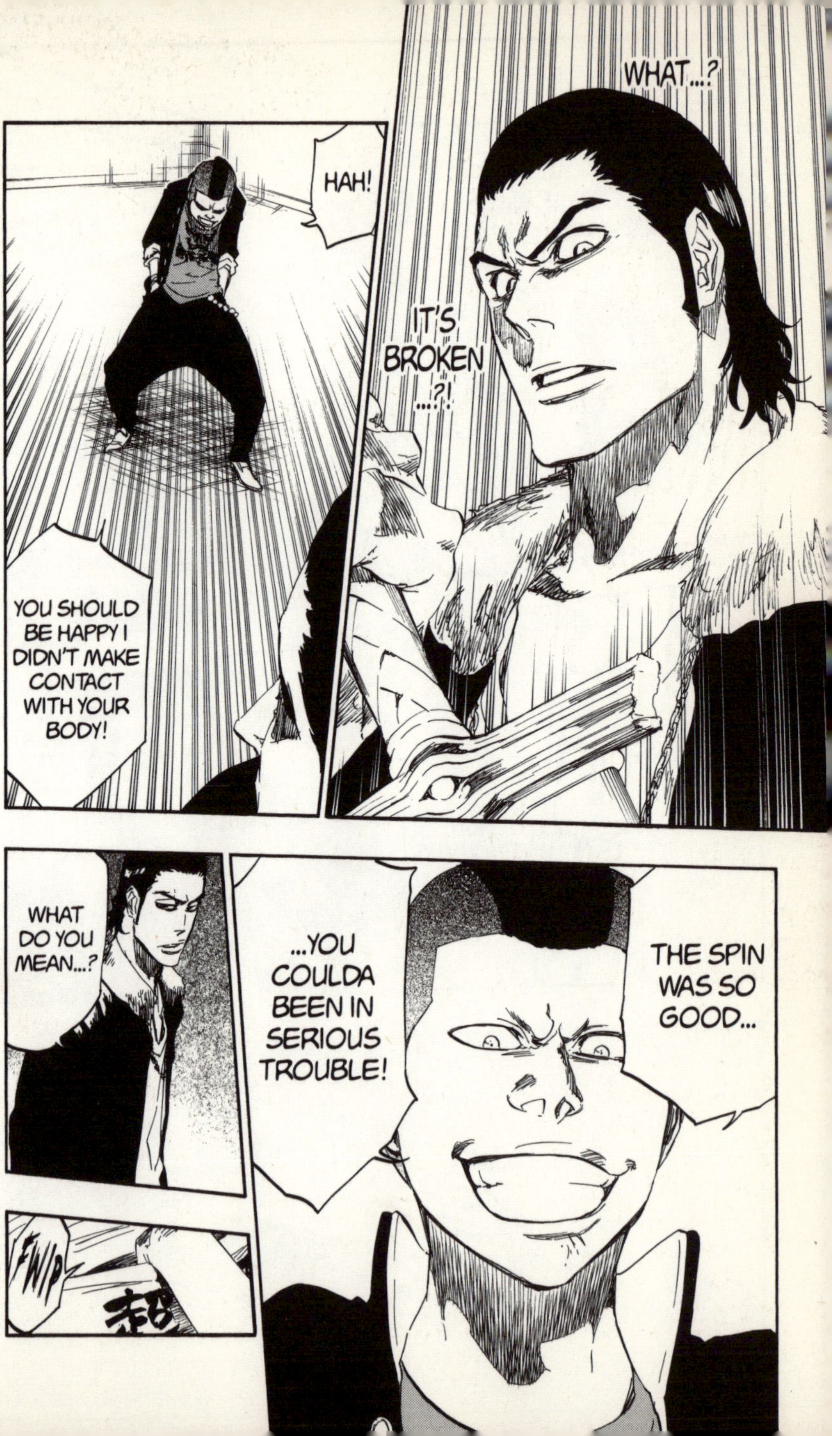
WHAT...?
IT'S BROKEN ...?!
HAH!
YOU SHOULD BE HAPPY I DIDN'T MAKE CONTACT WITH YOUR BODY!
THE SPIN WAS SO GOOD...
...YOU COULDA BEEN IN SERIOUS TROUBLE!
WHAT DO YOU MEAN...?
FWIP

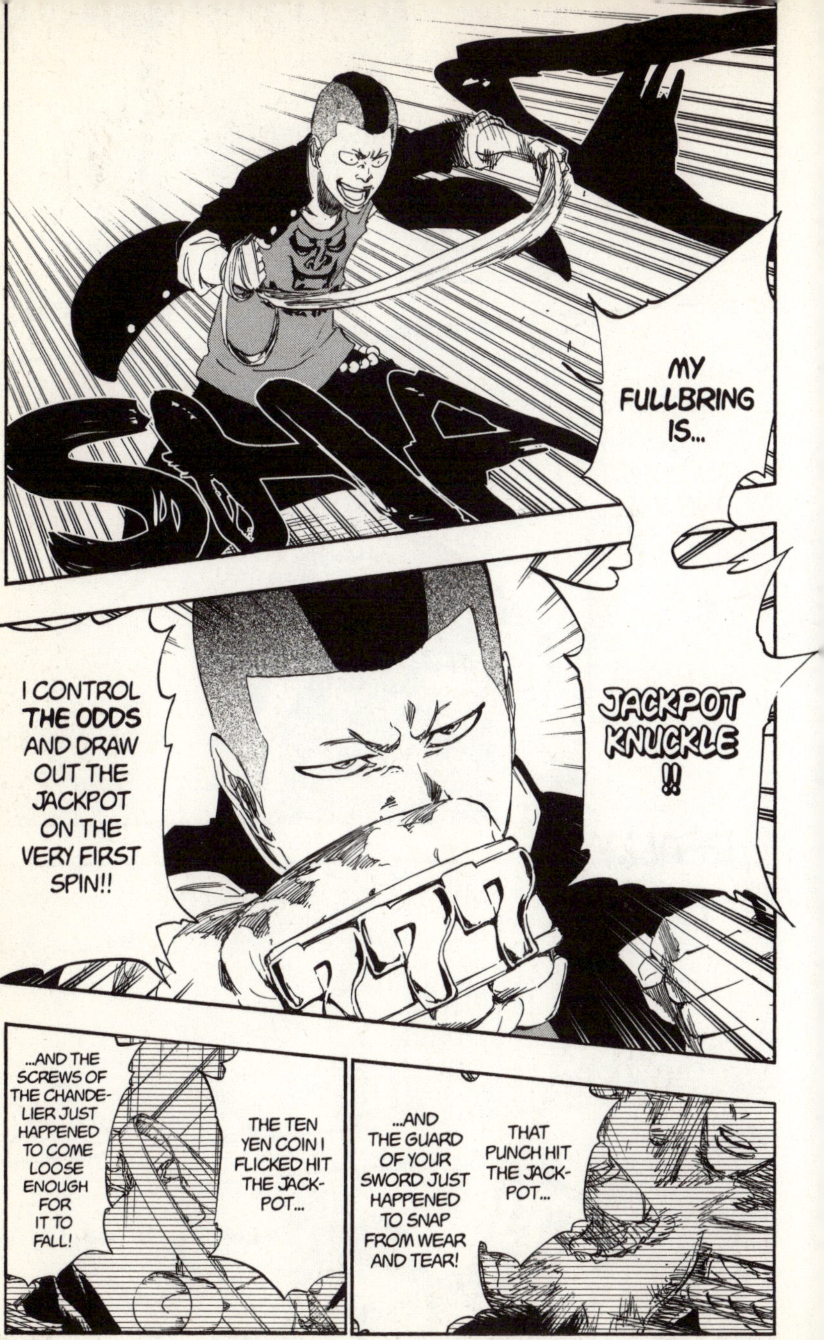
MY FULLBRING IS...
JACKPOT KNUCKLE!!
I CONTROL THE ODDS AND DRAW OUT THE JACKPOT ON THE VERY FIRST SPIN!!
THAT PUNCH HIT THE JACK-POT...
...AND THE GUARD OF YOUR SWORD JUST HAPPENED TO SNAP FROM WEAR AND TEAR!
THE TEN YEN COIN I FLICKED HIT THE JACK-POT...
...AND THE SCREWS OF THE CHANDE-LIER JUST HAPPENED TO COME LOOSE ENOUGH FOR IT TO FALL!

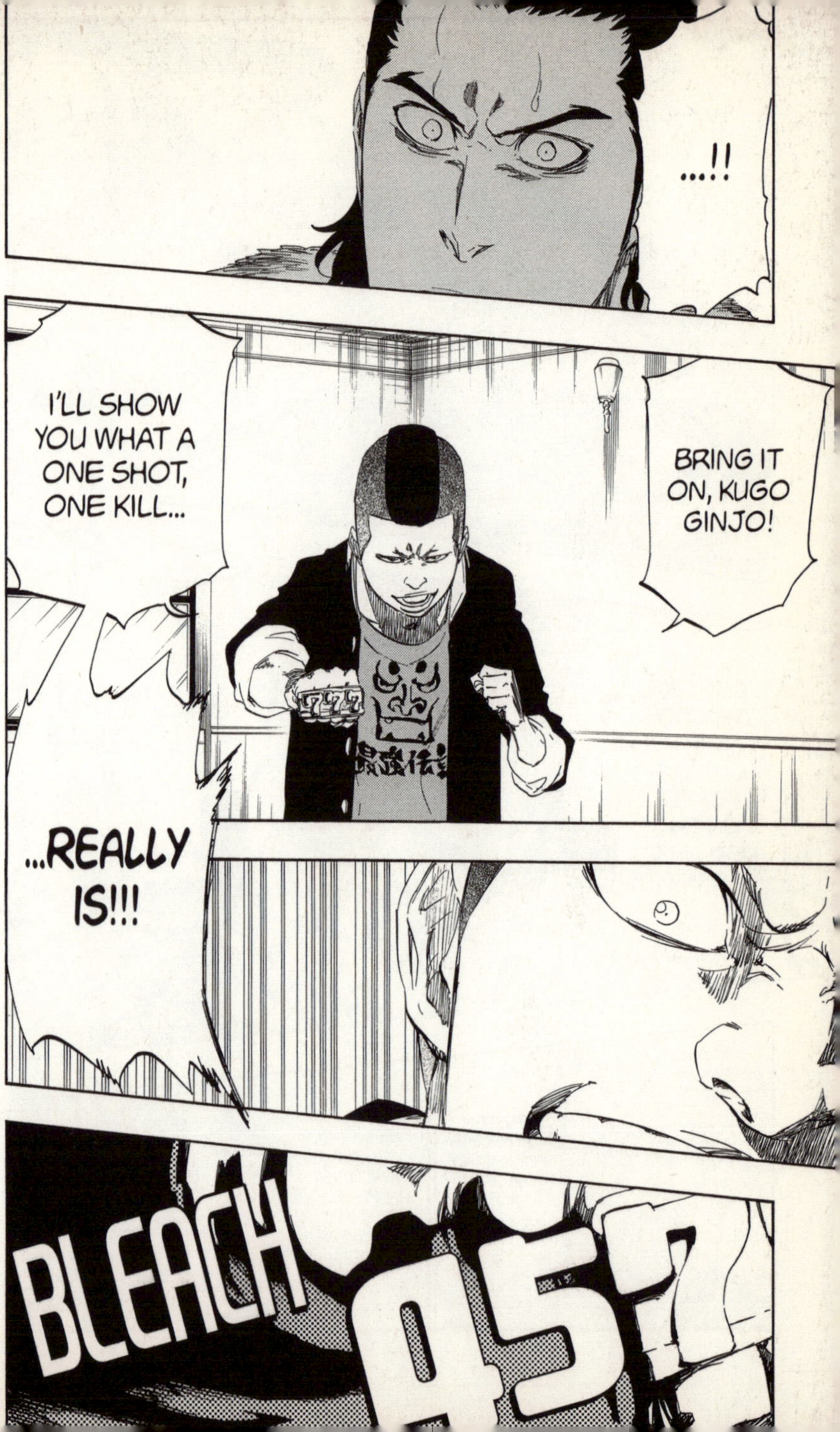
...!!
BRING IT ON, KUGO GINJO!
I'LL SHOW YOU WHAT A ONE SHOT, ONE KILL...
...REALLY IS!!!
BLEACH

# End of Bond 3

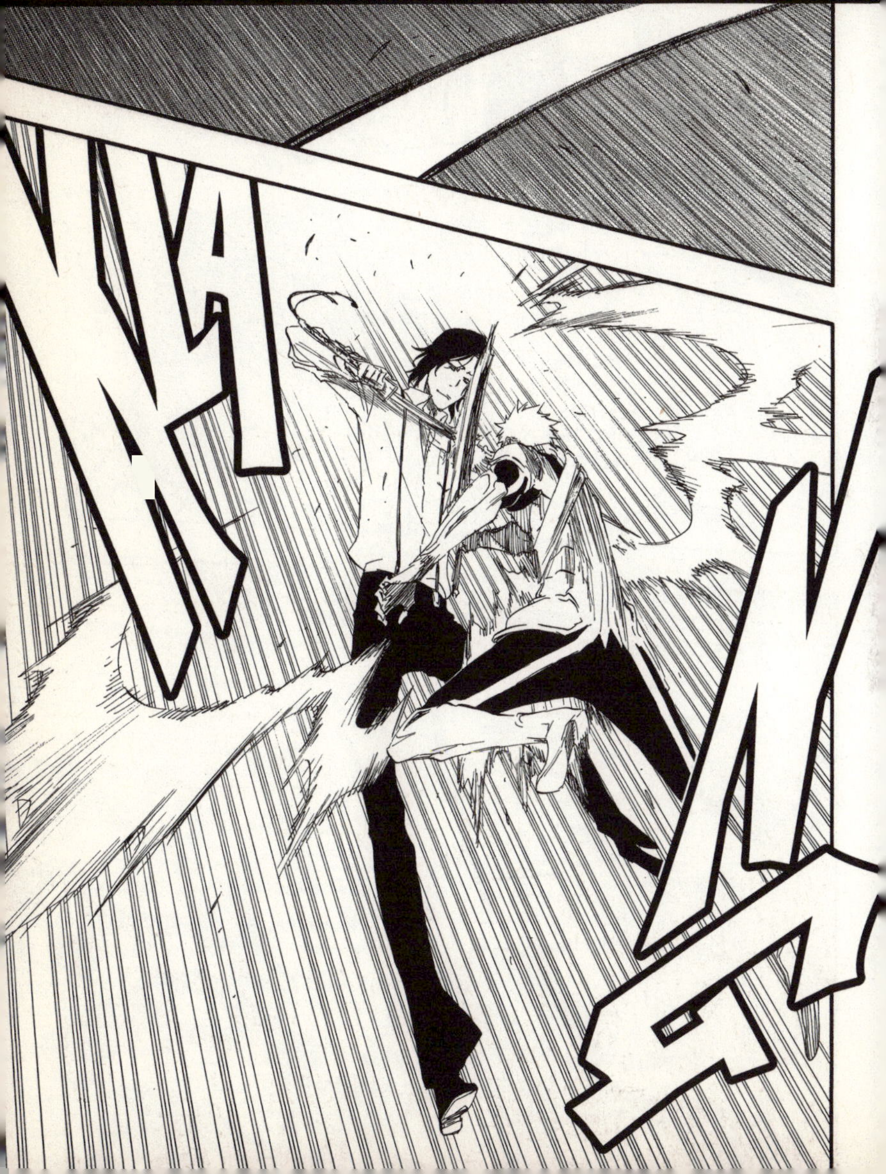

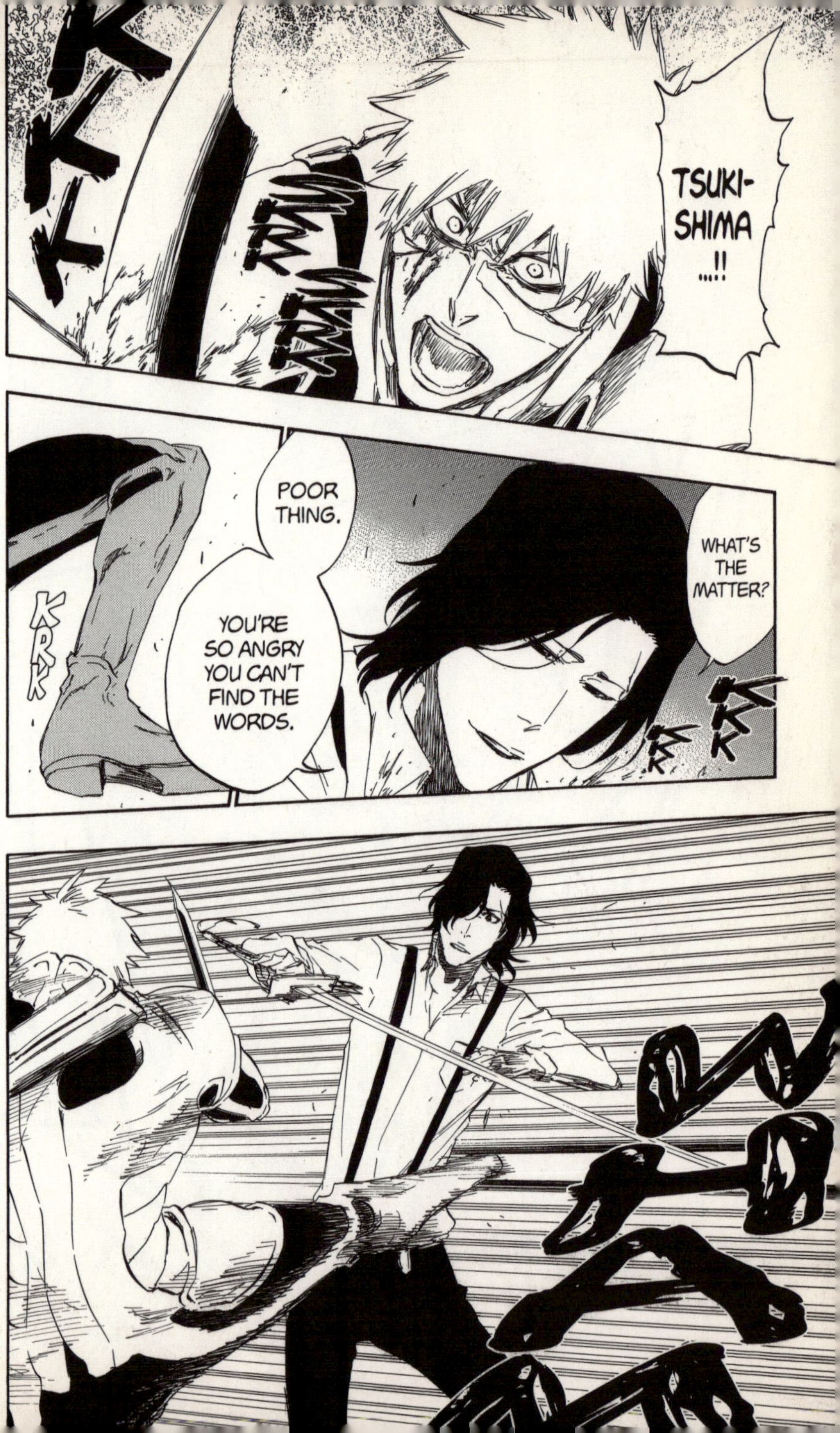
TSUKI-SHIMA ...!!
KRSSSH
K K K
WHAT'S THE MATTER?
KRK
POOR THING.
YOU'RE SO ANGRY YOU CAN'T FIND THE WORDS.
KRK

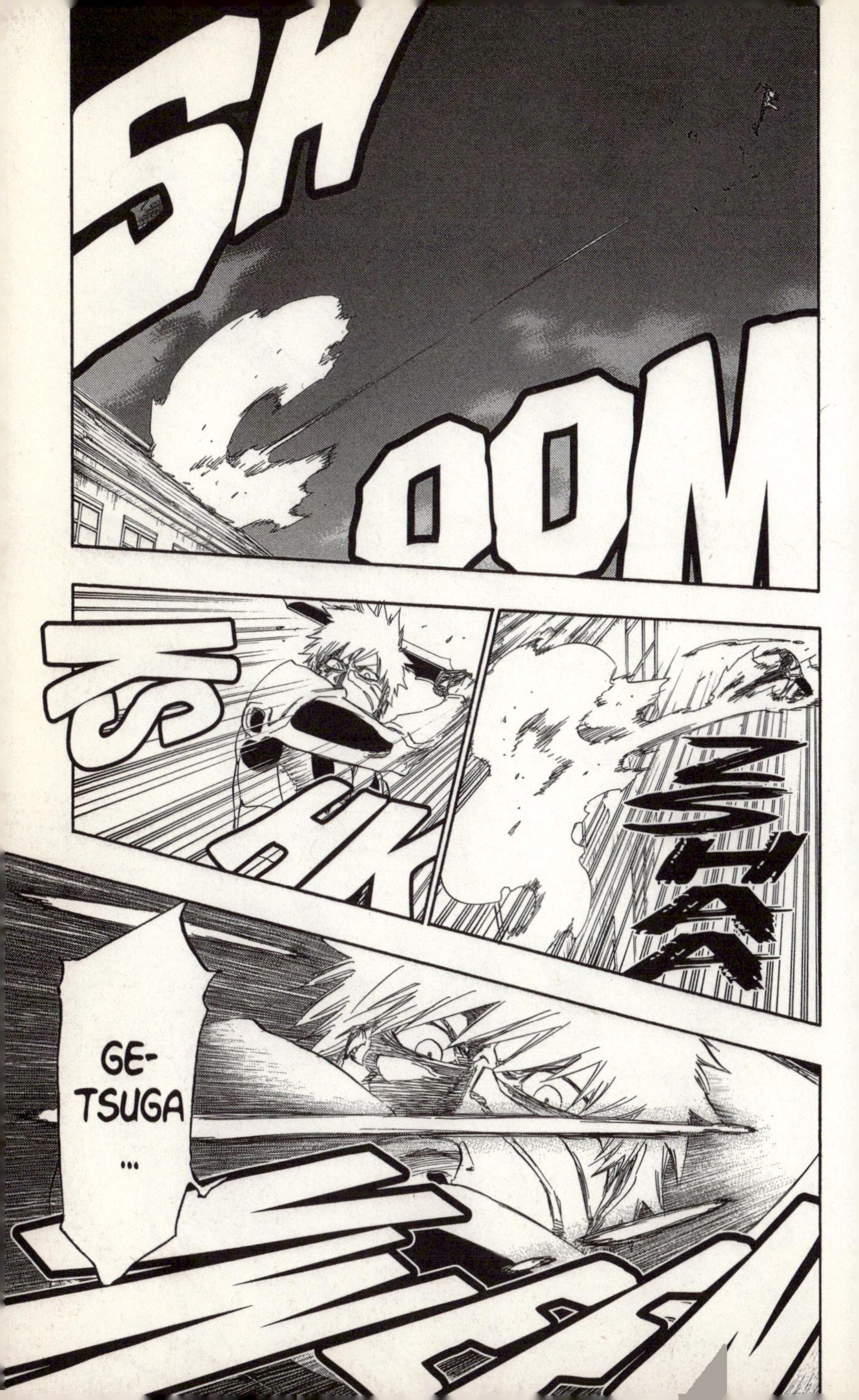

SHOOM
KSSHK
ZSHAA
GE-
TSUGA
...

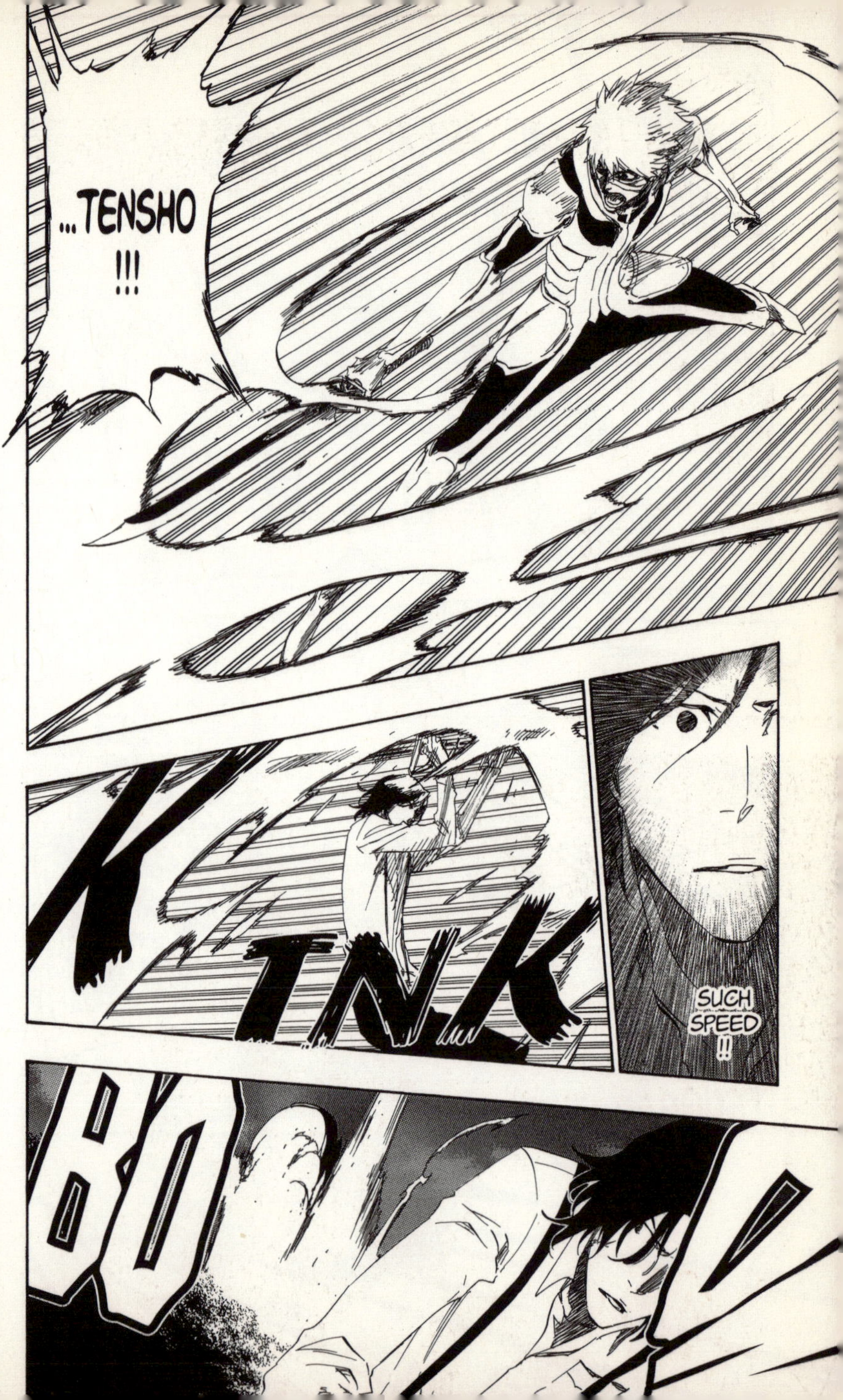
...TENSHO
!!!
SUCH SPEED
!!
TNK

READ THIS WAY

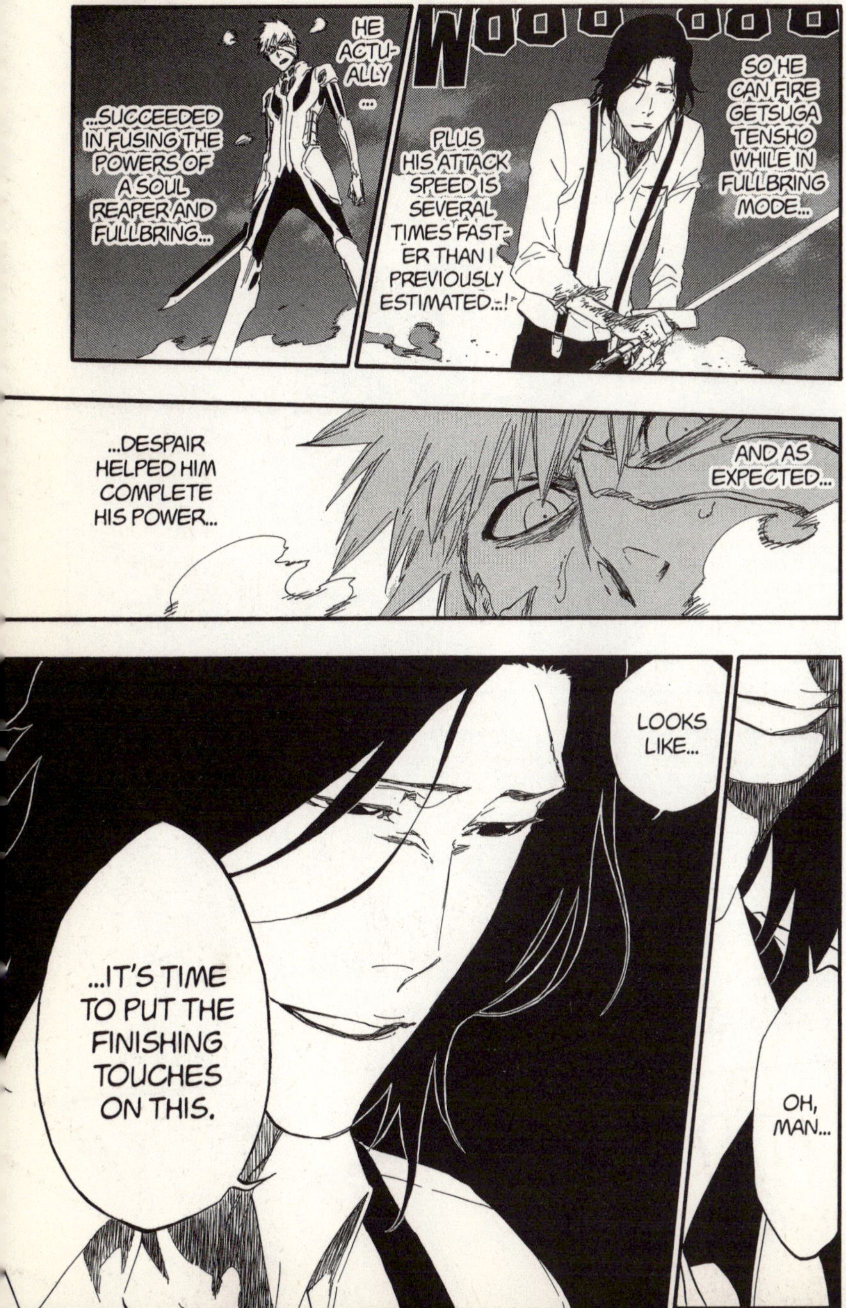
SO HE CAN FIRE GETSUGA TENSHO WHILE IN FULLBRING MODE...
PLUS HIS ATTACK SPEED IS SEVERAL TIMES FASTER THAN I PREVIOUSLY ESTIMATED...!
HE ACTUALLY...
...SUCCEEDED IN FUSING THE POWERS OF A SOUL REAPER AND FULLBRING...
AND AS EXPECTED...
...DESPAIR HELPED HIM COMPLETE HIS POWER...
OH, MAN...
LOOKS LIKE...
...IT'S TIME TO PUT THE FINISHING TOUCHES ON THIS.

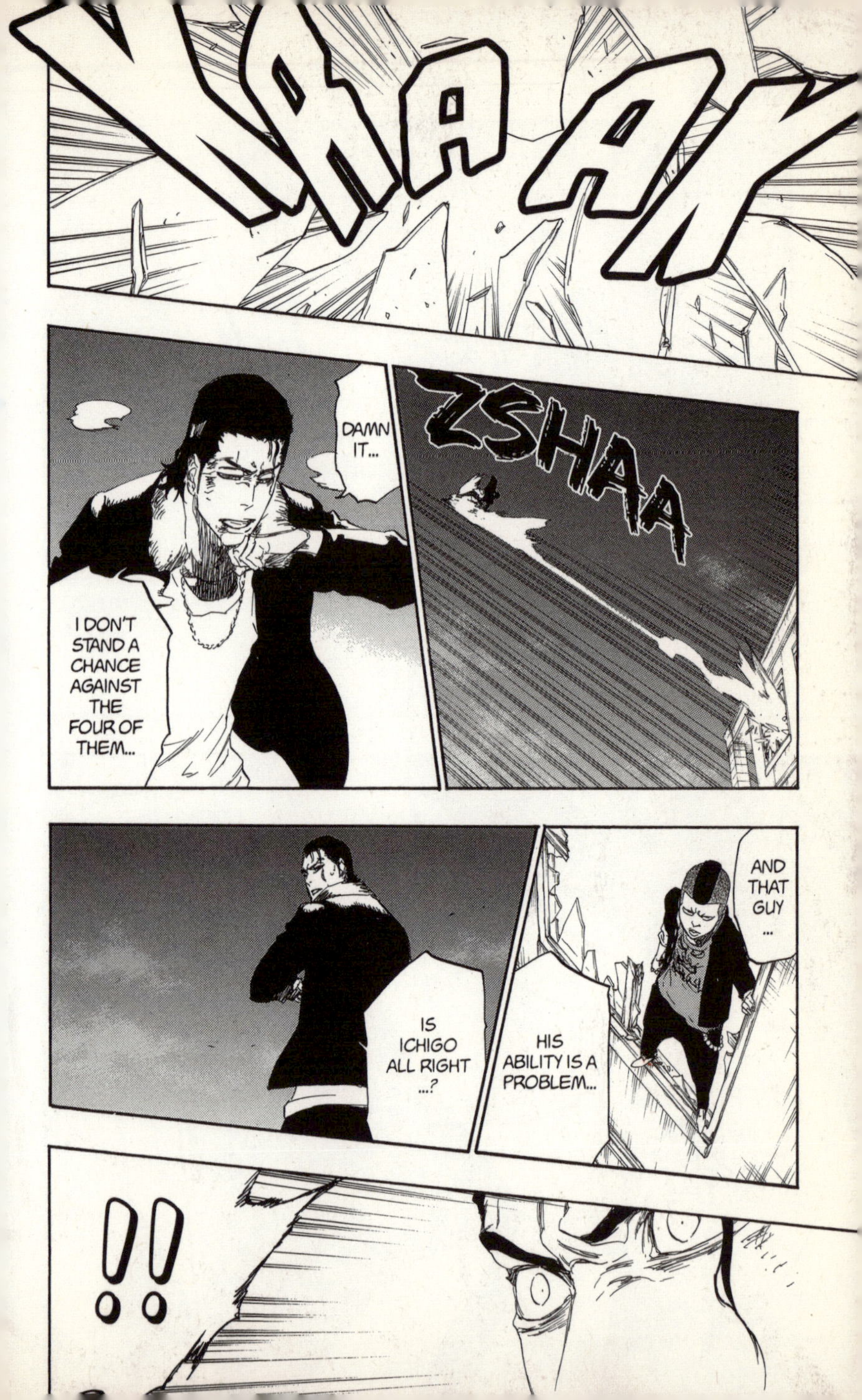
ZSHAA
DAMN IT...
I DON'T STAND A CHANCE AGAINST THE FOUR OF THEM...
AND THAT GUY ...
HIS ABILITY IS A PROBLEM...
IS ICHIGO ALL RIGHT ...?
!!

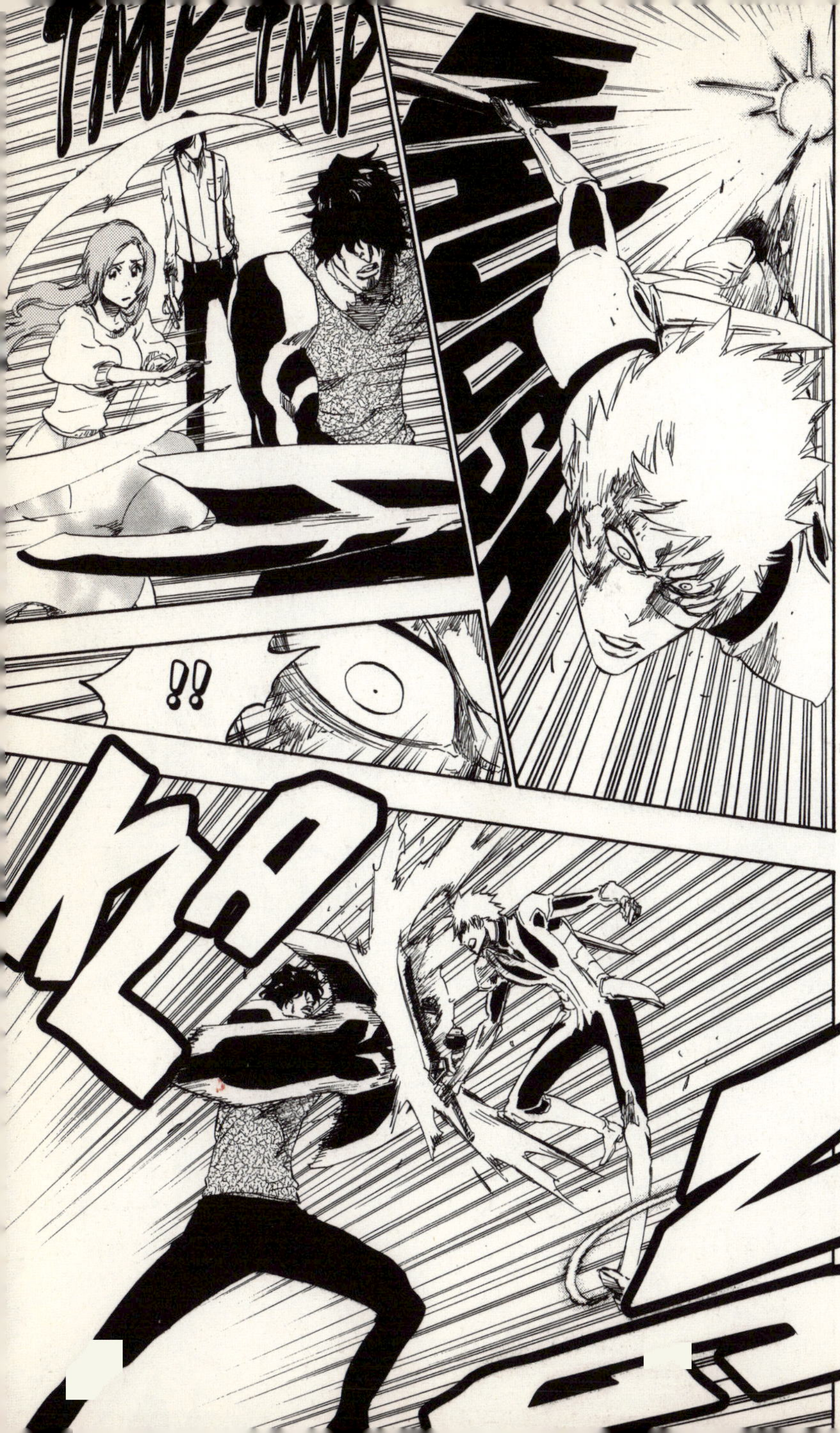
TMP TMP
!!
KA

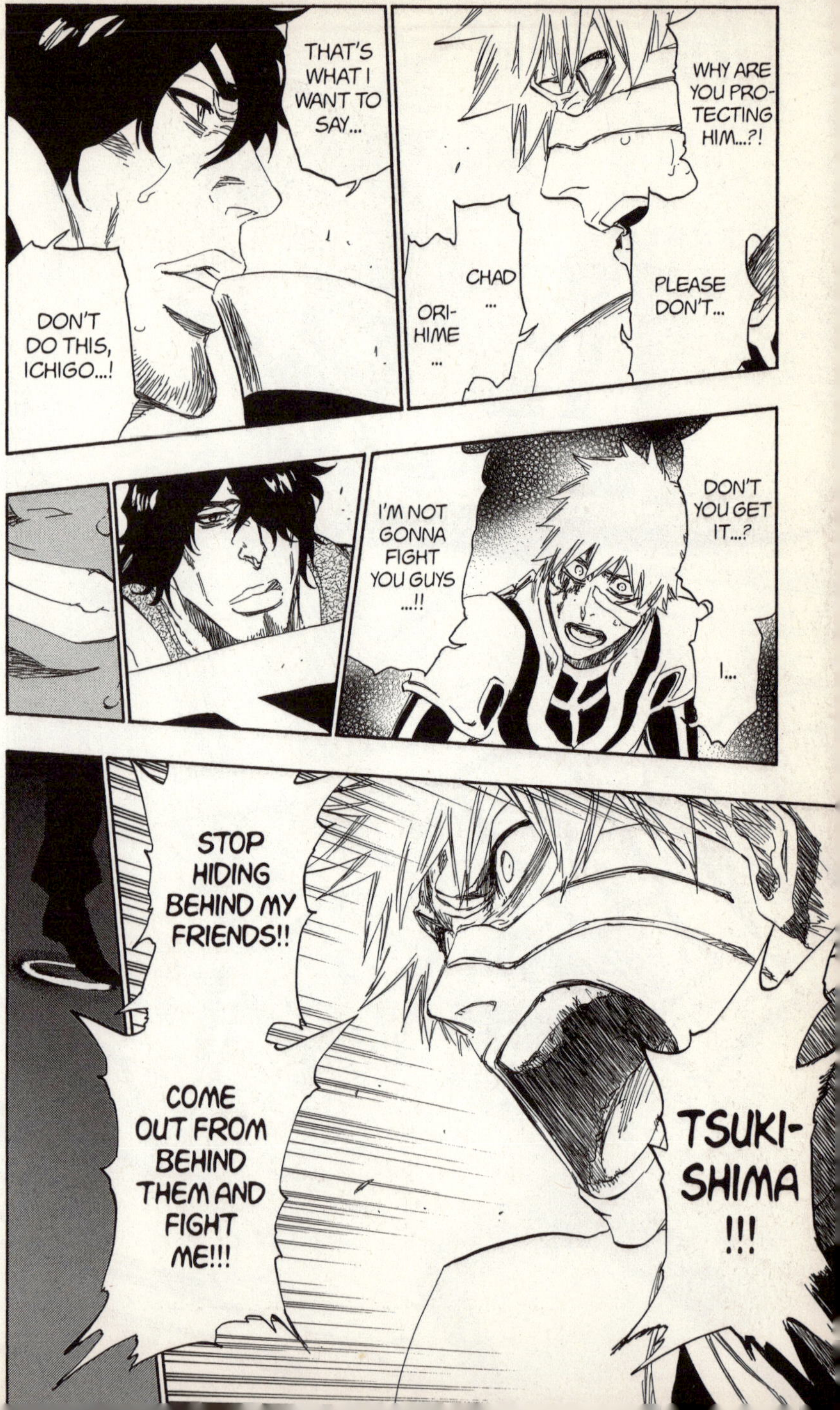
WHY ARE YOU PRO-TECTING HIM...?!
PLEASE DON'T...
CHAD ...
ORI-HIME ...
THAT'S WHAT I WANT TO SAY...
DON'T DO THIS, ICHIGO...!
DON'T YOU GET IT...?
I'M NOT GONNA FIGHT YOU GUYS ...!!
I...
STOP HIDING BEHIND MY FRIENDS!!
COME OUT FROM BEHIND THEM AND FIGHT ME!!!
TSUKI-SHIMA !!!

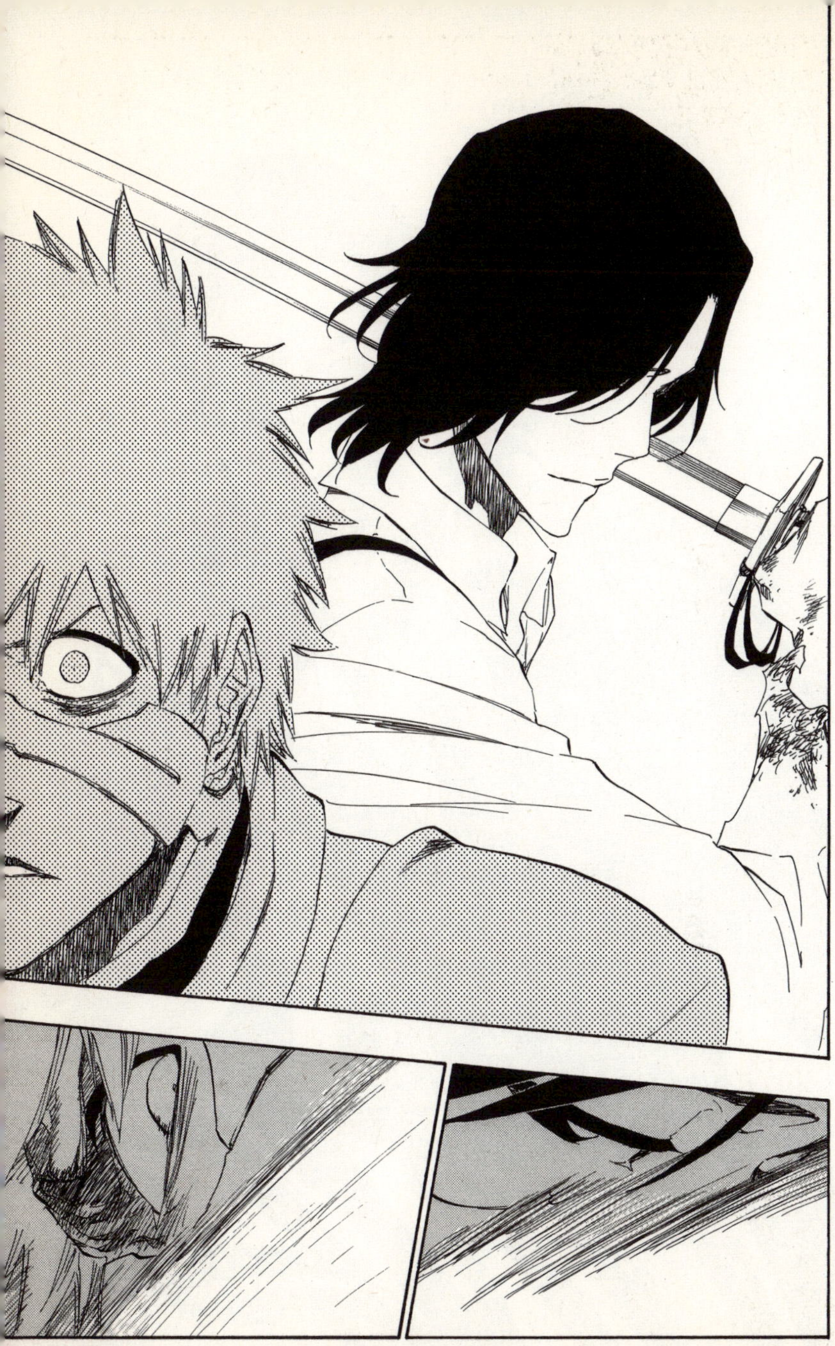

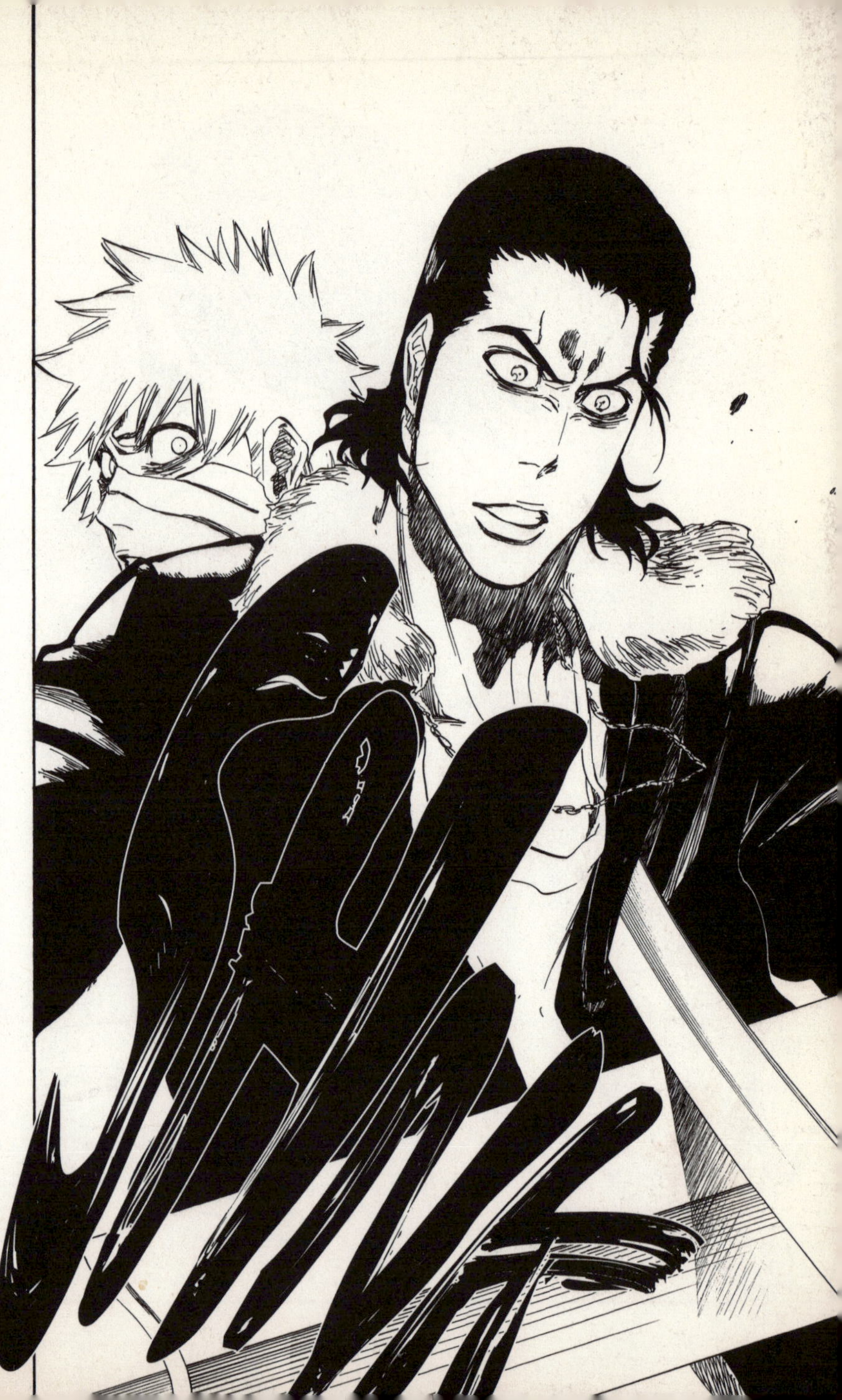

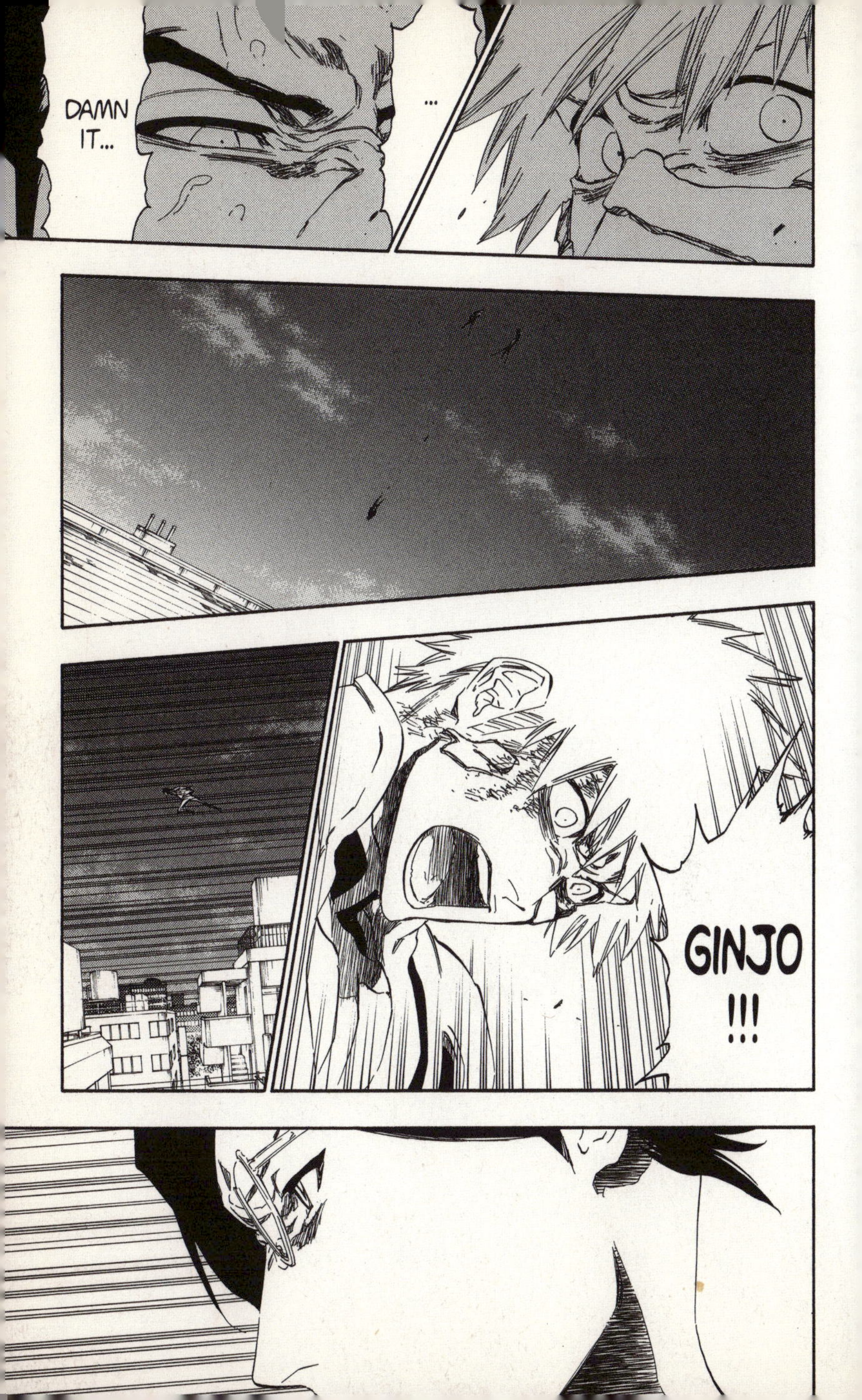
...
DAMN IT...
GINJO !!!

bury my

h e ar t

## 458. End of All Bonds

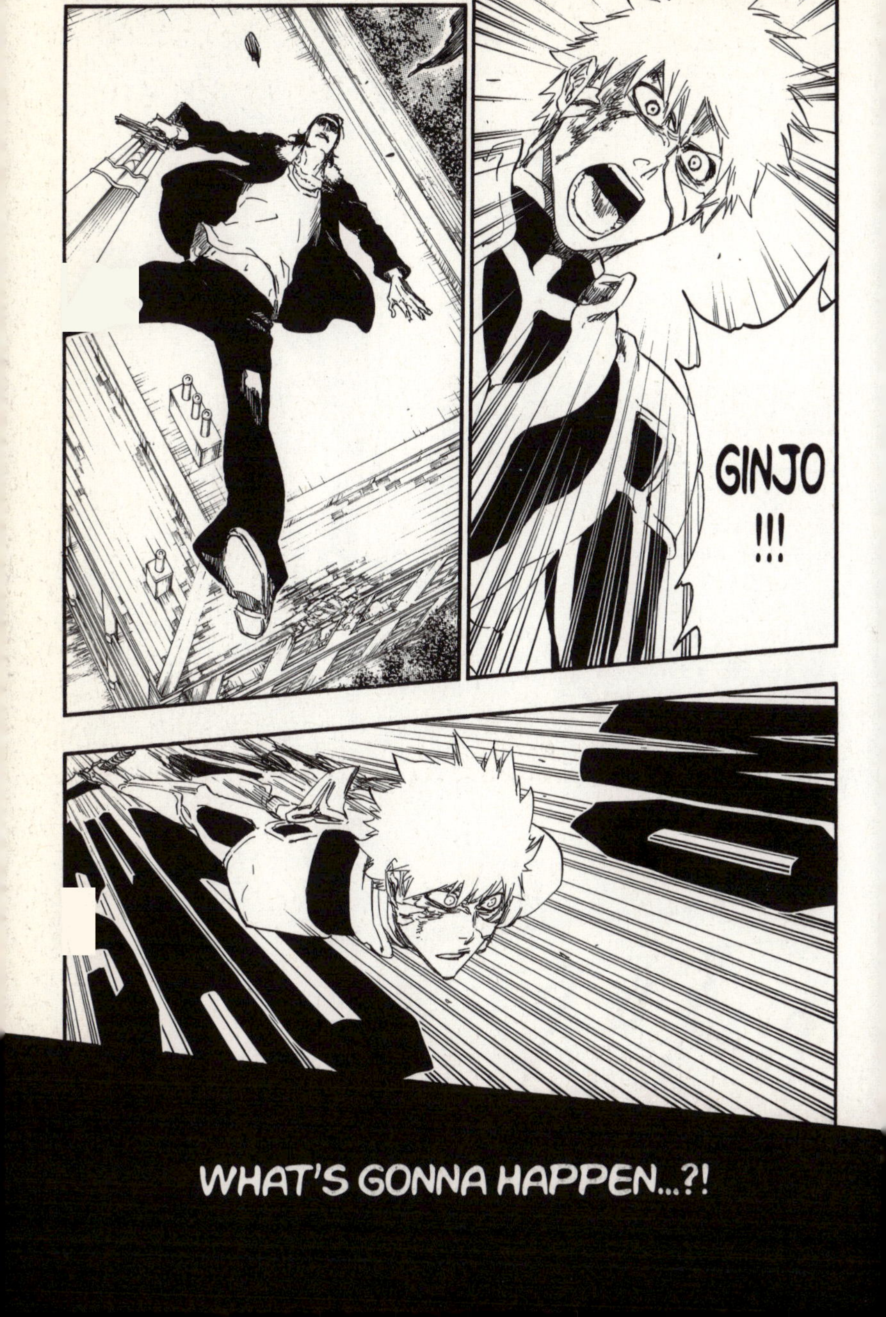
GINJO
!!!
WHAT'S GONNA HAPPEN...?!

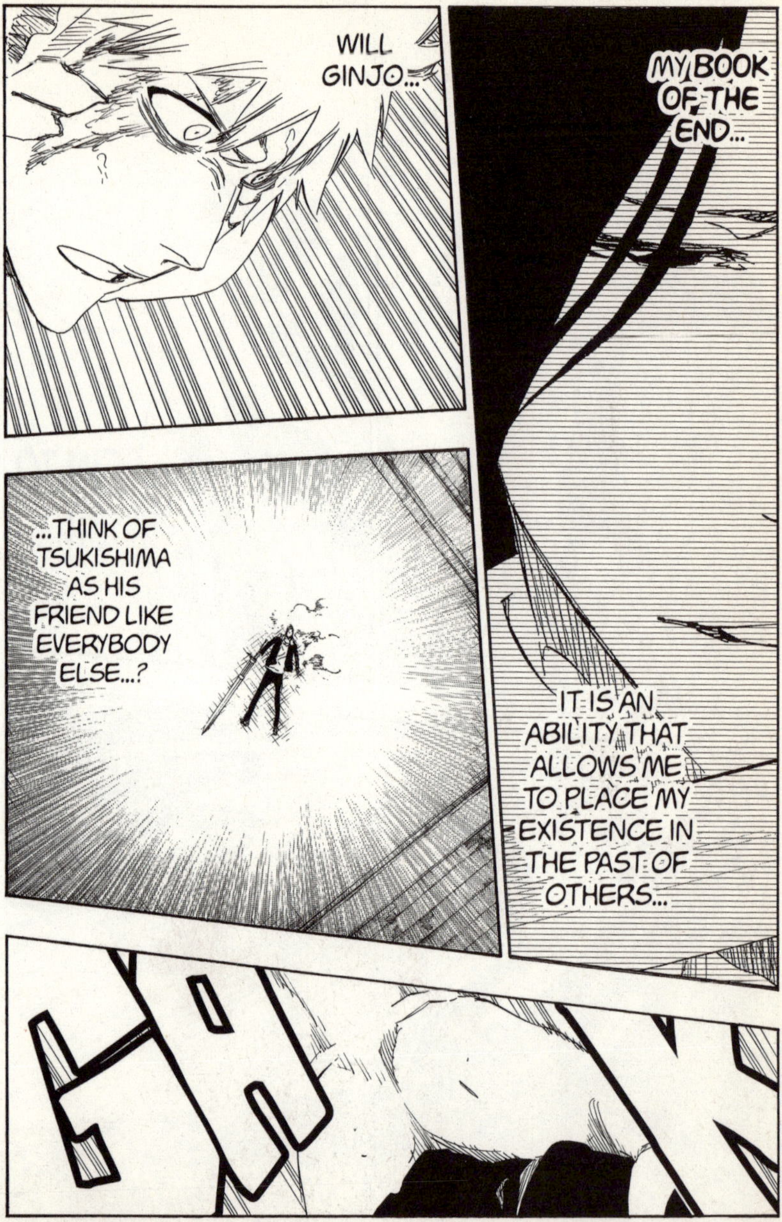
MY BOOK OF THE END...
IT IS AN ABILITY THAT ALLOWS ME TO PLACE MY EXISTENCE IN THE PAST OF OTHERS...
WILL GINJO...
...THINK OF TSUKISHIMA AS HIS FRIEND LIKE EVERYBODY ELSE...?

READ THIS WAY

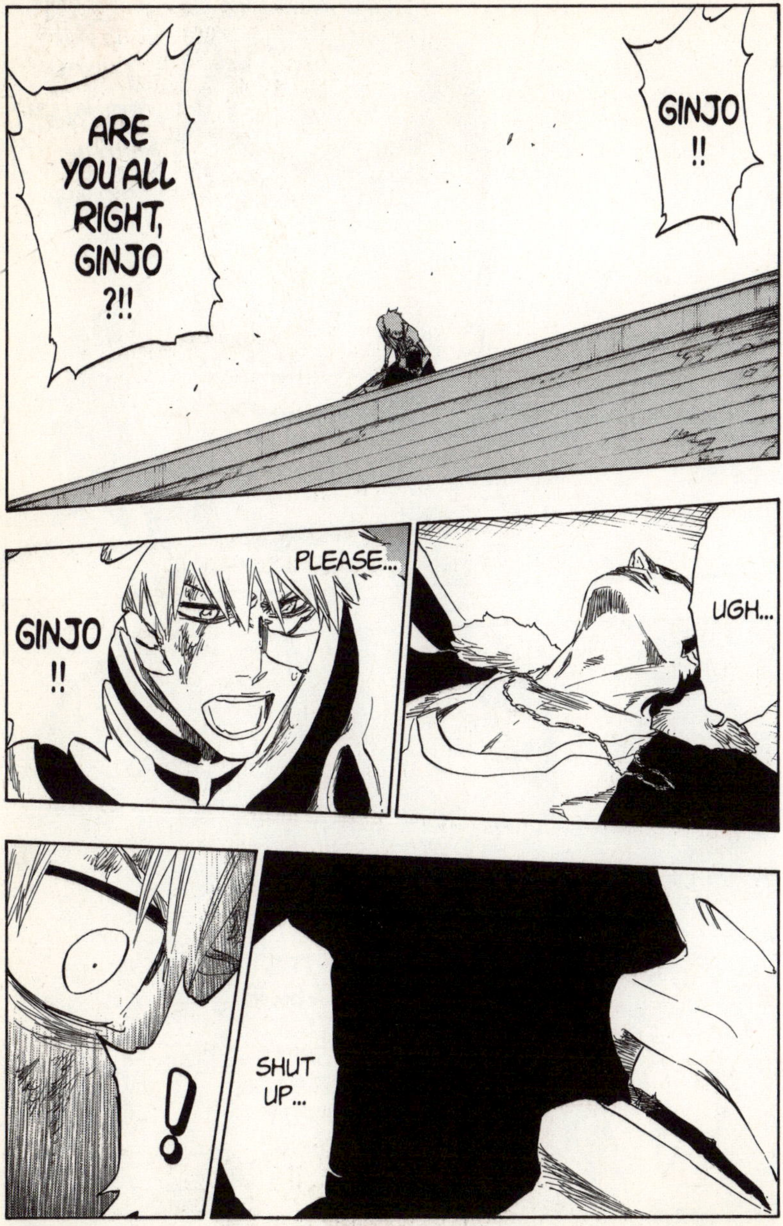
GINJO !!
ARE YOU ALL RIGHT, GINJO ?!!
UGH...
PLEASE...
GINJO !!
SHUT UP...
!

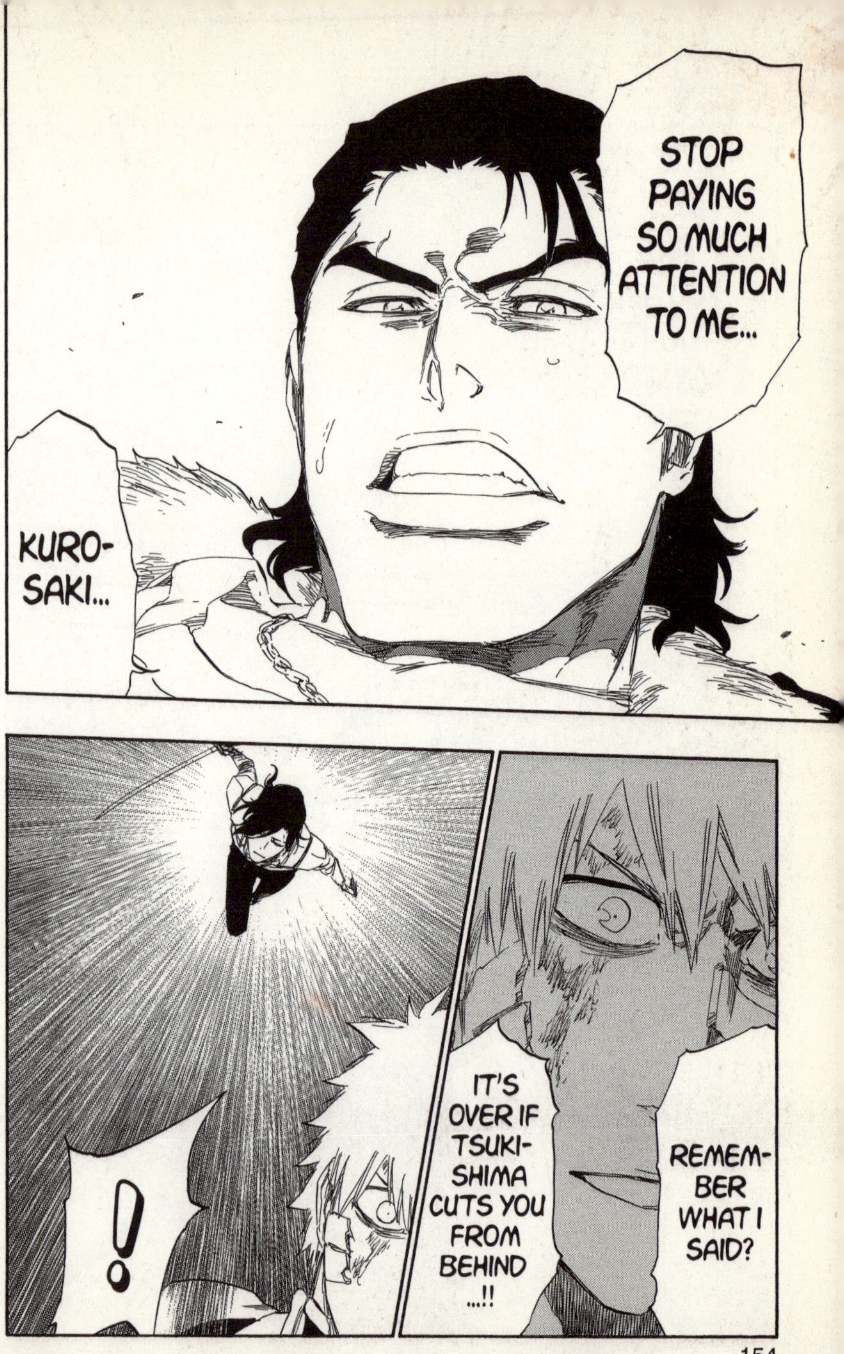
STOP PAYING SO MUCH ATTENTION TO ME...
KURO-SAKI...
REMEM-BER WHAT I SAID?
IT'S OVER IF TSUKI-SHIMA CUTS YOU FROM BEHIND ...!!
!

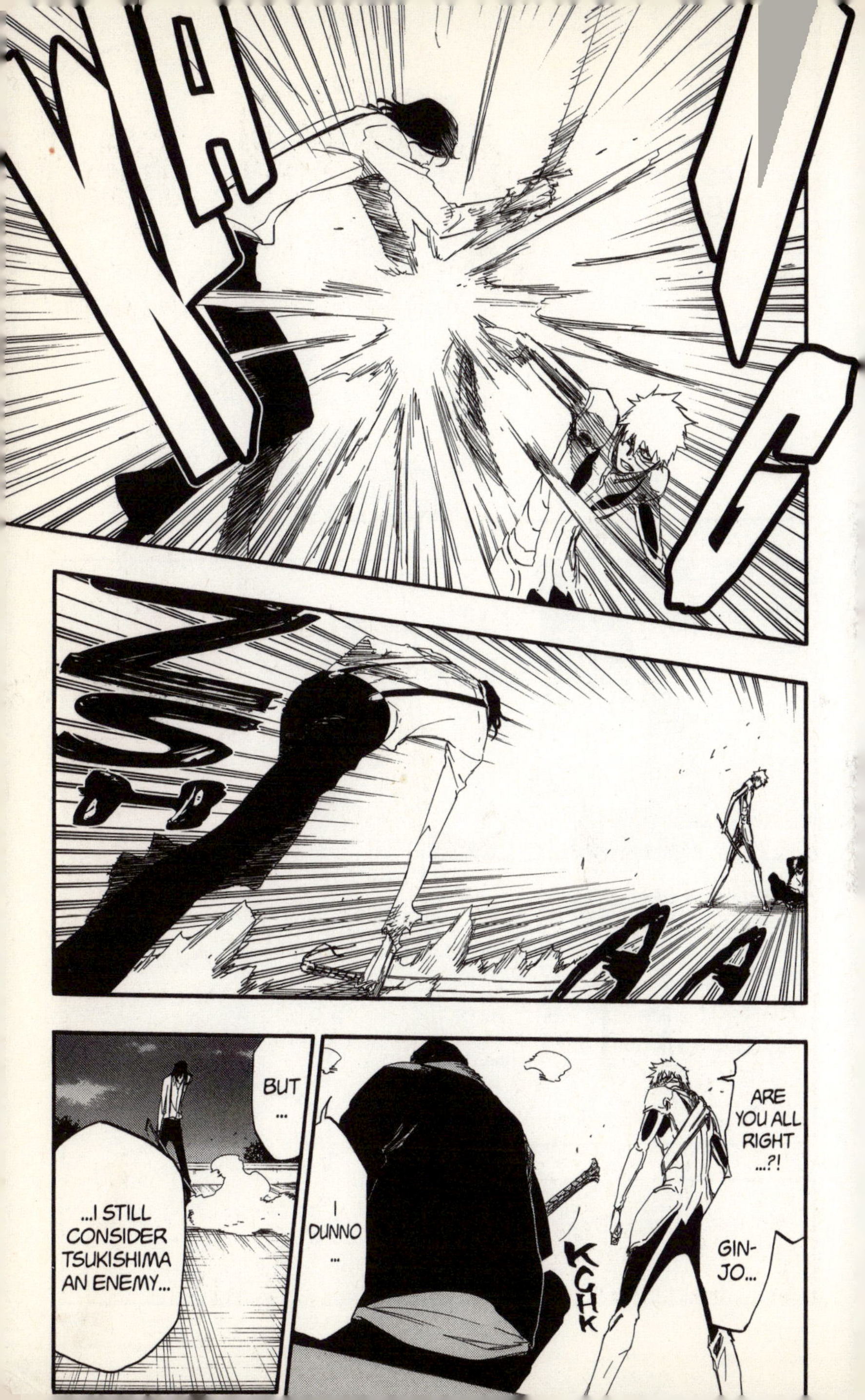
ARE YOU ALL RIGHT ...?!
GIN-JO...
KCHK
I DUNNO ...
BUT ...
...I STILL CONSIDER TSUKISHIMA AN ENEMY...

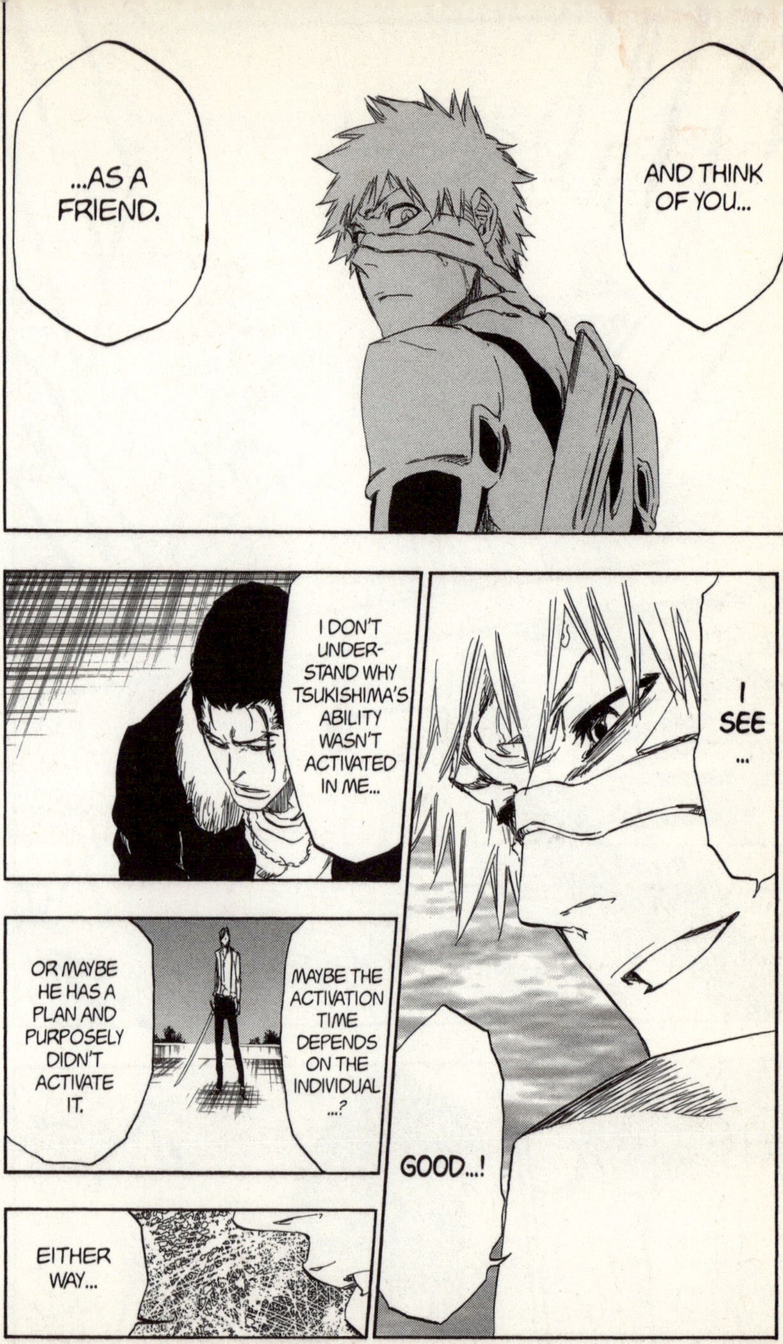
AND THINK OF YOU...
...AS A FRIEND.
I SEE ...
I DON'T UNDER-STAND WHY TSUKISHIMA'S ABILITY WASN'T ACTIVATED IN ME...
MAYBE THE ACTIVATION TIME DEPENDS ON THE INDIVIDUAL ...?
OR MAYBE HE HAS A PLAN AND PURPOSELY DIDN'T ACTIVATE IT.
GOOD...!
EITHER WAY...

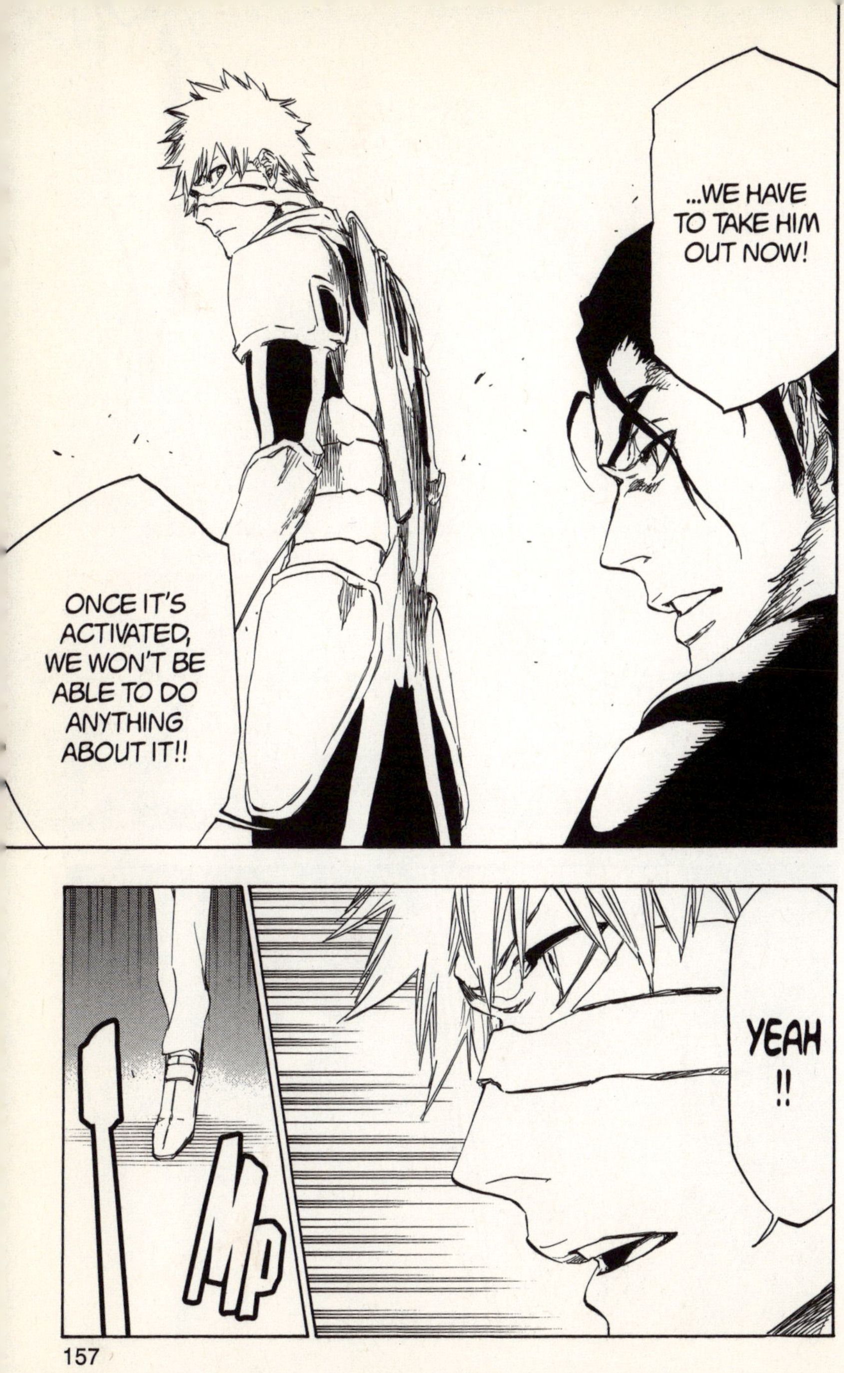
...WE HAVE TO TAKE HIM OUT NOW!
ONCE IT'S ACTIVATED, WE WON'T BE ABLE TO DO ANYTHING ABOUT IT!!
YEAH!!
MP

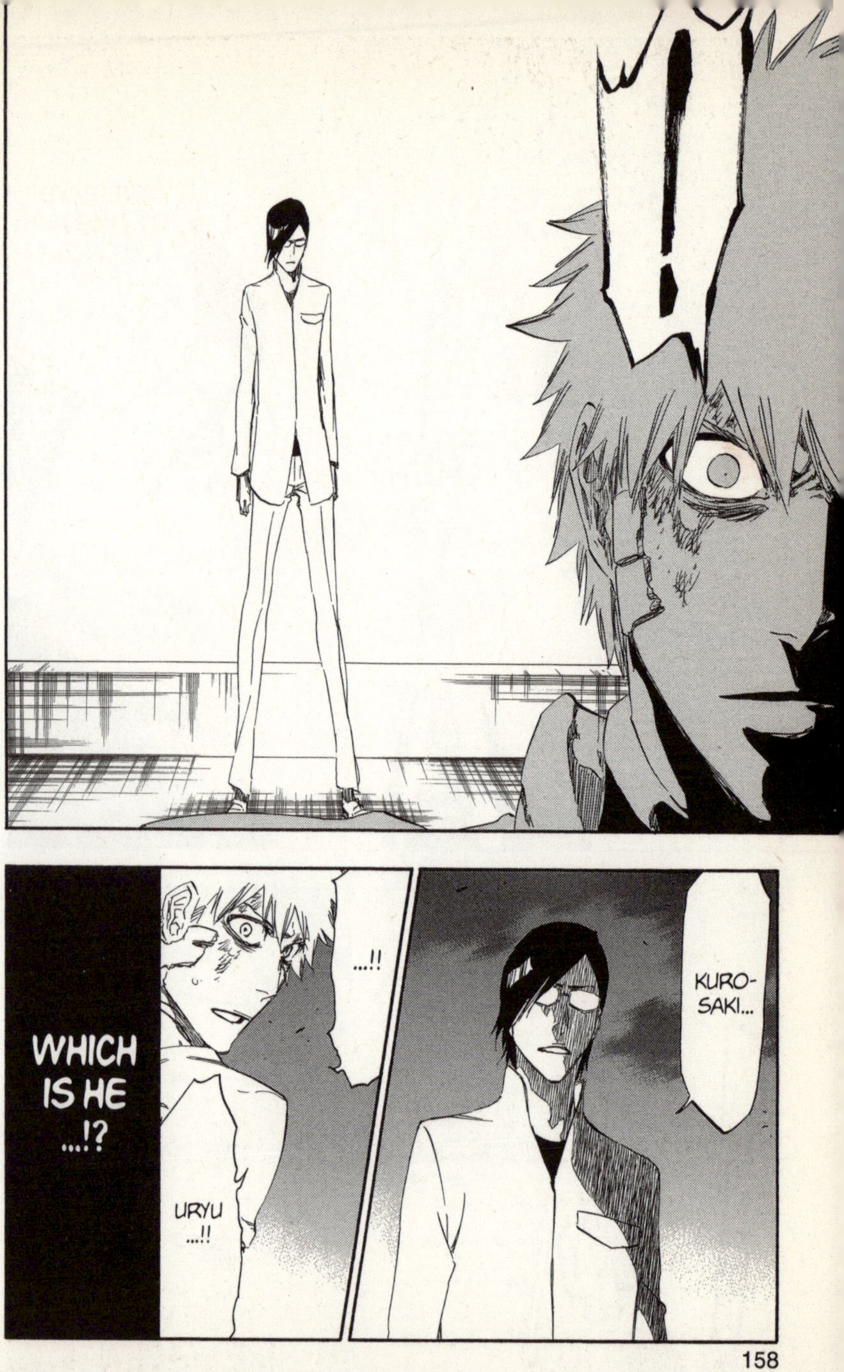
KURO-
SAKI...
...!!
URYU
...!!
WHICH
IS HE
...!?

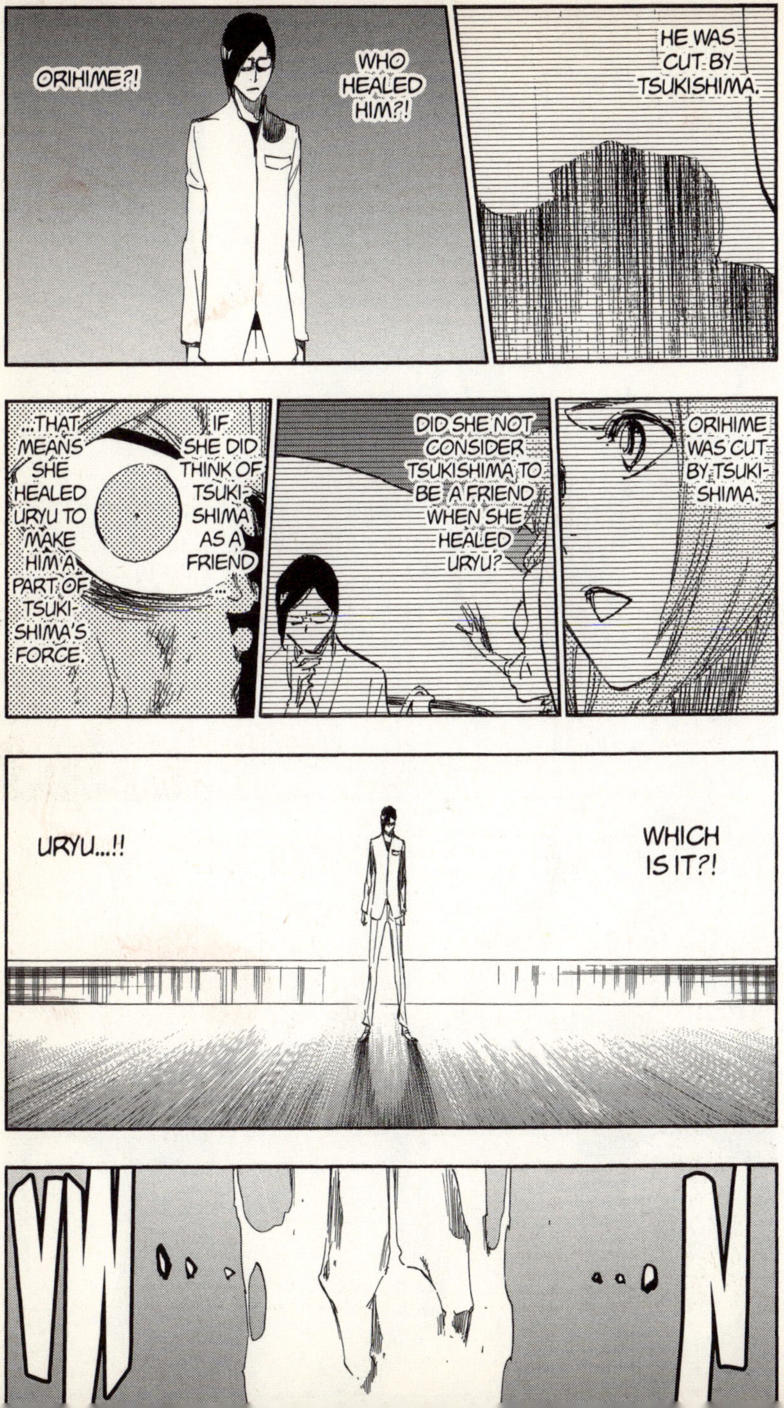
HE WAS CUT BY TSUKISHIMA.
WHO HEALED HIM?!
ORIHIME?!
ORIHIME WAS CUT BY TSUKISHIMA.
DID SHE NOT CONSIDER TSUKISHIMA TO BE A FRIEND WHEN SHE HEALED URYU?
IF SHE DID THINK OF TSUKISHIMA AS A FRIEND...
...THAT MEANS SHE HEALED URYU TO MAKE HIM A PART OF TSUKISHIMA'S FORCE.
WHICH IS IT?!
URYU...!!

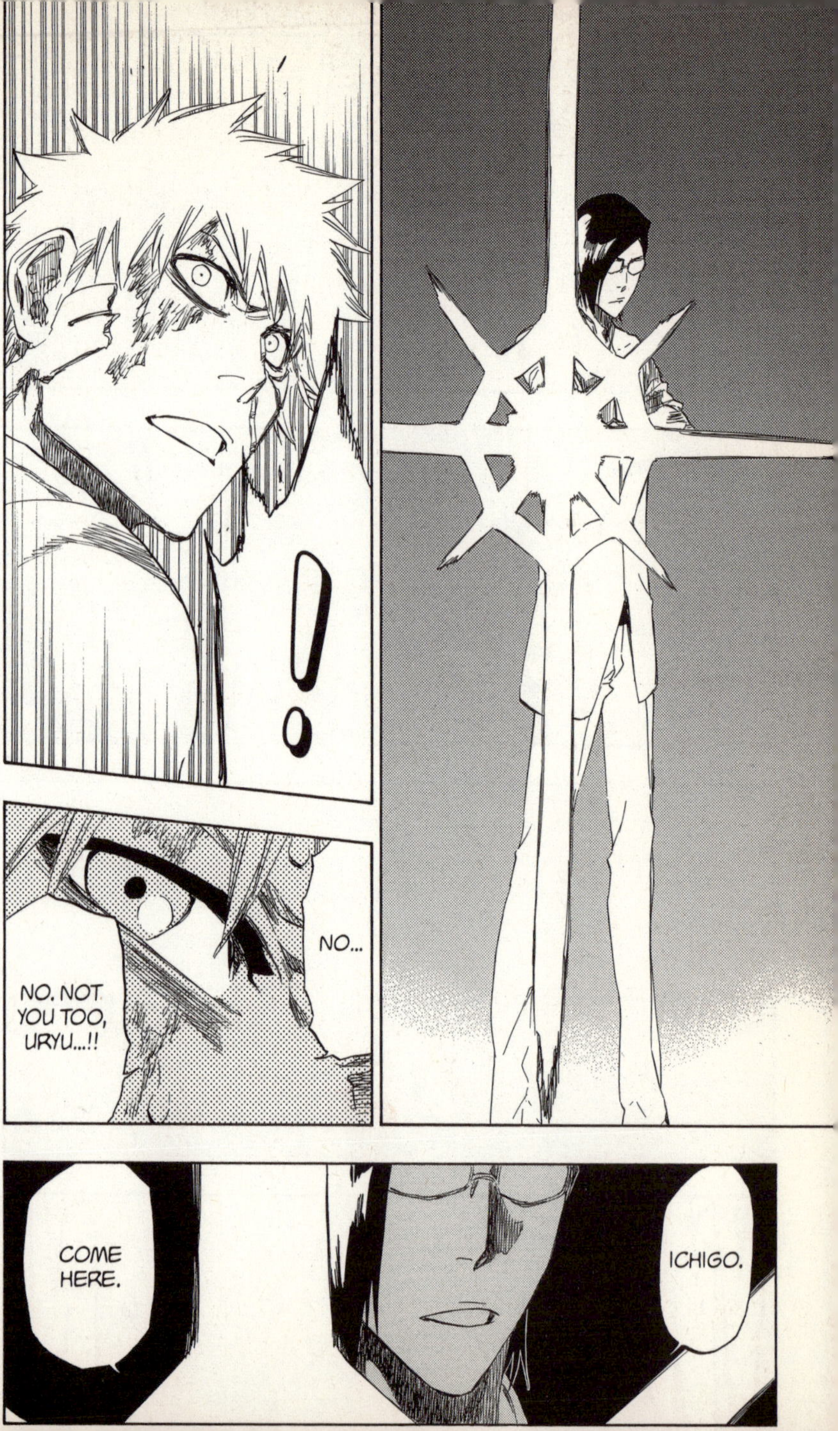

!
NO...
NO. NOT YOU TOO, URYU...!!
ICHIGO.
COME HERE.

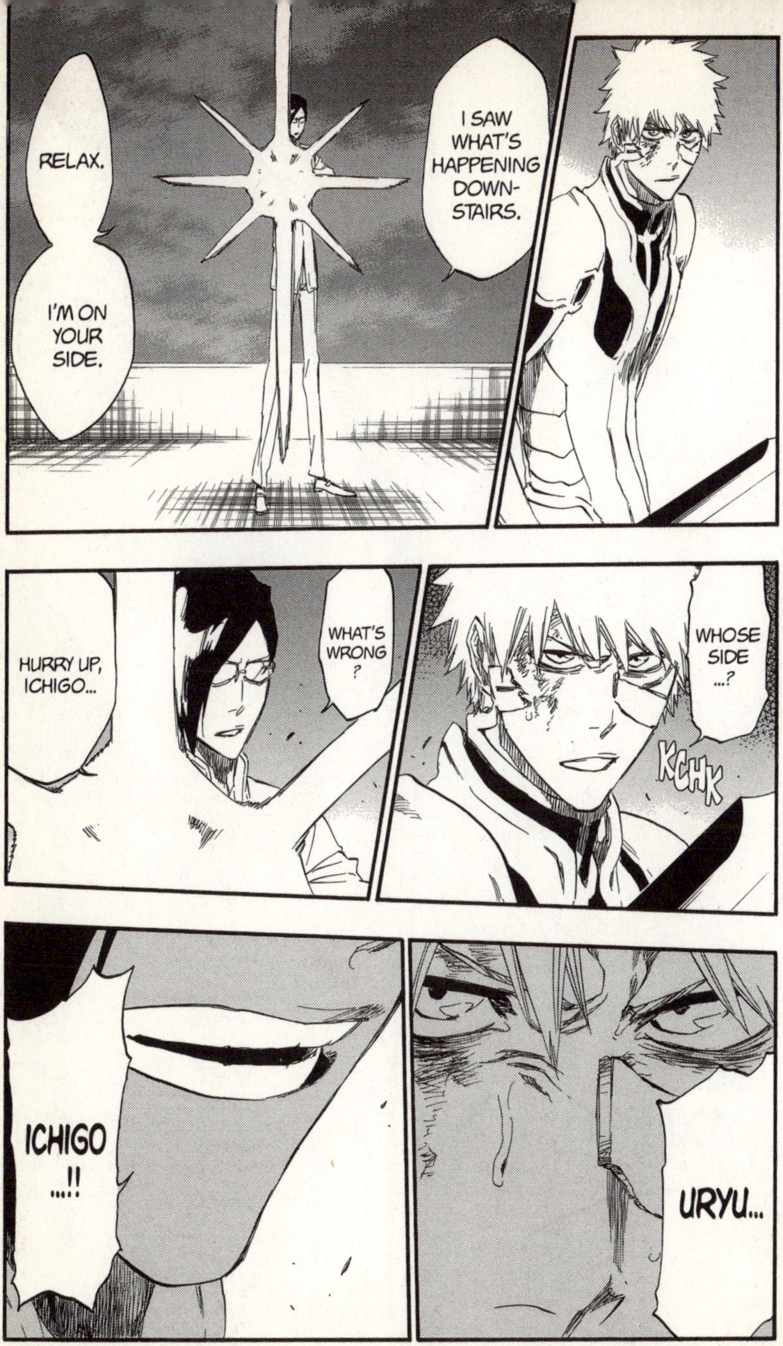
I SAW WHAT'S HAPPENING DOWN-STAIRS.
RELAX.
I'M ON YOUR SIDE.
WHOSE SIDE ...?
KCHK
WHAT'S WRONG?
HURRY UP, ICHIGO...
URYU...
ICHIGO ...!!

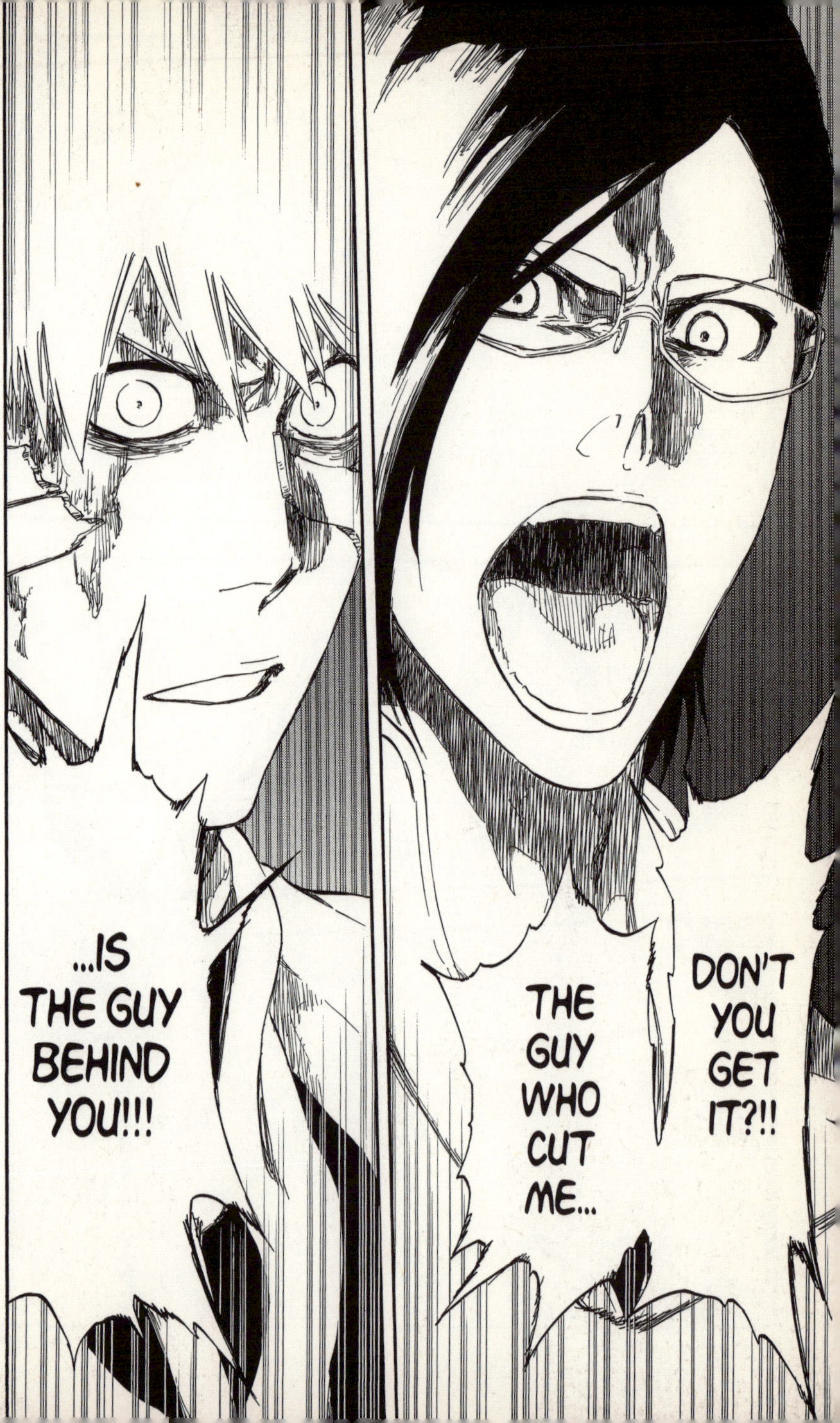
DON'T YOU GET IT?!!
THE GUY WHO CUT ME...
...IS THE GUY BEHIND YOU!!!

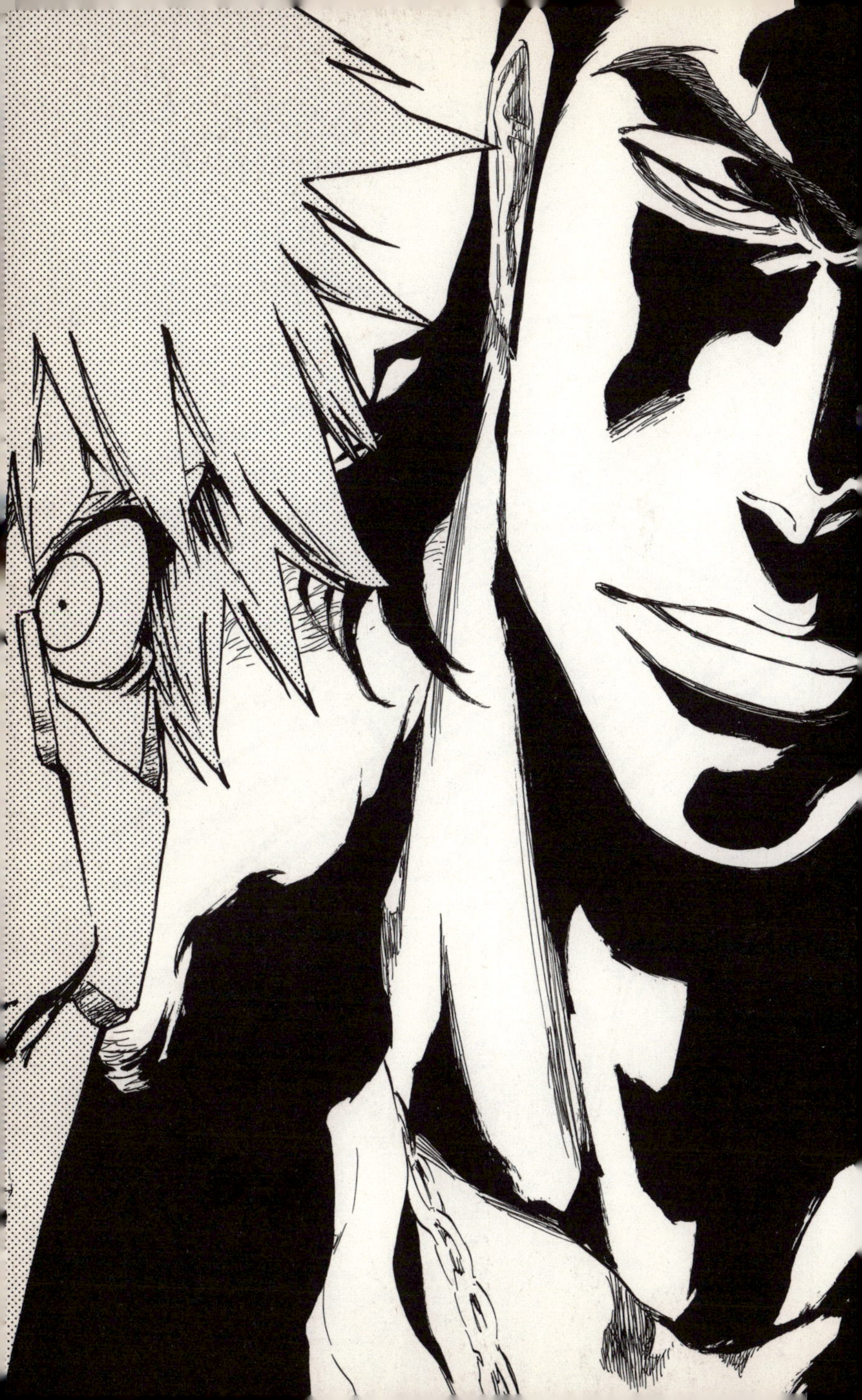

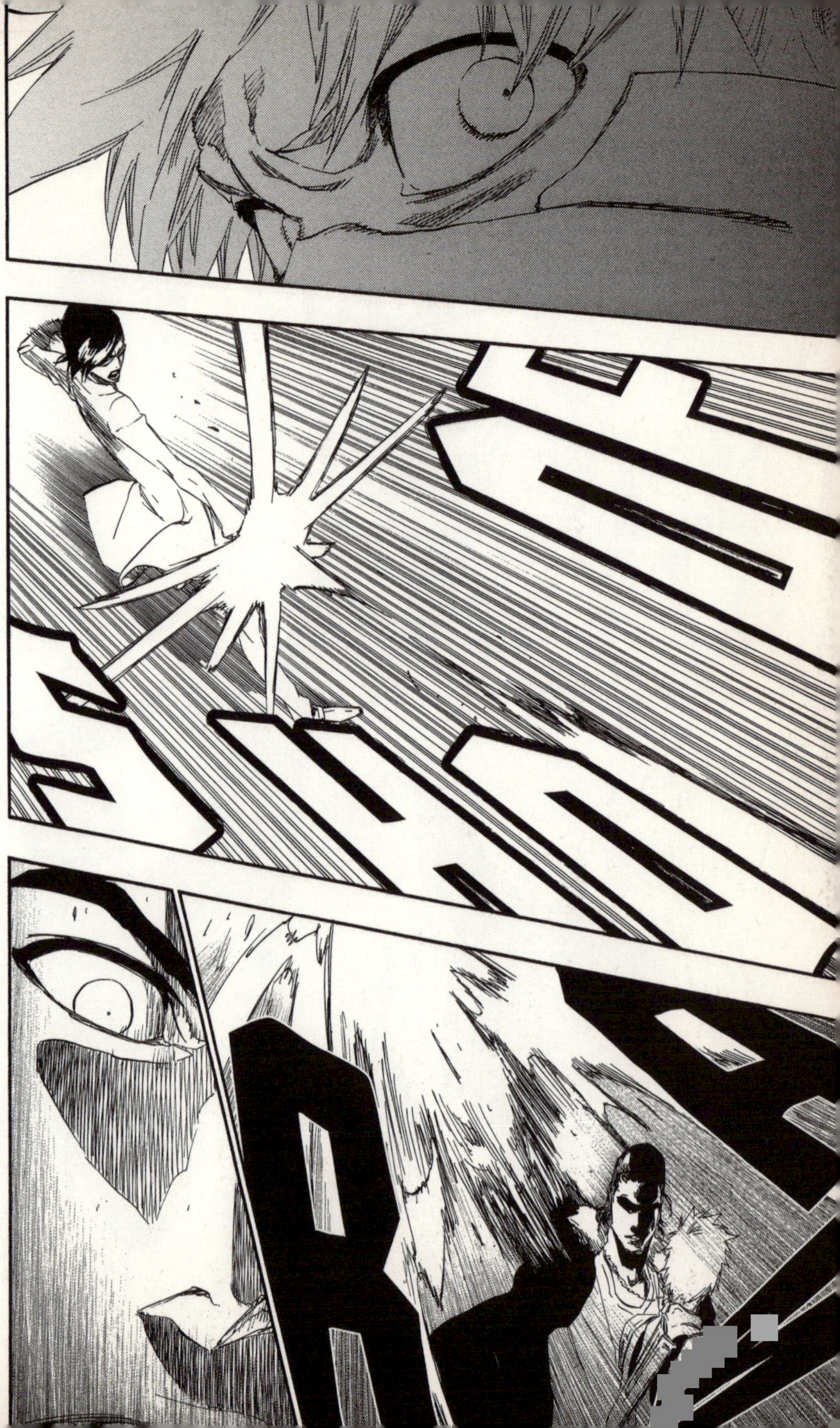

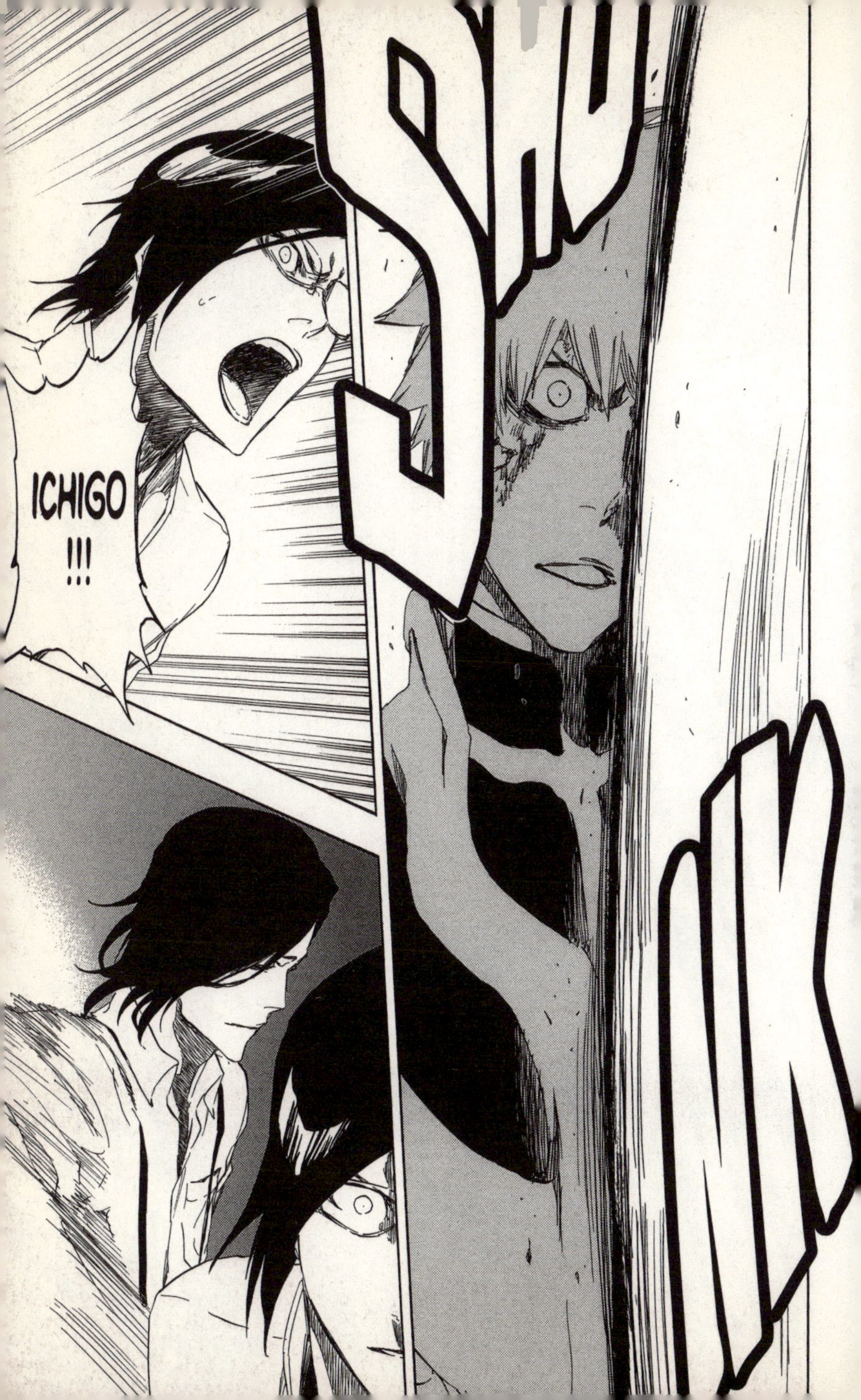
ICHIGO !!!
SHUNK

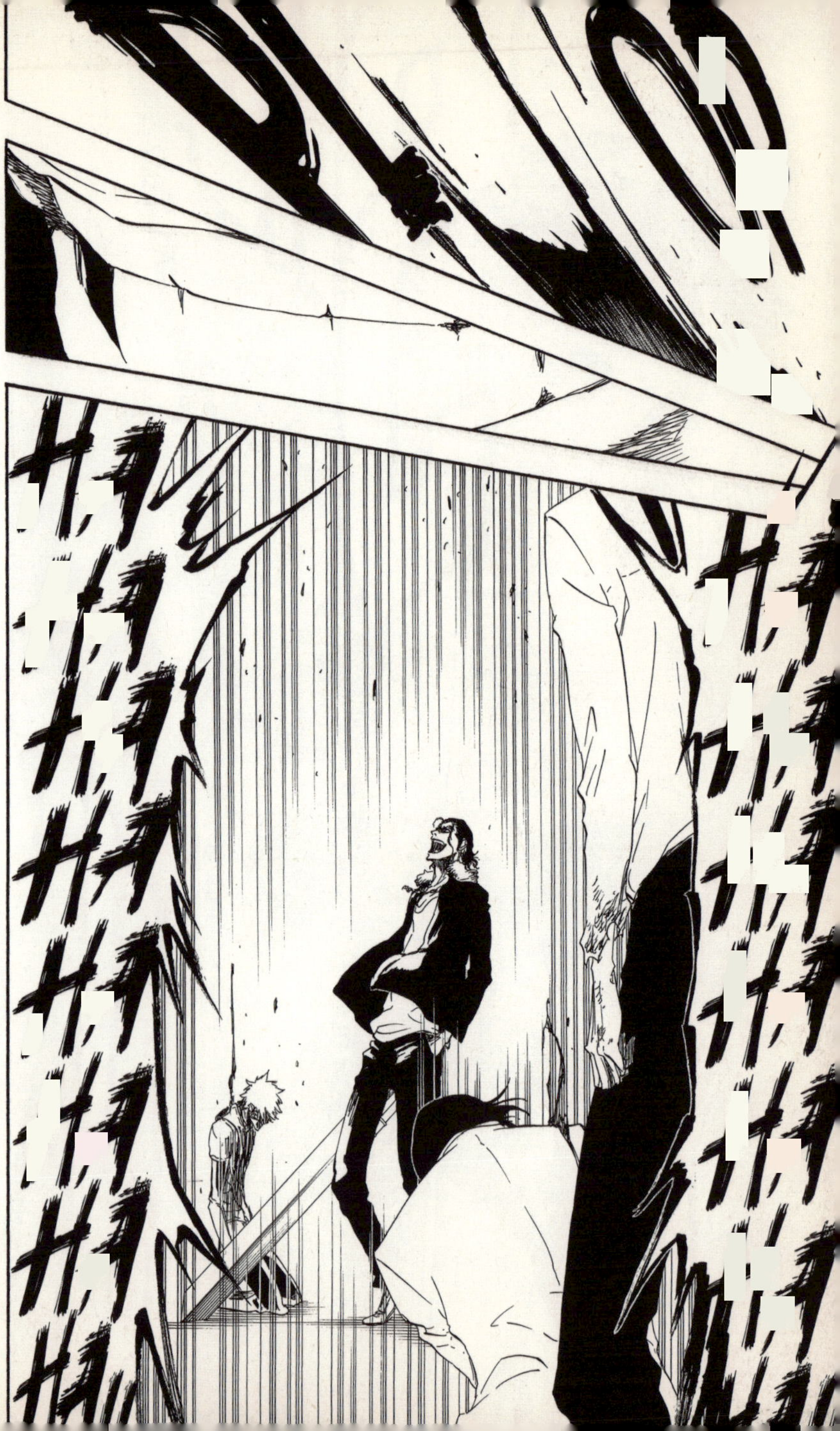

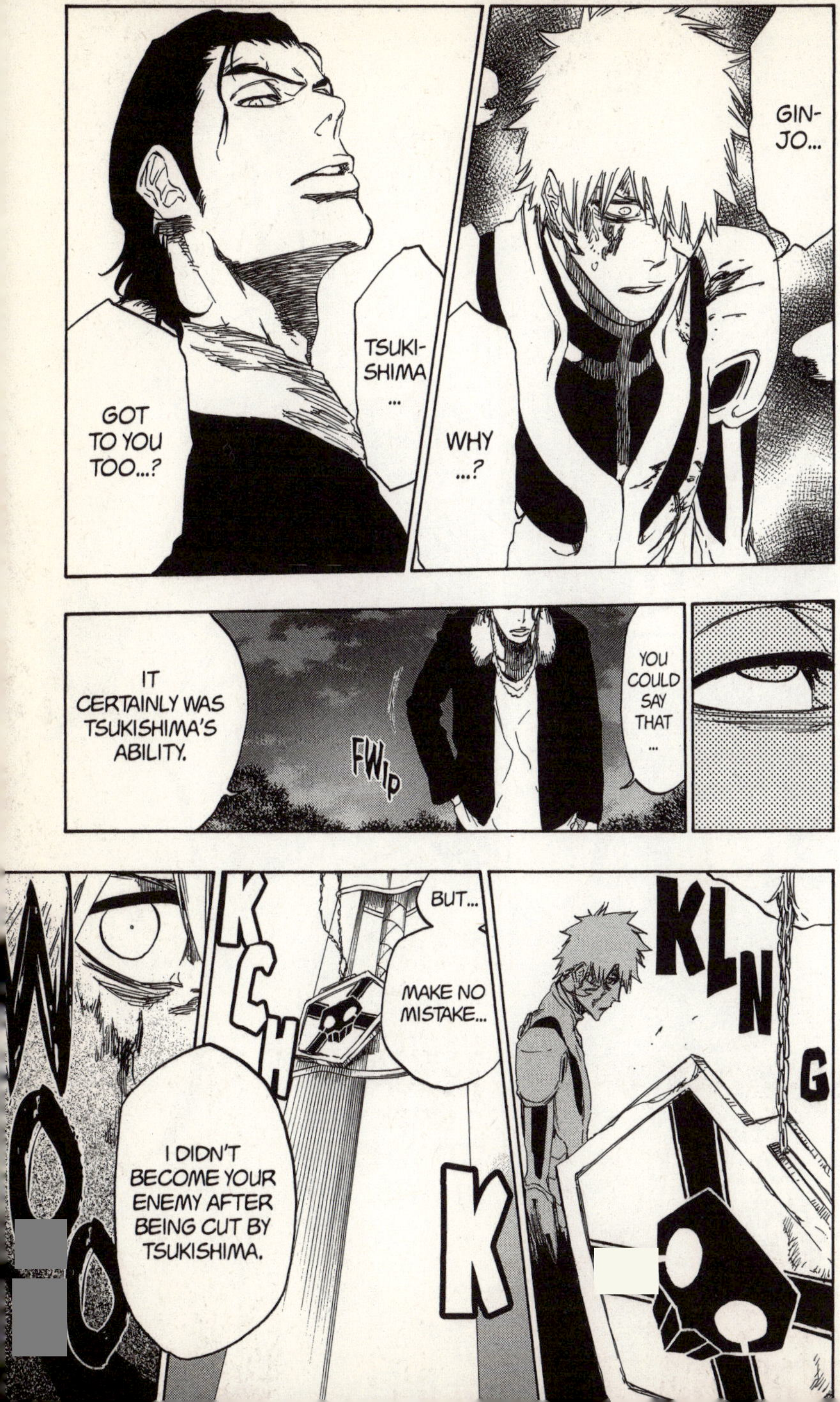
GIN-JO...
WHY ...?
TSUKI-SHIMA ...
GOT TO YOU TOO...?
YOU COULD SAY THAT ...
FWIP
IT CERTAINLY WAS TSUKISHIMA'S ABILITY.
KLNG
BUT...
MAKE NO MISTAKE...
KCH
K
I DIDN'T BECOME YOUR ENEMY AFTER BEING CUT BY TSUKISHIMA.

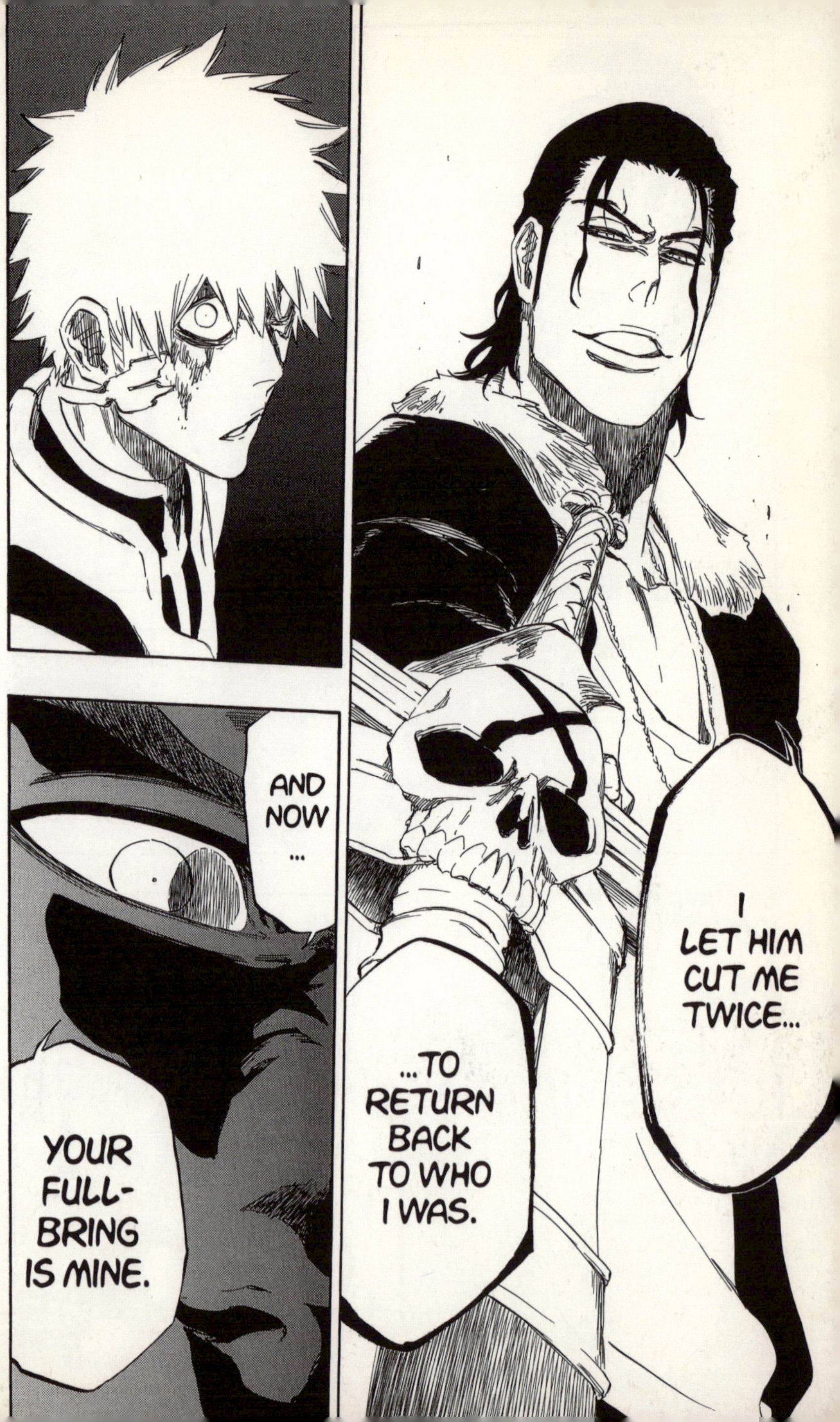
I LET HIM CUT ME TWICE...
...TO RETURN BACK TO WHO I WAS.
AND NOW ...
YOUR FULL-BRING IS MINE.

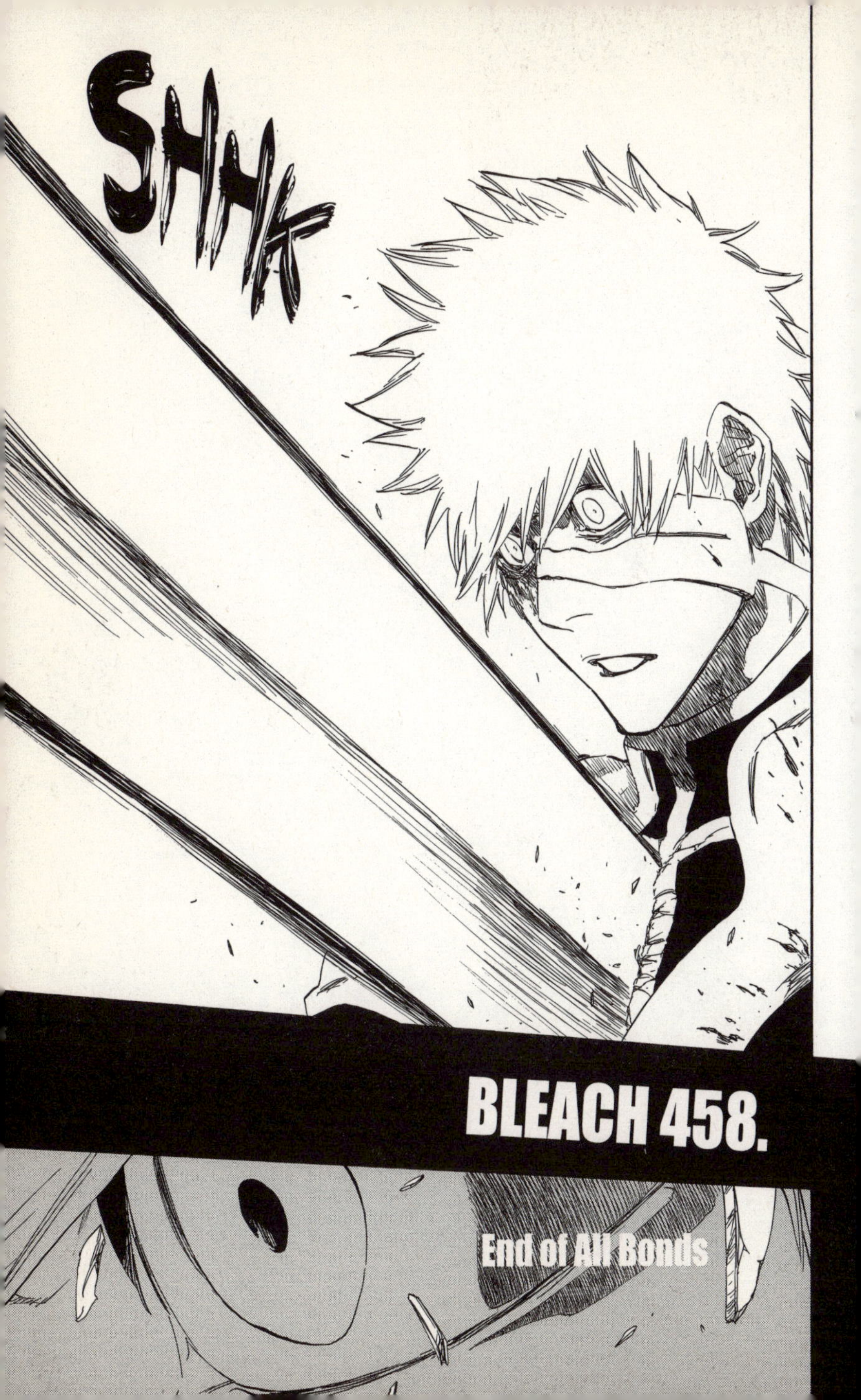
SHHK
BLEACH 458.
End of All Bonds

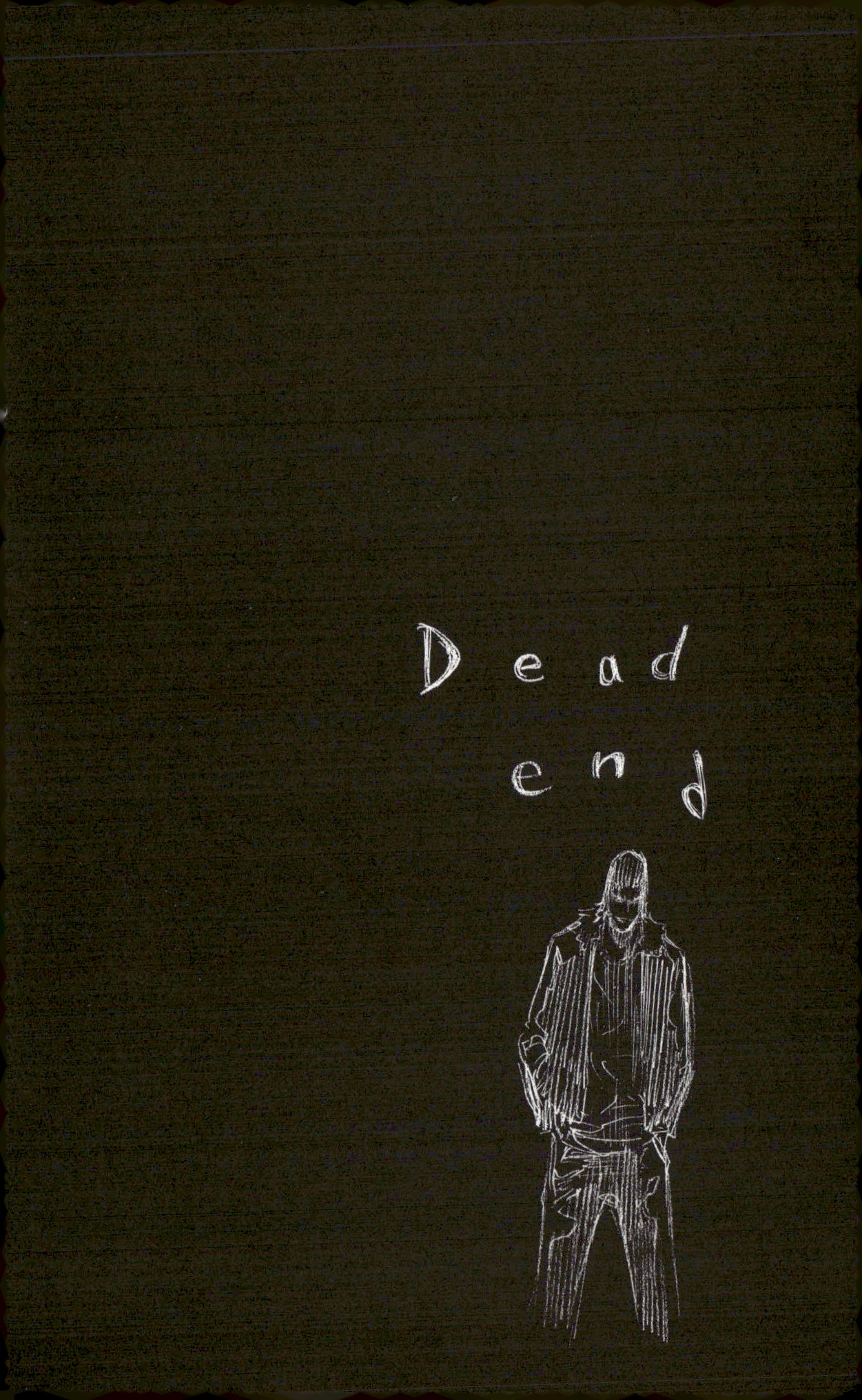
Dead
end

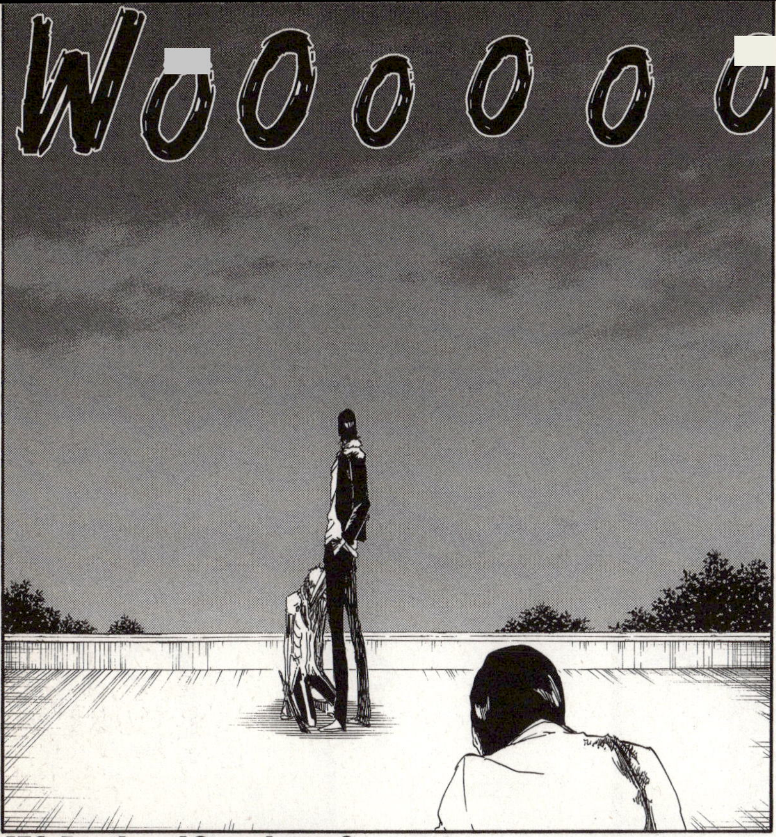
WOOOOOO

# 459. Death and Strawberry 2

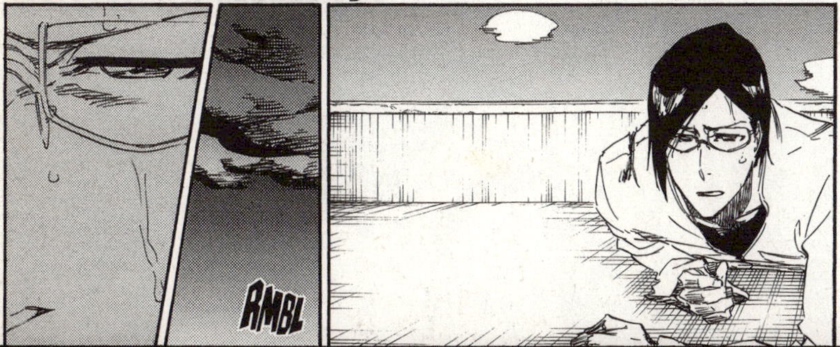
RMBL

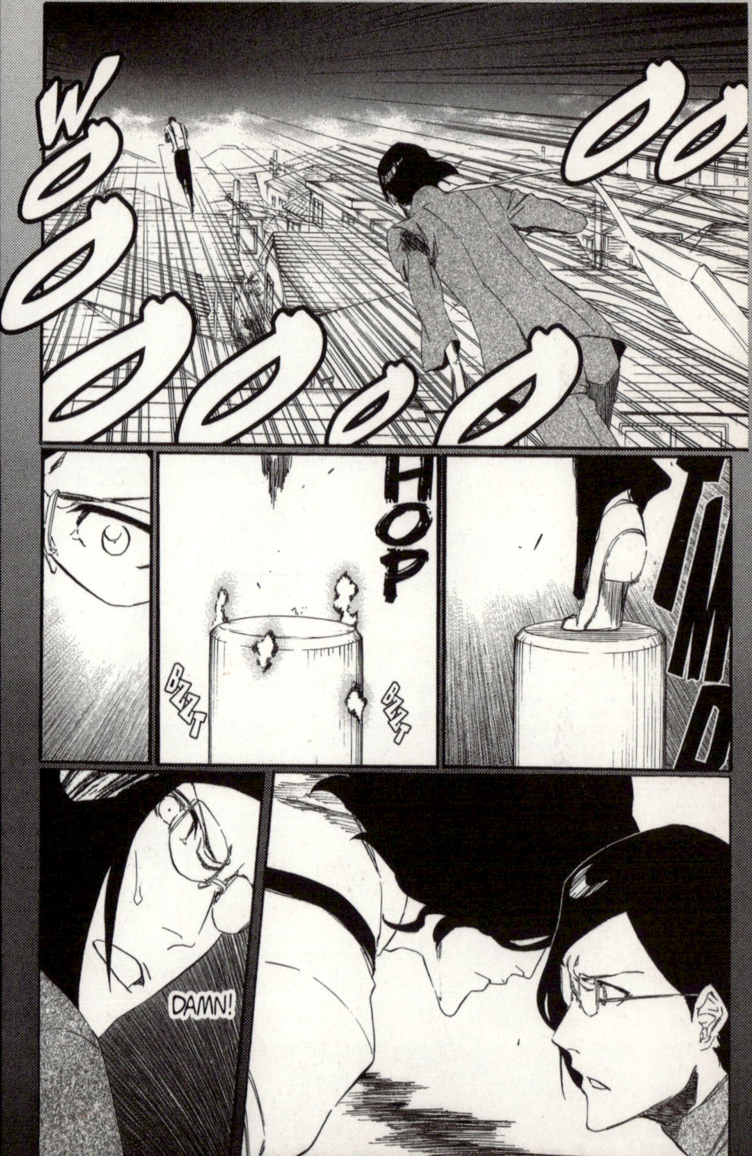
HOP
BZZT
BZZT
DAMN!

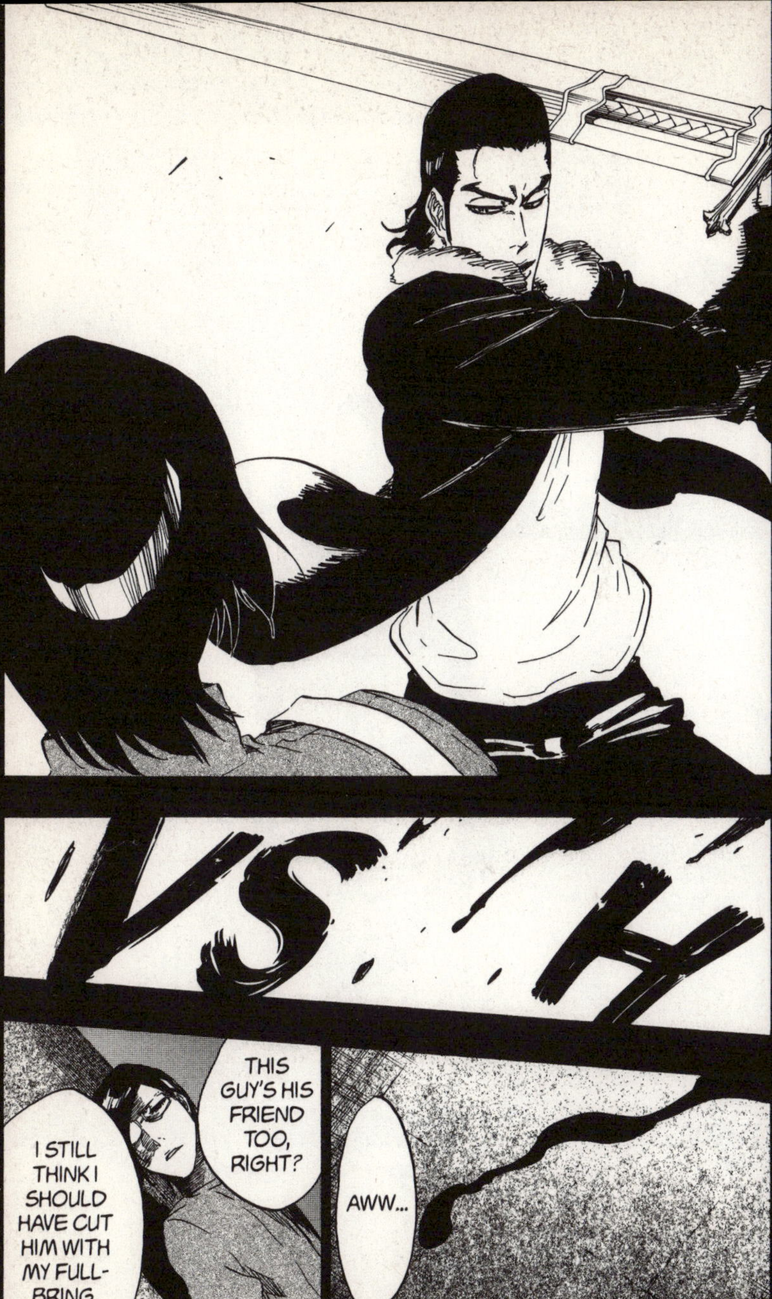
VS. H
THIS GUY'S HIS FRIEND TOO, RIGHT?
I STILL THINK I SHOULD HAVE CUT HIM WITH MY FULL-BRING.
AWW...

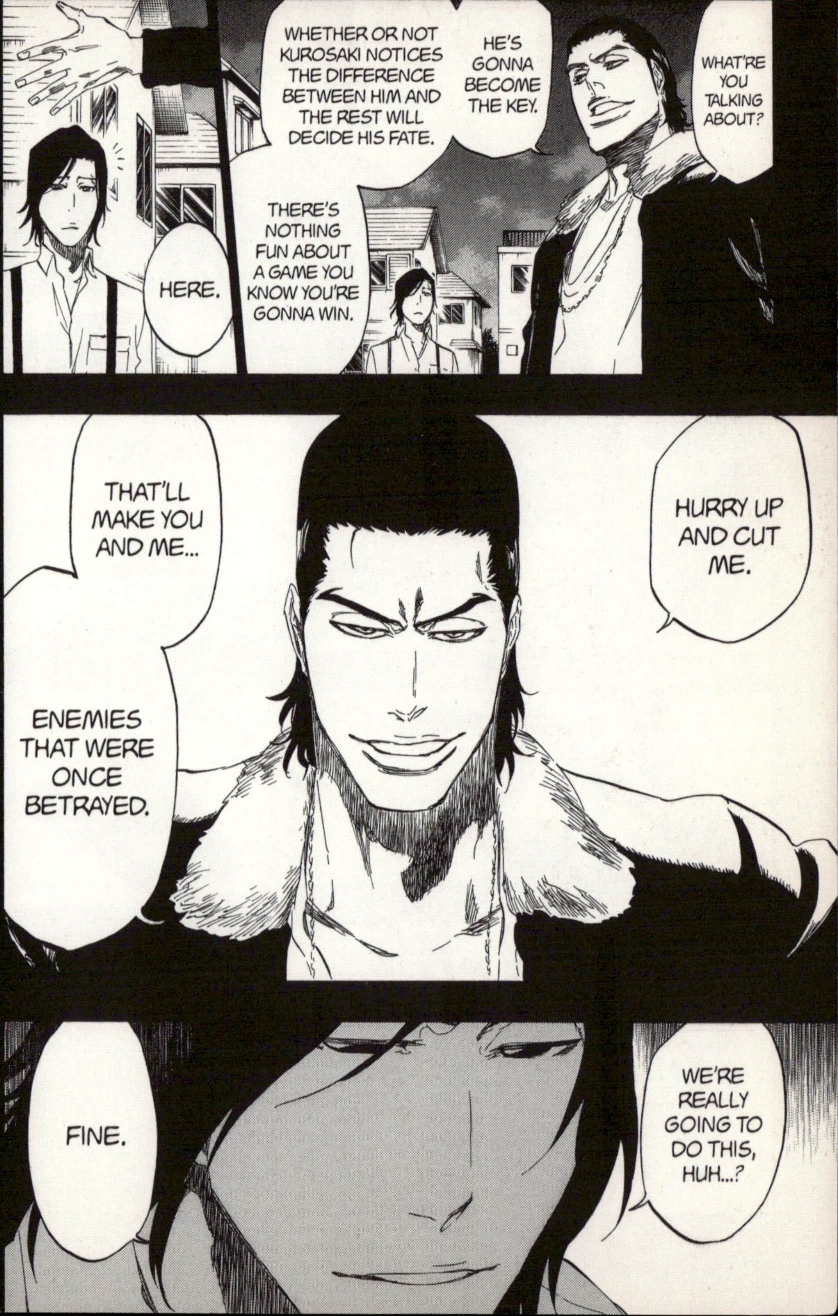
WHAT'RE YOU TALKING ABOUT?
HE'S GONNA BECOME THE KEY.
WHETHER OR NOT KUROSAKI NOTICES THE DIFFERENCE BETWEEN HIM AND THE REST WILL DECIDE HIS FATE.
THERE'S NOTHING FUN ABOUT A GAME YOU KNOW YOU'RE GONNA WIN.
HERE.
HURRY UP AND CUT ME.
THAT'LL MAKE YOU AND ME...
ENEMIES THAT WERE ONCE BETRAYED.
WE'RE REALLY GOING TO DO THIS, HUH...?
FINE.

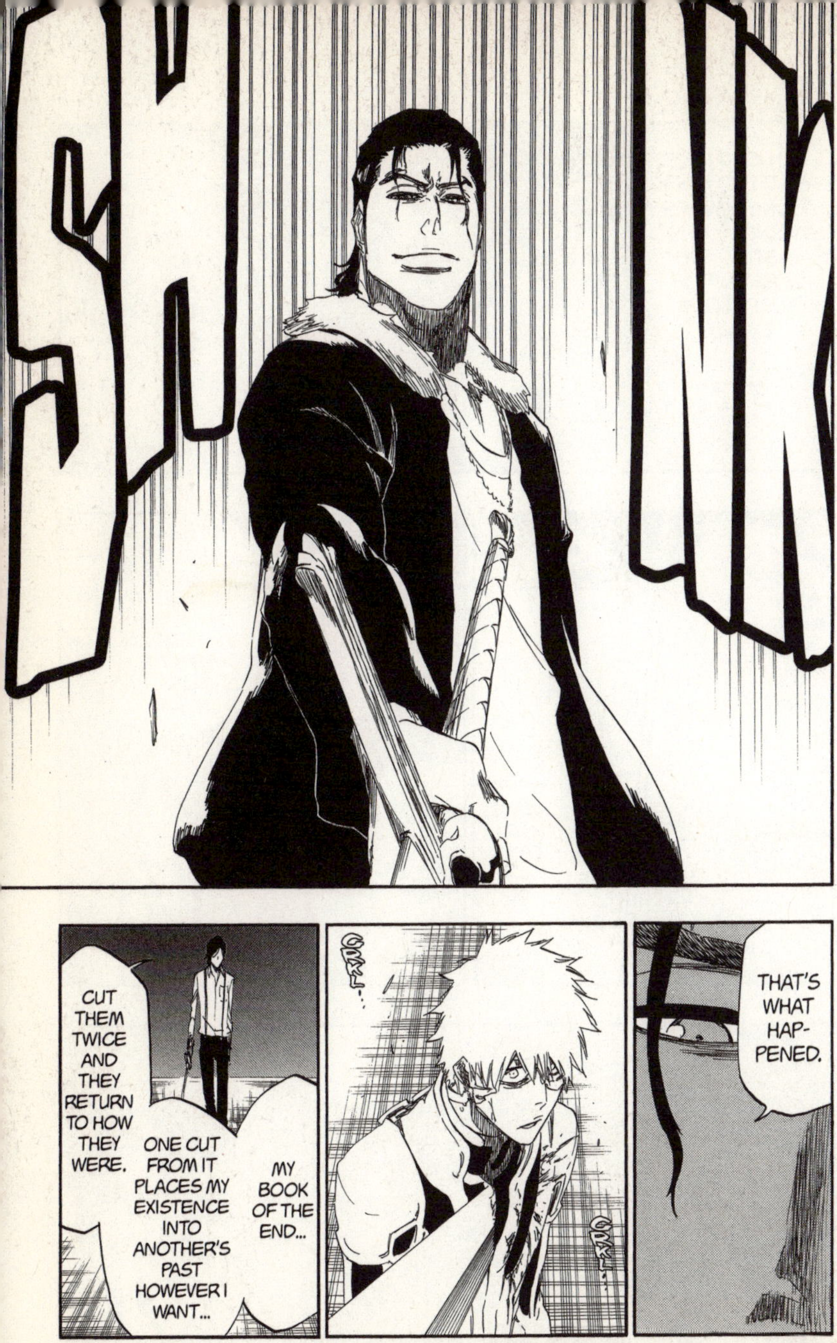
SHUNK
THAT'S WHAT HAP-PENED.
GRKL...
GRKL...
MY BOOK OF THE END...
ONE CUT FROM IT PLACES MY EXISTENCE INTO ANOTHER'S PAST HOWEVER I WANT...
CUT THEM TWICE AND THEY RETURN TO HOW THEY WERE.

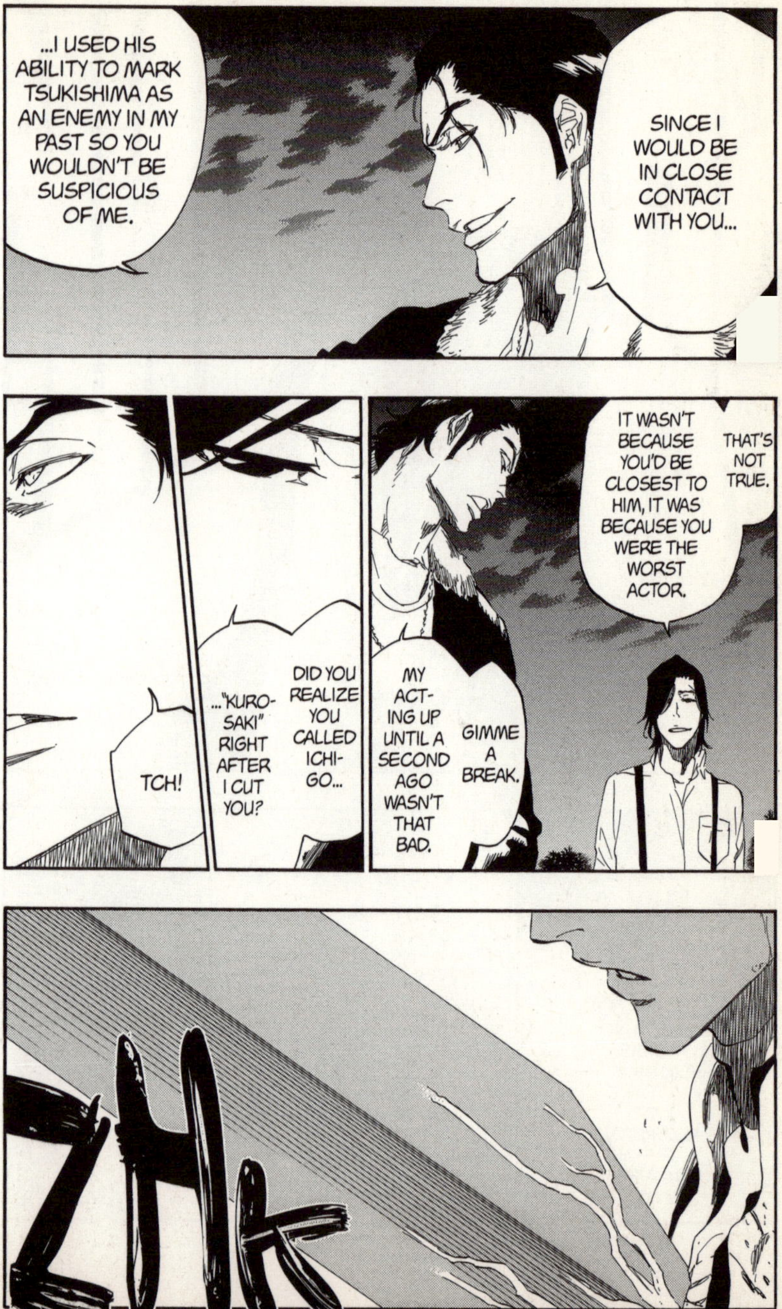
SINCE I WOULD BE IN CLOSE CONTACT WITH YOU...
...I USED HIS ABILITY TO MARK TSUKISHIMA AS AN ENEMY IN MY PAST SO YOU WOULDN'T BE SUSPICIOUS OF ME.
THAT'S NOT TRUE.
IT WASN'T BECAUSE YOU'D BE CLOSEST TO HIM, IT WAS BECAUSE YOU WERE THE WORST ACTOR.
GIMME A BREAK.
MY ACTING UP UNTIL A SECOND AGO WASN'T THAT BAD.
DID YOU REALIZE YOU CALLED ICHIGO...
..."KUROSAKI" RIGHT AFTER I CUT YOU?
TCH!
ZHK

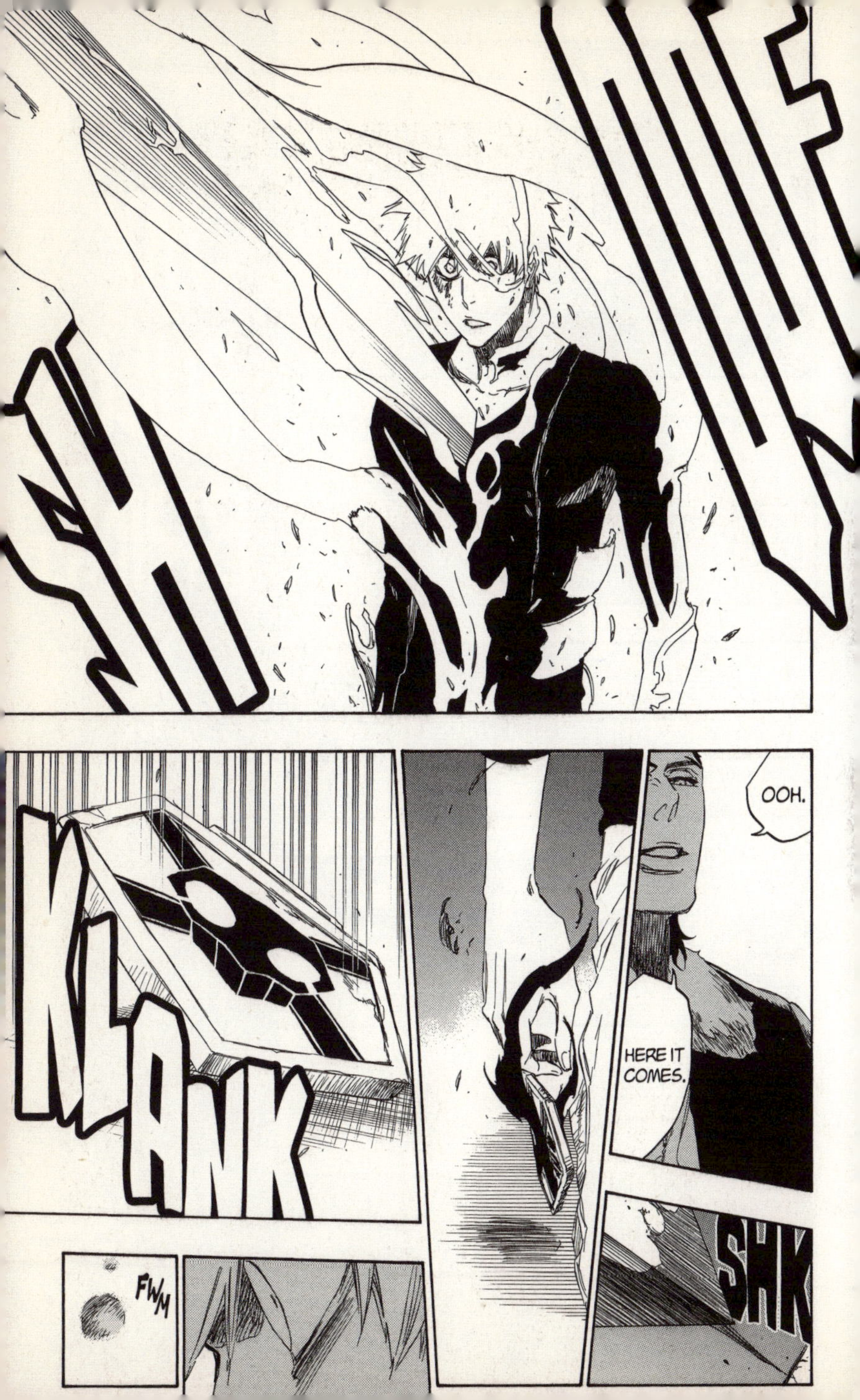

OOH.
HERE IT COMES.
SHK
KLANK
FWM

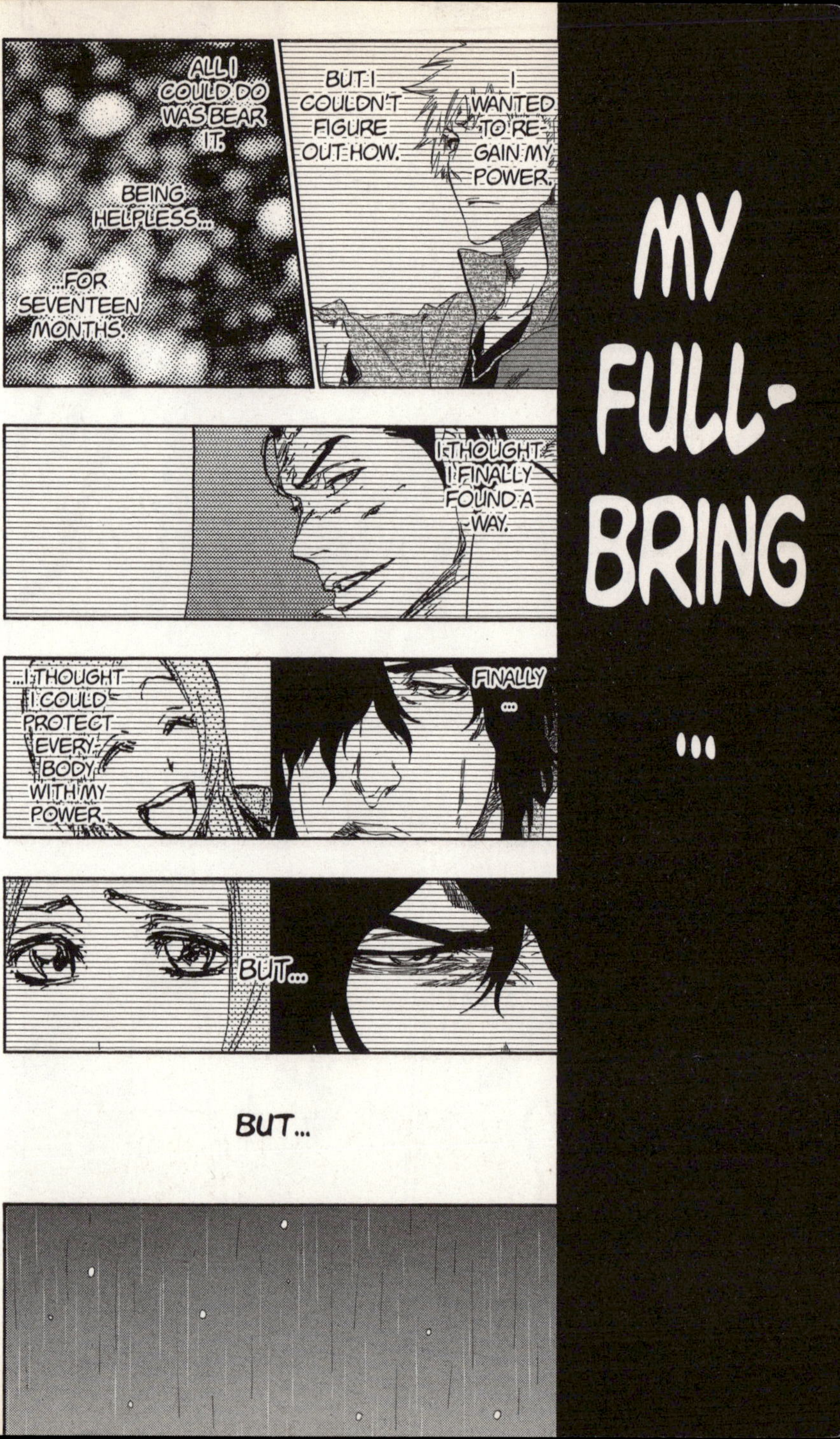
MY FULL-BRING...
I WANTED TO REGAIN MY POWER.
BUT I COULDN'T FIGURE OUT HOW.
ALL I COULD DO WAS BEAR IT.
BEING HELPLESS...
...FOR SEVENTEEN MONTHS.
I THOUGHT I FINALLY FOUND A WAY.
FINALLY...
...I THOUGHT I COULD PROTECT EVERYBODY WITH MY POWER.
BUT...
BUT...

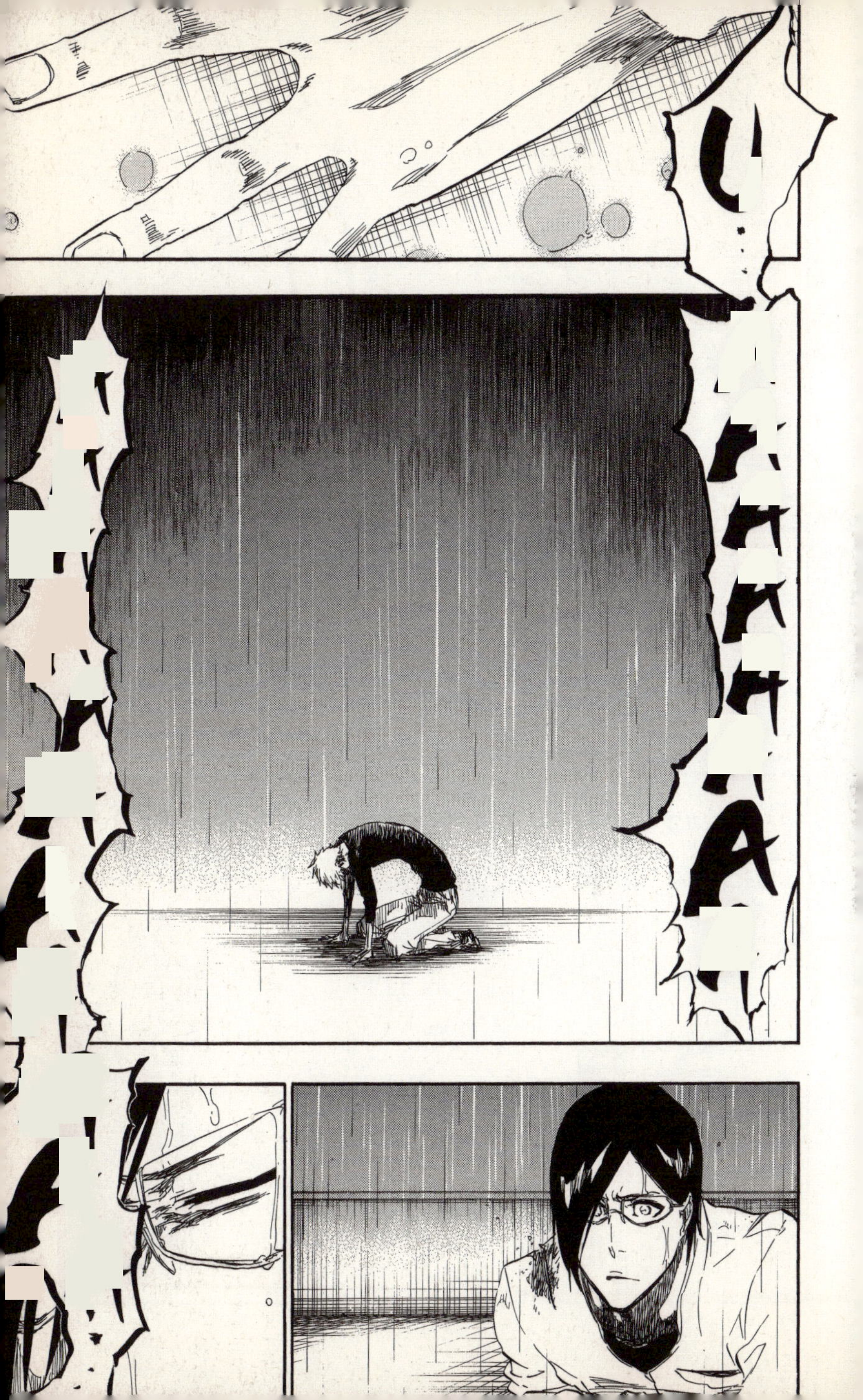

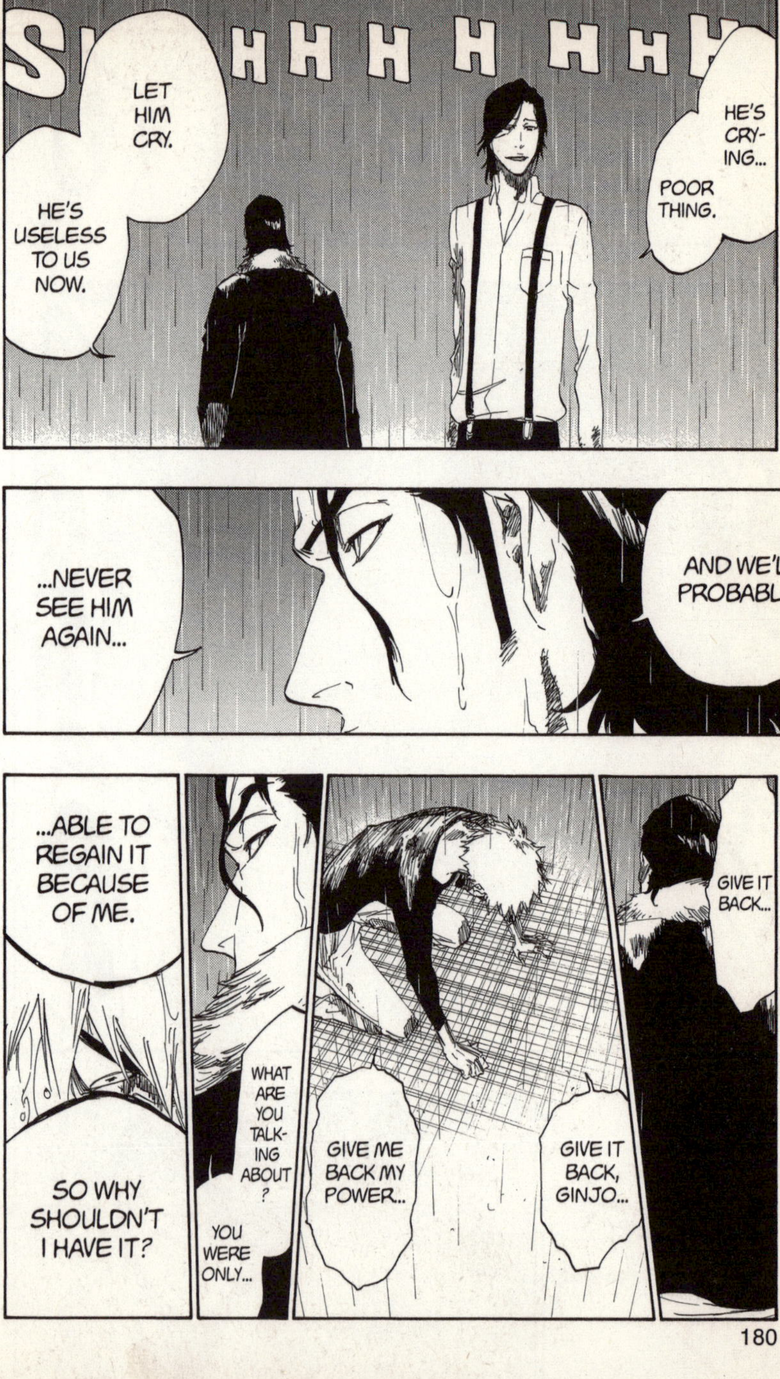
SHHHHHH
HE'S CRYING... POOR THING.
LET HIM CRY.
HE'S USELESS TO US NOW.
AND WE'LL PROBABLY...
...NEVER SEE HIM AGAIN...
GIVE IT BACK...
GIVE IT BACK, GINJO...
GIVE ME BACK MY POWER...
WHAT ARE YOU TALKING ABOUT?
YOU WERE ONLY...
...ABLE TO REGAIN IT BECAUSE OF ME.
SO WHY SHOULDN'T I HAVE IT?

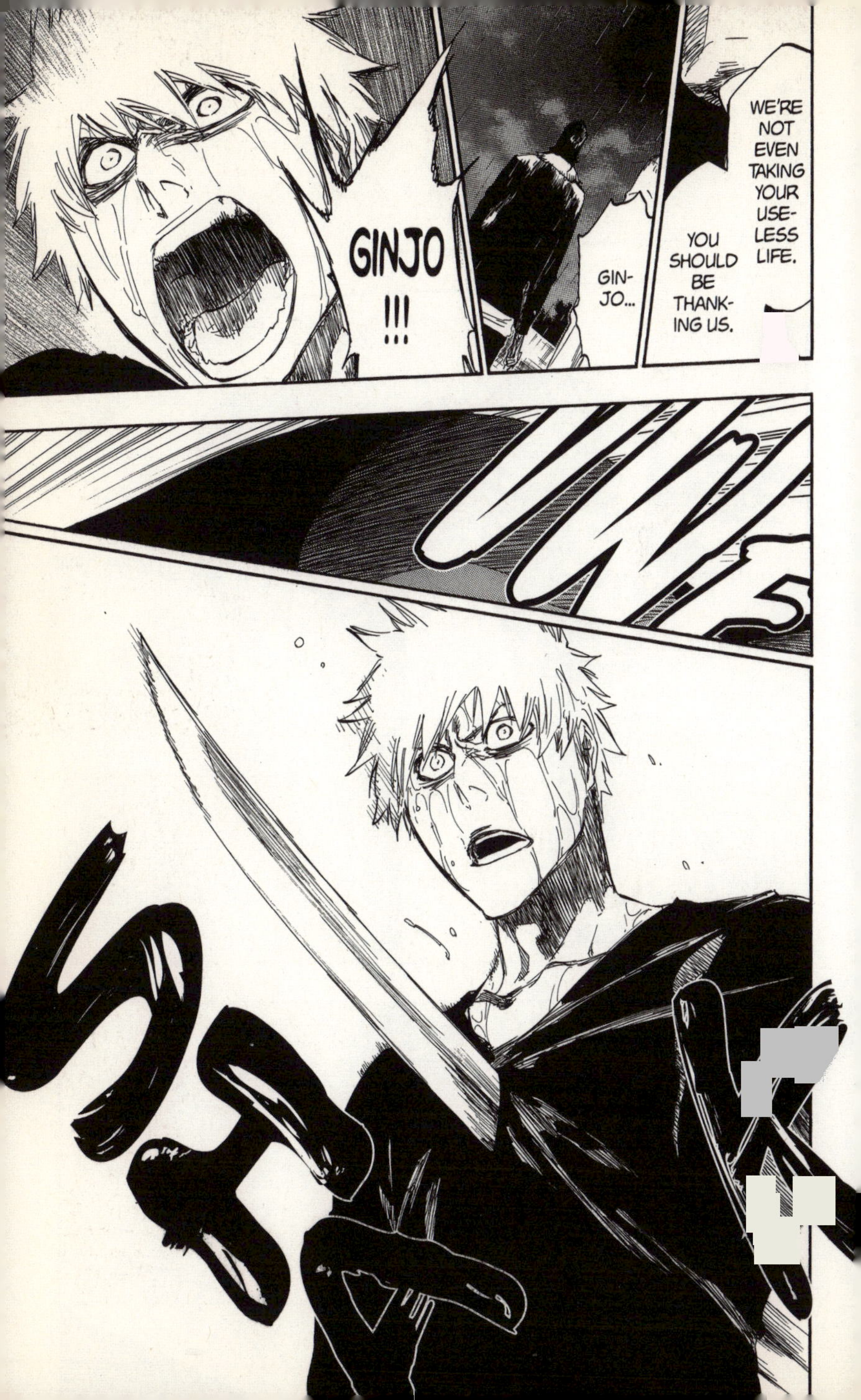
WE'RE NOT EVEN TAKING YOUR USE-LESS LIFE.
YOU SHOULD BE THANK-ING US.
GIN-JO...
GINJO !!!

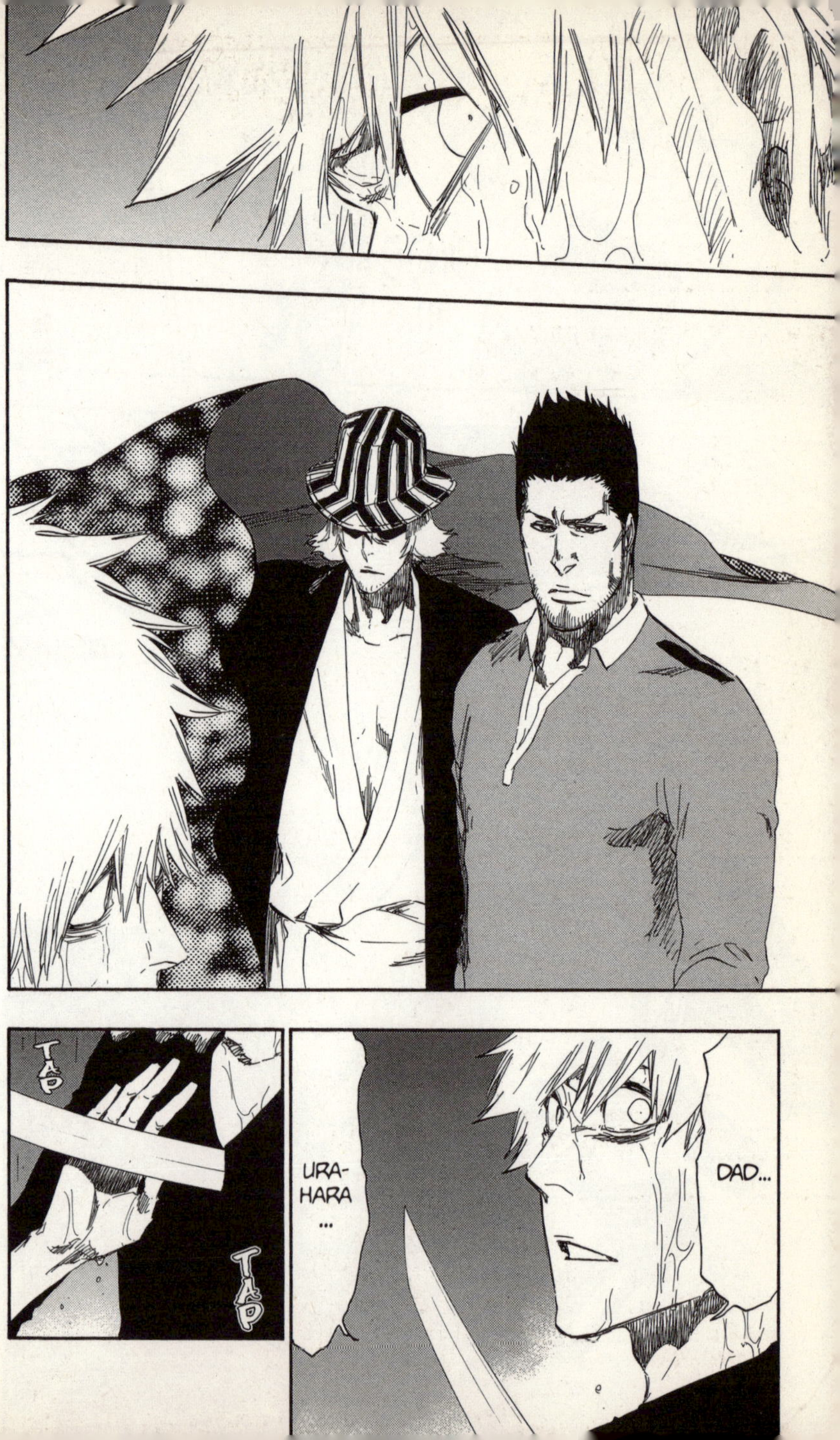
TAP
TAP
DAD...
URA-
HARA
...

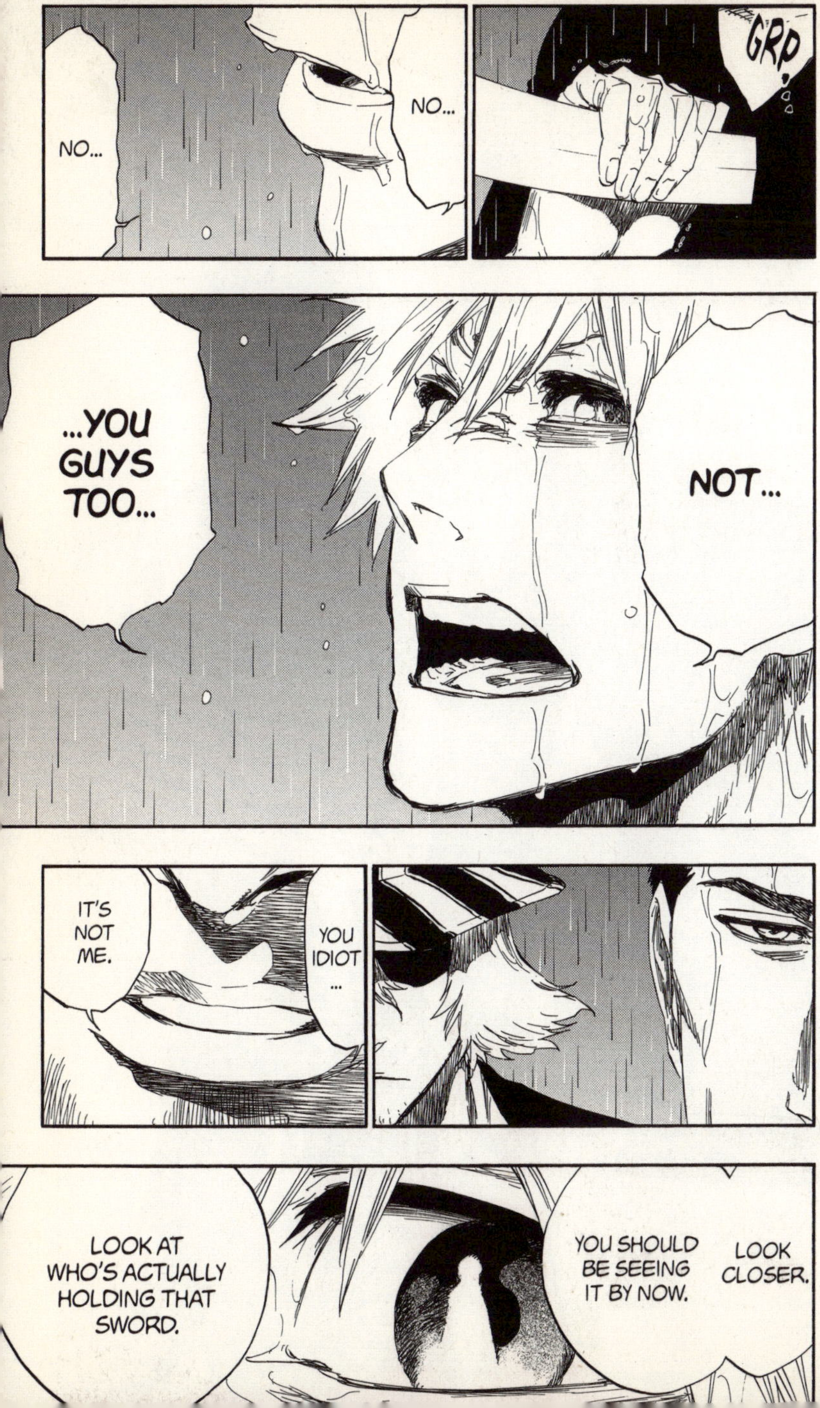
GRP
NO...
NO...
NOT...
...YOU GUYS TOO...
YOU IDIOT ...
IT'S NOT ME.
LOOK CLOSER.
YOU SHOULD BE SEEING IT BY NOW.
LOOK AT WHO'S ACTUALLY HOLDING THAT SWORD.

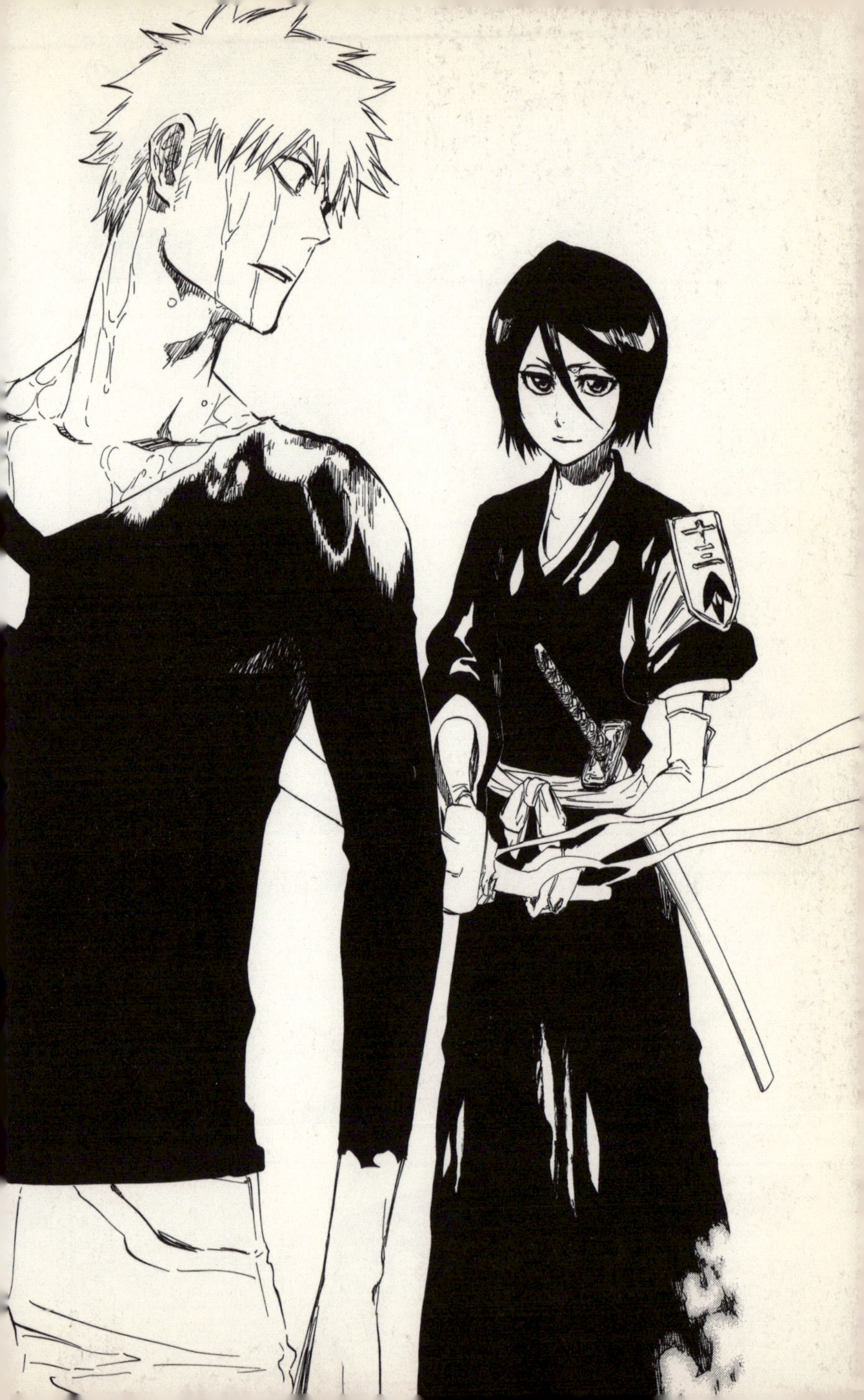
十三

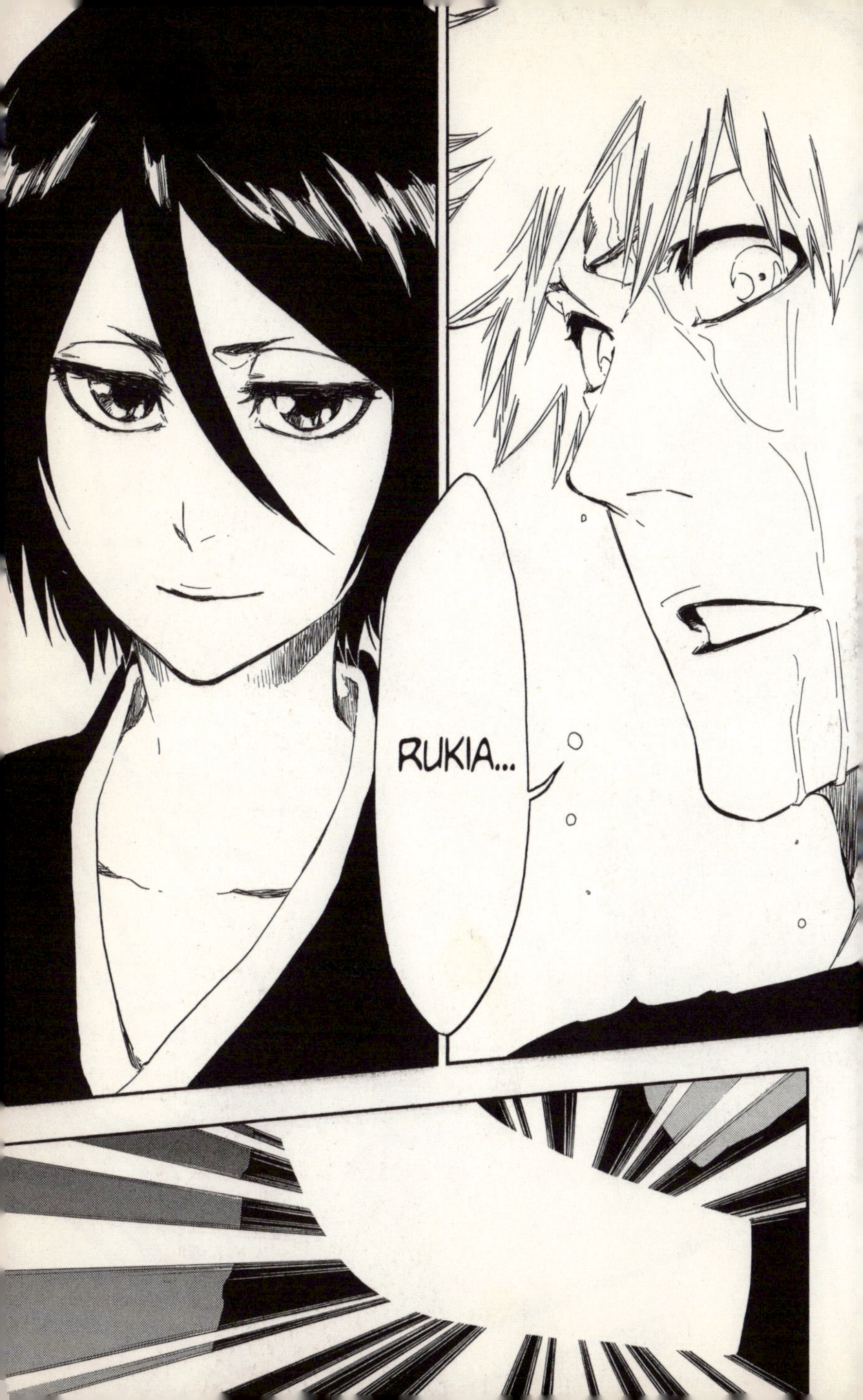
RUKIA...

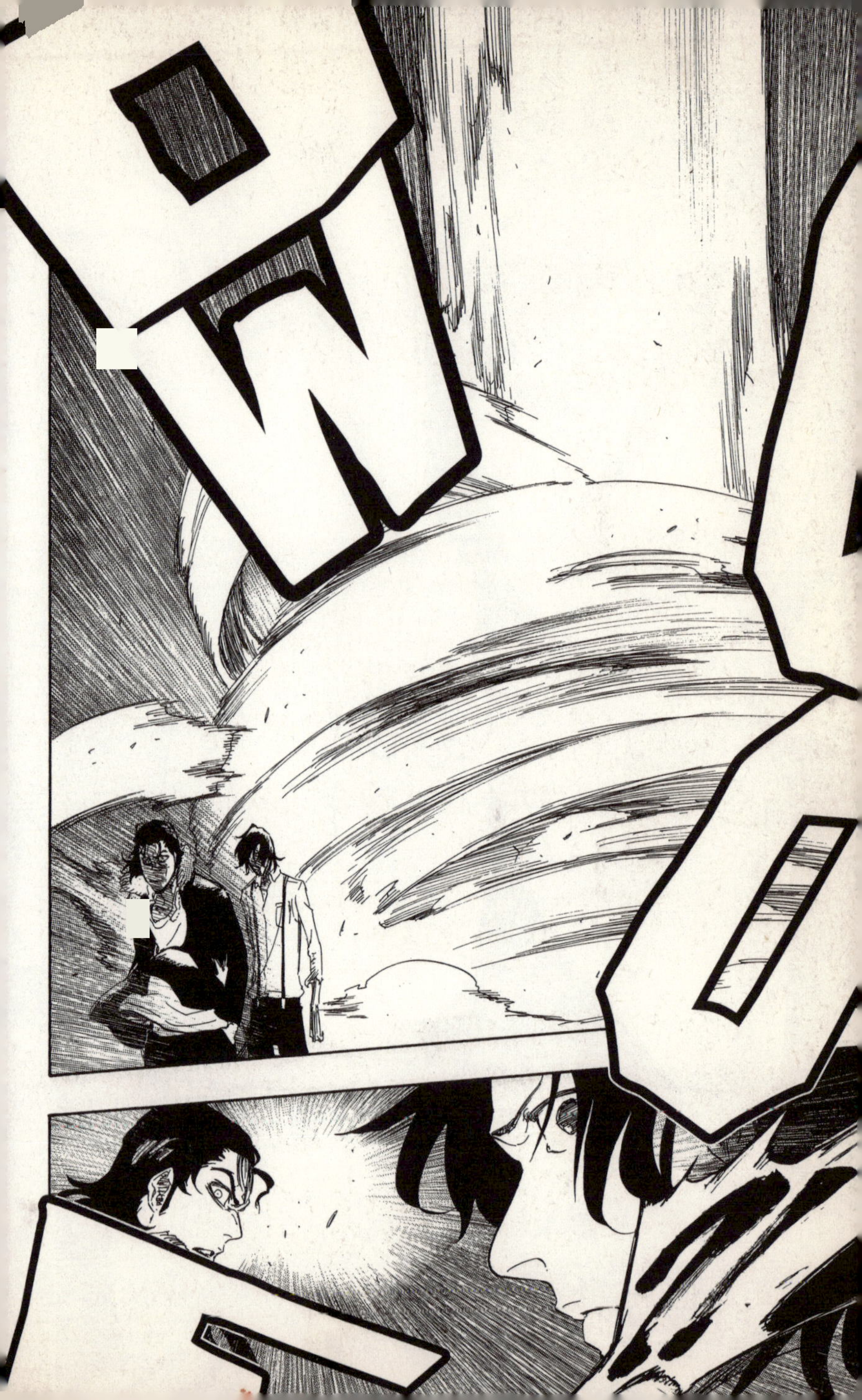

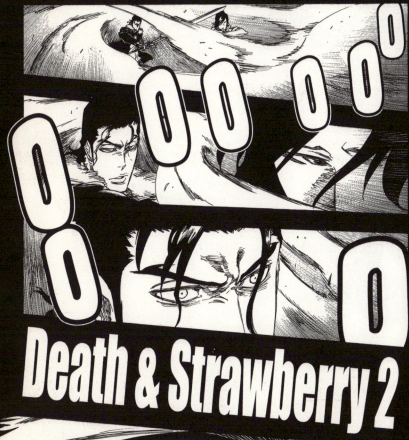

**BLEACH**             **459.**

# Death & Strawberry 2

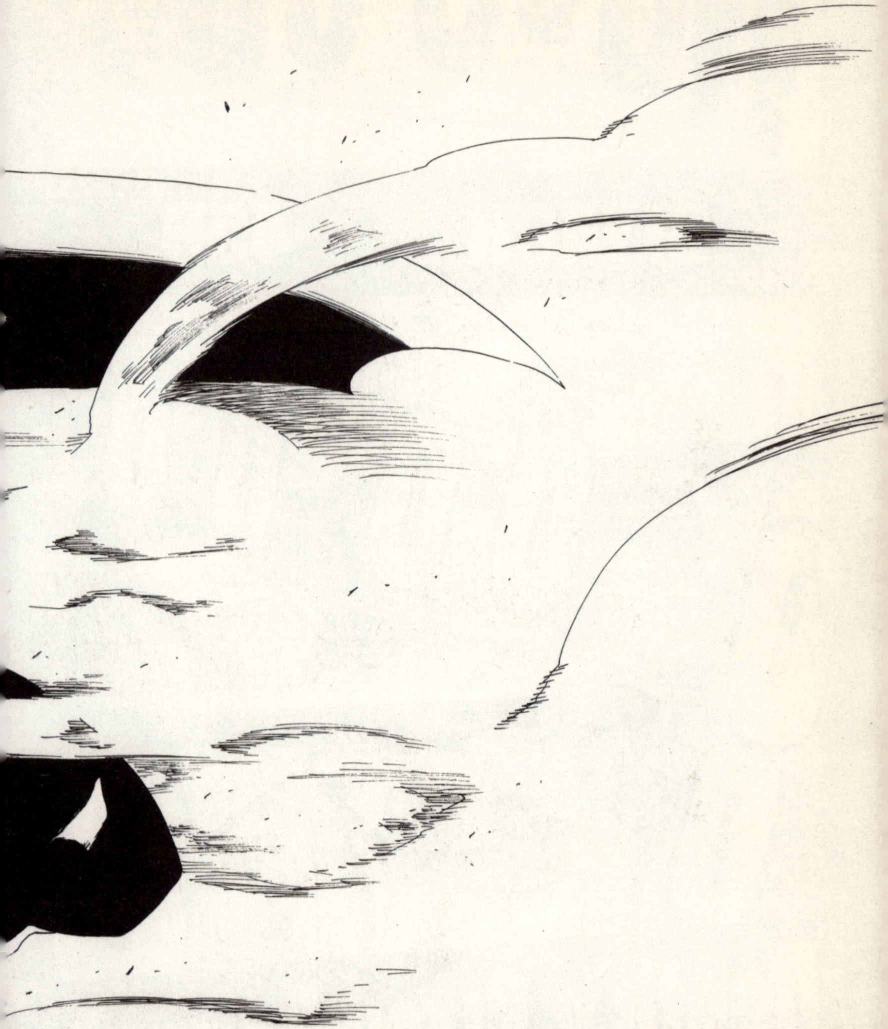

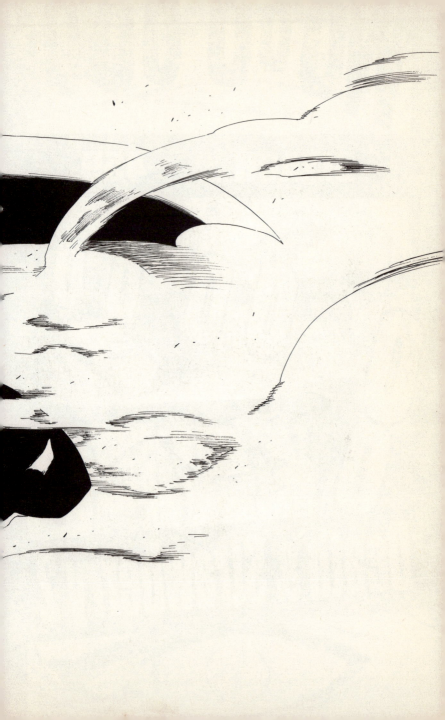

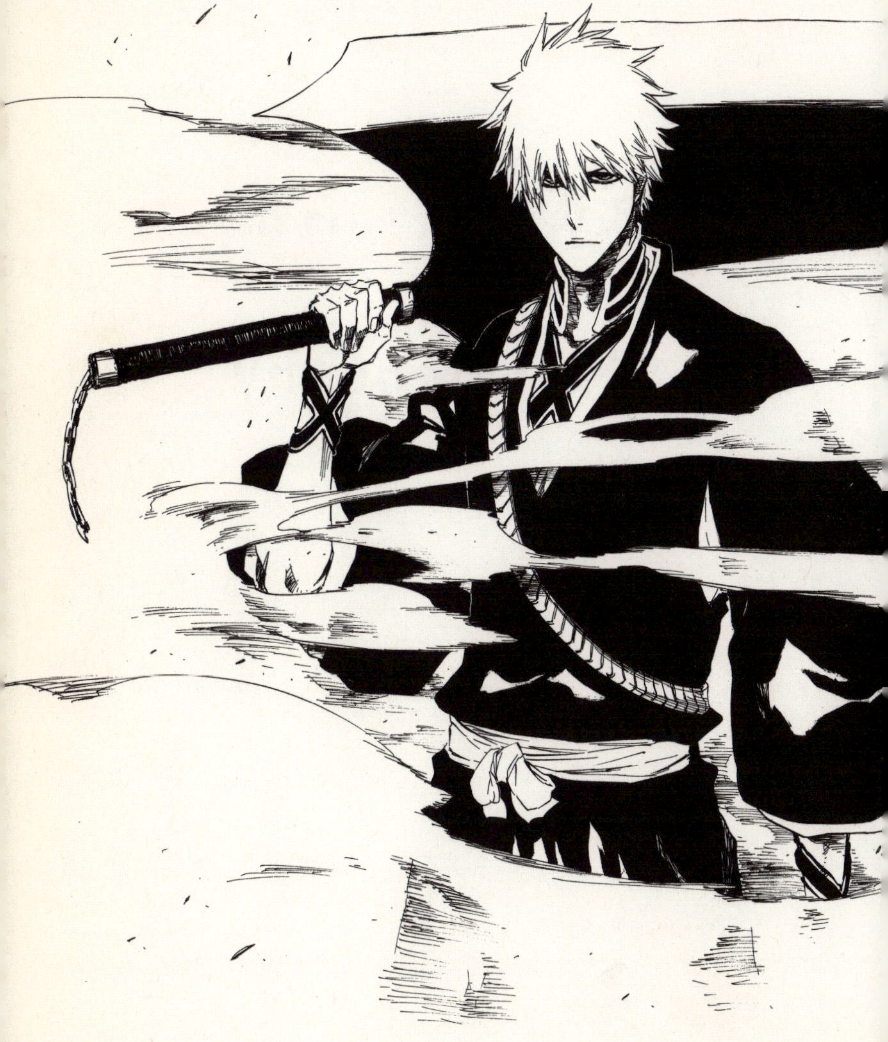

# Death and Strawberry